The Historical Novel

THE
HISTORICAL NOVEL

Georg Lukács

TRANSLATED FROM THE GERMAN BY
Hannah and Stanley Mitchell

Introduction by Fredric Jameson

University of Nebraska Press
Lincoln and London

First Bison Book printing: June 1983

Most recent printing indicated by the first digit below:
2   3   4   5   6   7   8   9   10

Library of Congress Cataloging in Publication Data

Lukács, György, 1885–1971.
   The historical novel.

   Translation of: A történelmi regény.
   Reprint. Originally published: Boston : Beacon
Press, 1963, c1962.
   "Bison book"—Verso t.p.
   Bibliography: p.
   Includes index.
   1. Historical fiction. 2. Historical drama.
I. Title.
[PN3441.L813 1983]   809.3'81   82-24772
ISBN 0-8032-7910-8 (pbk.)

Introduction
By Fredric Jameson

The Historical Novel is perhaps the single most monumental realization of the varied program and promises of a Marxist and a
dialectical literary criticism: something that can be argued by way
of the following checklist. First, Lukács's discussion of individual
works always presupposes a synthesis between analysis and evaluation: there is never found in these pages the dissociation between a
neutral formal (or semiotic) dissection of the text and a manifesto-
like defense of the interest, excitement, or "greatness" of this or
that cultural tendency—something only too frequent in bourgeois
criticism, and, indeed, for most of us, a situation or a dilemma
within which we find ourselves obligated to work, however much
we may deplore the limits and distortions it imposes on us.
Lukács's book may stand as a calm refutation of the often repeated
misconception that a Marxist historicism (with all the relativism
historicisms generally imply) can ultimately have no theory of
value in the area of culture.

Most obviously, however, *The Historical Novel* triumphantly
fulfills the central mission of any Marxist criticism, which lies in
the attempt to articulate what can very loosely be called the aesthetic text and its historical or social "context" (terms which presup-
pose a solution in advance and to that degree remain unhelpful).
For Lukács here, the elements of a solution are given in the coordi-
nation between an emergent new *form*, the historical novel, and an
emergent new type of *consciousness:* a new sense of history and a new
experience of historicity. If these last terms sound idealistic from
the perspective of contemporary theory (non-Marxist and Marxist
alike), it may be enough for the moment to suggest that *both*
elements in Lukács's articulation are mediatory—that is, neither is
a substance or terminal point in itself. Rather, attention to "form"
and "historical consciousness" opens up a further series of mediations and transcodings. "Historical consciousness" is not here some
final explanatory or causal datum, but rather something to be
explained in its turn, by mediations which must necessarily
address history, politics, social change, and ultimately the economic itself.

1

As for *form*, it is also a mediatory field. Lukács's magisterial exploration of the new *genre* of the historical novel, as it springs fully grown from Sir Walter Scott's imagination, may count as yet a third of the unique dialectical features of the present book. It is perhaps not sufficiently appreciated to what degree a dialectical approach to literature is deeply affiliated to the whole problematics of genre, which has, except in seminal work like that of Northrop Frye, undergone a crisis and an eclipse in contemporary theory. Not the least striking feature of Lukács's book, indeed, is the grand moment in which the formal specificity of the historical novel (and prose narrative itself) requires a turn of the theorist's attention, in elaborate and achieved detail, to the dialectical *other* of this genre, namely, the historical *drama*. Here, as Lukács shows, in a demonstration whose underpinnings draw on a whole aesthetics of the differentiation of the arts and forms, "world-historical figures," the so-called great men of history, are given to us directly, as the protagonists of the works in question. The historical novel, however—and it was Scott's originality to have grasped this in the very moment of emergence of the form—is populist and collective. The great yet enigmatic individual "subjects of history" must be approached by way of the average, anonymous consciousness of ordinary witnesses and merely representative "heroes," for whom the great of history offer only fitful and episodic contacts. "Balzac understood this secret of Scott's composition. Scott's novels, he said, marched towards the great heroes in the same way as history itself had done when it required their appearance. The reader, therefore, experiences the historical genesis of the important historical figures, and it is the writer's task from then on to let their actions make them appear the real representatives of these historical crises" (p. 39).

Yet this dialectical view of genre must necessarily be completed by the fourth indispensable feature of any dialectical approach to literature and culture, namely, its thoroughgoing historicism. Whoever speaks of the historical emergence of a new genre must at the same time take into account the possibility (and perhaps even the inevitability) of the historical decline and death of that same genre, whose idea can no longer exist in some eternal heaven of Platonic or Aristotelian forms but rather in the perpetual mutability of history itself. If, in other words, the historical novel, as a vital

2

new formal innovation, presupposes a certain kind of bourgeois historical consciousness (including, on the ideological level, a new bourgeois philosophical universalism), then it follows that key shifts, changes, or restructurations in that consciousness will have at least a symptomal effect on the form.

Here, as elsewhere, the great emblematic date or break that marks the most fundamental of these changes is for Lukács the revolution of 1848, where, in the June days, the "universal class" of the bourgeoisie suddenly confronts its own threatening class enemy, in the nascent industrial proletariat. The bourgeoisie must therefore, among other measures (which include brute force and bloody repression), also rework its own ideology in order to prevent its own universalism from becoming an incitement to the creation of a new and more universally democratic, classless society. (It is interesting that much of Jean-Paul Sartre's final work, particularly in his trilogy on Flaubert, also turns around this key crisis in mid-nineteenth-century bourgeois ideology.) With a new class-conscious defense of middle-class privilege, however, the historical novel also, as a form, loses its vitality and its vocation, and is degraded, as Lukács shows in a wealth of illustrations (mostly centering on Flaubert's *Salammbô*), into a narrative that is at once *archeologizing* and *modernizing*, which now takes the external world as a mere dead decorative spectacle (readers will here recognize Lukács's diagnosis of *naturalism*) and yet which at the same time paradoxically uses that decorative background as the pretext for a host of *projections* of contemporary psychological states (i.e., ennui, anxiety, neurosis), but also contemporary philosophical issues and concerns, into a past where they have no place.

The final section of Lukács's book will for contemporary readers be the most dated of all: yet this less because of the content of the analyses (which remain equal in interest and urgency to those elsewhere in the volume) than rather on account of the essentially Central European and indeed prewar literary frame of reference, whose great names (Anatole France, Charles de Coster, Leon Feuchtwanger, Heinrich Mann, Romain Rolland) are no longer household words for today's reading public. Indeed, one could go further in this vein and suggest that what may appear to us flawed in this architectonic monument which is *The Historical Novel* is less its theoretical consistency than the absence of writers and whole

3

cultures which lay outside Lukács's personal interests and background: the powerful later English language attempts at the form (George Eliot, Anthony Trollope, even Ford Madox Ford and James Joyce) are never addressed. The most elaborate and stunning of all European realizations of the historical novel, Pérez Galdós's enormous "National Episodes," are never mentioned, and the very remarkable Spanish and Latin American tradition of work in the genre is passed over in silence.

None of this, however, strikes in any esential way at Lukács's theoretical structure; and coming back to the now dated final section of the book, we can say that what seems to us archaic in Lukács's cultural references here is the other side of a final and supreme dialectical strength of the work itself, namely, its embattled engagement in the whole polemic field of contemporary art. *The Historical Novel* is indeed *not* an archeological narrative about an extinct form: it seeks, after its own fashion, and even in its analyses of the historical past and the radically different social and cultural situations of that past, to address the present with a partisan urgency. That present is no longer our own, but the urgency remains. In his final pages, Lukács calls for a revitalization of the historical novel in radically new social and political configurations—for him, those of post-revolutionary societies, for us, those of a new moment of multinational capitalism, which he could scarcely have anticipated. Lukács's book remains therefore a vital lesson for us in the dialectical unity of a criticism which, engaging the historical specificity of the past, never loses sight of its commitments and responsibilities in our own present.

There are many other things to be said in praise of this remarkable work, not least about its pedagogical spirit and the way in which, with its extensive quotations and references to both the Hegelian and Marxian philosophical traditions, it can be used as a virtual introduction or handbook to dialectical thinking. It may be wiser, however, in conclusion, to address some of the more traditional objections to Lukács's work in general, many of which are based on misconceptions and stereotypes about the historical figure himself, probably the central philosopher of the twentieth-century European communist movements and of the countries of so-called actually existing socialism.

These objections can be summed up in a twofold way: Lukács incarnates a *moralizing* approach to literary and cultural texts that has become repugnant to many of us; and he is at the same time irredeemably tainted by his association with Stalinism (*The Historical Novel*, along with the other more familiar literary studies of realism, naturalism, and modernism, were for the most part all written in Moscow during the Stalin era and contain any number of telltale passages in which obeisance is made to the "genius" of Stalin himself). Lukács's early career was indeed an exemplary evolution of an intellectual formed in the great middle-class philosophical traditions of Central Europe, and particularly of Germany (and an upper-class intellectual at that, a banker's son and a characteristic specimen of the Jewish aristocracy of the Austro-Hungarian Empire in its prewar heyday) toward a political commitment, first determined by revulsion against World War I, and then by an intellectual and emotional commitment to Marxism and to the ideals of the Soviet revolution in its early period. His great work, *History and Class Consciousness* (1923), virtually invents a properly Marxian *philosophy* and remains a rich, innovative, and still vital and hotly debated text. With the official party condemnation of this book, and the alarming growth of fascist power in all of the Central and Eastern European countries, Lukács faced a fundamental decision, which can be summed up in his famous remark, "My party card is my entry-ticket to History." The sad fate of neo-Marxists voluntarily or forcibly excluded from the Communist party (one thinks of Wilhelm Reich and Karl Korsch, but also of the Americans whose story Daniel Aaron's *Writers on the Left* has so persuasively reconstructed for us) lends a certain plausibility to this choice.

As for life in Moscow during the darkest days of the 1930s and '40s, the Abbé Siéyès's answer to an analogous question about the period of the Terror during the French Revolution may be the appropriate one. "What did you do during the Terror?" "I survived." Hardly less appropriate may be the well-known anecdote about the discussion that followed Krushchev's speech at the Twentieth Party Congress in 1956. To an anonymous question from the floor about what he, Krushchev, was doing while the enormities of Stalinism which he had just denounced were in full course, Krushchev is said to have drawn himself up aggressively and to have asked: "Who said that?" Silence. "Now," Krushchev is supposed to have remarked, "now you know what I was doing during the Stalin period."

The response would be less appropriate for Lukács, since he did continue to write and publish, although tactfully displacing his concerns from the political and the philosophical to the aesthetic. But what must be understood, particularly by those for whom his polemic against Berthold Brecht seems to mark Lukács as a traditionalist and also as a representative of some official Soviet cultural policy, is that the aesthetic works written and published during this period—the essays on realism as much as the present text—are all *coded* works. They are not the defense of a Zhdanovite "socialist realism" by a philosopher who, in capitulation, was content to become a party hack: they are rather explicit *critiques* of precisely that official Stalinist aesthetic of socialist realism, which for the obvious reasons of prudence and survival are in Lukács's work designated by the term *naturalism*. These books, then, involve a dual public: for the West, they are historical discussions of nineteenth-century literature which can stand on their own genuine merits as cultural history and analysis; for the East, they are coded interventions into a very real and urgent, dangerous zone which was that of culture and cultural revolution in a post-revolutionary "socialist" society, in a society at least officially still seeking to construct socialism. Lukács's traditional view of culture and cultural revolution, and of the heritage of progressive bourgeois literature, may well be open to criticism on those very grounds, but only if one shares his sense of urgency about the significance of culture and also about the commitment to socialism itself.

As for moralizing judgments, their flavor and the ethical habit is certainly present in Lukács's pages and in his stylistic mannerisms. It is interesting to note that it is precisely this kind of moralizing gesture which he shares with the only two critics of the Anglo-American tradition to have, in their very different ways, shared his concern with the relationship between cultural production and the vitality of the social community: the non-Marxists F. R. Leavis and Yvor Winters.

6

Still, I must feel—and this final remark returns us to the first point made above about Lukács's work, namely, the synthesis in it between analysis and value, between formal study and judgment—that Western, nondialectical or middle-class readers may tend to project their own moralizing habits into a dialectical thinking which is rather more complicated than that. Our training in the various literary "canons," for instance, accustoms us to habits of evaluation which are very close to outright ethical distinctions between the good and the bad: Balzac is thus, perhaps, a "great" writer, Flaubert is certainly a "great writer," while Scott—to whose vital contemporary reevaluation Lukács powerfully summons us, in a most timely way—would not normally be considered as such. Is not, therefore, the outright assault on Flaubert to be seen as the mere exercise of Lukács's own ideological prejudices? And the apologia for Scott to be seen, similarly, as an exercise in a certain perverse ideological sentimentalism?

But the critique of ideology, and particularly the related formal judgments as Lukács himself pioneered them, are by no means to be grasped as simple ethical pronouncements, which glorify or stigmatize, which read a given writer *into* or *out of* some eternal canon. Lukács's judgments on literary form are (even when they are couched in a simpler and more dogmatic Leninist language) philosophically intimately related to the concept of totality developed in his philosophical masterpiece, *History and Class Consciousness*. The "value" of a literary narrative is in this sense to be grasped in terms of its capacity to open a totalizing and mapping access to society as a whole: it is never what the work is able to elaborate that is "ideological"; what is "ideological" about a work of art, what solicits a seemingly "negative" judgment or an aesthetic (but also political and philosophical critique) is rather what the work finds itself obliged formally to *exclude*. Yet it would obviously be absurd to imagine that any narrative text can succeed in fully totalizing society (any more than individuals, with their own necessary class position, can be in a position of truth—or of Hegelian Absolute Spirit—with respect to society as a whole). It is therefore no surprise that even the greatest literary works and monuments—here, for example, Tolstoy—have determinate limits which are simultaneously formal *and* ideological: indeed, in a certain sense, the greater such a work the more urgent is the task of its formal and ideological specification, of the account of its determinate historical and social limits. Nothing is, then, ultimately further from the moralizing gesture than this difficult attempt to think the greatness and the ideological constraints of a given text together in the mind at one and the same time. Indeed, confronted with *The Historical Novel*, a Marxist classic with its own roots and determinations in a historical situation that is no longer ours today, we keep faith with Lukács's own method in evaluating it according to the rigorous standards it proposes.

Contents

ERRATA

page 11, head. *For* Translator's Note *read* Translators' Note

page 68, lines 7–8 from bottom. For (*Uproar in the Cevennes*) read (*The Revolt in the Cevennes*)

page 85, line 12. *For* with *read* which

page 118, para. 4, line 6. *For* Ocasionally *read* Occasionally

page 150, line 7 from bottom. *For* co-called *read* so-called

page 154, line 4. *For* with which is most familiar *read* with which he is most familiar

page 179, line 4 from bottom. *For* the injection a meaning *read* the injection of a meaning

page 180, para. 4, line 1. *For* historical solopism *read* historical solecism

page 197, para. 3, line 2. *For* Gegenwärtighkeit *read* Gegenwärtigkeit

page 221, line 4 from bottom. *For* Bismark *read* Bismarck

page 237, para. 3, line 2. *For* first half of the eighteenth century *read* first half of the nineteenth century

page 246, para. 2, line 9. *For* E.Th.A. Hoffmann's *read* E.T.A. Hoffmann's

page 285, para. 2, line 4 from bottom. *For* Nikola *read* Nicholas

Translator's Note

W E SHOULD like to draw attention to the following points. First, wherever possible we have translated quotations of non-German authors from their original language (e.g. French or Russian) rather than from the German in which they are given. This has sometimes produced certain slight divergences from their German renderings. Where verse quotations are concerned we have provided literal translations for the German passages, while for the French quotations (the only other language in question here), which are all given in the original, we have assumed a greater familiarity on the part of the reader and left them as they are.

Secondly, in omitting sources for quotations we have followed the practice of the original text.

Thirdly, with the exception of the term *Novelle* we have rendered all Lukács's specific literary and philosophic terms into English, varying their translation where a fixed word-for-word rendering would not adequately convey them. Sometimes we have indicated the original German word in parentheses.

Finally, a translator's apology: it has been difficult to produce a readable English version of a highly theoretical idiom in the German.

H. & S. M.

We add the following explanatory notes to aid the reader unfamiliar with certain names and references.

pp. 29, 90

Mikhail Lifschitz—a well-known Soviet critic who has written on Marx's philosophy of art.

p. 54

"social equivalent"—the phrase belongs to Plekhanov, the Russian Marxist critic, who wrote: "The first task of a critic is to translate the idea of a given work of art from the language of art into the language of sociology, to find what may be termed the social equivalent of the given literary phenomenon."

(Preface to the 3rd edition of the collection *The Past Twenty Years*, 1908.)

Plekhanov was criticised by Lenin and other Marxists for lapses into sociological relativism. The concept "social equivalent", derived perhaps from Taine, was used by the "vulgar sociology" which Lukács attacks.

p. 145

"for us"—Engels wrote: "If we are able to prove the correctness of our conception of a natural process by making it for ourselves, bringing it into being out of its conditions, and using it for our own purposes into the bargain, then there is an end of the Kantian incomprehensible 'thing-in-itself'. The chemical substances produced in the bodies of plants and animals remained just such 'things-in-themselves' until organic chemistry began to produce them one after another, whereupon the 'thing-in-itself' became a 'thing-for-us' . . ."

(*Ludwig Feuerbach*)

Lukács applies this idea *mutatis mutandis* to the literary treatment of reality.

pp. 246, 247, 249

Friedrich Gundolf—an influential German critic, associated with the Stefan George circle.

p. 247

Biedermeier—the period 1815-1848, i.e., from the end of the Napoleonic era to the 1848 Revolution. *Biedermeier* is the worthy, Philistine, middle-class German, so called after a poem by one Eichrodt which appeared in 1850.

p. 263

José Diaz—Secretary of the Spanish Communist Party from 1932-42.

Preface to the English Edition

THIS BOOK was composed during the winter of 1936/7 and published in Russian soon after its completion. If today I present it to the English reader without any changes, my decision requires some explanation. For, obviously, the past twenty-two years have considerably increased the material of the last chapter. To quote just one example: a detailed analysis of the concluding second part of Heinrich Mann's *Henri Quatre*, which has since appeared, would certainly heighten the concreteness and topicality of the last chapter. The same goes for the later novels of Lion Feuchtwanger. But even more important than this is the fact that the picture of the times and the perspective it reveals are those of twenty-two years ago. Certain expectations have proved too optimistic, have been belied by historical events. For example, the book pins exaggerated, indeed false, hopes on the independent liberation movement of the German people, on the Spanish revolution etc.

If I neither fill in the gaps nor correct the mistakes, but allow the book to appear as it was more than twenty-two years ago, it is chiefly because my present circumstances of work do not permit me to revise it to any worthwhile extent. I was thus faced with the choice either of publishing it unaltered or not at all.

This explanation, however, would be inadequate from a scholarly point of view were the literature of the past two decades able to affect the questions I deal with or the value and significance of my results in any decisive way. Which would indeed be the case if the question posed by my book were purely literary-historical, if its subject and theme were the development of the historical novel (or the historical drama) or even simply the unfolding of the historical spirit, its decline and rebirth.

However, as the reader will see, this is not the case. My aims were of a theoretical nature. What I had in mind was a theoretical examination of the interaction between the historical spirit and the great genres of literature which portray the totality of history—and then only as this applied to bourgeois literature; the change wrought by socialist realism lay outside the scope of my study. In such an enquiry it is obvious that even the inner, most theoretical, most abstract dialectic of the problem will have an historical character. My study is confined to working out the main lines of this historical dialectic: that is, it analyzes and examines only the typical trends, offshoots and nodal points of this historical development, those indispensable to a theoretical examination. Hence it does not aim at historical completeness. The reader must not expect a textbook on the development of the historical drama or the historical novel; he will find a discussion simply of writers, works and movements who are representative from this theoretical standpoint. Hence in some cases I have had to deal at length with lesser writers (i.e. from the purely literary point of view), while disregarding more important ones in other cases.

This approach also enabled me to leave the old conclusion unchanged. The book ended with the German anti-Fascist literature of 1937. This was made possible, I believe, by the fact that the theoretically important questions—in the first instance the strengths and given weaknesses of the time both in respect of outlook and politics as well as aesthetics—had found a sufficiently clear expression in precisely this literature. The new important historical novels, like Halldor Laxness's *The Bell of Iceland* and Lampedusa's *The Leopard* (particularly its first half) confirm the principles I arrived at in a positive direction. In a critical-negative respect these theoretical conclusions have perhaps stood the test even better. For the fact that the historical novels which make the most noise today are those which accommodate a purely belletrist treatment of life to the latest fashions cannot affect the foundations of the artistic form. Thus, although my political perspective of the time proved too optimistic, this in no way alters the significance of the theoretical questions raised and the direction in which their solution is to be sought.

This aim determines the methodological problem of my book. First of all, as already mentioned above, the choice of material. I do not trace an historical development in the narrow sense of the word, nevertheless I do try to clarify the main lines of historical development and the most important questions these have raised. The ideal, of course, would be to combine a thorough elaboration of the theoretical viewpoints with an exhaustive treatment of the totality of historical development. Then, and then alone, could the real strength of Marxist dialectics become tangible to all, could it be made clear to all that it is not something essentially and primarily intellectual, but the intellectual reflection of the actual historical process. But this again was not my aim in the present work; hence I regard my book simply as an attempt to establish the main principles and approaches in the hope that more thorough, more comprehensive works will follow.

The second important methodological approach is to examine the interaction between economic and social development and the outlook and artistic form to which they give rise. Here an entire series of new and hitherto barely analyzed problems is to be found : the social basis of the divergence and convergence of genres, the rise and withering away of new elements of form within this complicated process of interaction. In this respect, too, I consider my book no more than a beginning, a venture. In the concrete elaboration of Marxist aesthetics this question has as yet hardly arisen. However, no serious Marxist genre theory is possible unless an attempt is made to apply the theory of reflection of materialist dialectics to the problem of the differentiation of genres. Lenin, in his analysis of Hegel's logic, observes brilliantly that the most abstract deductions (syllogisms) are likewise abstract cases of the reflection of reality. I have attempted in my book to apply this idea to epic and drama. But here again, as in the treatment of history, I could go no further than give a methodological pointer to the solution of this problem. Thus this book no more claims to provide a complete theory of the development of dramatic and epic forms than it does to give a complete picture of the development of the historical novel in the domain of history.

Despite its extent it is, therefore, only an attempt, an essay: a preliminary contribution to both Marxist aesthetics and the materialistic treatment of literary history. I cannot sufficiently emphasize that I consider it, all in all, only a first beginning, which others, I hope, will soon extend, if necessary correcting my results. I believe, however, that in this still almost virgin territory even such a first beginning has its justification.

BUDAPEST, September, 1960.

Foreword

T HIS MONOGRAPH does not claim to give a detailed and complete history of the historical novel, Apart from the lack of real spade work for such an enterprise, this was not at all what I intended. I wished to deal with only the most important questions of principle and theory. Given the extraordinary role of the historical novel at present in both the literature of the USSR and the anti-Fascist popular front, such a study of principles seems to me as indispensable as it is topical. Especially so because the historical novel of our day, despite the great talent of its best exponents, still suffers in many respects from the remnants of the harmful and still not entirely vanquished legacy of bourgeois decadence. If the critic really wishes to uncover these shortcomings, then he must turn his attention not only to the principles of the historical novel, but to those of literature in general.

But there is an historical basis to our theoretical study. The difference of principles between the historical novel of the classics and of decadence etc. has its historical causes. And this work is intended to show how the historical novel in its origin, development, rise and decline follows inevitably upon the great social transformations of modern times; to demonstrate that its different problems of form are but artistic reflections of these social-historical transformations.

The spirit of this work then is an historical one. But it does not aim at historical completeness. Only those writers are dealt with whose works are in some respect representative, marking typical nodal points in the development of the historical novel. The same principle of selection applies to our quotations from older critics and aestheticians and from writers who have dealt theoretically with literature. In both spheres I have tried to show that with the historical novel as with all things else it is not a question of concocting something "radically new", but—as Lenin taught us—of assimilating all that is valuable in previous development and adapting it critically.

It is not for me to judge how successfully or not my intentions have been realized. I have simply wished to put these intentions clearly before the reader so that he should know at the outset what to expect and what not to expect from this book.

However, there is one gap to which I must draw the reader's attention before proceeding. As a result of my personal development I have been able to deal with the Russian historical novel only in translation. This is a serious and painful gap. In the older literature it was always possible to treat Russian literary works of universal importance. But translations of Soviet literature are only sporadic, and my critic's conscience forbids me to draw any conclusions on the basis of such scanty and incomplete material. For this reason I have been unable to deal with the historical novel in Soviet literature. Nevertheless, I hope that my remarks will do something to clarify these important problems for the Soviet reader, too, and hope especially that this gap in my work will be made good by others as soon as possible.

MOSCOW, September, 1937.

CHAPTER ONE

The Classical Form of the Historical Novel

1. Social and Historical Conditions for the Rise of the Historical Novel

THE HISTORICAL novel arose at the beginning of the nineteenth century at about the time of Napoleon's collapse (Scott's *Waverley* appeared in 1814). Of course, novels with historical themes are to be found in the seventeenth and eighteenth centuries, too, and, should one feel inclined, one can treat medieval adaptations of classical history or myth as "precursors" of the historical novel and indeed go back still further to China or India. But one will find nothing here that sheds any real light on the phenomenon of the historical novel. The so-called historical novels of the seventeenth century (Scudéry, Calpranède, etc.) are historical only as regards their purely external choice of theme and costume. Not only the psychology of the characters, but the manners depicted are entirely those of the writer's own day. And in the most famous "historical novel" of the eighteenth century, Walpole's *Castle of Otranto*, history is likewise treated as mere costumery: it is only the curiosities and oddities of the *milieu* that matter, not an artistically faithful image of a concrete historical epoch. What is lacking in the so-called historical novel before Sir Walter Scott is precisely the specifically historical, that is, derivation of the individuality of characters from the historical peculiarity of their age. The great critic Boileau, who judged the historical novels of his contemporaries with much scepticism, insisted only that characters should be socially and psychologically true, demanding that a ruler make love differently from a shepherd, and so on. The question of historical truth in the artistic reflection of reality still lies beyond his horizon.

However, even the great realistic social novel of the eighteenth century, which in its portrayal of contemporary morals and psychology, accomplished a revolutionary breakthrough to reality for world literature is not concerned to show its characters as belonging to any concrete time. The contemporary world is portrayed with unusual plasticity and truth-to-life, but is accepted naïvely as something given: whence and how it has developed have not yet become problems for the writer. This abstractness in the portrayal of historical time also affects the portrayal of historical place. Thus Lesage is able

19

to transfer his highly truthful pictures of the France of his day to Spain and still feel quite at ease. Similarly, Swift, Voltaire and even Diderot set their satirical novels in a "never and nowhere" which nevertheless faithfully reflects the essential characteristics of contemporary England and France. These writers, then, grasp the salient features of their world with a bold and penetrating realism. But they do not see the specific qualities of their own age historically.

This basic attitude remains essentially unchanged despite the fact that realism continues to bring out the specific features of the present with ever greater artistic power. Think of novels like *Moll Flanders*, *Tom Jones*, etc. Their broad, realistic portrayal of the present takes in here and there important events of contemporary history which it links with the fortunes of the characters. In this way, particularly in Smollett and Fielding, time and place of action acquire much greater concreteness than was customary in the earlier period of the social novel or in most contemporary French writing. Fielding indeed is to some extent aware of this development, this increasing concreteness of the novel in its grasp of the historical peculiarity of characters and events. His definition of himself as a writer is that of an historian of bourgeois society.

Altogether, when analyzing the prehistory of the historical novel, one must break with the Romantic-reactionary legend which denies to the Enlightenment any sense or understanding of history and attributes the invention of historical sense to the opponents of the French Revolution, Burke, de Maistre etc. One need only think of the extraordinary historical achievements of Montesquieu, Voltaire, Gibbon, etc., in order to cut this legend down to size.

What matters for us, however, is to concretize the particular character of this sense of history both before and after the French Revolution in order to see clearly what was the social and ideological basis from which the historical novel was able to emerge. And here we must stress that the history writing of the Enlightenment was, in its main trend, an ideological preparation for the French Revolution. The often superb historical construction, with its discovery of numerous new facts and connections, serves to demonstrate the necessity for transforming the "unreasonable" society of feudal absolutism; and the lessons of history provide the principles with whose help a "reasonable" society, a "reasonable" state may be created. For this reason the classical world is central to both the historical theory and the practice of the Enlightenment. To ascertain the causes of the greatness and decline of the classical states is one of the most important theoretical preliminaries for the future transformation of society.

This applies above all to France, the spiritual leader during the period of militant Enlightenment. The position in England is somewhat different. Economically, eighteenth century England indeed finds itself in the midst of the greatest transformation, the creation of the economic and social preconditions for the Industrial Revolution. Politically, however, England is already a post-revolutionary country. Thus where it is a question of mastering bourgeois society theoretically and subjecting it to criticism, of working out the principles of political economy, history is grasped as history more concretely than in France. But where it is a question of conscious and consistent application of such specifically historical viewpoints, they occupy an episodic position in the development as a whole. The really dominating economic theorist towards the end of the eighteenth century is Adam Smith. James Steuart, who posed the problem of capitalist economy far more historically and who investigated the process by which capital came into being, was soon forgotten. Marx characterizes the difference between these two important economists in the following way: Steuart's "contribution to the concept of capital is to have shown how the process of separation takes place between the conditions of production, as the property of definite classes, and labour-power. He gives a great deal of attention to this *process of the birth* of capital—*without as yet directly comprehending it as such* (my italics G.L.), although he sees it as the condition of large-scale industry. He examines the process particularly in agriculture; and he correctly presents manufacturing industry proper as dependent on this prior process of separation in agriculture. In Adam Smith's works this process of separation is assumed as already completed." This unawareness of the significance of the historical sense already present in practice, of the possibility of generalizing the historical peculiarity of the immediate present, which had been correctly observed by instinct, characterizes the position which the great social novel of England occupies in the development of our problem. It drew the attention of writers to the concrete (i.e. historical) significance of time and place, to social conditions and so on, it created the realistic, literary means of expression for portraying this spatio-temporal (i.e. historical) character of people and circumstances. But this, as in the economics of Steuart, was a product of realistic instinct and did not amount to a clear understanding of history as a process, of history as the concrete precondition of the present.

It is only during the last phase of the Enlightenment that the problem of the artistic reflection of past ages emerges as a central problem of literature. This occurs in Germany. Initially, it is true, the ideology of the German Enlightenment follows in the wake of that of France and England: the great achievements of Winckelmann and Lessing do not in the main diverge from the general trend of the Enlightenment. Lessing, whose important contributions to the clarification of the problem of historical drama we shall discuss at length later, still defines the relationship of writer to history entirely in the spirit of Enlightenment philosophy. He maintains that for the great dramatist history is no more than a "repertory" of names.

But soon after Lessing, in the *Sturm und Drang*, the problem of the artistic mastery of history already appears as a conscious one. Goethe's *Götz von Berlichingen* not only ushers in a new flowering of historical drama, but has a direct and powerful influence on the rise of the historical novel in the work of Sir Walter Scott. This conscious growth of historicism, which receives its first theoretical expression in the writings of Herder, has its roots in the special position of Germany, in the discrepancy between Germany's economic and political backwardness and the ideology of the German Enlighteners, who, standing on the shoulders of their English and French predecessors, developed the ideas of the Enlightenment to a higher level. As a result not only do the general contradictions underlying the whole ideology of the Enlightenment appear more sharply there than in France, but the specific contrast between these ideas and German reality is thrust vigorously into the foreground.

In England and France, the economic, political and ideological preparation and completion of the bourgeois revolution and the setting-up of a national state are one and the same process. So that in looking to the past, however intense the bourgeois-revolutionary patriotism and however important the works it produces (Voltaire's *Henriade*), the chief concern is inevitably the Enlightenment critique of the "unreasonable". Not so in Germany. Here revolutionary patriotism comes up against national division, against the political and economic fragmentation of a country which imports its cultural and ideological means of expression from France. For everything that was produced in the small German courts in the way of culture and particularly in the way of pseudo-culture was nothing more than a slavish imitation of the French court. Thus the small courts constitute not only a political obstacle to German unity, but also an ideological hindrance to the development of a culture stemming from the needs of German middle-class life. The German form of Enlightenment necessarily engages in sharp polemic with this French culture; and it preserves this note of revolutionary patriotism even where the real content of the ideological battle is simply the conflict between different stages in the development of the Enlightenment (Lessing's struggle against Voltaire).

The inevitable result of this situation is to turn to German history. Partly it is the reawakening of past national greatness which gives strength to hopes of national rebirth. It is a requirement of the struggle for this national greatness that the historical causes for the decline, the disintegration of Germany should be explored and artistically portrayed. As a result, in Germany, which in the preceding centuries had been no more than an object of historical changes, art becomes historical earlier and more radically than in the economically and politically more advanced countries of the West.

It was the French Revolution, the revolutionary wars and the rise and fall of Napoleon, which for the first time made history a *mass experience*, and moreover on a European scale. During the decades between 1789 and 1814 each nation of Europe underwent more upheavals than they had previously experienced in centuries. And the quick succession of these upheavals gives them a qualitatively distinct character, it makes their historical character far more visible than would be the case in isolated, individual instances: the masses no longer have the impression of a "natural occurrence". One need only read over Heine's reminiscences of his youth in *Buch le Grand*, to quote just one example, where it is vividly shown how the rapid change of governments affected Heine as a boy. Now if experiences such as these are linked with the knowledge that similar upheavals are taking place all over the world, this must enormously strengthen the feeling first that there is such a thing as history, that it is an uninterrupted process of changes and finally that it has a direct effect upon the life of every individual.

This change from quantity into quality appears, too, in the differences of these wars from all preceding ones. The wars of absolute states in the pre-Revolutionary period were waged by small professional armies. They were conducted so as to isolate the army as sharply as possible from the civilian population supplies from depots, fear of desertion, etc. Not for nothing did Frederick II of Prussia declare that war should be waged in such a manner that the civilian population simply would not notice it. "To keep the peace is the first duty of the citizen" was the motto of the wars of absolutism.

This changes at one stroke with the French Revolution. In its defensive struggle against the coalition of absolute monarchies, the French Republic was compelled to create mass armies. The qualitative difference between mercenary and mass armies is precisely a question of their relations with the mass of the population. If in place of the recruitment or pressing into professional service of small contingents of the declassed, a mass army is to be created, then the content and purpose of the war must be made clear to the masses by means of propaganda. This happens not only in France itself during the defence of the Revolution and the later offensive wars. The other states, too, if they transfer to mass armies, are compelled to resort to the same means. (Think of the part played by German literature and philosophy in this propaganda after the battle of Jena.) Such propaganda cannot possibly, however, restrict itself to the individual, isolated war. It has to reveal the social content, the historical presuppositions and circumstances of the struggle, to connect up the war with the entire life and possibilities of the nation's development. It is sufficient to point to the importance of the defence of Revolutionary achievements in France and to the connection between the creation of a mass army and political and social reforms in Germany and in other countries.

The inner life of a nation is linked with the modern mass army in a way it could not have been with the absolutist armies of the earlier period. In France the estate barrier between nobleman, officer and common soldier disappears: the highest positions in the army are open to all and it is well known that this barrier fell as a direct result of the Revolution. And even in those countries fighting against the Revolution, estate barriers were inevitably breached to some extent. One need only read the writings of Gneisenau to see how clearly these reforms were connected with the new historical situation created by the French Revolution. Further, the war inevitably destroyed the former separation of army from people. It is impossible to maintain mass armies on a depot basis. Since they have to maintain themselves by requisition they inevitably come into direct and permanent contact with the people of the country where the war is being waged. Of course, this contact very often consists of robbery and plunder. But not always. And it must not be forgotten that the wars of the Revolution and, to some extent, those of Napoleon were waged as conscious propaganda wars.

Finally, the enormous quantitative expansion of war plays a qualitatively new role, bringing with it an extraordinary broadening of horizons. Whereas the wars fought by the mercenary armies of absolutism consisted mostly of tiny manoeuvres around fortresses etc., now the whole of Europe becomes a war arena. French peasants fight first in Egypt, then in Italy, again in Russia; German and Italian auxiliary troops take part in the Russian campaign; German and Russian troops occupy Paris after Napoleon's defeat, and so forth. What previously was experienced only by isolated and mostly adventurous-minded individuals, namely an acquaintance with Europe or at least certain parts of it, becomes in this period the mass experience of hundreds of thousands, of millions.

Hence the concrete possibilities for men to comprehend their own existence as something historically conditioned, for them to see in history something which deeply affects their daily lives and immediately concerns them. There is no point in dealing here with the social transformations in France itself. It is quite obvious the extent to which the economic and cultural life of the entire nation was disrupted by the huge, rapidly successive changes of the period. It should be mentioned, however, that the Revolutionary armies and later those of Napoleon, too, did liquidate, completely or partially, the remnants of feudalism in many of the places they conquered, as for example in the Rhineland and Northern Italy. The social and cultural contrast between the Rhineland and the rest of Germany, still very noticeable at the time of the '48 Revolution, is a legacy handed down from the Napoleonic era, and the broad masses were conscious of the connection between these social changes and the French Revolution. To mention once again some of the literary reflexes: besides Heine's remembrances of his youth, it is most instructive to read the first chapters of Stendhal's *La Chartreuse de Parme* to see what a lasting impression was evoked by French rule in Northern Italy.

It is in the nature of a bourgeois revolution that, if seriously carried through to its conclusion, the national idea becomes the property of the broadest masses. In France it was only as a result of the Revolution and Napoleonic rule that a feeling of nationhood became the experience and property of the peasantry, the lower strata of the petty bourgeoisie and so on. For the first time they experienced France as their own country, as their self-created motherland.

But the awakening of national sensibility and with it a feeling and understanding for national history occurs not only in France. The Napoleonic wars everywhere evoked a wave of national feeling, of national resistance to the Napoleonic conquests, an experience of enthusiasm for national independence. To be sure, these movements are mostly, as Marx says, a compound of "regeneration and reaction", as in Spain, Germany etc. In Poland, on the other hand, the struggle for independence, the flare-up of national feeling is essentially progressive. But whatever the proportions of "regeneration and reaction" in individual national movements, it is clear that these movements— real mass movements—inevitably conveyed a sense and experience of history to broad masses. The appeal to national independence and national character is necessarily connected with a re-awakening of national history, with memories of the past, of past greatness, of moments of national dishonour, whether this results in a progressive or reactionary ideology.

Thus in this mass experience of history the national element is linked on the one hand with problems of social transformation; and on the other, more and more people become aware of the connection between national and world history. This increasing consciousness of the historical character of development begins to influence judgments on economic conditions and class struggle. In the eighteenth century it was only the odd critic of nascent capitalism, the wit and paradox-monger, who compared the exploitation of workers by Capital with forms of exploitation in earlier periods in order to expose Capitalism as the more inhumane form (Linguet). In the ideological struggle against the French Revolution a. similar comparison, admittedly shallow in economic terms and reactionary in tendency, between society before and after the Revolution or, on a wider scale, between Capitalism and Feudalism becomes the war-cry of Legitimist Romanticism. The inhumanity of Capitalism, the chaos of competition, the destruction of the small by the big, the debasement of culture by the transformation of all things into commodities—all this is contrasted, in a manner generally reactionary in tendency, with the social idyll of the Middle Ages, seen as a period of peaceful co-operation among all classes, an age of the organic growth of culture. But if mostly a reactionary tendency prevails in these polemical writings, it should not be forgotten that it was in this period that the notion of Capitalism as a definite, historical era of human development first arose, and this occurred not in the works of the great theorists of Capitalism, but in those of their enemies. It suffices to mention Sismondi here, who despite theoretical confusion over fundamental questions, raised certain individual historical problems of economic development with great clarity. One has only to think of his dictum that while in antiquity the proletariat lived at the expense of society, in modern times it is society which lives at the expense of the proletariat.

It is already clear from these remarks that the tendencies towards a conscious historicism reach their peak after the fall of Napoleon, at the time of the Restoration and the Holy Alliance. Admittedly, the spirit of historicism which at first prevails and gains official status is reactionary and by its nature pseudo-historical. The historical interpretation, publicist writings and *belles lettres* of Legitimism develop the historical spirit in radical opposition to the Enlightenment and the ideas of the French Revolution. The ideal of Legitimism is to return to pre-Revolutionary conditions, that is, to eradicate from history the greatest historical events of the epoch.

According to this interpretation history is a silent, imperceptible, natural, "organic" growth, that is, a development of society which is basically stagnation, which alters nothing in the time-honoured, legitimate institutions of society and, above all, alters nothing consciously. Man's activity in history is ruled out completely. The German historical school of law even denies nations the right to make new laws for themselves, it prefers to leave the old motley feudal laws of custom to their "organic growth".

Thus under the banner of historicism and of a struggle against the "abstract, unhistorical" spirit of the Enlightenment, there arises a pseudo-historicism, an ideology of immobility, of return to the Middle Ages. In the interests of these reactionary political aims, historical development is ruthlessly distorted. And the inner falsity of the reactionary ideology is intensified by the fact that the Restoration in France is compelled for economic reasons to come to terms socially with the Capitalism which has grown up in the meantime, indeed even to seek its partial support, economically and politically. (The situation of the reactionary governments in Prussia, Austria etc, is similar.) These then are the foundations on which history is to be written afresh. Chateaubriand tries hard to revise classical history in order to depreciate historically the old revolutionary ideal of the Jacobin and Napoleonic period. He and other pseudo-historians of reaction furnish a falsely idyllic picture of the unsurpassed, harmonious society of the Middle Ages. This historical interpretation of the Middle Ages determines the portrayal of feudal times in the Romantic novel of the Restoration.

Despite this ideological mediocrity of Legitimist pseudo-historicism, it exerts an extraordinarily powerful influence. Admittedly distorted and mendacious, it is nevertheless an historically necessary expression of the great period of transformation which sets in with the French Revolution. And the new stage of development, which begins precisely with the Restoration, compels the defenders of human progress to forge for themselves a new ideological armour. We have seen with what undaunted vigour the Enlightenment fought the historical legitimacy and continuity of feudal survivals. Similarly, we have seen how post-Revolutionary Legitimism regarded precisely their conservation as the content of history. The defenders of progress after the French Revolution had necessarily to reach a conception which would prove the *historical necessity* of the latter, furnish evidence that it constituted a peak in a long and gradual historical development and not a sudden eclipse of human consciousness, not a Cuvier-like "natural catastrophe" in human history, and that this was the only course open to the future development of mankind.

This, however, means a big change of outlook in the interpretation of human progress in comparison with the Enlightenment. Progress is no longer seen as an essentially unhistorical struggle between humanist reason and feudal-absolutist unreason. According to the new interpretation the reasonableness of human progress develops ever increasingly out of the inner conflict of social forces in history itself; according to this interpretation history itself is the bearer and realizer of human progress. The most important thing here is the increasing historical awareness of the decisive role played in human progress by the struggle of classes in history. The new spirit of historical writing, which is most clearly visible in the important French historians of the Restoration period, concentrates precisely on this question: on showing historically how modern bourgeois society arose out of the class struggles between nobility and bourgeoisie, out of class struggles which raged throughout the entire "idyllic Middle Ages" and whose last decisive stage was the great French Revolution. These ideas produce the first attempt at a rational periodization of history, an attempt to comprehend the historical nature and origins of the present rationally and scientifically. The first large-scale attempt at such a periodization had already been undertaken by Condorcet in the middle of the French Revolution, in his historico-philosophical major work. These ideas are further developed and scientifically enlarged in the Restoration period. Indeed, in the works of the great Utopians the periodization of history already transcends the horizon of bourgeois society. And if this transition, this step beyond Capitalism follows fantastic paths, its critical-historical basis is nonetheless linked—especially in the case of Fourier—with a devastating critique of the contradictions of bourgeois society. In Fourier, despite the fantastic nature of his ideas about Socialism and of the ways to Socialism, the picture of Capitalism is shown with such overwhelming clarity in all its contradiction that the idea of the transitory nature of this society appears tangibly and plastically before us.

This new phase in the ideological defence of human progress found its philosophical expression in Hegel. As we have seen, the central historical question was to demonstrate the necessity of the French Revolution, to show that revolution and historical development are not opposed to one another, as the apologists of feudal Legitimism maintained. The philosophy of Hegel provides the philosophic basis for this conception of history. Hegel's discovery of the universal law of transformation of quantity into quality is, seen historically, a philosophic methodology for the idea that revolutions constitute necessary, organic components of evolution and that without such a "nodal line of proportions" true evolution is impossible in reality and unthinkable philosophically.

On this basis, the Enlightenment conception of man is philosophically cancelled, preserved and raised to a higher level (aufgehoben). The greatest obstacle to an understanding of history lay in the Enlightenment's conception of man's unalterable nature. Thus, any change in the course of history had meant, in extreme cases, merely a change of costume and, in general, merely the moral ups and down of the same man. Hegelian philosophy draws all the inferences from the new progressive historicism. It sees man as a product of himself and of his own activity in history. And even if this historical process seems to stand idealistically upon its head, even if the bearer of the process is mystified into a "world spirit", Hegel nevertheless sees this world spirit as embodying the dialectics of historical development. "Thus the spirit opposes itself (i.e. in history G.L.) and has to overcome itself, as the really hostile obstacle to its own purpose: the evolution ... in the spirit ... is a hard, unceasing struggle against itself. What the spirit desires is to realize its own idea, yet it conceals this idea from itself, is proud and full of self-enjoyment in this alienation of its own self ... With the spiritual form it is different (from what it is in nature G.L.); here the change takes place not merely on the surface, but in the idea. It is the idea itself which is corrected." Hegel gives an apt description here—admittedly in an idealist and abstract fashion—of the ideological change which has occurred in his age. The thought of the earlier period oscillated antinomously between a fatalistic law-conforming conception of all social occurrence and an over-estimation of the possibilities of conscious intervention in social development. But on both sides of the antinomy the principles were considered to be "supra-historical", stemming from the "eternal" nature of "reason". Hegel, however, sees a process in history, a process propelled, on the one hand, by the inner motive forces of history and which, on the other, extends its influence to all the phenomena of human life, including thought. He sees the total life of humanity as a great historical process.

Thus there arose, in both a concrete historical as well as philosophic manner, a new humanism, a new concept of progress. A humanism which wished to preserve the achievements of the French Revolution as the imperishable basis of future human development, which regarded the French Revolution (and revolutions in history altogether) as an indispensable component of human progress. Of course, this new historical humanism was itself a child of its age and unable to transcend the limits of that age—except in a fantastical form, as was the case with the great Utopians. The important bourgeois humanists of this period find themselves in a paradoxical situation : while they comprehend the necessity of revolutions in the past and see in them the foundation for all that is reasonable and worthy of affirmation in the present, nevertheless they interpret future development in terms of a henceforth peaceful evolution on the basis of these achievements. As M. Lifschitz very rightly shows in his article on Hegel's aesthetics, they seek the positive things in the new world order created by the French Revolution and do not consider any new revolution to be necessary for the final realization of these positive things.

This conception of the last great intellectual and artistic period of bourgeois humanism has nothing to do with the barren and shallow apologia of capitalism which sets in later (and to some extent simultaneously). It is founded upon a ruthlessly truthful investigation and disclosure of all the contradictions of progress. There is no criticism of the present from which it will shrink. And even if it cannot consciously transcend the spiritual horizon of its time, yet the constantly oppressive sense of the contradictions of its own historical situation casts a profound shadow over the whole historical conception. This feeling that—contrary to the consciously philosophic and historical conception which proclaims unceasing and peaceful progress—one is experiencing a last brief, irretrievable intellectual prime of humanity manifests itself in the greatest representatives of this period in very different ways, in keeping with the unconscious character of this feeling. Yet for the same reason the emotional accent is very similar. Think of the old Goethe's theory of "abnegation", of Hegel's "Owl of Minerva" which takes flight only at dusk, of Balzac's sense of universal doom, etc. It was the 1848 Revolution which for the first time placed before the surviving representatives of this epoch the choice of either recognizing the perspective held out by the new period in human development and of affirming it, even if with a tragic cleavage of spirit, like Heine, or of sinking into the position of apologists for declining capitalism, as Marx, immediately after the 1848 Revolution, critically demonstrated in the case of such important figures as Guizot and Carlyle.

2. Sir Walter Scott

Such was the historical basis upon which Sir Walter Scott's historical novel arose. But one must never think of this relationship in terms of the idealist "history of the spirit" (Geistesgeschichte). In the latter we should find shrewd hypotheses to show the devious routes by which Hegelian ideas, for example, found their way to Scott; and some forgotten writer would be discovered who contained the common source of Scott's and Hegel's historicism. It is certain that Scott had no knowledge of Hegel's philosophy and had he come across it would probably not have understood a word. The new historical conception of the great historians of the Restoration actually makes its appearance later than the works of Scott and some of its problems are influenced by them. The fashionable philosophic-cum-philologic hunting down of individual "influences" is no more fruitful for the writing of history than the old philological hunting down of the effects of individual writers on one another. With Scott, in particular, it was the fashion to quote a long list of second and third-rate writers (Radcliffe, etc.), who were supposed to be important literary forerunners of his. All of which brings us not a jot nearer to understanding what was *new* in Scott's art, that is in his historical novel.

We have attempted to outline the general framework of those economic and political transformations which occurred throughout

Europe as a result of the French Revolution; in the preceding remarks we briefly sketched the latter's ideological consequences. These events, this transformation of men's existence and consciousness throughout Europe form the economic and ideological basis for Scott's historical novel. Biographical evidence of the individual instances which enabled Scott to become aware of these trends offers nothing of importance to the real history of the rise of the historical novel. The less so, as Scott ranks among those great writers whose depth is manifest mainly in their work, a depth which they often do not understand themselves, because it has sprung from a truly realistic mastery of their material in conflict with their personal views and prejudices.

Scott's historical novel is the direct continuation of the great realistic social novel of the eighteenth century. Scott's studies on eighteenth century writers, on the whole not very penetrating theoretically, reveal an intensive knowledge and detailed study of this literature. Yet his work, in comparison with theirs, signifies something entirely new. His great contemporaries clearly recognized this new quality. Pushkin writes of him: ... "The influence of Walter Scott can be felt in every province of the literature of his age. The new school of French historians formed itself under the influence of the Scottish novelist. He showed them entirely new sources which had so far remained unknown despite the existence of the historical drama of Shakespeare and Goethe ..." And Balzac, in his criticism of Stendhal's *La Chartreuse de Parme*, emphasizes the new artistic features which Scott's novel introduced into epic literature: the broad delineation of manners and circumstances attendant upon events, the dramatic character of action and, in close connection with this, the new and important role of dialogue in the novel.

It is no accident that this new type of novel arose in England. We have already mentioned, in dealing with the literature of the eighteenth century, important realistic features in the English novel of this period, and we described them as necessary consequences of the post-revolutionary character of England's development at the time, in contrast to France and Germany. Now, in a period when the whole of Europe, including its progressive classes and their ideologists, are swayed (temporarily) by a post-revolutionary ideology, these features in England must stand out with more than usual distinctness. For England has now once more become the model land of development for the majority of continental ideologists, though of course in a different sense from that of the eighteenth century. Then, the fact that bourgeois freedoms had actually been realized, served as an example to the Continental Enlighteners. Now, in the eyes of the historical ideologists of progress, England appears as the classic example of historical development in their sense. The fact that England had fought out its bourgeois revolution in the seventeenth century and had from then on experienced a peaceful, upward development, lasting over centuries, on the basis of the Revolution's achievements, showed England to be the practical, model example for the new style of historical interpretation. The "Glorious Revolution" of 1688, likewise, inevitably presented itself as an ideal to the bourgeois ideologists who were combating the Restoration in the name of progress.

On the other hand, however, honest writers, keenly observant of the real facts of social development, like Scott, were made to see that this peaceful development was peaceful only as the ideal of an historical conception, only from the bird's-eye view of a philosophy of history. The organic character of English development is a resultant made up of the components of ceaseless class struggles and their bloody resolution in great or small, successful or abortive uprisings. The enormous political and social transformations of the preceding decades awoke in England, too, the feeling for history, the awareness of historical development.

The relative stability of English development during this stormy period, in comparison with that of the Continent, made it possible to channel this newly-awoken historical feeling artistically into a broad, objective, epic form. This objectivity is further heightened by Scott's conservatism. His world-view ties him very closely to those sections of society which had been precipitated into ruin by the industrial revolution and the rapid growth of capitalism. Scott belongs neither with the ardent enthusiasts of this development, nor with its pathetic, passionate indicters. He attempts by fathoming historically the whole of English development to find a "middle way" for himself between the warring extremes. He finds in English history the consolation that the most violent vicissitudes of class struggle have always finally calmed down into a glorious "middle way". Thus, out of the struggle of the Saxons and Normans there arose the English nation, neither Saxon nor Norman; in the same way the bloody Wars of the Roses gave rise to the illustrious reign of the House of Tudor, especially that of Queen Elizabeth; and those class struggles which manifested themselves in the Cromwellian Revolution were finally evened out in the England of today, after a long period of uncertainty and civil war, by the "Glorious Revolution" and its aftermath.

The conception of English history in the novels of Scott thus gives a perspective (though not explicit) of future development in its author's sense. And it is not difficult to see that this perspective shows a marked affinity with that resigned "positivity" which we observed in the great thinkers, scholars and writers of this period on the Continent. Scott ranks among those honest Tories in the England of his time who exonerate nothing in the development of capitalism, who not only see clearly, but also deeply sympathize with the unending misery of the people which the collapse of old England brings in its wake; yet who, precisely because of their conservatism, display no violent opposition to the features of the new development repudiated by them. Scott very seldom speaks of the present. He does not raise the social questions of contemporary England in his novels, the class struggle between bourgeoisie and proletariat which was then beginning to sharpen. As far as he is able to answer these questions for himself, he does so in the indirect way of embodying the most important stages of the whole of English history in his writing.

Paradoxically, Scott's greatness is closely linked with his often narrow conservatism. He seeks the "middle way" between the extremes and endeavours to demonstrate artistically the historical reality of this way by means of his portrayal of the great crises in English history. This basic tendency finds immediate expression in the way he constructs his plot and selects his central figure. The "hero" of a Scott novel is always a more or less mediocre, average English gentleman. He generally possesses a certain, though never outstanding, degree of practical intelligence, a certain moral fortitude and decency which even rises to a capacity for self-sacrifice, but which never grows into a sweeping human passion, is never the enraptured devotion to a great cause. Not only are the Waverleys, Mortons, Osbaldistons and so on correct, decent, average representatives of the English petty aristocracy of this kind, but so, too, is Ivanhoe, the "romantic" knight of the Middle Ages.

In later criticism this choice of hero was sharply criticized, for example by Taine. Such later critics saw here a sympton of Scott's own mediocrity as an artist. Precisely the opposite is true. That he builds his novels round a "middling", merely correct and never heroic "hero" is the clearest proof of Scott's exceptional and revolutionary epic gifts, although from a psychological-biographical point of view, no doubt his own personal, petty aristocratic-conservative prejudices did play an important part in the choice of these heroes.

What is expressed here, above all, is a renunciation of Romanticism, a conquest of Romanticism, a higher development of the realist literary traditions of the Enlightenment in keeping with the new times. As a form of opposition to the degrading, all-levelling prose of rising capitalism the "demonic hero" makes his appearance even in the writings of politically and ideologically progressive writers who frequently, though unjustly, have been treated as Romantics. This hero type, particularly as he appears in the poetry of Byron, is the literary expression of the social eccentricity and superfluity of the best and sincerest human talents in this period of prose, a lyrical protest against the dominion of this prose. But it is one thing to acknowledge the social roots or even the historical necessity and justification of this protest and another to make of it a lyrical-sub-jectivist absolute. On this latter basis an objective portrayal is impossible. The great realistic writers of a somewhat later period who portrayed this type, such as Pushkin or Stendhal, overcame Byronism differently from Scott and in a higher form. They interpreted the problem of the eccentricity of this type in a social-historical, objective-epic way : that is, they saw the present historically and revealed all the social determinants of the tragedy (or tragi-comedy) of this protest. Scott's criticism and rejection of this type does not go as deep as this. His recognition or rather sense of the eccentricity of this type has the result of eliminating him from the sphere of historical portrayal. Scott endeavours to portray the struggles and antagonisms of history by means of characters who, in their psychology and destiny, always represent social trends and historical forces. Scott also extends this approach to the processes of declassing, always regarding them socially and not individually. His understanding for the problems of the present is not sufficiently deep for him to portray the problem of de-classing as it affects the present. Therefore he avoids this subject and preserves in his portrayals the great historical objectivity of the true epic writer.

For this reason alone, then, it is completely wrong to see Scott as a Romantic writer, unless one wishes to extend the concept of Romanticism to embrace all great literature in the first third of the nineteenth century. But then the physiognomy of Romanticism, in the proper, narrow sense, becomes blurred. And this is of great importance if we are to understand Scott. For the historical subject-matter of his novels is very close to that of the Romantics proper. However, we shall show subsequently in detail that Scott's interpretation of this subject-matter is entirely opposed to that of the Romantics, as is his manner of portrayal. This contrast has its first, immediate expression in the composition of his novels—with the mediocre, prosaic hero as the central figure.

Naturally, Scott's conservative philistinism is manifest here as well. Already Balzac, his great admirer and successor, took objection to this English philistinism. He says, for example, that with very few excep-tions all of Scott's heroines represent the same type of philistinely correct, normal English woman; that there is no room in these novels for the interesting and complex tragedies and comedies of love and marriage. Balzac is right in his criticism, and it applies far beyond the erotic sphere which he stresses. Scott does not command the mag-nificent, profound psychological dialectics of character which dis-tinguishes the novel of the last great period of bourgeois development. Nor indeed does he reach the heights scaled by the bourgeois novel in the second half of the eighteenth century, by Rousseau, Choderlos de Laclos and Goethe's *Werther*. His greatest successors in the historical novel, Pushkin and Manzoni, also far surpassed him in this respect by the depth and poetry of their characterization. But the change which Scott effects in the history of world literature is independent of this limitation of his human and poetic horizon. Scott's greatness lies in his capacity to give living human embodiment to historical-social types. The typically human terms in which great historical trends become tangible had never before been so superbly, straightforwardly and pregnantly portrayed. And above all, never before had this kind of portrayal been consciously set at the centre of the representation of reality.

This applies to his mediocre heroes as well. They are unsurpassed in their portrayal of the decent and attractive as well as narrow-minded features of the English "middle class". And as central figures they provide a perfect instrument for Scott's way of presenting the totality of certain transitional stages of history. This relationship was most clearly recognized by the great Russian critic, Belinsky. He accepts that the majority of the minor characters are more interesting and significant as human beings than the mediocre main hero, yet he strongly defends Scott. "This has indeed to be the case in a work of purely epic nature, where the chief character serves merely as an external central hub round which the events unfold and where he may distinguish himself merely by general human qualities which earn our human sympathy; for the hero of the epic is life itself and not the individual. In epic, the individual is, so to speak, subject to the event; the event over-shadows the human personality by its magnitude and importance, drawing our attention away from him by the interesting-ness, diversity and multiplicity of its images."

Belinsky is quite right in emphasizing the purely epic character of Scott's novels. In the entire history of the novel there are scarcely any other works—except perhaps those of Cooper and Tolstoy—which come so near to the character of the old epos. This, as we shall see, is very closely linked with the nature of Scott's historical subject-matter. And it is linked not with his interest in history as such, but with the specific nature of his historical themes, with his selection of those periods and those strata of society which embody the old epic self-activity of man, the old epic directness of social life, its public spontaneity. This it is that makes Scott a great epic portrayer of the "age of heroes", the age in and from which the true epic grows, in the sense of Vico and Hegel. This truly epic character of Scott's sub-ject-matter and manner of portrayal is, as we shall later show in detail, intimately linked with the popular character of his art.

Nevertheless, Scott's works are in no way modern attempts to galvanize the old epic artificially into new life, they are real and genuine novels. Even if his themes are very often drawn from the "age of heroes", from the infancy of mankind, the spirit of his writing is nevertheless that of man's maturity, the age of triumphing "prose". This difference must be stressed if only because it is intimately connected with the composition of Scott's novels, with the conception of their "hero". Scott's novel hero is in his way just as typical for this genre as Achilles and Odysseus were for the real epopee. The difference between the two hero types illustrates very sharply the fundamental difference between epic and novel, moreover in a case where the novel reaches its closest point to the epic. The heroes of the epic are, as Hegel says, "total individuals who magnificently concentrate within themselves what is otherwise dispersed in the national character, and in this they remain great, free and noble human characters". Thereby "these principal characters acquire the right to be placed at the summit and to see the principal event in connection with their individual persons". The principal figures in Scott's novels are also typical characters nationally, but in the sense of the decent and average, rather than the eminent and all-embracing. The latter are the national heroes of a poetic view of life, the former of a prosaic one.

It is easy to see how these contrasting conceptions of the hero spring from the fundamental requirements of epic and novel. Achilles is not only compositionally the central figure of the epic, he is also a head taller than all his fellow actors, he really is the sun round which the planets revolve. Scott's heroes, as central figures of the novel, have an entirely opposite function. It is their task to bring the extremes whose struggle fills the novel, whose clash expresses artistically a great crisis in society, into contact with one another. Through the plot, at whose centre stands this hero, a neutral ground is sought and found upon which the extreme, opposing social forces can be brought into a human relationship with one another.

Scott's simple, yet inexhaustible and superb inventiveness in this respect is generally, especially today, too little appreciated, although Goethe, Balzac and Pushkin clearly recognized this greatness. Scott presents great crises of historical life in his novels. Accordingly, hostile social forces, bent on one another's destruction, are everywhere colliding. Since those who lead these warring forces are always passionate partisans of their respective sides, there is the danger that their struggle will become a merely external picture of mutual destruction incapable of arousing the human sympathies and enthusiasms of the reader. It is here that the compositional importance of the mediocre hero comes in. Scott always chooses as his principal figures such as may, through character and fortune, enter into human contact with both camps. The appropriate fortunes of such a mediocre hero, who sides passionately with neither of the warring camps in the great crisis of his time can provide a link of this kind without forcing the composition. Let us take the best known example. Waverley is an English country squire from a family which is pro-Stuart, but which does no more than quietly sympathize in a politically ineffective fashion. During his stay in Scotland as an English officer, Waverley, as a result of personal friendships and love entanglements, enters the camp of the rebellious Stuart supporters. As a result of his old family connections and the uncertain nature of his participation in the uprising, which allows him to fight bravely, but never to become fanatically partisan, his relations with the Hanoverian side are sustained. In this way Waverley's fortunes create a plot which not only gives us a pragmatic picture of the struggle on both sides, but brings us humanly close to the important representatives of either side.

This manner of composition is not the product of a "search for form" or some ingeniously contrived "skill", it stems rather from the strengths and limitations of Scott's literary personality. In the first place Scott's conception of English history is, as we have seen, that of a "middle course" asserting itself through the struggle of extremes. The central figures of the Waverley type represent for Scott the age-old steadfastness of English development amidst the most terrible crises. In the second place, however, Scott, the great realist, recognizes that no civil war in history has been so violent as to turn the entire population without exception into fanatical partisans of one or other of the contending camps. Large sections of people have always stood between the camps with fluctuating sympathies now for this side, now for the other. And these fluctuating sympathies have often played a decisive role in the actual outcome of the crisis. In addition, the daily life of the nation still goes on amidst the most terrible civil war. It has to go on in the sheer economic sense that if it does not, the nation will starve and perish. But it also goes on in every other respect, and this continuation of daily life is an important foundation for the continuity of cultural development. Of course, the continuation of daily life certainly does not mean that the life, thought and experience of these non- or not passionately participant popular masses can remain untouched by the historical crisis. The continuity is always at the same time a growth, a further development. The "middle-of-the-road heroes" of Scott also represent this side of popular life and historical development.

But still further and very important consequences flow from this manner of composition. For instance what may sound paradoxical to the reader prejudiced by present-day traditions of the historical novel, but is nevertheless true, is the fact that Scott's incomparable ability to recreate the great figures of history was due to precisely this aspect of his composition. In Scott's life-work we meet with the most important personalities of English and even of French history: Richard *Coeur de Lion*, Louis XI, Elizabeth, Mary Stuart, Cromwell etc. All these figures appear in Scott in their real historical grandeur. Yet Scott is never prompted by a feeling of romantically decorative hero-worship à la Carlyle. For him the great historical personality is the representative of an important and significant movement embracing large sections of the people. He is great because his personal passion and personal aim coincide with this great historical movement, because he concentrates within himself its positive and negative sides, because he gives to these popular strivings their clearest expression, because he is their standard-bearer in good and in evil.

For this reason Scott never shows the evolution of such a personality. Instead, he always presents us with the personality complete. Complete, yet not without the most careful preparation. This preparation, however, is not a personal and psychological one, but objective, social-historical. That is to say, Scott, by disclosing the actual conditions of life, the actual growing crisis in people's lives, depicts all the problems of popular life which lead up to the historical crisis he has represented. And when he has made us sympathizers and understanding participants of this crisis, when we understand exactly for what reasons the crisis has arisen, for what reasons the nation has split into two camps, and when we have seen the attitude of the various sections of the population towards this crisis, only then does the great historical hero enter upon the scene of the novel. He may therefore, indeed he must, be complete in a psychological sense when he appears before us, for he appears in order to fulfil his historic mission in the crisis. The reader, however, never has the impression of anything rigidly complete, for the broadly drawn social struggles which precede the appearance of the hero show how at just such a time, just such a hero had to arise in order to solve just such problems.

Scott, of course, uses this manner of portrayal not only for the historically authenticated and well-known representative figures. On the contrary. In Scott's most important novels historically unknown, semi-historical or entirely non-historical persons play this leading role. Think of Vich Ian Vohr in *Waverley*, Burley in *Old Mortality*, Cedric and Robin Hood in *Ivanhoe*, Rob Roy and so on. These, too, are monumental historical figures, created according to the same artistic principles as the familiar historical figures. Indeed, the popular character of Scott's historical art manifests itself in the fact that these leader figures, who are directly interwoven with the life of the people, in general are more historically imposing than the well-known central figures of history.

But what is the connection between Scott's ability to portray the

historical greatness of an important figure and the minor compositional role which the latter plays? Balzac understood this secret of
Scott's composition. Scott's novels, he said, marched towards the great
heroes in the same way as history itself had done when it required their
appearance. The reader, therefore, experiences the historical genesis
of the important historical figures, and it is the writer's task from
then on to let their actions make them appear the real representatives
of these historical crises.

Scott thus lets his important figures grow out of the being of the
age, he never explains the age from the position of its great representatives, as do the Romantic hero-worshippers. Hence they can never
be central figures of the action. For the being of the age can
only appear as a broad and many-sided picture if the everyday life
of the people, the joys and sorrows, crises and confusions of average
human beings are portrayed. The important leading figure, who embodies an historical movement, necessarily does so at a certain level
of abstraction. Scott, by first showing the complex and involved
character of popular life itself, creates this being which the leading
figure then has to generalize and concentrate in an historical deed.

Scott's manner of composition here shows a very interesting
parallel to Hegel's philosophy of history. For Hegel, too, the "world-
historical individual" arises upon the broad basis of the world of
"maintaining individuals". "Maintaining individuals" is Hegel's all-
embracing term for men in "civil society", it describes society's uninterrupted self-reproduction through the activity of these individuals.
The basis is formed by the personal, private, egoistic activity of individual human beings. In and through this activity the socially general
asserts itself. In this activity the "maintenance of moral life" unfolds
itself. But Hegel does not only think of society in the sense of this
self-reproduction, as something stagnant; society also stands amid the
current of history. Here the new opposes itself hostilely to the old,
and the change "goes hand in hand with a depreciation, demolition
and destruction of the preceding mode of reality". There occur great
historical collisions in which, while the "world-historical individuals"
are conscious bearers of historical progress (or of the "spirit" according to Hegel), they are so only in the sense of granting consciousness
and clear direction to a movement already present in society. It is
necessary to emphasize this side of the Hegelian conception of history,
because it is here—despite Hegel's idealism, his over-rating of the
role of the "world-historical individuals"—that the contrast with the
Romantic hero cult comes out sharply. According to Hegel the function of the world-historical individual is to tell men what they want.
"He is," says Hegel, "the hidden Spirit knocking at the door of the
present, still subterranean, still without a contemporary existence and

wishing to break out, for whom the contemporary world is but a husk containing a different kernel from the old."

Scott's unequalled historical genius shows itself in the individual characteristics which he gives his leading figures so that they really concentrate in themselves the salient positive and negative sides of the movement concerned. The social and historical solidarity of leader and led in Scott is differentiated with extraordinary subtlety. Burley's single-minded, dauntless, heroic fanaticism marks the human summit of the rebellious Scottish Puritans at the time of Stuart Restoration, just as Vich Ian Vohr's peculiar, adventuresome compound of French courtly manners and clan patriarchalism represents the reactionary side of Stuart Restoration attempts after the "Glorious Revolution" which closely involved backward sections of the Scottish people.

This close interaction, this deep unity between the historical representatives of a popular movement and the movement itself is heightened compositionally in Scott by the intensification and dramatic compression of events. Here again the classical form of narrative must be shielded from modern prejudices. It is a general belief today that because epic portrays more extensively and broadly than drama, therefore it is pure extension, the chronicle-like succession and juxtaposition of all the events of a period which must constitute the essential character of epic art. Yet this is not the case even in Homer. Think of the composition of the Iliad. The poem begins with an extremely dramatic situation, the clash between Achilles and Agamemnon. And the actual narrative consists only of those events which are the direct consequence of this clash, namely the events up to Hector's death. Even classical aesthetics recognized a conscious principle of composition here. With the rise of the modern social novel such intensification has become even more necessary. For the inter-relationships between the psychology of people and the economic and moral circumstances of their lives have grown so complex that it requires a very broad portrayal of these circumstances and interactions if people are to appear clearly as the concrete children of their age. It is no accident that Scott's growing historical consciousness moved towards this kind of form. To awaken distant, vanished ages and enable us to live through them again he had to depict this concrete interaction between man and his social environment in the broadest manner. The inclusion of the dramatic element in the novel, the concentration of events, the greater significance of dialogue, i.e. the direct coming-to-grips of colliding opposites in conversation, these are intimately linked with the attempt to portray historical reality as it actually was, so that it could be both humanly authentic and yet be re-liveable by the reader of a later age. It is a question of the concentration of characterization. Only bunglers have maintained (and continue to do so) that the his-

torical characterization of people and events means the accumulation
of single, historically characteristic traits.

Scott never under-estimated the importance of picturesque, descriptive elements of this kind. Indeed, he used them so much that superficial critics have seen here the essence of his art. But for Scott the
historical characterization of time and place, the historical "here and
now" is something much deeper. For him it means that certain crises
in the personal destinies of a number of human beings coincide and
interweave within the determining context of an historical crisis. It
is precisely for this reason that his manner of portraying the historical
crisis is never abstract, the split of the nation into warring parties
always runs through the centre of the closest human relationships.
Parents and children, lover and beloved, old friends etc. confront one
another as opponents, or the inevitability of this confrontation carries
the collision deep into their personal lives. It is always a fate suffered
by groups of people connected and involved with one another; and it
is never a matter of one single catastrophe, but of a chain of catastrophes, where the solution of each gives birth to a new conflict.
Thus the profound grasp of the historical factor in human life demands a dramatic concentration of the epic framework.

The great writers of the eighteenth century composed much more
loosely. They were able to do so because they took the manners of
their time for granted and could assume an immediate and obvious
effect upon their readers. But do not forget that this applies to the
general structure of composition and not to the manner in which
individual moments and happenings are portrayed. These writers also
knew quite well that it was not completeness of description that mat-
tered—the enumeration of an object's constituents or of a sequence of
events forming a person's life, but the working-out of essential human
and social determinants. Goethe's *Wilhelm Meister* is conceived much
less dramatically than Scott's or Balzac's novels which come later.
But the individual events in this long story show a definite tendency
towards intensification. Wilhelm Meister's relationship to Serlo's
theatre, for instance, is almost entirely concentrated around the problem of the Hamlet production. In Goethe, too, there is no question of
a complete description of the theatre, nor of a complete chronicle of
events in the theatre.

The dramatic concentration and intensification of events in Scott
is thus in no way a radical innovation. It is merely a special summing-
up and extension of the most important artistic principles of the preceding period of development. But because Scott accomplished this
extension at a great historical turning-point, in keeping with the real
needs of the time, it signifies a turning-point in the history of the
novel. For the historical novel presents the writer with a specially

strong temptation to try and produce an extensively complete totality. The idea that only such completeness can guarantee historical fidelity is a very persuasive one. But it is a delusion, to which Balzac, in particular, drew sharp attention in his critical writings. In a review of Latouche's completely forgotten historical novel *Leo*, he says: "The entire novel consists of 200 pages on which 200 events are dealt with; nothing betrays the incompetence of the author more than the heaping-up of facts . . . . Talent flourishes where the causes which produce the facts are portrayed, in the secrets of the human heart, whose motions are neglected by the historians. The characters of a novel are forced to be more rational than historical characters. The former must be roused to life, the latter have already lived. The existence of the latter requires no proof, however bizarre their actions may have been, while the existence of the former requires general agreement." It is clear that the more remote an historical period and the conditions of life of its actors, the more the action must concern itself with bringing these conditions plastically before us, so that we should not regard the particular psychology and ethics which arise from them as an historical curiosity, but should re-experience them as a phase of mankind's development which concerns and moves us.

What matters therefore in the historical novel is not the re-telling of great historical events, but the poetic awakening of the people who figured in those events. What matters is that we should re-experience the social and human motives which led men to think, feel and act just as they did in historical reality. And it is a law of literary portrayal which first appears paradoxical, but then quite obvious, that in order to bring out these social and human motives of behaviour, the outwardly insignificant events, the smaller (from without) relationships are better suited than the great monumental dramas of world history. Balzac, in his criticism of Stendhal's *La Chartreuse de Parme*, enthusiastically praised Stendhal's genius, because he had undertaken a magnificent picture of court life within the framework of an Italian petty state. Balzac points out how in the petty struggles of the court of Parma all the social and spiritual conflicts which took place, for example, in the big struggles round Mazarin and Richelieu, are clearly manifest. And these struggles, according to Balzac, can be better portrayed in this way because the political content of the intrigues in Parma can be easily surveyed as a whole, can be translated directly into action and because its human spiritual reflexes can be revealed in an obvious, straightforward way, whereas the presentation of the big political problems which formed the substance of the intrigues round Mazarin or Richelieu, would create a dead and heavy ballast in a novel.

Balzac applies his argument to the smallest details involved in the epic treatment of history. He criticizes among other things a novel by Eugène Sue which deals with the rebellion in the Cévennes under Louis XIV. Sue gave an extensive description of the entire campaign from fight to fight in a modern dilettantist manner. Balzac attacks this enterprise with the greatest vigour. He says: "It is impossible for literature to go beyond a certain limit in painting the facts of war. To depict the Cévennes mountains, the plains between them, the flat expanse of Languedoc, and troop manoeuvres covering this entire area—this is something that Walter Scott and Cooper felt to b∟ beyond their powers. They never attempted a campaign in their works, but confined themselves to small encounters, revealing through them the spirit of the two contending masses. And even these small skirmishes which they undertook required lengthy preparation in their works." Balzac's description here of the intensive character of Scott's and Cooper's picture of history, applies also to the later development of the historical novel in the work of its great classical exponents.

Thus it would be a mistake to think that Tolstoy, for instance, really depicted the Napoleonic wars in extenso. What he does is, every now and then, to take an episode from the war which is of particular importance and significance for the human development of his main characters. And Tolstoy's genius as an historical novelist lies in his ability to select and portray these episodes so that the entire mood of the Russian army and through them of the Russian people gains vivid expression. Where he attempts to deal with comprehensive political and strategic problems of the war, for example in his description of Napoleon, he abandons himself to historico-philosophical effusions. And he does this not only because he misunderstands Napoleon historically, but also for literary reasons. Tolstoy was far too great a writer to be capable of offering a literary surrogate. Where his material could no longer be artistically embodied, he radically forsook literary means of expression and attempted to master his theme by intellectual means. And in so doing he furnishes a practical proof for the correctness of Balzac's analysis of the Scott novel and his criticism of Sue.

The historical novel therefore has to demonstrate by artistic means that historical circumstances and characters existed in precisely such and such a way. What in Scott has been called very superficially "authenticity of local colour" is in actual fact this artistic demonstration of historical reality. It is the portrayal of the broad living basis of historical events in their intricacy and complexity, in their manifold interaction with acting individuals. The difference between "maintaining" and "world-historical" individuals is expressed in this living connection with the existential basis of events. The former experience the smallest oscillations in this basis as immediate disturbances of their individual lives, while the latter concentrate the main features of events into motives for their own actions and for influencing and guiding the actions of the masses. The closer the "maintaining individuals" are to the ground, the less fitted they are for historical leadership, the more distinctly and vividly do these disturbances make themselves felt in their everyday lives, in their immediate, emotional responses. Obviously, such responses may easily become one-sided and even false. But a total historical picture depends upon a rich and graded interaction between different levels of response to any major disturbance of life. It must disclose artistically the *connection* between the spontaneous reaction of the masses and the historical consciousness of the leading personalities.

Such connections are of decisive importance for the understanding of history. One of the distinctive qualities of really great popular political leaders is their unusually sensitive understanding for such spontaneous reactions. Their genius manifests itself in the unusual rapidity with which they are able to perceive in quite small and insignificant reactions a change of mood, in the people or a class, and to generalize the connection between this mood and the objective course of events. This power of perception and generalization forms the basis of what leaders customarily call "learning from the masses". Lenin in his pamphlet *Will the Bolsheviks Retain State Power?* describes a very instructive instance of this interaction. After the suppression of the July rising of the Petrograd proletariat in 1917 Lenin is forced to live in illegality with a workers' family in the suburbs. He describes the preparation of the midday meal. "The wife brings in the bread. The husband says: 'Look at this lovely bread. They don't dare give us bad bread now. We had almost forgotten that there was good bread to be had in Petrograd'." Lenin adds: "I was amazed at this class estimate of the July days. My thoughts had revolved round the political significance of the events ... As a person who had never known want, I had never given a thought to bread ... Thought follows an uncommonly complicated and intricate path to reach, via political analysis, what is at the basis of everything, namely the class struggle for bread."

Here we can see such an interaction in wonderful plasticity. The Petrograd worker reacts with spontaneous class-consciousness to the events of the July days. Lenin learns from these reactions with the greatest sensitivity and turns them to account with remarkable speed and precision in the consolidation, substantiation and propagation of the correct political perspective.

It would, of course, be historically wrong if interactions of this kind were portrayed in novels dealing with the Middle Ages, 17th or 18th centuries. Besides, such interactions lay far beyond the horizon of the classical founders of the historical novel. Moreover, this example was only meant to illustrate the general structure of the interaction. But although all Scott's heroes acted with a "false consciousness" this is never a scheme, neither in its content nor its psychology. The difference, both in historical content and psychology, between close-to-life spontaneity and the capacity of generalization, which exists apart from the immediate necessities of earning a living, runs right through history. It is the task of the historical novelist to portray this concrete interaction, in keeping with the concrete, historical circumstances of the age he represents, as richly as possible. And this is one of Scott's greatest strengths.

The colourful and varied richness of Scott's historical world is a consequence of the multiplicity of these interactions between individuals and the unity of social existence which underlies this richness. The problem of composition already discussed, the fact, that the great historical figures, the leaders of the warring classes and parties are only minor characters in the story, now takes on a new light. Scott does not stylize these figures, nor place them upon a Romantic pedestal; he portrays them as human beings with virtues and weaknesses, good and bad qualities. And yet they never create a petty impression. With all their weaknesses they appear historically imposing. The primary reason for this is, of course, Scott's deep understanding for the peculiarity of different historical periods. But the fact that he is able to combine historical grandeur with genuine human qualities in this way depends upon the manner of his composition.

The great historical figure, as a minor character, is able to live himself out to the full as a human being, to display freely all his splendid and petty human qualities. However, his place in the action is such that he can only act and express himself in situations of historical importance. He achieves here a many-sided and full expression of his personality, but only insofar as it is linked with the big events of history. Otto Ludwig says very perceptively of Scott's Rob Roy: "He can appear all the more significant, because we do not follow his life step by step; we see him only at moments when he is *significant*; he surprises us by his omnipresence, he reveals himself only in the most interesting attitudes."

These remarks not only correctly describe Scott's manner of composition, they also point to general laws of portrayal: to the manner of representing important persons. Here there are deep differences between epic and novel. The all-national character of the principal themes of epic, the relation between individual and nation in the age of heroes require that the most important figure should occupy the central position, while in the historical novel he is necessarily only a minor character.

However, the choice of situation, noted by Otto Ludwig, where the leading figure only appears at significant moments also applies *mutatis mutandis* to epic. Hölderlin recognized this, correctly and profoundly, in the case of Achilles. He says: "One has often wondered why Homer who, after all, wanted to sing the anger of Achilles, hardly allows him to appear etc. ... He did not wish to profane the divine youth in the tumult outside Troy. The ideal must not appear commonplace. And he really could not sing him more gloriously and tenderly than by withdrawing him into the background ... , so that every loss of the Greeks from the day the matchless one is missed from the army recalls his superiority over the entire resplendent host of lords and servants, and the rare moments when the poet allows him to appear before us are thrown all the more into relief by his absence."

It is not too difficult to see the common factors here. Since all narrative art has to do with the small and even trivial details of life, it cannot allow the hero to figure personally in the foreground all the time for this would mean reducing him to the general level of the life portrayed; only a forced stylization could then effect the desired and necessary distance between him and the other characters. But this kind of stylization runs contrary to the real nature of epic which always seeks to create the impression of life as it normally is *as a whole*. This precisely is one of the many, never-fading charms of the Homeric epics, while the so-called literary epic, which almost consistently stylizes the distance between hero and surrounding world, elevating the central figure artificially, is epically lifeless, rhetorical and lyrical. In Homer a character like Achilles always has the same naturalness and human simplicity as any other figure. Homer lifts him from his surroundings by genuinely epic means, that is which are both artistic *and* true to nature: he creates situations where the significant emerges, so to speak, "of its own accord", situations in which the hero steps naturally, "of his own accord", on to a pedestal by contrasting with his own absence.

All these general epic functions are present in Scott, too. But, as we have seen, the relationship of the "world-historical individual" to the world in which he acts is quite different in the historical novel. The important features here are not the supreme manifestations of an essentially unchanging world order (as far as literature was concerned), but on the contrary the radical sharpening of social trends in an historical crisis. Further, the historical novel portrays a much more differentiated social world than the ancient epos. And with the increasing class divisions and class oppositions the representative role of the "world-historical individual", who concentrates the most important features of a society, takes on quite a different significance.

The antagonisms in the old epics are predominantly national ones.

The great national opponents, say, Achilles and Hector, represent socially, and therefore also morally, very similar orders: the moral scope of their actions is approximately the same: for the one, the human assumptions behind the actions of the other are fairly transparent and so on. All this is quite different in the world of the historical novel. Here the "world-historical individual" is, even viewed socially, a *party*, a representative of *one* of the many contending classes and strata. However, if he is to fulfil his function as the crowning summit of such an artistic world, then he must—in a very complex, very indirect way—also render visible the generally progressive features of the whole of society, of the whole age. These complicated preconditions of his representative role are portrayed in Scott by means of that broad prehistory which everywhere points towards his appearance; and the need for this prehistory would alone suffice to make him a minor character in the sense already explained.

This again then, as the reader has no doubt already gathered from the previous remarks, is not a matter of a clever technical trick on Scott's part, but of the artistic expression, in compositional terms, of his historical attitude to life. His admiration of the great personalities of history as decisive factors in the historical process leads him to this manner of composition. By renewing the old laws of epic poetry in his original way Scott discovers the only possible means whereby the historical novel can reflect historical reality adequately, without either romantically monumentalizing the important figures of history or dragging them down to the level of private, psychological trivia. Thus Scott humanizes his historical heroes, while avoiding what Hegel calls the psychology of the valet, namely the detailed analysis of small, human peculiarities which have nothing to do with the historical mission of the person concerned.

However, this manner of composition certainly does not mean that Scott's historical figures are not individualized down to their smallest human peculiarities. They are never mere representatives of historical movements, ideas etc. Scott's great art consists precisely in individualizing his historical heroes in such a way that certain, purely individual traits of character, quite peculiar to them, are brought into a very complex, very live relationship with the age in which they live, with the movement which they represent and endeavour to lead to victory. Scott represents simultaneously the historical necessity of this particular individual personality and the individual role which he plays in history. What results from this peculiar relationship is not merely whether the struggle will end in victory or defeat, but also the special, historical character of the victory or defeat, its special historical *valeur*, its class timbre.

One of the greatest feats of portrayal in world literature, for instance, is the way Mary Stuart concentrates all the features which from the outset condemn to failure her *coup d'état* and flight. The shadow of these qualities may already be felt in the composition and conduct of her supporters, who are preparing the *coup*, long before she herself is shown to the readers. Her own conduct adds consciousness to this feeling, and the defeat itself is only the fulfilment of an expectation which has been fostered for a long time. With equal mastery, but with quite different technical means, Scott depicts the superiority and victorious diplomacy of the French King, Louis XI. At the beginning the contrast, social and human, between the King and his retinue, still mostly feudal-chivalrous in sentiment, only appears in a few small preliminary skirmishes. Then for the entire middle action of the novel the King vanishes from the scene. He has cunningly saddled the correct, chivalrous hero, Quentin Durward, with a dangerous, indeed insoluble, task. And only at the end does he reappear in what is, outwardly, a completely desperate plight as a prisoner in the camp of the feudal-chivalrous, adventursome and politically stupid Duke of Burgundy, where purely by use of reason and cunning he extracts such advantages as to leave the reader in no doubt that, despite the draw with which the novel ends, the principle for which he stands has triumphed. These complex and yet straightforward interactions between the representatives of different classes, between the "above" and "below" of society create that incomparably truthful, historical atmosphere which in every novel of Scott reawakens a period; and which reawakens not only its historical-social content, but its human and emotional qualities, its particular redolence and ring.

This truthfulness of historical atmosphere which we are able to relive in Scott rests on the popular character of his art. This popular character met with growing incomprehension during the literary and cultural decadence. Taine asserts quite erroneously that Scott's art propagated feudal attitudes. This false theory was taken over whole by vulgar sociology and further extended, the sole difference being that Scott was now conceived as the poet, not of the feudal world, but of the English merchants and colonizers of contemporary English imperialism. Such "theories" of the historical novel—devised in order to erect a Chinese wall between the classical past and the present and so to deny the Socialist character of our present-day culture à la Trotsky—see in Scott nothing but the bard of the colonizing merchants.

The precise opposite is true. And this was clearly recognized by Scott's immediate contemporaries and important successors. George Sand quite rightly said of him : "He is the poet of the peasant, soldier, outlaw and artisan." For, as we have seen, Scott portrays the great transformations of history as transformations of popular life. He always starts by showing how important historical changes affect everyday life, the effect of material and psychological changes upon people who react immediately and violently to them, without understanding their causes. Only by working up from this basis, does he portray the complicated ideological, political and moral movements to which such changes inevitably give rise. The popular character of Scott's art, therefore, does not consist in an exclusive portrayal of the oppressed and exploited classes. That would be a narrow interpretation. Like every great popular writer, Scott aims at portraying the totality of national life in its complex interaction between "above" and "below"; his vigorous popular character is expressed in the fact that "below" is seen as the material basis and artistic explanation for what happens "above".

In *Ivanhoe* Scott portrays the central problem of medieval England, the opposition between the Saxons and Normans, in this way. He makes it very clear that this opposition is above all one between Saxon serfs and Norman feudal lords. But, in a true historical manner, he goes further than this opposition. He knows that a section of the Saxon nobility, though materially restricted and robbed of its political power, is still in possession of its aristocratic privileges and that this provides the ideological and political centre of the Saxons' national resistance to the Normans. However, as a great portrayer of historical, national life Scott sees and shows with eminent plasticity how important sections of the Saxon nobility sink into apathy and inertia, how others again are only waiting for the opportunity to strike a compromise with the more moderate sections of the Norman nobility whose representative is Richard *Coeur de Lion*. Thus, when Belinsky quite rightly says that Ivanhoe, the hero of this novel and likewise an aristocratic adherent of this compromise, is overshadowed by the minor characters, this formal problem of the historical novel has a very clear historical-political and popular content. For although one of the figures who overshadows Ivanhoe is his father, the brave and ascetic Saxon nobleman, Cedric, the most important of these figures are the latter's serfs, Gurth and Wamba, and above all the leader of the armed resistance to Norman rule, the legendary popular hero, Robin Hood. The interaction between "above" and "below", the sum of which constitutes the totality of popular life, is thus manifested in the fact that, while on the whole the historical tendencies "above" receive a more distinct and generalized expression, we find the true heroism with which the historical antagonisms are fought out, with few exceptions, "below".

The picture of popular life is drawn in just the same way in the other novels. Admittedly, in *Waverley* Vich Ian Vohr is the tragic hero, who for his loyalty to the Stuarts ends on the gallows. Yet we do not find the real, humanly stirring, unproblematic heroism in this —when all is said—ambiguous adventurer figure, but among his supporters in the Scottish clan. One of the greatest portrayals of simple, wordless heroism is the proposal of Evan Dhu, Vich Ian Vohr's fellow clansman, at the trial where they are both condemned to death: Evan Dhu whom the court would willingly pardon, suggests that he and a few other members of the clan should be executed in return for the release of their chief.

In touches such as these Scott's combination of popular spirit and historical authenticity emerges very clearly. Historical authenticity means for him the quality of the inner life, the morality, heroism, capacity for sacrifice, steadfastness etc. peculiar to a given age. This is the important, imperishable and—for the history of literature— epoch-making thing about Scott's historical authenticity and not the much-discussed, so-called "local colour" of the descriptions which is only one among many ancillary, artistic devices and could never on its own reawaken the spirit of an age. Both the great human qualities as well as the vices and limitations of Scott's heroes spring from a clearly embodied historical basis of existence. It is neither by analysis, nor by psychological explanation of its ideas that Scott familiarizes us with the peculiar historical qualities of the inner life of an age, but by a broad portrayal of its being, by showing how thoughts, feelings, modes of behaviour grow up out of this basis.

This is always shown in a masterly way in the course of some interesting happening. Thus Waverley becomes acquainted with the clansmen for the first time through a transaction between the clan and a Scottish landowner on the occasion of a cattle theft. They are still as unintelligible for him as they are for the reader. He then spends a considerable time among the clan, getting to know thoroughly the everyday life of the clansmen, their habits, joys and sorrows. When the clan then goes to war, and Waverley with it, both he and the reader are already familiar with the peculiar being and consciousness of these people still living in a gentile order. When in the first battle against the royal troops, Waverley wishes to save a wounded English soldier from his own estate, the clansmen first of all protest against this assistance to an enemy. Only when they realize that the wounded Englishman belongs to Waverley's "clan" do they help and honour Waverley as a provident chieftain. The breathtaking effect of Evan Dhu's heroism is only possible upon the basis of this broad display of the material and moral character of clan life, its being and behaviour. And one experiences other kinds of past heroism in Scott in a very similar way, for example the heroism of the Puritans etc.

Scott's great artistic aim, in portraying the historical crises of popular life, is to show the *human greatness* which is liberated in its important representatives by a disturbance of this all-embracing kind. There is no doubt that, consciously or unconsciously, it was the experience of the French Revolution which awoke this tendency in literature. It is already present, though very sporadically, in the period which directly prepared the Revolution, most significantly in Goethe's figure of Klärchen in *Egmont*. But this heroism, though occasioned by the Netherlands revolution, is nevertheless immediately called to life by Klärchen's love for Egmont. After the French Revolution Goethe himself finds a still more purely human expression for this tendency in his figure of Dorothea. Simple, strong, determined and heroic qualities spring to life in her as a result of the events of the French Revolution and the fate which her immediate environment suffers through these events. Goethe's great epic art shows itself in the way he draws Dorothea's heroism. It appears in complete accord with her simple and straightforward character : a quality which has always lain dormant in her as a potentiality and which is called to life by the great events of the time. Yet this heroism is not something which entails an irrevocable change in her life and psychological constitution. When the objective necessity for her heroic behaviour is over, Dorothea returns to everyday life.

Whether Scott knew these works of Goethe at all or to any extent is immaterial. The point is that, historically, he continues and extends this tendency of Goethe. His novels abound in such stories; everywhere we find this sudden blaze of great yet simple heroism among artless, seemingly average children of the people. Scott's extension of Goethe's tendency lies primarily in the fact that he brings out, much more strongly than Goethe, the historical character of this heroism, the peculiar historical quality of the human grandeur which it expresses. Goethe draws the general outlines of popular movements, of both the Netherlands and French Revolution, with extraordinary faithfulness to life. Nevertheless, while the minor characters in *Egmont* exhibit very definite contemporary historical features, while Klärchen, too, in every reaction provoked by her idyllic love for Egmont remains the child of her class and people, her heroic upsurge lacks a definite and emphatic historical character. It is true-to-life and authentic, for it shows human greatness within given historical circumstances, it follows organically from Klärchen's psychology, but its peculiar quality is not characterized historically. The same applies to the characterization of Dorothea. In neither case does the poet use specifically social-historical features when it comes to portraying the actual heroic upsurge. Such features are given prominence before in both cases (and, in the case of Dorothea, afterwards too). Yet they serve merely as a framework for the heroism itself and give it no historical colouring.

It is different in Scott. One sees this tendency at its clearest in *The Heart of Midlothian*. Here Scott has created his greatest female character in the figure of the Puritan peasant girl, Jeanie Deans. Events face the daughter of a radical soldier of Cromwell's army with a terrible dilemma. Her sister is charged with infanticide; according to the inhumane laws of the time, proof that she has kept her pregnancy secret is sufficient to condemn her to death. She was compelled to keep this secrecy, but was not responsible for the infanticide. Now Jeanie could save her sister by prejuring herself. But despite intense love for her sister, despite unending sympathy for her fate, her Puritan conscience triumphs and, accordingly, she declares the truth. Her sister is condemned to death. And so then the peasant girl, uneducated, penniless and unfamiliar with the world, walks to London in order to secure her sister's pardon from the King. The story of these inner battles and of this struggle to save her sister show the rich humanity and simple heroism of a really great human being. Yet Scott's picture of his heroine never for a moment obscures her narrow Puritan and Scottish peasant traits, indeed it is they which again and again form the specific character of the naïve and grand heroism of this popular figure.

Having successfully carried through her aim, Jeanie Deans returns to everyday life, and never again does she experience a similar upsurge in her life to betray the presence of such strengths. Scott draws this final stage in rather too broad and philistine a detail, while Goethe who aims at beauty of line and classical perfection, contents himself with indicating that Dorothea's heroic life is over and that she, too, must now recede into simple everyday life.

Both instances involve a formal epic requirement. But in both instances this formal requirement expresses a profound human and historical truth. The important thing for these great writers is to lay bare those vast, heroic, human potentialities which are always latently present in the people and which, on each big occasion, with every deep disturbance of the social or even the more personal life, emerge "suddenly", with colossal force, to the surface. The greatness of the crisis periods of humanity rests to a large extent on the fact that such hidden forces are always dormant in the people, and that they require only the occasion for them to appear on the surface. The epic requirement for such figures to recede after the accomplishment of their mission underlines just how general this phenomenon is. Neither Goethe, in the case of Dorothea, nor Scott, in the case of Jeanie Deans, wished to present an exceptional human being, an outstanding talent, who rises from the people to become the leader of a popular movement (Scott draws figures of this kind in Robin Hood and Rob Roy). On the contrary, they wished to show that the possibilities for this human upsurge and heroism are widespread among the popular masses, that endless numbers of people live out their lives quietly, without this upsurge, because no opportunity has come their way to evoke such an exertion of powers. Revolutions are thus the great periods of mankind because in and through them such rapid upward movements in human capacities become widespread.

Through this manner of human-historical portrayal Scott makes history live. As has been shown, he presents history as a series of great crises. His presentation of historical development, above all that of England and France, is of an uninterrupted series of such revolutionary crises. Thus if Scott's main tendency in all his novels—and which forms of them in a sense a kind of cycle—is to represent and defend progress, then this progress is for him always a process full of contradictions, the driving force and material basis of which is the living contradiction between conflicting historical forces, the antagonisms of classes and nations.

Scott affirms this progress. He is a patriot, he is proud of the development of his people. This is vital for the creation of a real historical novel, i.e. one which brings the past close to us and allows us to experience its real and true being. Without a felt relationship to the present, a portrayal of history is impossible. But this relationship, in the case of really great historical art, does not consist in alluding to contemporary events, a practice which Pushkin cruelly ridiculed in the work of Scott's incompetent imitators, but in bringing the past to life as the prehistory of the present, in giving poetic life to those historical, social and human forces which, in the course of a long evolution, have made our present-day life what it is and as we experience it. Hegel remarks: "The historical is only then ours ... when we can regard the present in general as a consequence of those events in whose chain the characters or deeds represented constitute an essential link .... For art does not exist for a small, closed circle of the privilegedly cultured few, but for the nation as a whole. What holds good for the work of art in general, however, also has its application for the outer side of the historical reality represented. It, too, must be made clear and accessible to us without extensive learning so that we, who belong to our own time and nation, may find ourselves at home therein, and not be obliged to halt before it, as before some alien and unintelligible world."

Scott's patriotism forms the premise of this living connection with the past. And only vulgar sociologists can see in this patriotism a glorification of the exploiting merchants. Goethe had an infinitely deeper and truer understanding of Scott's relationship to English

history. In a conversation with Eckermann he speaks of Scott's Rob
Roy, in which the central figure, interestingly enough, happens to be
both a hero of the Scottish people and a peculiar compound of rebel,
cattle thief and smuggler—hence a significant example of Scott's
"social equivalent". Goethe says of this novel: "Here, naturally everything is on the grand scale: material, content, characters, treatment.
. . . But one sees what English history is and what it means when such
a heritage falls to the lot of a capable poet." Goethe thus clearly senses
what it is that constitutes Scott's pride in English history: on the one
hand, naturally, the gradual maturing of national strength and greatness, the continuity of which Scott wishes to illustrate in his "middle
way"; but on the other, and inseparable from this, the crises of this
growth, the extremes whose struggle produce this "middle way" as
their end-result and which could never be removed from the picture of
national greatness without robbing it precisely of all its greatness,
wealth and substance.

Scott sees and portrays the complex and intricate path which led
to England's national greatness and to the formation of the national
character. As a sober, conservative petty aristocrat, he naturally
affirms the result, and the necessity of this result is the ground on
which he stands. But Scott's artistic world-view by no means stops
here. Scott sees the endless field of ruin, wrecked existences, wrecked
or wasted heroic, human endeavour, broken social formations etc.
which were the necessary preconditions of the end-result.

Undoubtedly, there is a certain contradiction here between Scott's
directly political views and his artistic world picture. He, too, like so
many great realists, such as Balzac or Tolstoy, became a great realist
despite his own political and social views. In Scott, too, one can establish Engels's "triumph of realism" over his personal, political and
social views. Sir Walter Scott, the Scottish petty aristocrat, automatically affirms this development with a sober rationality. Scott, the
writer, on the other hand, embodies the sentiment of the Roman poet,
Lucan: "Victrix causa diis placuit, sed victa Catoni" (the victorious
cause pleased the gods, but the vanquished pleased Cato).

It would be wrong, however, to interpret this contrast all too
rigidly, without interconnections: namely, to see in the sober affirmation of English reality, of the "middle way" of English development
something purely negative, something which could only have hindered the unfolding of Scott's great historical art. On the contrary,
we must see that this great historical art arose precisely out of the
interaction, out of the dialectical interpenetration of both these sides
of Scott's personality. It is precisely because of his character that Scott
did not become a Romantic, a glorifier or elegist of past ages. And it
was for this reason that he was able to portray objectively the ruina-

tion of past social formations, despite all his human sympathy for, and artistic sensitivity, to the splendid, heroic qualities which they contained. Objectively, in a large historical and artistic sense: he saw at one and the same time their outstanding qualities and the historical necessity of their decline.

This objectivity, however, only enhances the true poetry of the past. We have seen that the official representatives of earlier ruling classes by no means play the leading role in Scott's picture of history, quite contrary to the misrepresentations of later critics. Among the aristocratic figures of his novels—if one leaves out the correct "middle-of-the-road heroes", who can only very conditionally be called positive heroes—there are very few positively drawn figures. On the contrary, Scott very often shows in a humorous, satirical or tragic manner the weakness, the human and moral degeneration of the upper strata. Admittedly the Pretender in Waverley, Mary Stuart in The Abbot, even the Prince of Wales in The Fair Maid of Perth exhibit humanly attractive and winning features, but the chief tendency in their portrayal is to show their inability to fulfil their historic missions. In such cases Scott achieves his poetry by conveying to us the objectively historical, social reasons for this personal inability via the atmosphere of the whole, without pedantic analysis. Further, in a whole number of figures, Scott draws the repellently brutal sides of aristocratic rule (e.g. the Knight Templar in Waverley, etc.) as well as the already comic incapacity of the court nobility, increasingly severed from national life, to cope with the problems of their age. The few positive figures are made positive mostly by simple fulfilment of duty and gentlemanliness. Only a few great champions of historical progress, such as Louis XI in particular, are allowed historical monumentality.

In most cases where aristocratic figures play a positive role, whether completely positive or problematic, this rests upon their connection with the people, which of course usually takes the form of a living or, at least, not yet extinct patriarchal relationship (e.g. in the case of the Duke of Argyle in The Heart of Midlothian). The real life in Scott's historical reality is formed by the life of the people themselves. As an English petty aristocrat with strong ties both in tradition and individual habits of life with the bourgeoisie, Scott has a deep sympathy for the defiant self-assurance of the medieval English-Scots burgher and the independent, free peasant. In the character of Henry Gow in particular (The Fair Maid of Perth), he gives a fine picture of this medieval burgher courage and self-confidence. Henry Gow as a fighter is at least the equal of every knight, but he proudly declines the knighthood offered to him by the Earl of Douglas; burgher he is and free burgher he will live and die.

In Scott's life-work we find marvellous scenes and characters from the life of the serfs and the free peasants, from the fortunes of society's outlaws, the smugglers, robbers, professional soldiers, deserters and so on. Yet it is in his unforgettable portrayal of the survivals of gentile society, of the Scottish clans where the poetry of his portrayal of past life chiefly lies. Here in material and subject-matter alone, there is present such a powerful element of the heroic period of mankind, that Scott's novels at their height do indeed approach the old epics. Scott is a giant discoverer and awakener of this long vanished past. It is true that the eighteenth century already loved and enjoyed the poetry of primitive life. And in the wave of enthusiasm for Homer, in Homer's ousting of Virgil as the model, there is undoubtedly a dawning awareness of this infant period of mankind. Important thinkers such as Ferguson even saw the relationship between the Homeric heroes and the American Indians. Nevertheless this pre-dilection remained abstract and moralizing in quality. Scott was the first actually to bring this period to life, by introducing us into the everyday life of the clans, by portraying upon this real basis both the exceptional and unequalled human greatness of this primitive order as well as the inner necessity of its tragic downfall.

In this way, by bringing to life those objective poetic principles which really underlie the poetry of popular life and history, Scott became the great poet of past ages, the really popular portrayer of history. Heine clearly understood this quality and saw, too, that the strength of Scott's writing lay precisely in this presentation of popular life, in the fact that the official big events and great historical figures were not given a central place. He says: "Walter Scott's novels some-times reproduce the spirit of English history much more faithfully than Hume." The important historians and philosophers of history of this period, Thierry and Hegel, aspire to a similar interpretation of history. But with them it goes no further than a demand, a theo-retical pronouncement of this necessity. For in the field of theory and historiography only historical materialism is capable of intellectually unearthing this basis of history, of showing what the childhood of mankind was really like. But what in Morgan, Marx and Engels was worked out and proved with theoretical and historical clarity, lives, moves and has its being poetically in the best historical novels of Scott. For this reason Heine very rightly stresses this side of Scott, his popular side: "Strange whim of the people! They demand their history from the hand of the poet and not from the hand of the historian. They demand not a faithful report of bare facts, but those facts dissolved back into the original poetry whence they came."

We repeat: this poetry is objectively bound up with the necessary downfall of gentile society. We experience in the various novels of Scott the individual stages of this downfall in all its historical concreteness and differentiation. Scott did not—in the pedantic sense of Gustav Freytag's *Ahnen* (*Our Forefathers*)—wish to make a coherent cycle of his novels. But in regard to the fate of the clans this great historical connection, the inexorable necessity of their tragedy emerges into colossal relief—if only because their fortunes always spring from a living interaction with the social-historical world around them. They are never presented independently or in isolation, but always in the context of a general crisis of Scottish or English-Scottish popular life. The chain of these crises extends from the first great struggles between the rising Scottish middle class and the nobility, from Royalty's attempt to use these struggles in strengthening central power (*The Fair Maid of Perth*—end of the fourteenth century) to the last attempts of the Stuarts to turn back the clock of history, to restore outdated Absolutism in an already far advanced capitalist England (*Rob Roy*—end of the eighteenth century).

The clans are, of historical necessity, always the exploited, the cheated, the deceived. Their very heroic qualities which stem from the primitiveness of their social being, make them the toy of the humanly far inferior representatives of the ruling powers of the given stage of civilization. What Engels shows scientifically, namely how civilization achieves things beyond the powers of the old gentile society, this Scott portrays. In particular, he portrays the contrast in the human sphere, which Engels stresses in his analysis of this inevitable collapse of gentile society in face of civilization: "But it achieved them by setting in motion the lowest instincts and passions in man and developing them at the expense of all his other abilities."

As soon as absolute monarchy appears as a force within the class struggles of feudalism, it ruthlessly exploits the unimportant feud of the clans, turning them into mutual massacres. The mutual extermination of all the able-bodied men of two clans which forms the action of the first of the above-named novels is admittedly a crude and exceptional case of this and only Scott's great art is able to extract from it the typical. But Scott can do this only because, on a spontaneous, more isolated and episodic scale, the inability of the clans to defend their common interests against nobility or bourgeoisie and the dissipation of all their energies in the local insularity of such petty struggles are an inevitable result of the basis of clan life. The bodyguard of the French king, Louis XI, already consists of members of the old clans who have been more or less forcibly scattered and thrown on to their own resources (*Quentin Durward*). And the parties in the later civil wars, Parliament as well as the Stuarts, are already ruthlessly and extensively exploiting the courageous, devoted clan warriors as cannon fodder for political ends totally foreign to the clans (A *Legend of Montrose, Waverley, Rob Roy*).

With the suppression of the uprising of 1745—which is depicted in *Waverley*—the real downfall of gentile society in Scotland begins, says Engels. Several decades later (in *Rob Roy*) we see the clans already in a state of complete economic dissolution. One character in this novel, the shrewd merchant and bailiff of Glasgow, Jarvie, clearly sees that it has become a matter of economic necessity for the clans to wage their desperate and hopeless battles on behalf of the Stuarts. They are no longer able to maintain themselves on the basis of their primitive economy. They possess a surplus population, permanently armed and well seasoned who cannot be put to any normal use, who must resort to plunder and pillage, and for whom an uprising of this kind is the only way out of a hopeless situation. Thus we have here already an element of dissolution, the beginnings of class-uprooting which were as yet absent from the clan picture of *Waverley*.

Once more we must admire here Scott's extraordinarily realistic presentation of history, his ability to translate these new elements of economic and social change into human fates, into an altered psychology. His genuine popular feeling shows itself here in two ways. On the one hand he brings out these declassed features with implacable realism, particularly in the romantically adventurous behaviour of Rob Roy himself, who thereby differs very sharply, historically, from the primitive simplicity of the clan leaders of earlier periods. On the other he portrays this downfall of the clans with all the real popular heroism which attends it. Despite the declassing tendencies Rob Roy also concentrates in himself the magnificent human qualities of the old clan heroes. The downfall of gentile society in Scott is a heroic tragedy, not a wretched decline.

Scott then becomes a great poet of history because he has a deeper, more genuine and differentiated sense of historical necessity than any writer before him. Historical necessity in his novels is of the most severe, implacable kind. Yet this necessity is no otherworldly fate divorced from men; it is the complex interaction of concrete historical circumstances in their process of transformation, in their interaction with the concrete human beings, who have grown up in these circumstances, have been very variously influenced by them, and who act in an individual way according to their personal passions. Thus, in Scott's portrayal, historical necessity is always a resultant, never a presupposition; it is the tragic atmosphere of a period and not the object of the writer's reflections.

This does not mean, of course, that Scott's characters do not reflect upon their aims and tasks. However, these are the reflections of people acting in concrete circumstances. And the atmosphere of historical necessity arises out of the very subtly portrayed dialectic between the effectiveness and impotence of a correct insight in concrete historical circumstances. In A Legend of Montrose Scott portrays a Scottish episode in the great English Revolution. Both the Parliamentary army and the Royalists attempt to win over the warlike clans to themselves. Their instruments are the two great chieftains, Argyle and Montrose. Now it is extremely interesting that there is a small chieftain involved in this situation, who realizes quite clearly that to join either King or Parliament means his own inevitable downfall. His insight, however, is rendered impotent from the outset by the clan's adherence to the great leaders. The war between Argyle and Montrose begins.

This same inner necessity, however, which here favoured Montrose's plan, sets narrow clan limits to its realization. Montrose has defeated his opponent and would now like to join battle with the English enemies of the King; an army column with fresh forces might even change the course of the war in England. This, however, is objectively impossible. Only a Scottish clan war can be fought with an army of clan members. Montrose's followers will go through fire and water for him; yet in their conviction that the real enemy is not Parliament, but the hostile group of clans led by Argyle, they will yield neither to persuasion nor authority, however unlimited Montrose's power while he moves within the bounds of clan ideology. And one of the subtle and grand historical features in Scott's characterization is that he does not permit a merely external resolution of this opposition. Montrose is indeed an aristocrat, a convinced Royalist, an army commander of distinguished abilities, a man of great political ambition, yet at heart he is also a clan chieftain. The clansmen's way of thinking also affects him inwardly; necessity, outer and inner, makes him give up his great plans and squander his energies in a petty clan war against Argyle.

In portraying how historical necessity asserts itself in this way through the passionate actions of individuals, but often against their individual psychology, in showing how this necessity has its roots in the real social and economic basis of popular life Scott manifests his historical faithfulness. Measured against this authentic reproduction of the real components of historical necessity, it matters little whether individual details, individual facts are historically correct or not. Of course, Scott is particularly strong and authentic in respect of these details too. But never in the antiquarian or exotic sense of later writers. Detail for Scott is only a means for achieving the historical faithfulness here described, for making concretely clear the historical necessity of a concrete situation. This historical faithfulness in Scott is the authenticity of the historical psychology of his characters, the genuine *hic et nunc* (here and now) of their inner motives and behaviour.

Scott preserves this historical faithfulness in the human-moral conception of his characters. The most conflicting and divergent reactions to particular events always occur in his successful novels within the objective dialectical framework of a particular historical crisis. In this sense he never creates eccentric figures, figures who fall psychologically outside the atmosphere of the age. This would merit a detailed analysis on the basis of some outstanding examples. We shall only mention briefly Jeanie Deans's sister, Effie. Apparently she stands in the sharpest psychological and moral contrast to her father and sister. But Scott portrays with great subtlety how this contrast arose precisely out of opposition to the basic peasant-Puritan character of the family, how a number of circumstances in her upbringing provided the opportunities for this exceptional development and how, nevertheless, she retained many psychological traits which, even during her tragic crisis and later social rise, preserved what was common to the society and time in which she and her family lived. This manner of portrayal shows that Scott, in sharp contrast to the post-1848 development of the historical novel, *never modernizes* the psychology of his characters.

This modernizing is, of course, not a new "achievement" of the post-1848 historical novel. On the contrary. It is the false inheritance which Scott himself overcame. And the struggle between genuine historical psychology and psychological modernization forms the central problem on which minds divided in Scott's time, too. In the following we shall be dealing with this problem at length. Let it merely be said here that while the pseudo-historical novels of the seventeenth and eighteenth centuries simply equated naïvely the world of feeling of the past with that of the present, there is with Chateaubriand and German Romanticism a different, more dangerous trend of modernization. For the German Romantics, in particular, place extreme emphasis upon the historical faithfulness of every detail. They discover the picturesque charm of the Middle Ages and reproduce it with "nazarene" accuracy: everything, from medieval Catholicism to antique furniture is reproduced with craftsmanlike precision, which often becomes mere decorative pedantry. The human beings, however, who act in this picturesque world, have the psychology of a tormented Romantic or a freshly converted apologist of the Holy Alliance.

This decorative caricature of historical faithfulness was firmly rejected in Germany by the great champions of progress in literature and culture, Goethe and Hegel. The historical novel of Scott is the living counterpart of this at once false historicism and inartistic modernization. But does faithfulness to the past mean a chronicle-like, naturalistic reproduction of the language, mode of thought and feeling of the past? Of course not. And Scott's great German contemporaries, Goethe and Hegel, stated this problem with great theoretical clarity. Goethe brings up this question in a discussion of Manzoni's historical tragedy, *Adelchi*. He writes: "We pronounce in his defence what may seem paradoxical: that all poetry in fact moves in the element of anachronism. Whatever in the past we evoke, in order to recite it after our own fashion to our contemporaries, we must grant a higher culture to the ancient happening than it in fact had .... The *Iliad* and the *Odyssey*, all the great tragedians and all that has remained of true poetry lives and breathes only in anachronisms. To all conditions one lends the modern spirit, for only in this way can we see and, indeed, bear to see them. . . ."

How far these statements of Goethe directly influenced Hegel's aesthetics, we do not know. At any rate, Hegel in an aesthetic-conceptual generalization of the problem speaks already of *necessary anachronism* in art. But what he has to say regarding the concretization and historical dialectic of the problem goes, of course, considerably further than Goethe; he states theoretically those principles which determine Scott's historical practice. Hegel discusses necessary anachronism in the following way: "The inner substance of what is represented remains the same, but the developed culture in representing and unfolding the substantial necessitates a change in the expression and form of the latter."

This formulation sounds quite similar to Goethe's, but is really an extension. For Hegel already interprets the relation of present to past in a more consciously historical way than Goethe. Goethe is concerned chiefly with the break-through of universal human and humanist principles from the concrete basis of history. He wishes to remould the historical basis so as to allow for this break-through while preserving historical truth in its essentials. (We refer here to our earlier analysis of the portrayal of Dorothea and Klärchen.) Hegel, on the other hand, interprets this relation to the present historically. He maintains that "necessary anachronism" can emerge organically from historical material, if the past portrayed is clearly recognized and experienced by contemporary writers as the *necessary prehistory* of the present. Then the only kind of heightening required—in modes of expression, consciousness etc.—is such that will clarify and underline this relationship. And then the remoulding of events, customs etc. in the past would simply come to this: the writer would allow those tendencies which were alive and active in the past and which in historical reality have led up to the present (but whose later significance contemporaries naturally could not see) to emerge with that emphasis which they possess in objective, historical terms for the product of this past, namely, the present.

These ideas of Hegel sketch the aesthetic limits of historical subject-matter. He goes on for instance to contrast the necessary anachronism of the Homeric poems and the Greek tragedians with the medieval chivalric-feudal treatment of the *Nibelungenlied*. "This recasting takes a very different form when attitudes and ideas of a *later* development of religious and moral consciousness are transposed to an age or nation whose entire outlook *contradicts* such modern ideas." Modernization, therefore, arises of aesthetic and historical necessity, whenever this living connection between past and present is absent or only forcibly created. (We shall have a great deal to say about this problem in the following sections.)

There is, of course, an enormous historical difference, which is aesthetically reflected too, between the naïve unconsciousness and unconcern with which the poet of the *Nibelungenlied* refashioned the sagas of gentile times according to feudal-Christian ideas and the extravagant apologetics with which the reactionary Romantics transported the principles of Legitimism into the Middle Ages, turning them into a social idyll for decadent *déclassé* heroes.

Scott put Goethe's and Hegel's "necessary anachronism" into practice while we may be sure he had no knowledge of their reflections. All the more significant, therefore, is the fact that the important progressive poet and thinker of this period should agree with Scott's creative principles. Particularly so, when one considers that he was quite conscious about them artistically, though he gave them no philosophical foundation. In the Dedicatory Epistle to *Ivanhoe* he writes on this question: "It is true that I neither can nor do pretend to the observation of complete accuracy, even in matters of outward costume, much less in the more important points of language and manners. But the same motive which prevents my writing the dialogue of the piece in Anglo-Saxon or in Norman French, and which prohibits my sending forth to the public this essay printed with the types of Caxton or Wynken de Worde, prevents my attempting to confine myself within the limits of the period in which my story is laid. It is necessary for exciting interest of any kind that the subject assumed should be, as it were, *translated* (my italics G.L.) into the manners, as well as the language, of the age we live in . . .

"It is true that this licence is confined . . . within legitimate bounds . . . the author . . . must introduce nothing inconsistent with the manners of the age."

Scott's artistic faithfulness to history is an extension and application to history of the creative principles of the great English realist writers of the eighteenth century. And not only in the sense of a broadening of theme, an assimilation of historical material to the great tradition of realism, but in the sense of portraying men and events historically. What, for instance, was only latent in Fielding, becomes with Scott the driving spirit of literary portrayal. Scott's "necessary anachronism" consists, therefore, simply in allowing his characters to express feelings and thoughts about real, historical relationships in a much clearer way than the actual men and women of the time could have done. But the content of these feelings and thoughts, their relation to their real object is always historically and socially correct. The extent to which this expression of thought and feeling outstrips the consciousness of the age is no more than is absolutely necessary for elucidating the given historical relationship. At the same time Scott gives this expression the timbre, colour, cadence of the time, the class and so on. In this balance lies Scott's great poetic sensitivity.

3. The Classical Historical Novel in Struggle with Romanticism

Scott then gives a perfect artistic expression to the basic progressive tendency of this period, i.e. the historical defence of progress. And Scott did in fact become one of the most popular and widely read writers of his time on an international scale. The influence which he exercised over the whole of European literature is immeasurable. The most important writers of this period, from Pushkin to Balzac, are led on to fresh paths in their work by this new type of historical portrayal. But it would be a mistake to think that the great wave of historical novels in the first half of the nineteenth century is really based on Scott's principles. We have already seen that the historical conception of Romanticism is diametrically opposed to that of Scott. And there is, of course, much more than this to be said about the other trends in the historical novel. We shall mention only two important trends: on the one hand, liberal Romanticism, which in outlook and form has very much in common with the original basis of Romanticism, with the ideological struggle against the French Revolution, but which, nevertheless, upon these contradictory and uncertain foundations stands for the ideology of moderate progress; on the other, the trend represented by important writers like Goethe and Stendhal who preserved intact much of eighteenth century outlook and whose humanism contains to the end strong elements of Enlightenment. Our task here cannot, of course, be to give even the barest outline of the struggle of these trends. We shall simply analyse briefly a few important representative examples. We shall refer to writers, who are important either because they directly influence later development or because, like Scott, they offer contrasts to this development and hence are extremely topical for the present crisis of the historical novel.

We may disregard in this summary the English contemporaries and followers of Scott. Scott had only one worthy follower in the English language who took over and even extended certain of the principles underlying his choice of theme and manner of portrayal, namely the American, Cooper. In his immortal novel cycle *The Leather Stocking Saga* Cooper sets an important theme of Scott, the downfall of gentile society, at the centre of his portrayal. Corresponding to the historical development of North America, this theme acquires an entirely new complexion. In Scott it is a case of a centuries long, conflict-ridden development, of the various ways in which the survivals of gentile society are accommodated to the feudal system and later to rising capitalism, of the slow, crisis-ridden decline of this gentile formation. In America the contrast was posed far more brutally and directly by history itself; the colonizing capitalism of France and England destroys physically and morally the gentile society of the Indians which had flourished almost unchanged for thousands of years.

Cooper's concentration on this problem, on the physical decline and moral disruption of the Indian tribes gives his novels a large and broad historical perspective. Yet, at the same time, the directness and straightforwardness of the social contrast means an impoverishment of his artistic world, compared with Scott. This comes out in Cooper especially in his portrayal of the English and French, the bulk of whom are represented schematically, with superficial psychology and a monotonous and forced sense of humour. Balzac sharply criticized this weakness in Cooper, whom he otherwise held to be a worthy successor to Scott. The source of this weakness, in my opinion, lies in the fact that the individual Europeans who sporadically appear in Cooper's novels lead a far more isolated life than the feudal lords and town burghers of Scott and do not interact with one another socially.

Cooper's artistic interest is centred on the portrayal of the tragically declining gentile society of the Redskins. With truly epic grandeur Cooper separates the two processes of tragic decline and human and moral class-uprooting. He confines the movingly tragic features of decline to a few, great surviving figures of the Delawar tribe, while the symptoms of the Indians' moral disintegration are represented in breadth and detail in the hostile tribes. This admittedly simplifies his portrayal but in parts gives it an almost epic-like magnificence.

However, Cooper's greatest artistic achievement is his singular development of Scott's "middle-of-the-road hero". The central figure of these novels is the illiterate, simple English huntsman, Nathaniel

Bumppo, one of the pioneer colonizers of America who, nevertheless, as a plain man of the people, an Englishmen of puritan outlook, is deeply attracted to the simple, human nobility of the Indians and enters into an inseparable human bond with the survivors of the Delawars. It is true that his moral attitude on the whole remains that of a European, but his uncurbed love of freedom, his attraction to a simple, human life bring him closer to these Indians than to the European colonizers with whom he belongs in objective social terms. In this simple, popular figure who can only experience his tragedy emotionally, but not understand it, Cooper portrays the enormous historical tragedy of those early colonizers who emigrated from England in order to preserve their freedom, but who themselves destroy this freedom by their own deeds in America. Maxim Gorky expressed this tragedy very well: "As an explorer of the forests and prairies of the 'New World' he blazes new trails in them for people who later condemn him as a criminal because he has infringed their mercenary and, to his sense of freedom, unintelligible laws. All his life he has unconsciously served the great cause of the geographical expansion of material culture in a country of uncivilized people and—found himself incapable of living in the conditions of this culture for which he had struck the first paths." Gorky shows here very finely how a great historical, indeed world-historical tragedy could be portrayed through the destiny of a mediocre man of the people. Cooper shows that such a tragedy is rendered much more artistically moving if portrayed in a milieu where the immediate economic contrasts and the moral ones arising from them grow organically out of everyday problems. The tragedy of the pioneers is linked superbly here with the tragic decline of gentile society, and one of the great contradictions of mankind's journey of progress therewith acquires a wonderful and tragic embodiment.

This conception of the contradictions of human progress is a product of the post-Revolutionary era. We have already quoted Pushkin's remark where he points out, clearly and consciously, that Scott's portrayal of history signifies a new epoch even in comparison with Shakespeare and Goethe. This new historical situation can be studied most clearly in Goethe himself. Goethe was a passionate supporter of progress in every sphere to the very end. And to the very end he followed the new phenomena in literature with attentiveness and understanding. He studied and criticized in detail, not only Scott and Manzoni, but also, almost during the last days of his life, the first great works of Stendhal and Balzac.

Nevertheless, Goethe's relationship to Scott is problematic and Scott's influence on Goethe's creative method not at all decisive. In the portrayal of the historical *hic et nunc*, in the preservation of the real historical psychology of characters even at their supreme moments, Goethe is always a poèt of the pre-Scott period. It is not possible for us to analyse here Goethe's various pronouncements on Scott, their development and contradictoriness. Let it suffice to mention the contradictoriness itself. We have already quoted Goethe's enthusiastic comment on *Rob Roy*. One could quote a whole number of such comments. In his conversations with Chancellor von Müller Goethe, however, at one point rates Byron high above Scott, saying of the latter: "I have read two novels of Walter Scott and know now what he is after and what he can do. He would always entertain me, but I can learn nothing from him."

The statement to Eckermann which we quoted earlier dates from a later period, so that one would be justified in assuming that Goethe later revised this opinion of Scott. But the decisive works of the late Goethe show no trace of any effective influence of the new historical conception of men and events. The social horizon of late Goethe takes in more and more, his insight into the tragic dialectics of modern bourgeois life grows ever deeper, but as far as historical concretization of time and place and a consistent historical psychology are concerned, he never goes beyond the stage reached in his maturity. The historical character of works like *Egmont* remains in this respect the summit of his achievement. Indeed, even during his period of collaboration with Schiller, he still had a strong tendency to portray major topical events in accordance with their pure historical character; he would find an artistically concrete setting for their distilled social-human essence which did not bind him to any concrete historical time. This modified Enlightenment tradition can be clearly seen in different ways in *Reineke Fuchs* (*Reynard the Fox*) and in *Die natürliche Tochter* (*The Natural Daughter*). And the important social and historical events which come into *Wilhelm Meister*, for example (war etc.), are deliberately kept quite abstract; even more abstract than in Fielding or Smollett, for example. Goethe is here following the French rather than the English tradition. All these artistic tendencies which crystallized in Goethe before the period of Scott are preserved and become, indeed, more pronounced in his late period (*Wahlverwandtschaften* (*Elective Affinities*), *Faust II*). Even as a critical judge of the new developments, a strong Lessing tradition lives on in Goethe, as we shall see.

Thus Goethe's work belongs essentially to the pre-Scott stage of historical concretization. Nevertheless we have also seen that Goethe recognized certain conditions governing the rise of the historical novel and its subject-matter more clearly than any of his German contemporaries. He very rightly saw the significance of the continuous and, for the present generation, glorious history of England. This real basis of the historical novel is lacking in several important European countries, notably in Germany and Italy.

In the forties, Hebbel following on a review of one of his plays by Willibald Alexis writes very sharply and peremptorily of this relationship: "It is quite correct that we Germans have no connection with the history of our people ... But what is the reason for this? It is because this history has been *without result*, because we are unable to look upon ourselves as products of its organic development like the English and the French, for example, because what we needs must call our history is the history not of our *life*, but of our *illness* which has still to reach its crisis." And of the inevitable failure of German writers who had tackled Hohenstauffen themes he says with blunt vulgarity that these Emperors "had no other relationship" to Germany "than that of the *tape worm* to the *stomach*". This situation inevitably yields themes which are either fortuitous or indeed false unless writers are capable of making this critical condition, this fragmentariness, this tragedy of their own history itself the centre of their portrayal.

In Germany the ideological conditions did not exist for this kind of interpretation. The only approach to an historical narrative on a grand scale in which elements and hints of this tragic condition are unconsciously and instinctively present, Kleist's *Michael Kohlhaas*, remained a solitary episode not only in German literature, but also in the work of the writer himself. As Goethe before him in *Götz von Berlichingen*, so Kleist, with true historical feeling, goes back to a great crisis in German history, to the time of the Reformation. In both works the conflict results from the clash between the medieval independence of the individual (whose psychology and morality stem from a "heroic period" in the sense of Vico and Hegel) and the abstract justice of the emerging modern state form of Feudalism. And it is characteristic of the way in which German development is judged in both young Goethe and Kleist that the democratic continuation of the Reformation, i.e. the peasant war, is either missing from the total picture or appears only in the form of a negative tendency. In spite of all Kleist's politically and socially conservative views his *Novelle* clearly shows the ideological traces of the historical transformation which had taken place since Goethe's youthful drama. While in the latter the Reformation, including Luther, shows a purely progressive side, the liberation from medieval asceticism and unfreedom, in Kleist the problematic, indeed downright negative tendencies of the Reformation and its connections with the absolutism of petty states move into the foreground and become decisive factors in the central conflict.

The unique position which this *Novelle* occupies in German historical literature is due not least to the fact that it continues, intuitively, the concretization of the real problems of German history. This uniqueness manifests itself (*mutatis mutandis* as in Goethe) in the fact that this important approach to an artistic understanding of German history can have no follow-up in Kleist's life-work either. Goethe, of course, consciously draws all the necessary conclusions from this situation : with the exception of Acts One and Four of the Second Part of *Faust*, where the Götz motif, appropriately corrected, turns up again—in contrast now with Goethe's enriched and deepened historical experiences—he never again returns to the theme of German history. Kleist, on the other hand, incorporates the most varied material of German history in his dramatic work. But his manner of approach shows no trace of the central progressiveness of *Kohlhaas*; on the one hand it is episodic, treating the historical basis merely as a pretext for expressing purely personal, subjective experiences; on the other it gives reactionary answers to important questions of history. (The two series of motifs mostly cross; think of Homburg's sleep-walking.) The two so sharply contrasting cases of Goethe and Kleist thus pointedly stress the poverty of German history which we have indicated above.

The dominant line of historical literature in Germany was that of Romantic reaction, the apologetic glorification of the Middle Ages. This literature came into being long before Scott, with Novalis, Wackenroder and Tieck. The effect of Scott's influence here was at most to give a more realistic character to detail, a tendency which grew in the later work of Arnim and Tieck. But he did not and could not bring about a real change. And chiefly for political and ideological reasons; for it is clear from what has already been said that what was most important in Scott's composition and characterization could not possibly have been assimilated and applied by reactionary Romanticism. The reactionary Romantics could at best learn mere externals from Scott.

The situation is not very much better as regards the later liberal and liberalish Romanticism. Tieck in his later development freed himself from many of the subjectivist and reactionary whims of his early period. And his later historical tales are on a substantially higher level, at least in tendency, than the earlier ones, in particular the large fragment *Der Aufruhr in den Cevennen* (*Uproar in the Cévennes*). But here again Tieck was unable to take over anything of substance from Scott. The whole composition of this work starts out from the religious ideas of the last Huguenot uprising in France. The real action is formed by religious debates, bizarre forms of mystical belief, purely moral problems of behaviour (cruelty or mercy), religious conversions and so on. The fact that the rebellion is grounded in life, the problems affecting the life of the people themselves—these are as good as ignored. The life of the people is present merely as rather abstract illustrative material for spiritual and moral conflicts carried on in an isolated world "above".

The only German writer of whom one may say with some justice that he upholds the traditions of Scott is Willibald Alexis. He is a true storyteller with a true talent for what is historically authentic in the manners and feelings of people. With him history is far more than costume and decoration, it really determines the life, thought, feeling and behaviour of his characters. As a result Willibald Alexis's medieval world is also far removed from the idyll of reactionary Romanticism. But it is in precisely this gifted and clearsighted realist that the narrowness of German subject-matter makes itself most markedly felt. His novels suffer from the wretchedness of Prussian history, from the objective pettiness of the struggles between nobility, crown and bourgeoisie in Prussia. Just because Alexis is a true historical realist, these petty traits come out strongly in his writing, affecting both plot and characterization and depriving his correctly perceived and well-drawn works of that universality and convincingness which Scott's novels possessed. Despite his gifts he remains caught in the local world. Gutzkow recognized this very early on. And as frank an admirer of Alexis as Theodor Fontane associates himself unreservedly with this judgment. He quotes Gutzkow: "But that the local history of the Mark should be transformed into the history of the Reich ... for all Germany ... must forever remain a dream." Fontane sums up this idea as follows: "How great or slight was the historical and political significance of the events described in this novel? Perhaps not altogether slight, but certainly not very great either, and no amount of effort will ever make of the Mark that Promised Land which those gifted with the right insight knew to be Germany's destiny from the beginning. This idea, however, runs through all the novels, while in fact the Electorate of Brandenburg was a mere appendage to the Reich and the provincial glory of our towns, as far as wealth, power and culture were concerned, vanished beside the real Germany, beside the cities of the Reich and the Hansa."

In Italy historical themes were similarly unfavourable. Yet here Scott found a successor who, though only in a single, isolated work, nevertheless broadened his tendencies with superb originality, in some respects surpassing him. We refer, of course, to Manzoni's *I Promessi Sposi* (*The Betrothed*). Scott himself recognized Manzoni's greatness. When in Milan Manzoni told him that he was his pupil, Scott replied that in that case Manzoni's was his best work. It is, however, very characteristic that while Scott was able to write a profusion of novels about English and Scottish history, Manzoni confined himself to this single masterpiece. This is certainly not due to any limitation in

Manzoni's individual talent. His inventiveness in telling a story, his imaginativeness in presenting the most varied social classes, his feeling for historical authenticity in the inner and outer life rank at least equal to these gifts in Scott. Indeed, in diversity and depth of characterization, in the way he exhausts all the personal and psychological possibilities of great tragic collisions Manzoni is the superior of Scott. As a creator of individuals he is a greater artist than Scott.

As a truly great artist he also discovered a theme which enabled him to overcome the objective unfavourableness of Italian history and to create a real historical novel, that is, one which would rouse the present, which contemporaries would experience as their own prehistory. He sets the historical events even further in the background than Scott, although he draws them with an historical concreteness of atmosphere learned from Scott. But his basic theme is much less a given, concrete, historical crisis of national history, as is always the case in Scott, it is rather the critical condition of the entire life of the Italian people resulting from Italy's fragmentation, from the reactionary feudal character which the fragmented parts of the country had retained owing to their ceaseless petty internecine wars and their dependence on the intervention of the great powers. Thus, while Manzoni's immediate story is simply a concrete episode taken from Italian popular life—the love, separation and reunion of a young peasant boy and girl—his presentation transforms it into a general tragedy of the Italian people in a state of national degradation and fragmentation. Without ever departing from the concrete framework of time, place and the age- and class-conditioned psychology of the characters, the story of Manzoni's lovers grows into the tragedy of the Italian people as a whole.

As a result of this superb and historically profound conception Manzoni creates a novel in which the human comes out even more powerfully than in his master. But the inner nature of his theme shows that this had to be an only novel, that it could have been repeated only in a bad sense. Scott never repeats himself in his successful novels; for history itself, the representation of the particular crisis always produces something new. Italian history did not provide Manzoni's genius with this inexhaustible variety of subject-matter. Manzoni shows his artistic discretion in striking the one path that could lead to a grand conception of Italian history and in his realization that only one version of it was possible.

But this, of course, had its consequences for the novel itself. We have emphasized here those human and poetic features in Manzoni, wherein he excels in several respects over Scott. But the lack of that great historical substratum, which Goethe admired in Scott, cannot possibly be confined in its effects to subject-matter alone. It also had inner artistic consequences: the absence of that world-historical atmosphere which can be felt in Scott, even when he is presenting an extensive picture of petty clan wars, manifests itself in Manzoni in a certain limitedness of human horizon on the part of his characters. Despite all the human and historical authenticity, despite all the psychological depth which their author bestows upon them, Manzoni's characters are unable to soar to those historically typical heights which mark the summits of Scott's works. Compared with the heroic drama of Scott's Jeanie Deans or Rebecca, the fate of Lucia is really no more than an externally menaced idyll, while an inevitable pettiness attaches to the negative characters of the novel: their negativity is unable to reveal dialectically the historical limits of the whole period and therewith also the limits of the positive figures, as does, for example, that of the Knight Templar in *Ivanhoe*.

The position as regards the possibilities of the historical novel is quite different in the most backward country of the time, namely Russia. In spite of economic, political and cultural backwardness, Tsarist absolutism had created national unity and defended it against foreign enemies. For this reason the outstanding representatives of Tsarism could serve as characters in an historical novel, particularly if they stood for the introduction of Western culture into Russia. And the present, though far removed in time, though pursuing quite different social, political and cultural goals, would be able to feel in such a work its own prehistory, the real basis of its own existence. There is in the whole course of Russian history nothing, in a national respect, of the pettiness of conditions in German or Italian history. This historical generosity of national life gives the great class struggles, too, a significant, historical background, a significant historical scale. The peasant uprisings of Pugachov and Stenka Razin have a tragic, historical grandeur as have few peasant risings on this scale in Western Europe. Only the German peasant war surpasses them in tragic, historical splendour, as the moment of destiny of the German people, when the rescue from national degradation, the establishment of national unity appeared at least as a perspective on the horizon, only, of course, to perish tragically when the uprising was crushed.

Thus it is no accident that in Russia Scott's epoch-making revolution in the portrayal of history was understood perhaps more rapidly and profoundly than anywhere else in Europe. Pushkin and, later, Belinsky provided, together with Balzac, the most correct and searching analysis of the new principles of Scott's historical art. Pushkin, in particular, understands clearly and unerringly from the very first moment the diametrical opposition between Scott and the pseudo-historical novel of the French Romantics. He attacks fiercely every form of modernization, in particular the mannerism of bringing past and present together by clothing individual allusions to contemporary phenomena in historical costume, although the characters, despite their costume, retain modern sensibilities: "The Gothic heroines are educated at Madame Campan's and the statesmen of the sixteenth century read *The Times* and the *Journal des Débats*." Pushkin also combats the Romantic practice of Vigny and Victor Hugo of placing "great men" at the centre of their historical portrayals and of characterizing them by means of historically attested, or even invented, anecdotes. Thus he gives an ironic and devastating character-sketch of the figure of Milton in Hugo's *Cromwell* and Vigny's *Cinq Mars*. He contrasts here very sharply the hollow Romantic theatricality with the deep and genuine simplicity of Scott.

Pushkin's historical novel, *The Captain's Daughter*, and his novel fragment, *The Negro of Peter the Great*, show a very deep study of Scott's principles of composition. Pushkin is, of course, never a mere pupil of Scott. For his study of Scott and his assimilation of Scott's principles of composition are in no sense primarily a question of form. On the contrary, Scott's great influence on Pushkin lies, above all, in his strengthening of the popular tendency already present in Pushkin. Thus, if the latter constructs his historical novels in the same way as Scott, namely with a "middle-of-the-road hero" as the main figure and with the historically important figure only episodically present, their similar composition springs from an affinity in their attitude to life. Pushkin, like Scott, wished to depict in his historical novels important, critical turning-points in popular life. For him, too, the material and moral disturbance of popular life was not only the point of departure but also the central task of artistic portrayal. For him, too, the great man in history was not important in isolation, for himself alone, or because of some mysterious, psychological "grandeur", but as the representative of important currents in popular life. On this basis Pushkin, with wonderful historical authenticity and human truthfulness, portrays in Pugachov and Peter I unforgettable historical figures. And the artistic basis for this greatness is again the depiction of the decisive features of popular life, in their true historical complexity and intricacy. Pushkin also follows Scott in introducing his "middle-of-the-road" heroes into great human conflicts during an historical crisis, and in imposing exceptional tests and tasks upon them in order to show their growth under these strained conditions beyond their previous averageness, in order to bring out the true and humanly genuine qualities in them and in the people.

But Pushkin is by no means just a disciple of Scott. He creates an historical novel of an aesthetically higher type than his master. We stress the word "aesthetically" advisedly. For in the interpretation of history itself, Pushkin continues along Scott's path; he applies the latter's method to Russian history. But like Manzoni, though in a different way (in keeping with the personality of the two writers and the difference between their two countries), Pushkin far outstrips Scott in the artistry of his characterization and the aesthetic shaping of his story.

For whatever genius Scott displays in drawing the broad, historical outlines of a story or the social-historical psychology of his characters, as an artist he frequently drops below his own level. Here I am thinking not so much of the often banal and conventional characterization, especially of his principal figures, but chiefly of the final artistic working-through of every detail, the enticing-out of every hidden human beauty from the individual actions and responses of his characters. In such matters Scott is often, judged by the standards of a Goethe or a Pushkin, somewhat slight and superficial. His wonderful eye enables him to detect an almost unending profusion of historically and socially correct and humanly significant features in historical events. But he is often content to reproduce what he sees in a manageable and comfortable epic form, taking spontaneous pleasure in the telling of his story, and to go no further than this artistically. (That behind this brilliant spontaneity there is a rich and profound historical knowledge and a significant experience of life etc. does not, we think, require any further emphasis.)

Pushkin, however, goes beyond this stage of seeing and forming reality. He is not only a poet, who sees the world richly and rightly—Scott does this, too. He is at the same time, and first and foremost, an artist, a poet-artist, as Belinsky said. But it would be very superficial to interpret this artist character of Pushkin purely in the sense of artistic activity, of a restless striving after beauty (or even, as sometimes happens still today, in the sense of modern aestheticism). The desire for beauty, for artistic perfection, is something far deeper and more human in the case of Pushkin. There is in Pushkin present once again a "pure humanity", but unlike Goethe's it does not belong to a pre-Scott period of historical interpretation. For it never departs from what is historically conditioned, from what is determined by epoch and class, and yet, by its aesthetically clear and simple line, its classical restriction of story and psychology to the humanly necessary (while keeping its historical concreteness) it lifts every happening into the sphere of beauty. This beauty in Pushkin is not a merely aesthetic or indeed "aestheticist" principle. It proceeds not from abstract requirements of form, nor does it rest upon a separation of the poet from life, but, on the contrary, is the expression of the poet's very deep and unshaken bond with life. The peculiarity of Russian development made this unique, classical intermediary stage in modern art possible: an art on the ideological level of the entire previous European development, an art which, in content, fully absorbed the "problematic" of life, without, however, being compelled either to destroy its artistic purity of line, its beauty, because of this "problematic", or for the sake of beauty to turn aside from the richness of life.

The Pushkin period was soon superseded by other trends throughout the whole of Russian literature. In his embodiment of beauty Pushkin remains a solitary figure, and not only in Russian literature. His great younger contemporary, Gogol, approaches the historical novel in quite a different way from him. Gogol's great historical tale, *Taras Bulba*, continues the most important theme in Scott's work, i.e. the portrayal of the tragic downfall of pre-capitalist societies, the downfall of gentile order. Gogol's tale introduces two new elements into the theme, or rather, stresses certain aspects of the theme more vividly than Scott. Above all, the basic story, the struggle between the Cossacks and the Poles, is more national, more unified and more epic in character than even the stories of Scott. Gogol discovers the possibility of this grander, more epic-like portrayal in historical reality itself, for his Cossacks are able to appear and act more independently and in a more unified way than the Scottish clans, who in Scott are squeezed into a more advanced culture and were objectively no more than a toy in the decisive class struggle between England and Scotland. From this there grows a splendid, at times almost Homeric, national-epic breadth of theme whose possibilities Gogol as a really great artist is able fully to utilize.

But nevertheless Gogol is a modern writer who understands completely the tragic necessity for the downfall of the Cossack world. He portrays this necessity in a very original way, by inserting a tragic catastrophe, almost dramatic in its concentration, into the broad, epic composition of the whole: the tragedy of one of the principal hero's sons who, in love with a Polish aristocratic girl, becomes a traitor to his people. Already Belinsky noticed that the motif here is more dramatic than is generally the case in Scott. And yet this heightening of the dramatic element does not dissolve the broad, epic character of the whole. Gogol, with the true master's economy of line, understands how to fit this tragic episode *qua* episode organically into the whole and yet to let one feel that it is not a question here of one individual case, but of the fundamental problem of how a primitive society becomes infected by a more highly developed culture surrounding it, a tragedy of the necessary downfall of this entire formation.

However, the decisive intellectual struggles round the historical novel, the decisive steps in its further development take place in France, though not a single historical novel was written in French literature of this time which showed the kind of extension of Scott's tendencies as are to be found in the novels of Manzoni or Pushkin,

Cooper or Gogol. But on the one hand the historical novel of the Romantics in France produced more important figures than elsewhere in Europe, and the theoretical formulation of the Romantic historical novel also belongs on a more fundamental level than in the other countries. This is no accident, but the necessary consequence of the fact that during the Restoration period in France the struggle for a progressive or reactionary interpretation of history was much more directly the central social and political problem of the entire national development than anywhere else.

We cannot, of course, describe this struggle in extenso. We shall take only the most significant theoretical manifesto of the Romantic trend in the historical novel in order to illustrate the differences clearly. We shall analyse Alfred de Vigny's essay Sur la Vérité dans l'Art which appeared as a preface to his novel Cinq Mars.

Vigny starts from the extraordinary popularity of the historical novel and the preoccupation with history in general. He interprets this phenomenon entirely in the Romantic sense, saying: "We all have our eyes fixed on our Chronicles, as if, having reached maturity and moved on to greater things, we had stopped a moment to take account of our youth and its errors" (my italics, G.L.). This explanation is politically and ideologically of exceptional importance. For Vigny expresses here very frankly the aim of Romantic history writing: the manhood which France has reached as a result of the revolutionary struggles permits a retrospective glance at the errors of history. The preoccupation with history serves to disclose these errors in order to avoid them in the future. For Vigny, of course, the French Revolution is above all an error of this kind. But Vigny, like very many French Legitimists sees history sufficiently clearly to regard the French Revolution not as an isolated, sudden event, but rather as the final consequence of the "youthful errors" of French development, namely the destruction of the nobility's independence by the absolute monarchy, the furthering of the power of the bourgeoisie and therewith of capitalism. And in his novel he goes back to the time of Richelieu in order to reveal artistically the historical sources of this "error". In the establishment of the fact itself, there is no unbridgeable difference between Vigny and the progressive ideologists. Balzac regards Catherine de Medici as the precursor of Robespierre and Marat, and Heine on one occasion wittily groups Richelieu, Robespierre and Rothschild together as the three revolutionizers of French society. The Romantic, pseudo-historical principle in Vigny consists "merely" in the fact that he sees in this an "error" of history which could be made good by proper insight. Thus he belongs to those short-sighted ideologists of the Restoration era who do not see how, under the guise of reinstating the legitimate rule of monarchy and nobility,

French Capitalism, which set in vehemently with Thermidor, is soaring tempestuously ahead. (It is an essential mark of Balzac's genius that he fully recognized this economic reality of the Restoration period and portrayed it in all its complexity).

This interpretation of modern French history as a long path leading to the "error" of the French Revolution is, of course, not only a judgment on the social content of this development, but contains within it an entire methodology of approach to history, that is the whole question of whether one regards history as subjective or objective. Vigny, like every true artist, is not satisfied with immediate and empirically given facts. But he does not penetrate these facts in order to elicit their inner connections and then to find a story and characters which can express this inner connection better than what is immediately discoverable. He approaches the facts of history with a subjectivist, moral *a priori*, the content of which is precisely Legitimism. He says of historical facts: "They always lack a palpable and visible concatenation which could lead unerringly to a moral conclusion." Thus the deficiency of historical facts consists, according to Vigny, in their being unable to provide clear enough backing for the author's moral truths. From this standpoint Vigny proclaims the writer's freedom to transform historical facts and historical agents. This freedom of artistic imagination consists in "allowing the reality of the facts to yield sometimes to the *idea* which each of them must represent in the eyes of posterity".

There is thus in Vigny a marked subjectivism towards history, which at times amounts to saying that the outside world is fundamentally unknowable: "It is not given him" (i.e. man), says Vigny, "to see anything other than himself ..." The fact that he does not consistently follow through this extreme subjectivist conception alters its consequences very little, since the principles of objectivity in which he seeks support are, for their part, purely irrational and mystical. For what use is there his adding that only God can comprehend the totality of history? What use is there his assuming the unconscious activity of popular imagination in the adaptation of history, if this activity does nothing more than give rise to familiar sayings or historical anecdotes of the kind about Louis XVI's execution where somebody is heard to say: "Son of Saint Louis, ascend to heaven"? For by this alleged activity of popular imagination historical reality is converted into a disconnected sequence of fictional stories. This, according to Vigny, is a valuable process: "The adopted fact is always better composed than the true one ... because the *whole of humanity* requires that its destinies be a series of lessons for itself."

Given these principles, it is quite understandable that Vigny is a fundamental opponent of Scott's type of composition in the historical novel: "I believe too that I have no need to imitate those foreigners (the reference is to Scott, G.L.), who in their pictures barely allow the dominant figures of history to appear on the horizon. I have put ours right into the foreground, I have made them the chief actors of this tragedy ..." Vigny's artistic practice shows itself to be in complete agreement with this theory. The great historical figures of the age are in fact the heroes of his novels, and in accordance with the "activity of popular imagination", they are portrayed through a series of picturesquely fashioned anecdotes accompanied by moral reflections. The decorative modernization of history serves to illustrate a topical political and moral tendency. We have drawn upon this text of Vigny because it contains the most vivid expression of the specific tendencies of Romanticism in the historical novel. But the humanly and artistically incomparably more important Victor Hugo constructs his historical novels basically according to the same principle of decorative subjectivization and moralization of history, even long after he had broken with the political principles of reactionary Legitimism and had become the literary and ideological leader of liberal opposition movements. His criticism of Scott's *Quentin Durward* is extremely characteristic of his attitude to these problems. As a great man and writer, his attitude to Scott is naturally more positive than Vigny's. Indeed he sees quite clearly the realistic, contemporary tendencies in Scott's art, Scott's recognition of the prevailing "prose". Yet this great, realistic side of Scott's historical novel he considers the very principle to be overcome by his own practice, i.e. the practice of Romanticism. "After the picturesque but prosaic novel of Walter Scott there remains another novel to be created, more beautiful and more complete to our mind. It is a novel which is at once drama and epic, picturesque but poetic, real but ideal, true but great, which will enshrine Walter Scott in Homer."

It is clear to everyone who knows Victor Hugo's historical novels that he is not merely putting forward a criticism of Scott here, but outlining a programme for his own literary activity. In rejecting Scott's "prose", he renounces the only real approach to epic greatness, namely the faithful portrayal of the popular conditions and popular movements, the crises in popular life which contain the immanent elements of this epic greatness. In comparison, the Romantic "poeticization" of historical reality is always an impoverishment of this actual, specific, real poetry of historical life. Politically and socially, Victor Hugo goes far beyond the reactionary aims of his Romantic contemporaries. Yet he retains their moralizing subjectivism with a changed political and social content. For him, too, history is transformed into a series of moral lessons for the present. It is very characteristic that he should turn precisely this work of Scott—a model for the objective presentation of contending historical forces—by means of his interpretation into a moralizing fable intended to demonstrate the superiority of virtue over vice.

There are, of course, anti-Romantic tendencies in the France of the time, too. But these tendencies do not simply become part of the new conception of history and so lead to a development of the new historical novel. In France, more than in any other country, the tradition of the Enlightenment remained potent and alive. It was France which offered the sharpest ideological resistance to Romantic obscurantism, it was she who defended most vigorously the traditions of the eighteenth century and, with them, those of the Revolution, against the claims of Restoration Romanticism. (These traditions in France are extremely strong and manifold. Since the Englightenment had also its courtly aristocratic wing, these tendencies are active in Romanticism too, as Marx pointed out in the case of Chateaubriand; the reader will find in Vigny's ahistoricism many such modified elements of Enlightenment.) Of course, the important representatives of Enlightenment traditions did not remain unaffected by the new situation and its tasks. For this reason their struggle against reaction required to be more consciously historical than the conceptions of the old Enlighteners. Nevertheless, their conception retained either strong elements of an unilinear conception of human progress or tendencies towards a general scepticism regarding the "rationality" of history.

The most important representatives of the continuation of Enlightenment traditions in this period are Stendhal and Prosper Mérimée. We can only examine their views here in relation to the problem of the historical novel. Mérimée states his views clearly both in the foreword to his historical novel *Chronique du Regne de Charles IX* as well as in one of its chapters, in a dialogue between author and reader. He takes the sharpest stand against the Romantic conception of the historical novel, namely that the great figures of history should provide the principal heroes. He refers this task to the field of history writing. He ridicules the reader who, in accordance with Romantic traditions, demands that Charles IX or Catherine de Medici should bear a demonic stamp in each of their personal features. Thus in the dialogue the reader demands: "But let her (i.e. Catherine) say a few memorable words. She has just had Jeanne d'Albert poisoned or at least so it is rumoured, and this should be apparent." The author replies: "Not at all; for if this were apparent, where would be the famous dissimulation?" With these and similar remarks Mérimée very rightly ridicules the Romantic monumentalization and dehumanization of historical figures.

Here then, we have a very serious attempt to continue the historical novel on the basis of an unbiassed exploration of the real life of the past. The contrast to reactionary Romanticism is obvious at every point. Admittedly the contrast to classicist convention is just as sharp, to both the rhetorical, hero-worshipping manner of presenting historical figures as well as to the narrowing traditions of form which prevent a faithful rendering of historical life. This opposition made possible the temporary literary alliance between Mérimée and his friends and a section of the Romantics. But their common opposition to the limitations of classicism, their common fierce criticism of the latter should not obscure the inner divisions between the allies.

Nor the ideological and literary divisions in the progressive camp, that is, the different ways in which history is interpreted, adapted by literature, and utilized in the defence of progress against reaction. We have already mentioned the fact that Mérimée and his friends were rooted in the philosophic traditions of the Enlightenment. In regard to the historical novel this had the disadvantage of leaving the dualism between empirical reality and abstract general laws both ideologically and artistically unresolved. That is, Mérimée wishes to draw general lessons from history which hold good for all time (including the present), but he draws them *directly* from a keen and detailed observation of the empirical facts of history; he does not draw out those specific, concrete modifications of the laws of life, the structure of society, the relations of men to one another etc. from which Scott (unaware, naturally, of the general, methodological significance of his discoveries) derived the realism of his historical pictures. Mérimée, therefore, is more empirical than Scott, adhering more closely to individual features and detail; at the same time he draws more directly general conclusions from historical facts than the latter.

The empiricism is shown above all in the way Mérimée presents historical events. Instead of viewing them from the distance of a present-day narrator, as individual stages in the prehistory of the present, as Scott did, he aims at the intimate closeness and familiarity of the contemporary observer who can catch each accidental and scurrying detail.

Vitet, young Mérimée's comrade-in-arms and friend, whose historical scene-sequences strongly influenced Mérimée's *Jacquerie* in particular, declares this aim very clearly in a preface: "I imagined myself in May 1558 walking about in Paris during the stormy day of the barricades and the days preceding; I entered, one after the other, the halls of the Louvre, the Hotel de Guise, the taverns, churches, abodes of citizens belonging to the parties of the League, the politicians or the Huguenots, and each time a picturesque scene, a picture of manners, a trait of character presented itself, I sought to retain its image while I sketched a scene. One feels that only a series of portraits could arise from this, or, as the painters say, *studies, sketches* which have no right to claim any other merit than that of resemblance."

Vitet made these remarks with reference to his own dramatic scenes from history. The consequences of such views for the historical drama —and Vitet's *Jacquerie* represents an attempt in this direction—we shall discuss later. Mérimée's historical novel follows directly upon these dramatic experiments, but shows a greater, more conscious stylistic concentration. This concentration, however, applies essentially to the purely literary expression and does not indicate a real move towards the classical conception of the historical novel. Mérimée's concentration here is of a novella-like, anecdotal quality. He says in the foreword from which we have already quoted: "The only thing I like in history are anecdotes, and of them I prefer those in which I think I have found a true painting of the manners and characters of a given epoch."

For this reason memoirs have more to offer him than historical works, for they are intimate conversations between author and reader and hence give a picture of the age that has all the closeness and intimacy of direct observation, which Mérimée (like Vitet) see as the decisive factor in the presentation of history.

Thus Mérimée's conception is not the recognition of the concrete and complex intricacy of the historical process itself. He deprives the leading historical figures of their heroism with rightful scepticism. But in so doing he makes the course of history private. By portraying in his novel the purely private destinies of average human beings he aims to present the manners of the age realistically. And in detail he succeeds admirably. His story, however, has two weaknesses, both very closely connected with his sceptical Enlightenment attitude. First, the private events are not linked closely enough with the real life of the people; they are too confined at their important points to the higher social regions. Thus, while they give a subtle psychological portrait of the manners of these classes, they fail to show the relationship of the latter to the real, decisive problems of the people. As a result the crucial ideological questions of the epoch, above all the opposition between Protestantism and Catholicism, appear as purely ideological problems, and this character is only further underlined by the author's sceptical, anti-religious attitude which comes out clearly in the course of the story. Secondly, and in close connection with this, there is no really organic link between the great historical event which Mérimée wishes to portray—the night of St. Bartholomew—and the private destinies of the principal heroes. The night of St. Bartholomew has something here of the character of a Cuvier-like "natural catastrophe"; that it should happen, and happen as it does, is not shown by Mérimée as an historical necessity.

Mérimée's scepticism conceals a deep contempt for the bourgeois society of the Restoration period which emerged from the "heroic period" of the Enlightenment and the Revolution. Hence the ironic comparison between present and past in Mérimée's depiction of manners which is so different from the Romantic comparison. Mérimée says in his foreword: "It is interesting, it seems to me, to compare these manners with our own, and to observe in the latter the decline of vigorous passions in favour of tranquillity and perhaps happiness."

Here, the close connection between Mérimée's and Stendhal's conception of history is plainly visible. In French literature Stendhal is the last great representative of the heroic ideals of the Enlightenment and the Revolution. His criticism of the present, his picture of the past rest essentially on this critical contrasting of the two great phases of bourgeois society. The implacable nature of this criticism has its roots in the living experience of the past heroic period and in the unshaken belief—despite all scepticism—that the development of history will yet lead to a renewal of this great period. Thus the passion and rightness of Stendhal's criticism of the present is linked in the closest possible way with the Enlightenment limits of his conception of history, with his inability to recognize the end of the "heroic period" of bourgeois development as an historical necessity. This is the source of a certain abstract psychologism in his important historical portrayals; an admiration for the great, unbroken and heroic passion in and for itself. Hence his tendency to abstract from historical circumstances an extremely general essence and to present them in this general form. But the chief product of this attitude is to concentrate his energies on a criticism of the present. Stendhal's contact with the historical problems of the epoch produces less a new historical novel than a further development of the social-critical novel of the eighteenth century, with certain elements of the new historicism worked in as a means of intensifying and enriching its realistic features.

This continuation of the historical novel, in the sense of a consciously historical conception of the present, is the great achievement of his outstanding contemporary, Balzac. Balzac is the writer who carries forward in the most conscious fashion the tremendous impetus which the novel received from Scott, and in this way he creates a higher and hitherto unknown type of realistic novel.

Scott's influence on Balzac is extremely strong. Indeed, one may say that the specific form of the Balzac novel emerged in the course of his coming to grips, ideologically and artistically, with Scott. We are thinking here not so much of the historical novels themselves which Balzac wrote or at least planned at the commencement of his career;

although Balzac's youthful novel *Le Dernier Chouan*, despite the somewhat romantically exaggerated love story at its centre, represents a worthy successor to Scott in its portrayal of popular life. In Balzac it is neither the aristocratic leadership of the reactionary peasant uprising nor a group of leaders of Republican France who are at the centre of the action, but the primitive, backward, superstitious and fanatical people of Bretagne on the one hand and the deeply convinced, straightforwardly heroic and simple soldier of the Republic on the other. This novel is devised entirely in the spirit of Scott, even if at times Balzac surpasses his master in the realistic portrayal of such scenes, showing the hopelessness of the counter-revolutionary uprising precisely in terms of this social and human contrast between the contending classes on both sides. He depicts with extraordinary realism the egoistic greed and moral degeneration of the aristocratic leaders of the counter-revolution, among whom the old aristocrats who support the King's cause out of real conviction are fish out of water. And this in Balzac is not simply an historical picture of manners, as it is not in Scott's *Redgauntlet*, where the model of these scenes is obviously to be sought. Rather this moral disintegration, this complete absence of selfless devotion to one's own cause, is intended to bring out the cause of the defeat, the sympton of an historically lost and retrograde struggle. Further, Balzac shows—again, very much like Scott with the clans—that though the peasants of Bretagne may be very adept at guerrilla warfare in their mountains, they are quite unable despite their wild courage and predatory cunning to oppose successfully the regular armies of the Republic. And above all he shows the unshakeable courage of the Republicans in unfavourable situations involving personal tragedies; their simple, humorous, human superiority which springs from the deep conviction that to fight for the good cause of the Revolution is to fight for the cause of the people themselves.

This example would alone suffice to illustrate the extent of Scott's influence upon Balzac. Balzac not only expressed himself theoretically about this relationship many times, but in *Les Illusions Perdues* represented this influence, and the tendency which was to supersede the Scott historical novel, artistically. In Lucien de Rubempré's conversations with D'Arthez on the former's historical novel, Balzac treats the great problem of his own transition period: the plan to present modern French history in the form of a coherent cycle of novels which would embody the historical necessity of the emergence of modern France. In the foreword to the *Comédie Humaine* the idea of a cycle appears in the form of a cautious and sympathetic criticism of Scott's conception. Balzac sees in the lack of cyclical cohesion in Scott's novels a lack of system in his great predecessor. This criticism, together with Balzac's other criticism—that Scott presented the passions too primitively, because he was the prisoner of English hypocrisy—constitutes the formal aesthetic point at which Balzac passes from the portrayal of *past history* to the portrayal of the *present as history*.

Balzac himself, in one of his prefaces, stated his view clearly on the thematic side of this change: "The only possible novel about the past was exhausted by Walter Scott. This is the struggle of the serf or citizen against the nobility, of the nobility against the Church, of the nobility and Church against the monarchy."

The relationships and circumstances depicted are relatively simple here: they are those of the estates. "Today, equality in France has produced endless nuances. Formerly, the caste gave every person his physiognomy which dominated his individuality; today the individual receives his physiognomy from himself."

Balzac's deepest experience was the necessity of the historical process, the necessity for the present to be as it was, although he saw more clearly than anyone else before him the infinite net of chance which formed the precondition of this necessity. It is no accident that his first important historical novel goes back no further into the past than the great Revolution. The stimulus of Scott transformed this tendency to portray historical necessity into a conscious one. And so it became Balzac's task to present this section of France's history, from 1789 to 1848, in its historical connections. Only occasionally does he go back to earlier ages. The great original plan to present this development in a connected form, starting from the class struggles of the Middle Ages and going on to the rise of the absolute monarchy and bourgeois society in France right through to the present, recedes more and more behind this central theme, behind the portrayal of the last crucial act of this great tragedy.

The unified character of the social and historical conception which led aesthetically to Balzac's idea of a cycle, was only realizable given this concentration in time. The youthful plan of D'Arthez for a cycle of historical novels could only have been realized in a pedantic manner; the continuity of the figures participating could only have been the continuity of families. Thus it would have turned out to be a cycle in the style of Zola or even of Gustav Freytag's *Ahnen* (*Our Forefathers*) and not at all in the free, generous and inevitable manner of the *Comédie Humaine*. For the individual novels of such a cycle could not possibly have been connected in an organic and living way, that is through their action. The structure of the *Comédie Humaine* shows precisely how little the family and the connections between families suffice to depict such links; not even when the time-span of the cycle embraces only a few generations. With the extremely radical transformation of important social groups in the course of historical development (destruction and extinction of the old nobility in the class struggles of the Middle Ages, ousting of the old patrician families in the towns during the early rise of Capitalism etc.) the individual novels would have had to make use of very contrived and, socially, often very untypical human material in order to preserve the family continuity of sons, grandsons etc.

But the last act of roughly fifty years, which Balzac portrayed, breathes entirely the great historical spirit of his predecessor. However, Balzac goes beyond Scott not only in the freer and more differentiated psychology of the passions, as he states programmatically, but also in historical concreteness. The compression of historically portrayed events into a relatively brief period, full of big changes following one another in rapid succession, forces Balzac to characterize almost each year of the development individually, to give quite short phases an historical atmosphere peculiar to them, whereas it was sufficient for Scott to present the general character of a longer epoch with historical faithfulness. (Think, for instance, of the sultry atmosphere preceding Charles X's *coup d'état* in *Splendeurs et Misères des Courtisans.*)

This extension of the historical novel into an historical picture of the present, this extension of the portrayal of prehistory into the portrayal of self-experienced history has, of course ultimately, not aesthetic, but social and historical causes. Scott himself lived in a period of English history in which the progressive development of bourgeois society seemed assured, and thus he could look back upon the crises and struggles of the prehistory with epic calm. The great experience of Balzac's youth is the volcanic character of social forces, concealed by the apparent calm of the Restoration period. He recognized with greater clarity than any of his literary contemporaries the profound contradiction between the attempts at feudal-absolutist Restoration and the rapidly growing forces of Capitalism. The change from his plan to present French history in the manner of Scott to portraying the history of the present coincides roughly and not accidentally with the July Revolution of 1830. For these antagonisms exploded in the July Revolution, and the apparent balance between them in Louis Philippe's "bourgeois monarchy" was such an unstable equilibrium that the contradictory and vacillating character of the entire social structure inevitably became the focus of Balzac's conception of history. The historical orientation towards the necessity of progress, the historical defence of progress against Romantic reaction essentially comes to a close with the July Revolution: for Europe's greatest minds the central problem now becomes the understanding and portrayal of the historical "problematic" of bourgeois society itself. It was no accident for example that the July Revolution also gave the first signal for the break-up of the greatest historical philosophy of this period, the Hegelian system.

Thus with Balzac the historical novel which in Scott grew out of the English social novel, returns to the presentation of contemporary society. The age of the classical historical novel is therewith closed. But on no account does this mean that the historical novel becomes a closed episode in the history of literature, henceforth only of historical interest. Quite the contrary; the peak reached by the contemporary novel in Balzac is understandable only if seen as a continuation of this stage of development, as its elevation to a higher level. Once the historical consciousness with distinguishes Balzac's conception of the present weakens as a result of the class struggles of 1848, the decline of the realistic social novel sets in.

The normative character of this transition from the historical novel of Scott to the artistic history of contemporary bourgeois society is emphasized once again by its repetition in Tolstoy's development. The complex problems which occur in Tolstoy's work because he is both the contemporary—and greatly influenced contemporary—of post-'48 Western European realism and yet lives in a country whose bourgeois Revolution is only just developing during his long lifetime, have been discussed by us in other contexts (see *Studies in European Realism*). As far as the question here is concerned it is sufficient to record that Tolstoy, the powerful depicter of Russia's period of transformation from the 1861 Emancipation of the peasants to the 1905 Revolution, turns in the first instance to the major historical problems which formed the prehistory of this transformation and created its social preconditions. In portraying primarily the Napoleonic Wars, he was acting as consistently as previously Balzac had done when, in portraying the French Revolution, he sought (unconsciously) the social foundations of his *Comédie Humaine*.

And without stretching the parallel too far—for this inevitably leads to distortion and exaggeration—it is very characteristic that both great writers originally went even further back into the past, that both were drawn by the great, initial turning-points of history which ushered in the modern development of their country—Balzac by Catherine de Medici, Tolstoy by Peter the Great. However, Balzac wrote only one interesting and significant essay on Catherine de Medici, while Tolstoy got no further than beginnings and fragments. For the powerful pressure of contemporary problems was too great for either of them to dwell for long on the prehistory of these questions.

There, of course, the parallel ends in a literary respect. Indeed, it was only intended to bring out the social necessity which in the careers of these two foremost representatives of transitional epochs in the lives of two great nations, impelled them first towards the classical type of historical novel and then led them away from it. Artistically *War and Peace* occupies a quite different position in Tolstoy's career from that of *Le Dernier Chouan* in Balzac's; nor is it possible to compare their literary merit, so highly does Tolstoy's work rank in the entire history of the historical novel.

To call *War and Peace* an historical novel of the classical type shows how important it is not to interpret this term in a narrow literary-historical or formal-artistic sense. In contrast to important writers like Pushkin, Manzoni or Balzac, no direct, literary influence of Scott is traceable in Tolstoy. Nor as far as I know did Tolstoy ever study Scott very thoroughly. He created an historical novel of a unique kind out of the real conditions of life in this transitional period, and only in terms of the *most general and ultimate* creative principles does it constitute a brilliant renewal and development of Scott's classical type of historical novel. This unifying, ultimate principle is that of *popular character*. Apart from Balzac and Stendhal, Tolstoy also had a very high regard for Flaubert and Maupassant as writers. But the real and decisive features of his art go back to the classical period of bourgeois realism, for the social and ideological springs of his personality draw their strength from a deep bond with the central problems of national life during a great transitional period and his art still has the contradictorily progressive character of this period as its central theme.

War and Peace is the modern epopee of popular life even more decisively than the work of Scott or Manzoni. The depiction of popular life is broader, more colourful, richer in characters. The emphasis on popular life as the real basis of historical happenings is more conscious. Indeed, this manner of presentation acquires a polemical accent in Tolstoy which it did not and could not have in the first classics of the historical novel. The latter portrayed above all the *connection*; the historical events emerged as the crowning peaks of the contradictory, vying forces in popular life. (It is a consequence of the special development of Italy that certain historical events were presented by Manzoni in a purely negative way, as disturbances of popular life.) At the heart of Tolstoy is the contradiction between the protagonists of history and the living forces of popular life. He shows that those who despite the great events in the forefront of history, go on living their normal, private and egoistic lives are really furthering the true (unconscious, unknown) development, while the consciously acting "heroes" of history are ludicrous and harmful puppets.

This basic conception of history determines the greatness and limitation of Tolstoy's work. The individual lives of the characters unfold with a richness and liveliness scarcely equalled before in world literature. But while they are aroused, while their sympathies may be excited by the events in the foreground, they are never wholly absorbed by these events. The historical concreteness of feelings and thoughts, the historical genuineness of the peculiar quality of reaction, in sufferings and deeds, to the outer world—all this is on a magnificent level. But the basic Tolstoyan idea—that these individual strivings, spontaneous in their operation, unconscious of their significance and consequences, which together constitute popular forces, equally spontaneous in their operation, that these strivings really motivate the course of history—this idea remains problematic.

We have already said that Tolstoy successfully created a real popular hero in the figure of Kutuzov: a man who is important because he *wants* to be nothing else and nothing more than a simple, collective, executive organ of these powerful forces. His most personal and intimate qualities are concentrated wonderfully—precisely because they are often contradictory, indeed paradoxical—round this source of social greatness. His popularity "below", his divided position "above" are always vividly and strikingly explained by this position. But for Tolstoy the necessary content of this greatness is—passivity, a biding of time, which allows history itself, the spontaneous stirring of the people, the spontaneous course of things to act and does not wish to interfere with the free working-out of these forces.

This conception of the "positive" historical hero shows how far class antagonisms had sharpened—even in Tsarist Russia—since the days of Scott. It is part of Tolstoy's greatness that he has no confidence in the "official leaders" of history, neither in the open reactionaries nor in the liberals. But it is a limitation—the limitation of the growing revolt of the peasant masses—that this historically justified mistrust stops short at a passive mistrust of all conscious historical action, that Tolstoy completely fails to understand the movement of revolutionary democracy already beginning in his time. This failure to understand the role of conscious action by the people leads Tolstoy into an extreme and abstract denial of the significance of conscious action by the exploiters, too. His abstract exaggeration thus does not lie in his criticism and repudiation of the social content of such action, but in the fact that it is denied any significance at all. It is no accident that the best characters portrayed here by Tolstoy move visibly towards Decembrism; or that Tolstoy busied himself for a long time with a plan for a Decembrist novel, but it is also no accident that this remains only a move towards Decembrism and that the Decembrist novel was never in fact completed.

This contradictory, two-sided character of Tolstoy's historical portrayal of popular life itself argues a shift from past to present.

War and Peace, by broadly depicting the economic and moral life of the people, raised the great Tolstoyan problem of the peasantry and how different classes, strata and individuals were related to it. *Anna Karenina* presents the same problem after the emancipation of the peasants when antagonisms have sharpened still further: the present is made so historically concrete that the novel surpasses all previous Russian literature in the same way as Balzac's picture of French capitalism surpassed its predecessors. With *War and Peace* Tolstoy became "his own Walter Scott". But *War and Peace* is just as much a product of the previous realistic social novel of Russia and France as Scott's portrayal of history is of the English social-critical realism of the eighteenth century.

CHAPTER TWO

Historical Novel and Historical Drama

O UR ARGUMENT may now prompt the following question: given the historical basis of the new historicism in art, why did the latter produce the historical novel and not the historical drama?

An answer to this question requires a serious and detailed examination of the relation of both genres to history. The first thing one realizes is that really historical and fully artistic historical dramas existed long before this period, whereas most of the so-called historical novels of the seventeenth and eighteenth centuries have no significance either as reflections of historical reality or as art. Even quite apart from French classicism and the bulk of Spanish drama, it is obvious that both Shakespeare and a number of his contemporaries produced real and important historical dramas e.g. Marlowe's *Edward II*, Ford's *Perkin Warbeck* etc. In addition there comes, at the end of the eighteenth century, the second great flowering of historical drama in the early work and the Weimar period of Goethe and Schiller. All these dramas are not only of an incomparably higher artistic order than the so-called precursors of the classical historical novel, but are also historical in quite a different, deep and genuine sense. On the other hand, one must also point out that the new historical art beginning with Scott only very rarely produces really important works in the field of drama, above all Pushkin's *Boris Godunov*, Manzoni's dramas etc. The artistic flowering of the new, historical conception of reality is concentrated in the novel and, apart from that, only in the long story.

In order to understand this uneven development we must establish the difference between the drama's and the novel's relationship to history. This question is complicated by the fact that in modern times a very considerable interaction has occurred between drama and novel. Naturally, there are close connections between great epic and tragedy; it is no accident that Aristotle should have already pointed this out. But in classical times Homeric epic and classical tragedy belong to quite different epochs and, however related they may be in certain fundamental questions affecting content and form, their formal paths nevertheless diverge very clearly. Classical drama arises out of the epic world. The historical growth of social antagonisms in life produces tragedy as the genre of portrayed conflict.

This historical and formal relationship changes a great deal in modern times. The flowering of drama precedes the great development of the novel, despite Cervantes and Rabelais, despite the not unimportant influence of the Italian *novella* on Renaissance drama. On the other hand modern drama—including that of the Renaissance, even of Shakespeare—has from the outset certain stylistic tendencies which in the course of development take it evermore in the direction of the novel. And conversely, the dramatic element in the modern novel, particularly in Scott and Balzac, though arising primarily from the concrete historical and social needs of the time, is nevertheless by no means uninfluenced artistically by the preceding development of drama. Shakespearean drama, in particular, as Mikhail Lifschitz rightly pointed out in the discussion on the theory of the novel, exercised a decisive influence on the development of the modern novel. This connection between Scott and Shakespeare was clearly recognized already by Friedrich Hebbel, who saw Scott as the modern successor of Shakespeare. "What of Shakespeare came alive again in England was manifested in Walter Scott . . . for he combined the most admirable instinct for the basic conditions of all historical circumstances with the most subtle psychological insight into each individual characteristic and the most lucid understanding for the moment of transition, in which general and particular motives coincide, and it was to the combination of these three qualities that Prospero's wand owed its omnipotence and irresistibility."

But this extensive and complex historical interlocking of the two genres—which after all did not develop in a vacuum, metaphysically separated from one another—should not obscure the fundamental divisions between them. One has thus to return to the basic differences of form between drama and novel, uncovering their source in life itself, in order to comprehend the differences of both genres in their relationship to history. Only if we begin here can we understand the historical developments in both genres—emergence, flowering, decline etc.—historically and aesthetically.

1. *Facts of Life underlying the Division between Epic and Drama.*

Both tragedy and great epic—epic and novel—present the objective, *outer* world; they present the inner life of man only insofar as his feelings and thoughts manifest themselves in deeds and actions, in a visible interaction with objective, outer reality. This is the decisive dividing line between epic and drama, on the one hand, and lyric, on the other. Further, great epic and drama both give a *total picture* of objective reality. This distinguishes them both as regards form and content from the other epic genres, of which the *Novelle* in particular has become important in modern development. Epic and novel are distinguished from all other minor varieties of the epic by this idea of totality: the difference is not a quantitative one of extent, but a qualitative one of artistic style, artistic form, a difference which informs all the individual moments of the given work.

However, the important difference between dramatic and epic form must be mentioned forthwith: there can be only one "total" genre in drama. There is no dramatic form to correspond to the *Novelle*, ballad, tale etc. The one-act plays which appear from time to time and were looked upon as a special genre at the end of the nineteenth century mostly lack real dramatic elements. Since the drama had become a loosely composed narrative, broken up into dialogue, it was an easy step to turn the shorter *Novelle* type of sketch into a scene with dialogue. But the decisive question is of course not one of mere form; just as the difference between novel and *Novelle* is not one of extent. From the standpoint of a really dramatic portrayal of life Pushkin's short dramatic scenes are complete and finished dramas. For their brevity of extent is that of the uttermost dramatic concentration of content and outlook; they have no connection with the modern episode in dialogue form.

We have only the problem of tragedy to deal with here. (In comedy the problem is somewhat different for reasons which cannot be explained here.) This affinity between epic and drama is emphasized by Aristotle, when he says: "He, therefore, who is a judge of the beauties and defects of tragedy is, of course, equally a judge with respect to those of epic poetry...."

Tragedy and great epic thus both lay claim to portraying the totality of the life-process. It is obvious in both cases that this can only be a result of artistic structure, of formal concentration in the artistic reflection of the most important features of objective reality. For obviously the real, substantial, infinite and extensive totality of life can only be reproduced mentally in a relative form.

This relativity, however, acquires a peculiar form in the artistic reflection of reality. For to become art, it must never appear to be relative. A purely intellectual reflection of facts or laws of objective reality may openly admit this relativity and must in fact do so, for if any form of knowledge pretends to be absolute, ignoring the dialectical character of the merely relative, i.e. incomplete, reproduction of the infinity of objective reality, it is inevitably falsified and distorts the picture. It is quite different with art. Obviously, no literary character can contain the infinite and inexhaustible wealth of features and reactions to be found in life itself. But the nature of artistic creation consists in the ability of this relative, incomplete image to appear like life itself, indeed in a more heightened, intense and alive form than in objective reality.

This general paradox of art is sharpened in those genres which are compelled by their content and form to appear as living images of the totality of life. And this is what tragedy and great epic must do. They owe their deep effect, their central and epoch-making importance in the entire cultural life of mankind to their ability to arouse this feeling in the recipient. If they have been unable to do so, they have completely failed. No naturalist authenticity of individual manifestations of life, no formalist "mastery" of structure or individual effects can replace this feeling of the totality of life.

It is clear that the immediate question here is a formal one. But the absolute appearance of the relative image of life must, of course, be founded on content. It requires a real grasp of the essential and most important normative connections of life, in the destiny of individuals and society. It is just as clear, however, that the mere knowledge of these essential connections can never suffice. These essential features and all-important laws of life must appear in a new immediacy as the unique personal features and connections of concrete human beings and concrete situations. To achieve this new immediacy, to re-individualize the general in man and his destiny is the mission of artistic form.

The specific problem of form in great epic and tragedy is to give this immediacy to the totality of life, to conjure up a world of illusion which requires—even in the most extensive epic—a very limited number of men and human destinies to arouse the feeling of the totality of life.

Aesthetic theory of the post-1848 period failed any longer to understand problems of form in this wide sense. Where it did not nihilistically and relativistically deny all distinction between forms, it simply classified them in an external, formalist way according to their superficial distinguishing marks. We have to go to classical German aesthetics to find these questions dealt with in their real essentials, though of course the Enlightenment pioneered many important individual questions.

The most fundamental and profound definition of the difference between totality in epic and totality in drama is to be found in Hegel's aesthetics. Hegel lays down as the first requirement of the world of epic the "totality of objects which" is created "for the sake of connecting the particular action with its substantial basis". Hegel stresses sharply and rightly that this does not mean an antonomous object-world. If the epic poet makes the object-world antonomous, then it loses all poetic value. In poetry things are important, interesting and attractive only as objects of human activity, as transmitters of relations between human beings and human destinies. But in epic they are there neither as decorative background nor as technical instruments for directing the action, of no real interest in themselves. An epic work which presents only the inner life of man with no living interaction with the objects forming his social and historical environment must dissolve into an artistic vacuum without contours or substance.

The truth and depth of Hegel's definition lies in the emphasis on interaction, in the fact that the "totality of objects", represented by the epic poet, is the totality of a stage of historical development in human society; and that human society cannot possibly be represented in its entirety, unless the foundations encompassing it, the surrounding world of things forming the object of its activity, is also represented. Hence things precisely because they depend on, and are permanently related to, the activity of men not only become important and significant, but thereby acquire their artistic independence as objects of representation. The demand for a "totality of objects" in epic is essentially a demand for an artistic image of human society which produces and reproduces itself in the same way as the daily process of life.

Drama, too, as we already know, aims at a total embodiment of the life-process. This totality, however, is concentrated round a firm centre, round the dramatic collision. It is an artistic image of the system, so to speak, of those human aspirations which, in their mutual conflict, participate in this central collision. "Dramatic action," says Hegel, "therefore rests essentially upon colliding actions, and true unity can have its basis only in *total movement* (my italics G.L.). The collision, in accordance with whatever the particular circumstances, characters and aims, should turn out to conform so very much to the aims and characters, as to cancel out its contradiction. The solution must then be like the action itself, at once subjective and objective."

Hegel hereby counterposes "totality of movement" in drama to "totality of objects" in epic. What does this mean with regard to epic and dramatic form? Let us try to illustrate this difference with a notable historical example. In *King Lear* Shakespeare creates the greatest and most moving tragedy of the break-up of the family *qua* human community known to world literature. No one can come away from this work without a sense of all-embracing totality. But by what means is this impression of totality achieved? Shakespeare portrays in the relations of Lear and his daughters, Gloster and his sons, the great typical, human moral movements and trends, which spring in an extremely heightened form from the problematicalness and break-up of the feudal family. These extreme and—in their very extremity—typical movements form a completely closed system, the dialectics of which exhaust all the possible human attitudes to the collision. It would be impossible to add a further link to this system, a further avenue of movement, without committing a psychological and moral tautology. This psychological richness of the contending characters grouped around the collision, the exhaustive totality with which, complementing one another, they reflect all the possibilities of this collision, produces the "totality of movement" in the play.

What, however, is *not* included here? The entire life surroundings of parents and children is missing, the material basis of the family, its growth, decline etc. One need only compare this play with the great family portraits depicting the "problematic" of the family in an epic manner—e.g. Thomas Mann's *Buddenbrooks*, Gorky's *House of Artamonov*. What breadth and abundance here of the real circumstances of family life, what generalization there of the purely human moral qualities, the wills which can be brought into collision! Indeed, Shakespeare's extraordinary art of dramatic generalization is to be admired because he embodies the older generation of the family only through Lear and Gloster. Had he provided either Lear or Gloster or both with a wife, which an epic writer would certainly have had to do, he would have had either to weaken the concentration round the collision (if the conflict with the children had produced a conflict between the parents) or the wife would have been a dramatic tautology—she could only have served as a diminishing echo of her husband. It is characteristic of the rarefied atmosphere of dramatic generalization that this tragedy affects the beholder as a moving spectacle and that the question of the missing wives, for instance, simply does not arise. Whereas in a corresponding epic work a situation of this kind with two such parallel destinies would inevitably appear contrived and would need to be specially argued, if it could be convincingly argued at all. This analysis could naturally be extended to the portrayal of the smallest detail. What is important for us here is to bring out the contrast in its general outlines.

By concentrating the reflection of life upon a great collision, by grouping all manifestations of life round this collision and permitting them to live themselves out only in relation to the collision, drama simplifies and generalizes the possible attitudes of men to the problems of their lives. The portrayal is reduced to the typical representation of the most important and most characteristic attitudes of men, to what is indispensable to the dynamic working-out of the collision, to those social, human and moral *movements* in men, therefore, out of which the collision arises and which the collision dissolves. Any figure, any psychological feature of a figure, which goes beyond the dialectical necessity of this connection, of the dynamics of the collision, must be superfluous from the point of view of the drama,

Hence, Hegel is right to describe a composition which resolves itself in this way as the "totality of movement".

How rich and broad this typicality is depends on the phase of historical development to which the drama belongs and, within this phase, obviously on the individuality of the dramatist.

Yet most important of all is the inner, objective dialectic of the collision itself which as it were, independently of the dramatist's consciousness, circumscribes the "totality of movement". Let us take, for instance, the *Antigone* of Sophocles. Creon has decreed that Polyneices shall not be buried. Given this situation the dramatic collision requires two, but only two, sisters of Polyneices. Were Antigone the only sister, then her heroic resistance to the king's decree might give the impression of a socially average and matter-of-course reaction. The figure of her sister, Ismene, is vital in order to show that Antigone's action is indeed a heroic and matter-of-course expression of an earlier morality which has already perished, but which in the present circumstances of the drama is no longer a spontaneously matter-of-course reaction. Ismene condemns Creon's prohibition just as Antigone does, but she demands of her heroic sister that, as the weaker one, she should submit to the power of authority. It is, I believe, just as obvious that without Ismene Antigone's tragedy would not be convincing, that it would not be an artistic image of the social-historical totality, as it is that a third sister would be dramatically a pure tautology.

Lessing, therefore, in his polemic against the *tragédie classique* is absolutely right in stressing that Shakespeare's principles of dramatic composition are fundamentally the same as those of the Greeks. The difference between the two is an historical one. As a result of the increasing objective, social-historical complexity of human relations, the structure of the collision in reality itself became more involved and manifold. The composition of Shakespearean drama is just as faithful and grand a reflection of this new state of reality as the tragedy of Aeschylus and Sophocles was for the simpler state of things in ancient Athens. This historical change signifies something qualitatively new in Shakespeare as regards dramatic structure. The newness is, naturally, not a simple, external increase of richness in the world portrayed. On the contrary, Shakespeare has invented an entirely new and original system of social and human movements, typical and diverse, but with the diversity reduced to what is typically necessary. It is precisely because the innermost nature of Shakespeare's drama is built upon the same principles as that of the Greeks that his dramatic form was necessarily completely different.

The correctness and depth of Lessing's analysis however, shows itself more particularly in negative examples. There is a widespread prejudice that an outward concentration of action, a reduction of the number of characters to a few persons etc. represents a purely dramatic trend, while a colourful and frequent change of scene, a large number of characters etc. represents an epic trend in drama. This conception is both superficial and mistaken. Whether the character of a drama is truly dramatic or "novelized" depends on how the problem of the "totality of movements" is solved and not on purely formal distinguishing marks.

On the one hand, let us take the manner of composition of the *tragédie classique*. It attempts to realize the famous unity of time and place. The figures who appear are reduced to a minimum. But within this minimum there are characters who, without exception, are completely superfluous dramatically, namely the notorious "confidants". Alfieri, himself an adherent of this manner of composition, not only criticizes the undramatic role of these figures theoretically, but eliminates them in practice from his dramas. But what is the result? Alfieri's heroes may have no "confidants", but instead they have long and often quite undramatic monologues. Alfieri's criticism exposes a pseudo-dramatic side of the *tragédie classique* and puts a patently undramatic motif in its place. The real error of composition at the basis of this entire problem is that these writers rendered the collision abstract in a mechanical and brutal fashion (this happens in different ways, for different historical and individual reasons, in different representatives of this trend). As a result the living dynamic of the "totality of movement" is lost. Think again of Shakespeare. Even his "most solitary" heroes are not alone. Yet Horatio is no "confidant" of Hamlet, but an independent and necessary driving force of the total action. Without the system of contrasts between Hamlet, Horatio, Fortinbras and Laertes, the concrete collision of this tragedy would be unthinkable. In the same way Mercutio and Benvolio have independent and necessary functions in *Romeo and Juliet*.

Naturalist drama may serve as a counter example. Given a composition which is to some extent dramatic, such as Hauptmann's *Die Weber (The Weavers)*, the majority of the characters are necessary, representing a live component of the concrete totality of the weavers' uprising. As against this, most naturalist dramas, even those which manage with relatively few characters and heavily concentrate their plots temporally and spatially, always include a number of characters who serve only to illustrate the social *milieu* for the spectator. Every such character, every such scene "novelizes" the drama, for it expresses an element of that "totality of objects" which is alien in nature to the aim of drama.

This simplification seems to distance drama from life and this apparent distance has given rise to a variety of false theories about drama : in the past, the various theories justifying the *tragédie classique*; in our own time, the theories of the special "convention" of dramatic form, of the theatre's "autonomy" etc. The latter are no more than reactions to the necessary failure of naturalism in drama and, landing themselves in the opposite extreme, move inside the same false, magic circle as naturalism itself.

However, one must see this very "distance" of drama as a *fact of life*, as an artistic reflection of how life itself is *objectively at certain moments* and how it *necessarily appears* accordingly.

It is generally accepted that the central theme of drama is the collision of social forces at their most extreme and acute point. And no special perceptiveness is needed to see the relation between social collision in an extreme form, on the one hand, and social transformation, i.e. revolution, on the other. Every genuine and deep theory of the tragic stresses as the characteristic of the collision the necessity, on the one hand, for each of the conflicting forces to take action and, on the other, for the collision to be forcibly settled. If, however, one translates these formal requirements of the tragic collision into the language of life, then one can see in them the most highly generalized features of revolutionary transformations in life itself, reduced to the abstract form of movement.

It is certainly no accident that the great periods of tragedy coincide with the great, world-historical changes in human society. Already Hegel, though in a mystified form, saw in the conflict of Sophocles' *Antigone* the clash of those social forces which in reality led to the destruction of primitive forms of society and to the rise of the Greek polis. Bachofen's analysis of Aeschylus' *Oresteia*, though pressing the mystifying tendencies even further than Hegel, nevertheless formulates this social conflict more concretely, i.e. as a tragic collision between the dying matriarchal order and the new patriarchal social order. The deep and trenchant analysis of this question given by Engels in *The Origin of the Family* stands Bachofen's mystical and idealistic theory materialistically on its feet. It substantiates in a manner, equally clear theoretically and historically, the necessity of the connection between the rise of Greek tragedy and this world-historical transformation in the history of mankind.

The position is similar with regard to the second flowering of tragedy during the Renaissance. This time the world-historical collision between dying feudalism and the birth pangs of the final class society provides the preconditions in subject-matter and form for the resurgence of drama. Marx pointed out this connection quite clearly in regard to the drama of the Renaissance. He also mentions in various writings the social necessity for the rise and close of tragic periods. Thus in the Introduction to the *Contribution to the Critique* of *Hegel's Philosophy of Right* (1844) he underlines the element of necessity and the deep sense of justification which arises from this necessity among the dying section of society, as the precondition of tragedy. "As long as the *ancien régime*, as an existing world order, struggled against the world that was only coming into being, there was on its side a world-historical error, not a personal one. That is why its downfall was tragic."

In this youthful essay, as well as later in the *Eighteenth Brumaire*, Marx give a penetrating analysis of why in the course of history certain social collisions, from being tragic conflicts, become the subjects of comedy. And it is extremely interesting and of fundamental importance for the theory of drama that the objective result of the historical developments investigated by Marx always consists, as it does in this case, in the cancelling out, socially and historically, of the tragic necessity of action on the part of one of the conflicting sections, i.e. on the part of the opponent of human progress.

It would, however, be too narrow to restrict the facts of life underlying dramatic form, in a mechanistically rigid fashion, to the great historical revolutions themselves. This would entail an intellectual isolation of revolution from the general and permanent tendencies of social life, it would turn the phenomenon of revolution once more into a Cuvier-like "natural catastrophe". On the other hand, one must above all take note that not all those social collisions which have borne the seeds of revolution have in fact led to revolutions in historical reality. Marx and Lenin pointed out repeatedly that there have been situations which, though objectively revolutionary, have not led to a revolutionary outbreak, because of the insufficient development of the subjective factor. For example, the period at the end of the 1850's and the beginning of the 1860's in Germany (the "new era" and the subsequent constitutional conflict in Prussia).

But this by no means exhausts the problem of social collisions. A real popular revolution never breaks out as a result of a single, isolated social contradiction. The objective-historical period preparatory to revolution is filled with a whole number of tragic contradictions in life itself. The maturing of the revolution then shows with increasing clarity the objective connection between these isolatedly occurring contradictions and gathers them into several central and decisive issues affecting the activity of the masses. And, in the same way, certain social contradictions can continue unresolved even after a revolution or, indeed, emerge strengthened and heightened as a result of the revolution.

All this has very important consequences for the question which interests us here. On the one hand, we see the important connection in life between dramatic collision and social transformation. Marx's and Engels's conception of the connection between a great dramatic period and revolution proves itself here completely; for it is clear that the social-historical concentrating of contradictions in life necessarily demands a dramatic embodiment. On the other hand, we see that the trueness-to-life of dramatic form cannot be "localized", as it were, in a narrow and mechanical way, round the great revolutions of human history. It is true that a real dramatic collision gathers together the human and moral features of a great social revolution, but since the portrayal aims at the human essence, the concrete conflict by no means has to reveal immediately a transformation underlying it. The latter forms the general basis of the collision, but the connection between this basis and the concrete form of the collision can be a very complex one, with many intermediary stages. We shall see later on that the historicism of Shakespeare's most mature and outstanding dramas manifests itself in this way. The contradictoriness of social development, the intensification of these contradictions to the point of tragic collision is a *general* fact of life.

Nor does this contradictoriness of life come to an end with the social resolution of class antagonisms through the victorious Socialist revolution. It would be thoroughly shallow and undialectical conception of life to believe that with Socialism there is only the monotonous serenity of self-satisfaction without problems, struggle or conflict. Dramatic collisions, naturally, take on an entirely new aspect, since with the social disappearance of class antagonism, of antagonistic contradictions, the necessary tragic downfall of the hero in drama, to take one example, no longer plays the same role as before.

But also in regard to the drama of class society, it is worse than superficial to see in this tragic downfall solely the brutal destruction of human life, to see only something "pessimistic", which one then counters with a just as shallowly conceived "optimism" in our own drama. It should never be forgotten that, in the really great dramatists of the past, the tragic downfall has always released the greatest human energies, the supremest human heroism; and this ennoblement of man was only possible because the conflict was fought out to the end. Antigone and Romeo, indeed, perish tragically, but the dying Antigone and the dying Romeo are much bigger, richer and nobler people than they were before being swept into the whirlpool of the tragic collision.

Today it is specially important to stress this side of the tragic collision, to see how dramatic form generalizes a typical fact of life and makes of it an intense experience. And this human side of the dramatic collision, which is by no means necessarily linked with tragic downfall, is present, too, as a fact of life, in Socialist society and can thus become the basis of a significant dramatic work.

Thus, in recognizing the truthfulness of dramatic form, the problem of collision as a fact of life must be kept very clearly in view. Without pretending to anything like completeness, we shall list several, typical facts of life, which, reflected artistically, necessarily take on dramatic form.

Let us begin with the problem of the parting-of-the-ways in the lives of individuals and of society. In Hebbel's tragedy *Herodes und Mariamne* (*Herod and Mariamne*) the Queen says to the King:

> Du hast vielleicht
> Gerade jetzt dein Schicksal in den Händen
> Und kannst es wenden, wie es Dir gefällt !
> Für jeden Menschen kommt der Augenblick,
> In dem der Lenker seines Sterns ihm selbst
> Die Zügel ubergibt. Nur das ist schlimm,
> Dass er den Augenblick nicht kennt, dass jeder
> Es sein kann, der vorüberrollt !
>   (You have perhaps
> Even now your destiny in your hands
> And can direct it as you please !
> To every man there comes the moment
> When the pilot of his star
> Hands him the reins. The misfortune is
> He does not know the moment, each
> Which passes by may be the one.)

Only the adherents of a mechanistic fatalism can doubt the reality of such "moments" in life. The necessity of social life asserts itself not only through coincidences, but also through such decisions, made by human beings and groups of human beings. Of course, these decisions are not free in the sense of an idealist voluntarism, they do not represent human independence in a vacuum. But within the historically given, necessarily prescribed framework of all human activity and as a result of the contradictory basis of all social and historical development, such "moments" arise of necessity.

We have put this word in quotation marks because, if taken too literally, it has a fetishist character. However, it is an essential feature of reality that this parting-of-the-ways crops up again and again with the possibility and necessity of a decision, whichever path one takes. But in the first place such a choice does not always exist, for it presupposes a certain crucial sharpening of social or personal circumstances; in the second place the length of time for such a decision is always relatively limited. This must be known to everyone from his personal experience.

Lenin's writings, especially those belonging to the acute revolutionary periods, show what a significant role such moments play in history itself and how very limited is their duration. When Lenin, after the July rising of 1917, proposes to the Social Revolutionaries and Mensheviks the formation of a government responsible to the Soviets, he writes: "Now and only now, perhaps *only during a few days* or for only one or two weeks would it be possible to form and consolidate such a government in perfect peace." The political importance of this proposal lies outside the scope of our discussion. We have quoted such a strategist and tactician of class struggle as Lenin simply to show that the "parting-of-the-ways", the "moment" of decision, is not something that idealist dramatists have invented and over-stylized, nor any sort of "requirement of dramatic form", which it has become in the hands of the neo-classical theorists of drama in the age of imperialism, but an extremely important and ever recurring fact of life which plays a very important part in both the destiny of individuals and of classes.

The second group of facts of life comes under the heading of "calling to account". What does this mean? The causal intricacy of life is extremely complicated. Obviously, every act of a person or group of persons affects their further fortunes; these are largely dependent on which line of action they take in historically given circumstances. But in life these consequences often set in very slowly and always unevenly and contradictorily. Many people end their lives or have long since followed a different path before the consequences of their earlier actions come upon them in such a form. But it is a general and frequent fact of life that these necessary consequences of earlier deeds and, especially, of the general attitude to life which inspired these deeds, concentrate themselves with tremendous force in life, and the individual then has to settle his accounts. Here again, the connection between the dramatic facts of life and the revolutionary crises of society is evident. For particularly in the case of social groups, e.g. parties, the "day of reckoning" usually dawns in a time of crisis. Parties have gradually ceased to be real representatives of the class interests in whose defence they were founded, and have heaped failure upon failure in this respect without incurring any real consequences. Then "suddenly" there is a social crisis, and a party which yesterday was powerful is "suddenly" discredited and abandoned before the eyes of its previous supporters. History is full of such facts, and, obviously, not only with regard to political parties in a narrow sense. The great French Revolution, in particular, is full of such catastrophes which are already dramatic in life itself. From the "sudden" collapse of absolutism on the day of the storming of the Bastille, a chain of such collapses leads from the fall of the Gironde, the Dantonists and Thermidor right through to the fall of the Napoleonic Empire.

Such moments already have a dramatic character in life itself. It is not surprising, therefore, if the "day of reckoning" constitutes one of the central problems of drama. From Sophocles' *Oedipus*, for two thousand years the tragic model of drama, to Büchner's *Danton's Death*, we can trace this problem as a leitmotif of great tragedy. And it is especially characteristic of drama not to portray the slow and gradual amassing of consequences, but to take usually a relatively brief and decisive period of time, in fact, that dramatic moment in life itself, in which the accumulation of consequences is transformed into action. It is customary, starting from the formal example of Oedipus, to connect this kind of drama with the classicist concentration of events, on the one hand, and the Ancients' "idea of destiny", on the other. Neither corresponds to the facts. Büchner's masterpiece, for example, is conceived formally entirely in Shakespeare's sense and not in that of the Greeks. And yet the tragedy of Danton rests upon the same basis. Neither the powerful tactician of revolutionary victory, nor the vacillating bourgeois politician who turns away from the continuation of the revolution stands at the centre of the drama. All this has long since taken place in Büchner's play. What he portrays, with unique dramatic power, is how Danton, the great revolutionary, having estranged himself from both the people and his mission, is "called to account" for thus turning his back upon history.

Let us proceed. Lenin says repeatedly that in a situation demanding action one must choose from among the endless possibilities one particular link in the chain, which one must firmly grasp in order to keep a real hold on the entire chain. Therewith, Lenin not only describes incomparably an important principle of political action, especially in periods of necessary change, but at the same time a feature of human behaviour in general. Or rather, a certain kind of human behaviour, a kind of human response at certain turning-points in life. We just wish to mention briefly that the act of choosing and grasping the link in a chain is closely related to the parting-of-the-ways problem which we dealt with earlier. But we should like to draw attention to the specific character of this fact of life. What is specific to the link-in-the-chain problem is, above all, the stress given to the chosen link, which is made central. Thereby, life, to further its own ends, simplifies and generalizes itself. This simplification and generalization gives life a pulsating, vigorous character, forming contrasts and driving them to their extremes.

Grasping the link in the chain need not in itself be connected with a collision, nor grow out of one, but the concentration of life's problems around such a centre does in most cases produce collisions. After all, in individual life as well, things do not concentrate in a vacuum, but in live interaction with the acts of other human beings. And, naturally, the concentration of one's own actions round one decisive point provokes a similar concentration about this point by the personal and human forces opposed to oneself. The effect of grasping the link is, of course, particularly visible in political life. When such a "link" problem arises and takes up the centre of political life, the often amorphous nature of the different tendencies and trends acquires a distinct and clearcut physiognomy on all sides. Just think of the extreme differentiation among the various standpoints occasioned by Lenin's great speeches at the introduction of NEP. *Mutatis mutandis* this problem plays a kindred role in the life of the individual.

Finally, let us mention another problem which is closely related to this question: a person's deep involvement with his work. Even in the purely personal life, this produces collisions, dramatic conflicts and entanglements. For however central a man's life-work may be to all his endeavours, there is no person in and for whom other forces in life are not crucially important. The deeper a person's devotion to his life-work on the one hand, the more genuine a human being he is on the other, i.e. the more and the closer are the threads which bind him to life and its various trends, the more dramatic will this collision be.

But a person's attachment to his life-work is not always, not even in the rarest cases, simply a matter of concern to himself. If the work in question belongs to the domain of art or science, then superficially and psychologically it may give this appearance. But if this life-work is directly tied to social life, then a set of complications arises which by their nature bear a direct social character.

This brings us back to the problem which we have already treated in the first section, the problem of "world-historical individuals" in Hegel's sense. There we began with the historical process itself and examined the role of these "world-historical individuals" in its epic portrayal. We came to the conclusion that their historical significance was best brought out epically when, viewed compositionally, they played minor parts in the story. Now we approach the problem from a different angle, from the inner life of the individual. We see how a deep human involvement with society and with an individual's tasks therein make for the type of the "world-historical individual", in whom both the individual's involvement with his social work, his absorption therein, as well as the extensive and intensive significance of this task appear at their highest point. Hegel says of this relationship: "These are the great human beings in history whose own particular purposes contain the substantial, which is the will of the world spirit. This content is their true power. . . ."

If we have already seen in the complete personal devotion to a task a dramatization of life in life itself, it is clear that such a supreme case of involvement represents a high point dramatically both in life and art. In life, too, this basic personal unity between the individual, his life-work and its social content sharpens the concentrated sphere in which the "world-historical individual" moves, drawing it around significant collisions which are materially linked with the realization of this life-work. The "world-historical individual" has a dramatic character. He is destined by life itself to be a hero, to be the central figure in drama.

For the social collision, as the centre of drama, round which everything revolves and to which all components of the "totality of movement" refer, requires the portrayal of individuals, who in their personal passions directly represent those forces whose clash forms the material content of the "collision". It is clear that the more a person is a "world-historical individual" in Hegel's sense, that is, the more his personal passions centre upon the content of the "collision" and merge with it, the more suited he is to be the hero, the central figure of drama. Again, this truth of dramatic form is, as we have seen, a truth about life and not a piece of formalist subtlety.

For this reason it must never be explained in too mechanical a sense. For instance, many theorists of the *tragédie classique* and their modern neo-classicist imitators consider that only the great figures of history, or of myth, are suited to be heroes of drama. Neither life, nor drama, as its artistic image, is interested in formal-decorative representation, but in an objective-thematic concentration of forces, in a real, personal compression of a colliding social force.

Hebbel on one occasion makes a witty and fine comparison between tragedy and a world clock, which points to successive historical crises as its hands go round. Developing the simile, he adds: "It makes no real difference whether the clock's hands are of gold or brass, nor does it matter whether an action which is significant in itself, that is symbolic, takes place in a lower or socially higher sphere." Hebbel wrote these words in the preface to his bourgeois tragedy, *Maria Magdalene*, as a theoretical defence of the play. And he is quite justified in this defence. Characters such as the peasant, Pedro Crespo, in Calderon's *Judge of Zalamea*, the bourgeois characters in *Emilia Galotti*, *Kabale and Liebe* (*Intrigue and Love*), Ostrovsky's *Thunderstorm* and in Hebbel's tragedy as well are "world-historical individuals" in this sense. The fact that the concrete personal conflict which is treated in these plays has no wide historical dimension, that is, that it does not directly decide the fate of nations or classes, in no way alters this fact. The important thing in these plays is that the inner social substance of the collision makes of it a decisive event, historically and socially; and that the heroes of such plays have within themselves that combination of individual passion and social substance which characterizes the "world-historical individuals". It is the absence of both these dramatic elements of life which makes most bourgeois and, unfortunately, most proletarian plays so banal, tedious and insignificant. The unfavourableness of the material is due, above all, to the difficulty of bringing out dramatically the world-historical character of the conflict and of the hero within it without stylizing, without introducing falsely momumentalizing elements. But modern drama during the period of the general decline of realism takes the line of least resistance; that is, it accommodates its artistic means to the most trivial side of its material, to the most prosaic moments of modern daily life. In this way the grey banality of life becomes the subject of representation, underlining those very sides of the material which are the least favourable for drama. Plays are written which dramatically are on a lower level than the life which they portray.

We repeat : we have mentioned here only a few striking examples from among the large number of "facts of life" of which drama is the concentrated and conscious reflection, exhausting all the possibilities of this concentration. The formal laws of drama arise out of the material of actual life; the form being the most universal and supremely generalized artistic reflection of this material. Hence great writers in different periods create entirely different types of drama. Yet, for this very reason, the same inner laws of form are operative in these very different works of art. These are the laws of movement of life itself, of which the plays are artistic images. Hence the laws of *artistic* reflection are operative, and the drama is a true work of art, if these are applied and observed.

Any theory of drama which, even though unconsciously, like the idealist aesthetics of earlier periods, has as its starting-point not these facts of life, but problems of dramatic "stylization", of whatever kind, is inevitably side-tracked into formalism. For such theories do not recognize that the so-called "distance from life" of dramatic form is only a heightened and concentrated expression of certain tendencies in life itself. The failure to understand this phenomenon, that is, to start from the formal distance between dramatic expression and the general and average forms in which daily life manifests itself, produces not only a false theory, but also false dramatic practice, distorts not only the form of drama, but also its social and human content.

Many critics of the *tragédie classique*, from Saint Evremond to Voltaire, have felt somewhat uneasy about even the greatest of Corneille's and Racine's plays. They felt a certain abstractness, remoteness from life, a want of "nature". But despite Lessing's very fundamental criticism, which in many instances treats the most important problems of form, it was Manzoni who first put his finger on the weakest spot of the *tragédie classique*. We quote his criticism here because it shows most vividly how the task of dramatic concentration is the correct reflection of actual "facts of life", actual tendencies in life; because it shows most distinctly the distorting effect of formal concentration upon the human content of drama.

Throughout his life Manzoni fought against the formal requirements of the unities of time and place. He saw in them an insuperable obstacle to the task of his time, to the historical drama. But like his great contemporary, Pushkin, he combats them neither in the name of "naturalness", nor in that of probability or improbability. He starts instead from the fact that the characters and their passions are inevitably deformed by the confinement of the action to twenty-four hours. "It was necessary, therefore, to bring this will to life more rapidly by exaggerating the passions, by denaturing them. For a character to come to a final decision within twenty-four hours, an altogether different degree of passion is required than in the case of one with which he has been battling for a month." All nuances are thereby eliminated. "The tragic poets were in a way reduced to painting only this small number of clearcut, dominant passions ... the theatre became filled with fictitious characters who figured as abstract types of certain passions rather than as passionate beings ... Hence the exaggeration, the conventional tone, the uniformity of the tragic character ..." The concentration of time and place compels these tragedians to "give these causes a power which the real causes would not have had ... Brutal shocks are necessary, terrible passions, precipitate resolves ..." And Manzoni goes on to show convincingly how the immoderate predominance of the love motif, which other critics have also attacked, is connected with these formal problems and their distorting effect.

This distorting tendency obviously has its immediate social and historical causes. But artistic form is never a simple mechanical image of social life. Admittedly, it arises as a reflection of social tendencies, but within this framework it has its own dynamic, its own direction which takes it towards or away from truthful representation. Thus, Manzoni—great dramatist and profound critic—rightly criticized the distorting effect of a particular form by considering the problems of dramatic form in general in close connection with those of historical life.

2. The Peculiarity of Dramatic Characterization

At this point one might ask: granted that all these facts of life (whose artistic reflection we take dramatic form to be) are real and important—are they not in fact *general* facts of life? Must not epic also reflect them? The question is perfectly justified. Indeed, in this general and therefore too abstract form, it may be answered in the affirmative. As general facts of life they must naturally be portrayed by all literature reflecting life. The question is, simply, what role and significance is allotted them in the various forms of literature. And here we must concretize the question. We have selected these facts from the entire range of life, because, thus selected, they form the central problems of drama; because in drama everything revolves round the reflection of such critical and crisis-producing heightenings and climaxes of life; because this is the centre whence the parallelogram of forces of the "totality of movement" arises; because drama reflects life in its actual heightening.

Of course, all these facts of life occur similarly in epic's reflection of reality. The difference is "merely" that here they occupy the position which is theirs in the *total* process of life. Here, they are not the centre round which everything is grouped. Furthermore, since drama portrays these heightened moments of life, all such manifestations of life as are not immediately connected with these moments disappear from dramatic representation. The driving forces of life are represented in drama only insofar as they lead to these central conflicts, insofar as they are motive forces of these actual collisions. In epic, on the other hand, life appears in all its breadth and wealth. Dramatic high points may occur, but they form peaks which include not only the mountain range, but also the hills and the plain. And this kind of reflection naturally yields new aspects. It is obvious that the "normal" proportions of life are observed much more strictly in epic than in drama, so that it is not surprising if the new and singular problems of form make their appearance in drama. This connection was already clearly recognized by Aristotle. He goes on, after the passage we have already quoted, in which he spoke of the common basis of epic and tragedy, to say: "for all the parts of the epic poem are to be found in tragedy; not all those of tragedy in the epic poem."

The isolation of certain moments of life which takes place in drama must itself be a form in which life manifests itself in order to serve as the basis for the constitution of a literary form. For the question we have raised has yet another aspect, which is important both historically and aesthetically. Since it is clear that the facts of life which drama reflects can and must be represented in epic, too, it seems equally obvious that these facts occur *permanently* in life; which would mean that life is constantly providing the possibility for genuine, great drama.

This, however, contradicts what has actually happened in the historical development of literature. Admittedly, dramatic form has never experienced so thoroughgoing a change as the transformation of the old epos into the modern bourgeois novel. Dramatic form has a much more perennial character, its essential laws are better preserved in its various guises. But this continuity asserts itself within a very discontinuous, very disconnected development. It is characteristic of the history of drama that it has experienced relatively short, intensive periods of flowering, which have been preceded and followed by century long periods, producing virtually nothing bearing a remote resemblance to drama. And this phenomenon is all the more striking because the outer prerequisite for drama, namely the stage and acting, shows a much more continuous development. The more closely we connect in our minds drama and stage (from the standpoint of the inner laws of dramatic form), the more seriously must we raise the question of the social and historical reasons for the discontinuous appearances of drama.

The bare fact of this discontinuity alone indicates that, while the moments of life which we have enumerated are reflected in drama and form the basis of its specific problems of form, nevertheless something else must be added to them, rather, they must be produced by a life in a definite, specific manner, if their adequate artistic representation is to be that of true drama. And the discontinuity of the development of life is then explained by the fact that these additional specific factors whose presence is necessary for the emergence of true drama can only manifest themselves in very special social and historical conditions. Thus, they contribute nothing new in principle to the "facts of life" which we have investigated. But they help to bring out the dramatic character, always present in them, distinctly, visibly and adequately.

The necessity as well as direction and nature of this concretization may be made clear by reference to a few significant (positive and negative) examples. Let us take the case, for instance, which we described earlier on by the term "calling to account". This motif crops up in the course of literature in the most varied forms without necessarily taking on a really dramatic character in every case. So, for example, in the medieval mystery plays which are outwardly constructed on the basis of dialogue and scene. A theme which frequently occurs here, and which was most notably embodied in the English mystery play, *Everyman*, is that of Man, in his dying hour, being called to account by Death: in the hour of death the bankruptcy of an erring life is revealed in a compressed and concentrated form. Despite the dialogue and scene construction of this mystery play, despite its (in the abstract) dramatic motif, nothing dramatic ever emerges. Why is this? Because in such conditions the consequences of the "calling to account" can only be purely inward, psychological and moral and cannot be translated into action and struggle. The collision is enacted exclusively in the hero's soul, in the form of fear, repentance, inner struggle with himself etc. Its mode of expression, therefore, can only be that of lyricism or of didactic rhetoric. Despite the scenic objectification, the collisions which occur have no visible dramatic character; despite the dialogue form, no dramatic struggle ensues between two social-human forces. (And it is interesting to observe how powerfully the inner drama of this motif makes itself felt when this kind of "calling to account" is portrayed epically, as in Tolstoy's short story masterpiece, *The Death of Ivan Ilyich*.) In the mystery play, with its outwardly dramatic form, the "calling to account" is so general that it cannot be expressed in a dramatically individualized case. The relation of the agent's individuality to the universality of the problem is that of an example, cited at random and replaceable at will, to a law, not the dramatic embodiment of one of the colliding forces.

This abstract universality of the colliding forces need not necessarily take the form of such a rigid confrontation of life and death in general, of a religious relationship to reality. On the contrary, this special type of pseudo-dramatic portrayal is bound up with dying feudalism, and has only since found some few imitators, significantly enough, in imperialist decadence.

However, the newly-awakened sense of history induced many writers to give their works such a breadth of empirical detail, of mere facts, that historical necessity could again only appear abstractly amidst their abundance. For every historical force or historical necessity represented in drama is abstract in an artistic sense, if it is not adequately and obviously embodied in concrete human beings and concrete human destinies. This the progressive historical movement represented by Mérimée, Vitet and their friends, for example, which we have already treated, neither wished nor were able to do. They, misunderstanding the Shakespeare history plays, which they chose for their model, wished to create a drama based on an extensive, broad and complete representation of historical detail.

Vitet, the most consistent exponent of this trend, recognized fairly clearly the contradiction which this presented to the nature of drama. He expresses this openly in the preface to his historical play *Les Barricades*, from which we have already quoted: "All the same, these scenes are not separate from one another: they form a whole; there is an action to whose development they contribute; but this action is only there, as it were, in order to produce them and serve as a link to them. If, on the other hand, I had wanted to create a drama, it would have been necessary to have had regard above all to the course of the action; to have sacrificed painting a multitude of details and accessories in order to give it more life; to have excited curiosity by being silent on certain matters; *to have set several principal characters and events*

*in relief at the expense of truth, and to have allowed the others to be
seen only in perspective.* I have preferred to leave things as I found
them, to place in the foreground all the people and all the events just
as they occurred, contriving nothing and allowing myself to interrupt
the action with frequent digressions and episodes, as happens in real
life. I resigned myself to stimulating interest the less, in order to copy
with the more exactitude." (My italics, G. L.)

We have already seen that Mérimée never went as far as Vitet,
his friend and comrade-in-arms, in his adherence to the empirical data
of all historical happenings, in the conscious sacrifice of poetic truth
and historical faithfulness to individual facts. In spite of this, his historical play *La Jacquerie* is built upon very similar principles. His great
and lasting merit is not only to have been the first to go back to the
great peasant uprising, which historians had cast into oblivion, and
thus to counter the Romantic idyllization of the Middle Ages with a
tangible picture of the sharpest and most violent class struggles. More
than this, Mérimée gave a genuine and artistically alive picture
of *all classes* during the crumbling Middle Ages; for the different
classes he found and portrayed important, typical representatives; he
presented the clash of the different classes in situations alive as they
were typical.

Despite this genuinely poetic portrayal, however, which went
far beyond mere historical faithfulness *à la* Vitet, no compelling drama
resulted. Charles Rémusat, a contemporary critic who was close to
the Mérimée circle at this time, sensibly argued the causes of this
failure. Having dealt in detail with all the the good points of *La Jacquerie*, he turns to Goethe's *Götz von Berlichingen*, which likewise
gives a broad period picture of the life of all classes in the declining
Middle Ages and also presents a peasant uprising. Rémusat sees in
the genuine and deep human qualities of the figure of Götz the
secret "of his poetic greatness, which enchants and elevates the imagination", a portrayal of character which is lacking in all later literary
attempts, those of Mérimée included, which have arisen upon a
similar formal basis and strive after a similar faithfulness to history.
Rémusat goes on to give a detailed analysis of the figure of Götz in
all his individual richness, summing up his judgment as follows: "He
(i.e. Götz—G.L.) is the most important man of all times with the physiognomy of his century. In this way poetry and history may be reconciled in drama. By means of such works those of the modern theatre
may achieve a place at the side of the old national theatre. Art would
be incomplete and untruthful, if it did not reproduce in its fiction
everything, which nature permits and includes, just as well and perhaps even better than she."

It is immaterial for our present purposes how we assess the historical

Götz von Berlichingen and Goethe's conception of him, whether, like Hegel, we see in him one of the last representatives of the "heroic age" or, like Marx, a "miserable fellow". For Hegel and Marx (the latter with a polemical emphasis directed against Lassalle) agree that Goethe succeeded in creating a figure in whom the deepest individual and personal traits merge with historical authenticity and truth to form an organic, inseparable, directly effective unity. And this, too, is the sense of the Rémusat remarks we quoted. The destiny which Götz encounters as a result of historical circumstances is thus not only appropriate in a general sense—that is, seen poetically, from an abstract, historical point of view—but, losing none of its historical character (on the contrary, deepening and concretizing this historical character), it is the specific, *individual destiny* of Götz in all its most personal uniqueness.

Therefore, Manzoni, the most important exponent of historical drama at the time in Western Europe, very consistently sees its mainspring in this individualization of characters and destinies; and this historical drama he polemically opposes to the abstracting method of classicism. In sharp contrast to Vitet and also to Mérimée, he asserts that there neither is, nor can be, any fundamental contradiction between historical faithfulness and dramatic individualization. Historical tradition informs us of the facts and the general trends of development. The dramatist has no right to alter any of this. Nor has he any cause to, for if he really wishes to portray his characters as living individuals, then he will find his most important clues and aids in the historical facts, and the deeper he penetrates into history, the more will this be the case. "Now, where can true drama better be found than in what men have really done? A poet finds in history an imposing character who arrests him and seems to say : observe me, I shall teach you something about human nature; the poet accepts the invitation; he wishes to draw this character, to develop him : where can he find external deeds which conform more to the true idea of the man he is proposing to depict than in the deeds actually performed by this man?"

But what then remains for the writer to do, asks Manzoni. "What remains? Poetry; yes, poetry. For, after all, what does history give us? Events, which, so to speak, are known only from the outside; what men have performed : but what they have thought, the feelings which have accompanied their deliberations and their plans, their successes and their misfortunes; the conversations by which they have impressed or tried to impress their passions and their wills upon other passions and other wills, by which they have expressed their anger, poured forth their grief, by which, in a word, they *have revealed their individuality* : all this history passes by almost in silence; and all this is the domain of poetry." (G.L.'s italics—translators).

The struggle of true historical drama with the obstacles formed by
what for art is the abstract appearance of things in history shows very
clearly, in positive and negative examples, that the *individuality of the
dramatic hero* is the decisive problem. All those facts of life which find
their appropriate reflection in drama can only crystallize in answer to
their inner requirements if the colliding forces, whose clash is caused
by these facts, are so constituted that their struggle concentrates itself
in persons whose individual and social-historical physiognomies are
equally in evidence.

To clarify fully the correctness of this concretization of our earlier
remarks, we must analyse a few more cases in which the presence of
dramatic facts of life again does not lead to real drama, though for
opposite reasons. Only then can we clearly outline the concrete area
of specific, dramatic reflection of life, where dramatic form arises out
of the inner needs of the material given it to portray.

Let us, therefore, now take the opposite extreme : collisions which
are grounded on a similar emotional basis, but which, though embodied
in different individuals, do not possess social universality. In Shakespeare, when the love of Romeo and Juliet comes into conflict with
the social circumstances of declining feudalism, situations arise,
inner changes occur etc. which everyone can experience directly. And
the more individually the principal characters are portrayed, the more
overwhelming is one's feeling of sympathy. The individualization of
the principal heroes cannot weaken, but only strengthen the universally social character of the collision. Indeed, it is precisely individual
love here which breaks through the bounds of feudal family enmities.
It is necessary to heighten the passions to the utmost in order to give
the collision its tragic sublimity and render every compromise, every
temporary solution impossible from the outset. And the effect of this
heightening is necessarily to individualize the love and so to underline the personal, subjective characteristics of the principal figures.
Shakespeare's poetic depth and tragic wisdom are revealed here in the
inseparable, organic unity between the uttermost emphasis of individual qualities, of the subjectivity of the passion, and the universality
of the collision.

But this is by no means the case with every passion, however irresistible subjectively. John Ford, the extremely gifted, younger contemporary of Shakespeare, chose the incestuous passion of a brother and
sister for the tragic subject of his play *'Tis Pity She's a Whore*. Ford
not only has considerable dramatic talent, but a special ability for portraying extreme passions forcefully and realistically. Individual scenes
in this play attain to an almost Shakespearean magnificence by the
simplicity, directness and authenticity with which these total passions
dominate the heroes' lives. But the overall dramatic impression never-

theless remains very problematic and divided. We cannot possibly sympathize with the passion of his heroes. It is, and remains, humanly foreign to us. The author, too, does not seem to have been entirely unaware of the foreign nature of this passion. For dramatically, in terms of action, the incestuous character of the passion is only a perverse accessory. The actual collision, however, arises dramatically simply out of the clash between the passion (whatever its nature) and external circumstances; most scenes, the really dramatic ones would still be possible, almost unaltered, if it were a case of an ordinary play about forbidden and separated love (whatever the reasons) or of any play about love, marriage and adultery. The love of the brother and sister is too eccentric, too subjective to be able to carry a dramatic action. The action takes refuge in the heroes' souls, whose passion is thus opposed, dramatically, merely by a prohibition in general, an obstacle in general, thus something quite foreign and abstract in relation to the passion.

Every action, every translation of a collision into deeds requires a certain common territory between the opponents, even if this "community" is one of sworn social enmity. Exploiter and exploited, oppressor and oppressed may have this territory for their struggle; sexual abnormality, however, has no such battleground in its collision with society. Such a passion also lacks the relative, subjective justification either of being rooted in the social order of the past, or of anticipating the future. The struggle of successive systems of love, marriage, family etc., thus has nothing to do with the "problematic" of this drama. All conflicts occurring in ancient tragedy, which in a modernized interpretation would appear to be "similar", are, in reality, clashes between two social orders.

How little Ford's failure with this subject was accidental, for he was a gifted dramatist, may be seen by studying another, more recent example, Alfieri's *Myrrha*. Alfieri is a tragedian who thinks deeply about theory. He disdains every effect which does not result directly from the tragic nature of his given subject. Thus when he chooses the theme of sexual abnormality, a daughter's fatal passion for her father, he avoids all the general effects of forbidden love, all the obstacles which this love endeavours to overcome. He dispenses with all the means whereby Ford, with his spontaneously dramatic instinct, was able to bestow apparent action and apparent suspense upon his material. Alfieri wishes to dramatize the spiritual, the human collision of abnormal passion, of incestuous love. And his intentions therein are pure and noble: but what happens in the actual tragedy? In brief, Alfieri transforms the entire drama into a suppressed monologue. He paints his heroine, dramatically and very rightly, as a sensitive and highly moral person, horrified by her own passion and yet, despite heroic resistance, invincibly subjected to it. Throughout the play we see this noble creature struggling against a dark, unspoken fate, making one senseless resolve after another in order to bury within herself, undeclared and hidden from the world, the passion of which we are only dimly aware and whose nature is never disclosed. Until finally Myrrha, threatened with the curse of the father she loves, involuntarily gives herself away and puts an end to her suffering by committing suicide.

Alfieri is superior to Ford dramatically, insofar as he places at the centre the real, inner tragic collision of the abnormal passion, constructing his plot around this and this alone. Yet in so doing he reveals the deeply anti-dramatic character of such a theme. The single, really dramatic moment in his play can only, indeed, be Myrrha's final confession. But, strictly speaking, the drama of this scene goes no further than the heroine's half-stammered-out confession, the father's exclamation of horror and the daughter's suicide. Everything else is simply preparation, simply cleverly arranged retardation.

A real dramatic conflict, however, must contain a whole chain of such moments, which are capable of continuous heightening and permit a rich variety of ups and downs in the outward struggle of the colliding social forces, too. But the fruitfulness of a really dramatic theme depends on how deep the inner connection is between the persons at the centre of the drama and the concrete collision of the social-historical forces, i.e. on whether and in what way these characters are engaged with their whole personality in the conflict. If their tragic passion coincides at its heart with the decisive, social moment of the collision, then, but only then, can their personalities acquire a fully unfolded and rich, dramatic relief. The emptier, the more abstract and peripheral this relationship, the more must the dramatic hero undergo his development *alongside* the drama proper; that is from an artistic point of view: lyrically, epically, dialectically, rhetorically etc.

The greatness of *dramatic characterization*, the ability to make characters *live dramatically* does not only depend, therefore, on the playwright's ability to create character, in itself, but rather, indeed above all, upon how far it is given him, subjectively and objectively, to discover the characters and collisions in reality that will correspond to these inner requirements of dramatic form.

It is clear that this is not only a question of talent, but a social problem at the same time. For even the most outstanding dramatist cannot *invent* such plots freely, just as he pleases (plot understood here as the unity of character and collision). Rather, and this Manzoni, in particular, was quite right to emphasize, he must *find* them, discover them in society, in history, in objective reality.

It is obvious, however, that not only is the social content of the colli-sions of an age the product of its economic development, but that the forms of these collisions are produced by the same historical-social forces. Admittedly, these latter relations are far less directly deducible from the economic basis, from the economic tendencies of the period. But all that this means, in regard to our problem, is that the great dramatist has more room here for invention. Not that any degree of invention could concoct socially non-existent forms of collision, re-placing perhaps dramatically unfavourable qualities by imaginary favourable ones, without destroying the realistic character of drama. The true dramatic genius is revealed "only" by his ability to select from the vast, complex tangle of empirical forms those in which the inner dramatic content of the period may be adequately reflected, in keeping with the demands of dramatic form.

In comparing Shakespeare and Ford the emphasis was chiefly on the difference in dramatic talent. But only chiefly, for with the rapid re-grouping of social forces during this period, the age difference of about twenty years between the two playwrights also meant a changed social environment. To examine this question, even in outline, would take us beyond the limits of this study. What we wished to show here was that the possibility of portraying colliding social forces in an adequate dramatic form, i.e. in fully developed, fully individ-ualized personalities, is not given automatically or immediately by any collision, but presupposes very complex subjective and objective conditions.

We now continue our concretization of the area in which dramatic development is possible for those facts of life, which, as it were, tend towards drama in life itself. In our remarks hitherto, where we have examined the dangers for real drama of an over-objective or exagger-atedly subjective collision, we deliberately left out of account the extent to which writers have been able to provide their characters with real and appropriate *means of self-expression*.

This is indispensable to drama. But the history of drama shows that this endeavour has not always been guided by a similar necessity. Influenced by the modern naturalistic development and the skilfully imitated "natural" stammer of its stage figures, we tend to see here alone the source of the non-dramatic manner of expression. This, how-ever, restricts the question, for it is a matter of the character's *personal* expression. The character must give adequate expression to those thoughts, feelings, experiences, etc., which move *precisely him* in precisely this situation. It is equally dangerous from the standpoint of drama whether expression extends beyond the concrete situation and the concrete human being because of intellectual abstraction (as often happens in *tragédie classique* or, at times, in Schiller) or, on the other hand, whether it is confined to an ordinary everyday level out of a mistaken striving after a closeness and trueness to life.

We are not primarily concerned here with language; although, obviously, dramatic dialogue is the concrete outward form of all these problems. Neither in Schiller nor in Gerhart Hauptmann, to take two complete extremes, can there be any question of literary incapacity to express adequately in language what they are aiming at artistically. Both, naturally in very different ways and on very different artistic levels, are masters of the word; as far as linguistic technique is concerned, they are able to do everything they wish. But, in the case of Schiller, what he wishes passes over the heads of his characters, describing something else, beyond, more general than, the given acting or suffering characters. In the case of Gerhart Hauptmann, on the other hand, the dialogue expresses adequately the "here and now" of the characters, but remains so entirely a prisoner of this "here and now" as to fall below the level of generalization required of the characters if they are to give their personalities the necessary plasticity.

The dramatic hero is continuously summing up his life, that is, the different stages of his path to tragedy. There must always be a tendency, therefore, towards generalization in his utterances and an intellectual, emotional and linguistic realization of this tendency. But, and this is essential, the generalization must never be permitted to become detached from the concrete person and the concrete situation; it must in all respects be the generalization of the thoughts, feelings, etc. of *just this* person in *just this* situation.

This means that the dramatic dialogue throughout, and especially at its peak moments, must also achieve an intellectual concentration and condensation in which (without detriment to the deeply personal character of the content and form of expression, indeed, as a result of its very highest intensification) all moments which make of this man's destiny a *general destiny* must be directly manifest. In this respect, too, Shakespeare is the summit of drama's history. To illustrate this not so simple matter by a single example, think of Othello's words, when Iago persuades him of Desdemona's infidelity. He begins with a purely subjective expression of disillusion, rage and revenge; but his speech culminates with the words:

> O, now, for ever
> Farewell the tranquil mind! farewell content!
> Farewell the plumed troop, and the big wars,
> That make ambition virtue! O, farewell!
> Farewell the neighing steed, and the shrill trump,
> The spirit-stirring drum, th'ear piercing fife,
> The royal banner, and all quality,

Pride, pomp, and circumstance of glorious war !
And, O you mortal engines, whose rude throats
Th' immortal Jove's dread clamours counterfeit,
Farewell ! Othello's occupation's gone !

The power of such words is obviously not only a matter of language. Above all the writer has to create *such people* and place them in such situations that words such as these will "naturally" follow. I have discussed at length elsewhere the social and human, the philosophical and artistic preconditions for this use of language (cf. *The Intellectual Physiognomy of Literary Characters, Problems of Realism*, Berlin, 1955). Here, we can only dwell on a few important and special factors in relation to drama.

This brings us to age-old arguing points about drama—what should be the nature of its heroes, what is their relationship to people in everyday life? These questions already played a role in antiquity. They form a principal theme in the satirical discussion between Aeschylus and Euripides in Aristophanes' *Frogs*. Euripides praises himself for having introduced private life and everyday manners into drama, describing this as a very bold undertaking. And this same point, together with the formal and linguistic questions connected with it, is the principal theme of Aeschylus's attack upon his art. The theoretical discussions of the *tragédie classique* period, too, always return to these questions. Their formulation here is whether, in fact, only kings, generals etc. can be the heroes of tragedy and what the real reasons are for this "law". Then, the question is renewed from a fresh standpoint when bourgeois drama is born, namely whether a person from the "third estate" may become the hero of tragedy etc.

All these discussions about drama naturally spring directly from the class struggles of the given epochs. But whether any given trend can become artistically fruitful depends upon very complex influences, exercised by the social foundations of drama, upon its formal and thematic potentialities. The motor, the primary driving force are the social forces; but the field in which they are realized is fenced round by the laws of dramatic form.

Earlier, when speaking of bourgeois drama, we touched upon the problem of the "world-historical individual" as the necessary hero of drama. Here, dealing with the social and human preconditions of adequate dramatic expression—that is, neither too elevated, too low, too abstract, nor too subjective—we must once again return to this question. That the dramatic hero and the "world-historical individual" are near to one another in conception does not, of course, make them identical. There are highly important figures in history whose lives contain no potentiality for drama, just as there are dramatic heroes, who can only be called "world-historical individuals" in that extended and figurative sense which we established in our remarks on bourgeois drama.

But, given these reservations, we must hold firmly to the factors which do converge. First of all, the historical height at which the collision is pitched. In drama as in epic this is by no means identical with the outward historical significance of the events represented. The greatest historical occurrence may appear thoroughly empty and unreal in drama, while less important events, as perhaps have never taken place in history, can evoke the impression of the downfall of an epoch or the birth of a new world. It is enough to think of the great tragedies of Shakespeare, Hamlet or Lear, to see clearly how much a personal destiny can evoke the impression of a great historical change.

The example of Shakespeare's great tragedies is particularly instructive, because in them the *specifically dramatic* character of historical changes, of *dramatic historicism*, is clearly manifest. As a true dramatist Shakespeare does not try to paint a detailed picture of historical and social circumstances. He characterizes the period through his actors. That is, all the qualities of a character, from the ruling passion down to the smallest "intimate", yet dramatic, subtlety, are coloured by the age. Not necessarily in a broad or epic historical sense, but certainly in the historical conditioning of the collision; its essence must derive from the specific determinants of the epoch.

Of course, this historicity is general to an entire epoch. Think of our earlier example of *Romeo and Juliet*. The colour and atmosphere of the play is Italy at the close of the Middle Ages. But it would be quite wrong to look for the kind of concretization of the *here and now* in this tragedy which we find in Scott and which gives his novels their incomparable historical spirit. Ocasionally time and place are more concrete in Shakespeare, and this is truer still of later dramatists such as Goethe or Pushkin. But, on the one hand, this very possibility reveals an important characteristic of drama—the fact that it can do without this concreteness in certain circumstances and that its absence does not rule out dramatic historicism. On the other hand, the later and more concrete drama also endeavours to characterize the most general traits of an epoch; and in a much more direct way than the historical novel, transcending much more the particular qualities of individual phases and the complex, capillary character of all the different trends.

Viewed from a different angle, we see that this broad historical conception of an epoch is only possible if all the characteristic factors of the time have been thoroughly and organically assimilated into the characters, becoming factors in their personal behaviour. And we may see here particularly clearly the similarity, which Lessing perceptively pointed out, between the classical tragedians and Shakespeare as regards ultimate principles. Both reduce the world of human action to pure and direct relations of people to one another. The mediating role of things, institutions etc. is confined to a minimum; they appear simply as props, background etc. and play no dramatic part at all. They are important only indirectly, when their mediating role is indispensable to the clarification of human relations. (Epic, likewise, never fetishizes the relations of people. But it portrays their relations to one another *with* these mediations, and uses them very liberally.) The wealth and depth of characterization and situation in drama serves one end: to create characters, who in the self-containment of their personalities, can yet bear and reveal the fullness of their world.

Hegel drew attention to the plastic character of the heroes of drama. This, for him, is not a mere comparison, but part of his historical philosophy of art: the conception of plastic art and tragedy as the leading arts of antiquity, in contrast to painting and the novel, as the arts of modern times. There is a certain idealistic one-sidedness in this conception, but this is not the place to discuss it. What concerns us here rather is to grasp the profound aesthetic truth in this parallel beween plastic art and drama. Both are art forms in which the world of man is realized *exclusively* through the portrayal of man himself. And we must grasp how from this "reduction" to man there springs an enriched representation of man's whole world. In these remarks we have tried to indicate how this dramatic plasticity, individualization and, at the same time, historicism are realized. The social conditons for such a conception and embodiment of man, for such individualization are the conditions for true drama.

The Hegelian definition of "world-historical individuals", namely that their "own, particular purposes contain the substantial, which is the will of the world spirit", thus comes very near to characterizing the dramatic hero. One has only to translate the whole mysticism of the "spirit" into materialist, historical reality and to conceive as *directly* as possible this coincidence between the personality of the hero and the historical essence of the collision. The directness is the decisive thing. The faithfully drawn historical figures of a Vitet or Mérimée, however much they agree with the facts, never achieve the dramatic pathos of world history, because they lack this directness, while Calderon's peasant Pedro Crespo or Schiller's *petits bourgeois* in *Kabale and Liebe* (*Intrigue and Love*) are imbued throughout with this historical pathos amidst the trivial everyday reality surrounding them. It is surely unnecessary to point to examples of a higher order, such as Romeo, Hamlet or Lear.

To sum up the entire position by means of a negative example, let us consider as important a modern dramatist as Friedrich Hebbel. His Judith liberates the hard-pressed Jewish people by killing their enemy's leader, Holofernes. In order to perform this heroic national deed, to bring about the salvation of her people, she must, however, sacrifice her woman's honour by giving herself to Holofernes. There is undoubtedly present a genuinely tragic collision. Hebbel indeed has his heroine say, before she resolves to go to Holofernes: "If you (the God of the Jews, G.L.) place a sin between me and my deed, who am I that I should quarrel with you about it, that I should shun you!" But the tragedy between Judith and Holofernes then evolves quite differently. After Judith has killed Holofernes, the following, very characteristic dialogue develops between her and her companion, Mirza:

"*Judith*: Why did I come? My people's misery drove me here, the impending famine, the thought of that mother who tore open her wrist to suckle her languishing child. Oh, now I am once again at peace with myself. All this I forgot in thinking of myself!

Mirza: You forgot it. Then it was not that which drove you, when you plunged your hand in blood!

Judith (slowly, crushed). No—no, you are right, it was not that—nothing but the thought of myself drove me. Oh, what confusion is here! My people are delivered, yet if Holofernes had been dashed to pieces by a stone, they would have owed more gratitude to thàt stone than they do now to me!"

And, upon her return to Bethulia, surrounded by the jubilant, thankful people she has saved, she says: "Yes, I have killed the first and last man in the world, so that you (to the one) may let your sheep graze in peace, that you (to a second) may plant your cabbages, and you (to a third) may practise your craft and beget children like yourselves!"

The figure of Judith is conceived by Hebbel with real psychological mastery; the scenic-dramatic structure of the tragedy is powerfully built up; the language (apart from a few bombastic aberrations) is strong, expressive, dramatically alert. Yet, for all that, it is precisely dramatic individualization which is lacking in Judith's tragic words. Her historic mission in the life of her people is simply a chance starting-point for her personal, tragic fate as a woman; and, conversely, the salvation of the Jewish people is not something which stems organically from their own lives; from their standpoint it is no less a matter of chance.

Accidents *of this kind* cancel out the dramatic. Shakespeare treats the accidental connections between individual events with sovereign ease (for example, the tragic denouement of *Romeo and Juliet*). As a born dramatist, he knew that dramatic necessity is neither dependent upon the flawlessness of individual causal connections, nor cancelled out by individual accidents in the plot. Dramatic necessity, the supreme persuasive force of drama depends precisely upon the inner accord (briefly analyzed above) between the character (with his dominant passion which evokes the drama) and the social-historical essence of the collision. If this connection is present, then every individual accident, as at the close of *Romeo and Juliet*, occurs in an *atmosphere of necessity*, and in and through this atmosphere its accidental character is dramatically erased. On the other hand, if this necessity, produced by the dramatic convergence of character and collision, is not present, as in the case of Hebbel's *Judith*, then however well assembled the causal motivation, its effect will be one of mere cleverness; instead of strengthening the tragic impact, it will make it appear cold.

This convergence of character and collision is the fundamental basis of drama. The more deeply thought out, the *more direct* is its effect. We used the expression "atmosphere of necessity" advisedly, wishing to describe the organic, direct nature of this connection between character and collision that is far removed from any kind of sophistication. The fate against which the hero of drama struggles comes as much "from without" as "from within". His character, so to speak, "predestines" him for the particular collision. For there is no collision which is inescapable in itself. The majority of cases in life, where a social-historical collision occurs, are not resolved in a dramatic form. Only when the collision meets with a person like Antigone, Romeo or Lear, does drama result. This is what Aristophanes' Aeschylus says when he protests against Euripides' conception of Oedipus in the prologue to *Antigone*, namely, that Oedipus was happy at first and then became the unhappiest of mortals. He did not become this, says Aeschylus, he never ceased to be such.

It would of course be a dangerous exaggeration to take this polemical sally too literally, to stretch it too far. Aeschylus is protesting here, quite rightly, against the external character of Euripides' conception, whereby Oedipus's destiny becomes a "destiny" in the sense of a mechanically inescapable fate. The majority of heroes of the really great tragedies are in no way inevitably doomed simply because of their character. They are in no way, to use a modern phrase, "problematic beings". Take Antigone, Romeo, Lear, Othello, Egmont etc. Before their dramatic essence can be released they have to encounter a concrete and *definite* collision. They do not encounter just any collision which might embody, as it were by accident, an abstract-general principle of the tragic as many theorists of the eighteenth century believed.

It follows that the dramatic collision and its tragic outcome must not be conceived in an abstract pessimistic sense. Naturally, an abstract denial of the pessimistic elements in the drama given to us by the history of class society would be senseless. The horror of the conflicts in class society, the fact that for most people there is clearly no solution to them, is certainly *one* motif, and by no means an unimportant one, in the rise of drama. But it is by no means supreme. Every really great drama expresses, amid horror at the necessary downfall of the best representatives of human society, amid the apparently inescapable, mutual destruction of men, an *affirmation of life*. It is a *glorification of human greatness*. Man, in his struggle with the objectively stronger forces of the social external world, in the extreme exertion of all his powers in this unequal battle, reveals important qualities which would otherwise have remained hidden. The collision raises the dramatic hero to a new height, the possibility of which he did not suspect in himself before. The realization of this possibility produces the enthusing and uplifting qualities of drama.

This side of drama must also be specially stressed because bourgeois theories—particularly those which became dominant during the latter half of the nineteenth century—give increasing, one-sided prominence to the pessimistic aspects, while our polemic against them often simply counters this abstract and decadent pessimism scholastically with an abstract and shallow optimism.

In reality the one-sided pessimistic theory of drama is closely connected with the destruction of the specific historicism of drama, of the direct unity between man and deed, between character and collision. Schopenhauer, the founder of these theories, sums up the nature of tragedy as follows: "that the purpose of this supreme poetic achievement is the representation of the terrible side of life, that the nameless pain, the anguish of humanity, the triumph of evil, the mocking rule of chance and the irremediable fall of the just and the innocent are here paraded before us." Thereby, Schopenhauer degrades the concrete, social-historical collision to a more or less accidental *occasion* for "universal human tragedy" (of the futility of life in general). He voices philosophically a tendency which, from the middle of the last century onwards, acquires increasing prominence in drama and leads increasingly to the dissolution of dramatic form, to the disintegration of its really dramatic elements.

We have seen these disintegrating tendencies at work in the drama of so exceptionally talented a writer as Friedrich Hebbel. We saw that the very centre of dramatic unity was attacked—the unity of hero and collision. In this way dramatic expression is faced with the following dilemma: the most deeply personal and characteristic features of the main figure have no inner and organic connection with the concrete collision. These features, therefore, require on the one hand a relatively broad exposition, if they are to be at all noticeable and intelligible on the stage; on the other hand, very complicated means are necessary if a connection is to be made between the inner, psychological "problematic" of the hero and the social-historical collision. (Hebbel's Judith, for example, is a widow, who yet remained a virgin in her marriage. The complex psychology arising from this singular situation provides the bridge to her tragic deed in the play.) These tendencies have an epic effect. They are an important factor in the development which we have called the general "novelization of drama".

However, the *a posteriori* establishment of complex psychological connections between hero and social-historical collision is not sufficient for drama. In the case of nearly all talented playwrights, who fail in the vital question, this is still further supplemented by a lyrical ecstasy at the high moments, especially at the end. These ecstasies may vary very much in content. But for the most part they take the form of a lyrical-psychological insight into the necessity of the tragic downfall. This kind of subjective lyricism is an attempt to replace and restore, subsequently and artificially, the lack of objective dramatic unity. And it is clear that the more this unity is broken up by playwrights, the less naturally historical their collision and conception of character, the more their connecting general link approaches Schopenhauer's ideas, the greater will be the abyss separating subjective psychology from universality of destiny and the more indispensable the lyrical ecstasy as a substitute for the dramatic.

It is no accident that Schopenhauer himself saw in the opera *Norma* the model of tragedy. Nor that his pupil, Richard Wagner, attempted to conquer the problematic rock of modern drama by means of music. His music-drama however, is only a marginal instance in modern drama as a whole. Various able observers, most recently Thomas Mann, have clearly seen the close connection between the Wagnerian music-drama and, say, the prose drama of Ibsen.

We believe we have now given the desired concretization of the dramatic tendencies in life, listed earlier. Without claiming any historical or systematic completeness, which would only be possible in a full dramaturgy, we nevertheless believe that the specific, dramatic embodiment of these facts of life is now clear to us. They are embodied in the fully developed, plastic personality of the "world historical individual", who is portrayed in such a way that he not only finds an immediate and complete expression for his personality in the deed evoked by the collision, but also draws the general social, historical and human inferences of the collision—without losing or weakening in the least either his personality or its immediacy.

The decisive dramatic question here is whether a person can express himself immediately and completely through a deed. Epic, in all its forms, presents the growth of events, the gradual change or gradual revelation of the people taking part in them; its maximum aim is to awaken this convergence of man and deed in the work as a whole, which it portrays, therefore, *at most as a tendency*. In contrast, dramatic form requires immediate and direct proof of this coincidence at every stage of its journey.

To give a concrete historical picture of the facts of life tending towards drama, enumerated in the previous section, we should thus have to examine the social-historical conditions of the individual periods and see whether and in what way their economic structure, the nature of their class struggles etc. favoured or did not favour a genuinely dramatic realization of such facts.

If the preconditions are lacking in social life for these dramatic tendencies to launch into real drama, then they will break through in other directions. On the one hand, they will make dramatic form problematic; on the other, they will carry dramatic elements into other literary forms. Both trends are particularly visible in nineteenth century literature. Goethe and Schiller were the first to establish the reciprocal influence of epic and dramatic form as the essential characteristic of modern literature (cf. my essay on the correspondence between Goethe and Schiller, *Goethe and seine Zeit*, (*Goethe and his Age*), Berlin, 1955). Then Balzac, with special reference to Scott as the initiator, stressed the dramatic as a distinguishing mark of the new type of novel in contrast to previous types. This penetration of the dramatic element was extremely fruitful for the modern novel. Not only did it enliven the action, enrich and deepen characterization, beyond that it created an adequate form of literary reflection for the specifically modern manifestations of life in a developed bourgeois society; namely, for the tragic (and tragi-comic) dramas of life, which though dramatic in themselves, appear in an undramatic way, because they would be unintelligible and unportrayable, except by distortion, without their small, even trivial, capillary movement onwards.

These same social forces, however, could not help exerting a very dangerous influence on drama. For the greater the playwright, the more intimately bound up with the life of his time, the less inclined he will be to do violence to important manifestations of life which are closely connected with his heroes' psychology and the nature of his collisions for the sake of dramatic form. Inevitably, these tendencies added increasingly to the "novelization" of drama. Maxim Gorky, the greatest writer of our time, underlined these factors forcefully in a quite unjustly harsh criticism of many of his own plays: "I have written nearly twenty plays, and they are more or less loosely connected scenes in which the plot is never sustained and the characters are insufficiently developed, vague and unconvincing. A drama must be bound by its action, strictly and throughout; only with this condition can it serve to arouse contemporary emotions."

The trends in the present disfavouring drama are sharply and accurately described here. And to show quite clearly how fundamentally right this criticism is (irrespective of its exaggerated self-criticism), let us recall the decisive scene in one of the best plays of the representative playwright of the second half of the nineteenth century— Henrik Ibsen's *Rosmersholm*. Rebecca West loves Rosmer. She wishes to remove every obstacle between them; thus, she induces his half-mad wife, Beate, to commit suicide. But her life with Rosmer awakens and clarifies her moral instincts; she now feels her deed to be an insuperable obstacle between herself and the man she loves. Now when her change brings her to explain and confess, it happens as follows:

"*Rebecca* (vehemently): You think then that I was cool and calculating and self-possessed at the time! I was not the same woman then that I am now, as I stand here telling it all. Besides, there are two sorts of will in us, I believe! I wanted Beate away, by one means or another; but I never really believed that it would come to pass. As I felt my way forward, at each step I ventured, I seemed to hear something within me cry out: No farther! Not a step farther! And yet I could not stop. I had to venture to the least little bit farther. Only one hair's breadth more. And then one more—and always—one more.—And then it happened.—That is the way such things come about."

Here, with the unflinching honesty of a great writer, Ibsen declares why *Rosmersholm could not become a real drama*. Whatever could be elicited from the material by a judicious artistic intelligence, this Ibsen accomplished. But at the decisive moment we see that the actual drama, namely Rebecca West's struggle, tragic collision and conversion, is, as far as subject-matter, structure, action and psychology are concerned, really a novel, the last chapter of which Ibsen has clothed in the outward form of drama with great mastery over scene and dialogue. Despite this, however, the basis of the play is still, of course, that of a novel, full of the undramatic drama of modern bourgeois life. As drama, therefore, *Rosmersholm* is problematic and fragmentary; as a picture of the times it is authentic and true-to-life.

As with Hebbel, whom we touched on earlier, so with Ibsen here, what interests us is only their typical and symptomatic sides. The different ways in which novel and drama reflect the dramatic moments of life, and which are to be seen in Ibsen and Hebbel, take us back to a central problem of our study—the ways in which the "world-historical individual" is portrayed in drama and in the novel.

We have already discussed at length why the classics of the historical novel always represented the great figures of history as minor characters. Our present observations show afresh that drama, by its very nature, demands for them the central role. Both types of composition, however much they contrast, spring from the same feeling for genuine historicity, for real historical greatness; both endeavour to grasp in an adequate artistic form what is humanly and historically *significant* in the important figures of our development.

The very sketchy analysis of dramatic form given so far shows how the latter's aim all the time is to bring out immediately and visibly all that is significant in man and his deeds, how the prerequisites for its realization are concentrated in a plastic, self-contained unity of hero and action. But the "world-historical individual" is already marked by such a unifying tendency in reality itself.

Since drama then concentrates the decisive moments of a social-historical crisis in the collision, it must be so composed that what determines the grouping of the figures, from centre to periphery, is the degree to which they are caught up in the collision. And since the process of driving the essential moments of such a crisis towards a collision is achieved by vigorously bringing out their human and historical importance, this compositional ordering must at the same time create a dramatic hierarchy. Not in a crude and schematic sense, whereby the central figure of a play necessarily has to be the "greatest person" in every conceivable respect or from some abstract point of view. The hero of drama is superior to his surroundings rather because of his closer connection with the problems of the collision, with the given concrete historical crisis. It is the way in which the latter is chosen and portrayed, the manner in which the hero's passion is linked with this force, which determines whether the formal significance bestowed upon the characters by the representational means of drama is charged with a content that is real and true, historical and human. But for this social content to make itself felt the formal tendencies, which provide the structure of drama, are, as we have seen, indispensable; that is, the singling out of the significant factors from the entire complex of reality, their concentration and the creation out of their connections of an image of life upon a heightened level.

It is quite different in epic. The significant factors here are portrayed as parts, elements of a broader, more extensive, comprehensive totality. We see their complex rise and decline, their inseparable connection with the slow and confused growth of the whole of popular life, the capillary interplay of the great and small, the significant and the insignificant. Earlier we showed how the historically and humanly significant qualities of the "world-historical individuals" in the classics of the novel grew precisely out of these complex connections. We also showed, in reference to the important observations of Balzac and Otto Ludwig, that a quite special kind of composition is required here, so that neither the significant is submerged in the unfathomable infinity of life, levelled to the average by the often inevitably petty detail of life, nor the authenticity and richness of social reality lost because of artificial stylization, because of an exaggerated heightening of life.

For it is not an essential need of the novel to portray significant people in significant situations. In certain circumstances it can quite dispense with this or it can present the significant persons in a form which gives their features a purely inward-moral expression, so that the peculiar charm of the novel will lie precisely in the contrast between the petty everyday character of life and this purely inward significance of the person, that is, in the disproportion between person and action, between the inner and the outer.

The historical novel does not differ from the novel in general even as regards these possibilities and means; it does not form any genre or sub-genre of its own. Its specific problem, the portrayal of human greatness in past history, has to be solved within the general conditions of the novel. And these—as the practice of the classic authors has proved to us—provide all that is necessary for the successful accomplishment of this task. For the form of the novel by no means excludes the possibility of portraying significant people in significant situations. It can in certain circumstances succeed without these; but it also allows for their portrayal. It is only a question of creating a plot in which these significant situations become necessary, organic parts of a much broader and richer total action; and a plot which is so contrived that its own inner logic impels it towards such situations, because they provide its real fulfilment. And further the "world-historical" figure must be so fashioned that he appears in such and only such situations of his own inner necessity. We are outlining here in different terms and from a different angle what we have already argued before, namely that the "world-historical individual" in the historical novel must be a minor figure.

The diametrically opposed types of composition in drama and the novel thus spring from a similar representational aim with regard to the "world-historical individual": that is, to see his significance and greatness artistically and not to oblige us with domestic platitudes about his "all too human" qualities. But this similar aim is realized by very different artistic means, and, as in all art, the formal difference conceals a very important content. The interesting and difficult task of the historical novel is to represent the significant qualities of the "historical individual" in such a way that it neglects none of the complex, capillary factors of development in the whole society of the time; that, on the contrary, the significant features of the "world-historical individual" not only grow organically out of this development, but at the same time explain it, give it consciousness and raise it to a higher level. What in historical drama is necessarily presupposed, i.e. the concrete mission of the hero (the hero himself gives subsequent proof by his behaviour during the play that he has this mission and is equal to it), this in the historical novel is unfolded in breadth and evolved gradually, step by step. Balzac, as we have shown, quite rightly pointed out that, in the classical historical novel, not only is the "world-historical individual" a minor figure, but in most cases he only ever appears when the action is nearing its climax. His appearance is prepared by a broad picture of the times, which allows us to perceive, re-experience and understand this specific character of his significance.

This portrait of the age is held together at the centre by the historical novel's "middle-of-the-road" hero. Those very social and human characteristics which banish such figures from drama or permit them only a subordinate, episodic role, qualify them for their central position in the historical novel. The relative lack of contour to their personalities, the absence of passions which would cause them to take up major, decisive, one-sided positions, their contact with each of the contending hostile camps etc. make them specially suited, to express adequately, in their own destinies, the complex ramification of events in a novel. Otto Ludwig was perhaps the first to recognize this difference between drama and the novel which he illustrated very precisely by several examples. "This is the chief difference between the hero of the novel and the dramatic hero. If one were to think of *Lear* as a novel, then Edgar would probably have to be the hero... If, on the other hand, one wanted to turn *Rob Roy* into a drama, then Rob Roy himself would have to be the hero, but the story would have to be considerably changed, Francis Osbaldiston would have to be omitted entirely. Similarly, in *Waverley* Vich Ian Vohr would be the tragic hero and in *The Antiquary* the Countless Glenallen."

3. The Problem of Public Character

It seems we are once again confronted with a formal problem, a compositional problem, but again what is in fact form here is only an artistically generalized reflection of regularly recurring facts of life. From the standpoint of content the difference we have established so far is explained by the *public character* of drama. Epic of course was also a public art, as far as its historical origins are concerned. This is certainly one of the reasons why the formal divergence between epos and drama in antiquity was slighter than between novel and drama (despite the greater mutual influence of the latter). But this public character of the ancient Greek epos is the same as that of the whole of life in a primitive society. And it was bound to disappear as society developed. If we keep the definition of epic as the "totality of objects" (and the Homeric epics provide the basis and best practical confirmation of this definition), then it is clear that such a world, as a whole, can retain its public character only at a very primitive stage of social development. Think of Engels's observations on the public character, for example, of the household in a primitive society and of how all matters and functions connected with the maintenance of life necessarily take on a private character at an already slightly higher stage of development. And do not forget here the role played by the public character of these phenomena in the Homeric epics.

The dramatic factors in life as such, however, as independent, heightened segments of the life process, are necessarily public in *every* society. Again this division must not be treated pedantically; in particular, it must never lead to a classification of facts of life into public and non-public, dramatic and epic. Almost every fact of life may, under certain conditions, manifest itself at sufficiently high a level to acquire a public character; it has a side which concerns the public *directly*, which requires a public for its representation. Precisely here we see the transformation of quantity and quality very clearly. Dramatic conflict is not distinguished from other events in life by its social content, but by the manner in which contradictions sharpen and the degree to which they do so. This sharpening then produces a new, original quality.

This unity of unity and diversity is indispensable if drama is to be immediately effective. The dramatic conflict must be experienced by spectators as something immediate, with no need of special explanation, otherwise it can have no effect. Thus it must possess a great deal in common with the normal conflicts of everyday life. At the same time it must represent a new and peculiar quality, so that upon this common basis it can exercise the broad and deep impact of true drama upon the publicly assembled multitude. The examples of the important bourgeois dramas which we cited earlier on, such as *The Judge of Zalamea, Kabale und Liebe (Intrigue and Love)* etc., show this transformation at its clearest. They show that what is in itself an everyday incident is forced out before the forum of the public precisely as a result of this sharpening. But this again is a process which occurs with great frequency in life itself. Drama, as the art of public life, therefore presupposes the kind of subject-matter and treatment that will correspond in every respect to this level of generalization and intensification.

The public character of drama has a dual nature. Pushkin pointed this out with the greatest clarity. He says first of the content of drama: "What element is unfolded in tragedy? What is its aim? Man and the people. The destiny of man, the destiny of the people." And in close connection with this definition Pushkin speaks of the public origin and public effect of drama: "Drama was born in a public square, it formed a popular entertainment. The people, like children, require diversion, action. Drama presents them with an unusual, strange occurrence. The people require strong sensations—even an execution is a spectacle for them. . .

"Tragedy depicted in the main heinous crimes, supernatural sufferings, even physical (e.g. Philoctetes, Oedipus, Lear). But habit blunts the sensations—the imagination grows accustomed to murders and executions, regards them with indifference; whereas in the representation of the passions and outpourings of the human soul it can always find something new, something diverting, great and instructive. Drama came to govern the passions and the human soul."

In connecting these two aspects of the public character of drama, Pushkin goes to the heart of drama in a deep and comprehensive manner. Drama deals with human destinies, indeed there is no other species of literature which concentrates so exclusively upon the destinies of individuals, and in particular upon such as arise from men's antagonistic relations with one another and from these alone. But drama deliberately stresses this exclusiveness. This is why the individual destinies are conceived and represented in such a special way. They give *direct* expression to general destinies, destinies of whole nations, whole classes, indeed whole epochs. The high generalization of the significance and worth of individuals is coupled inseparably with the immediate mass impact. Goethe formulated this connection very precisely: "But to be exact, nothing is theatrical which does not appear simultaneously symbolic, an important action indicating one yet more important."

We have seen how closely this question of the public character of drama's content is connected with the question of form, with the necessarily public nature of performance. The essence of dramatic effect is *immediate*, direct impact upon a *multitude*. (This social prerequisite of dramatic form crumbles with capitalist development. On the one hand a more or less "purely literary drama" arises which either lacks these necessary characteristics of dramatic form or includes them only very dilutedly. On the other hand, a substanceless, pseudo-theatrical art appears which exploits with formalist cleverness the elements of suspense deriving from the original dramatic principle to provide trifling entertainment for the ruling class. Thus there is in some sense a return here to the initial period of the theatre indicated by Pushkin. However, what was then the primitive crudeness which could in time give birth to a Calderon or Shakespeare is now the hollow and refined brutality which amuses a decadent public.) The actual, immediate dependence of dramatic form on immediate mass impact has very deep consequences for its entire structure, for the organization of its whole content, in sharp contrast to the formal requirements of all large epic works which lack this *direct* connection with the multitude, this necessity of immediate impact upon the multitude.

As the conclusion to his long oral and written discussion with Schiller on the common and dividing characteristics of epic and dramatic form, Goethe sums up his views in a short basic essay. Goethe proceeds from a very general concept of the epic and dramatic. Thus he does not give theoretical consideration to the nature of modern epic, to the disappearance of public recitation. But even in the very generalized picture which Goethe gives of the recitation of epic poetry by the rhapsodist, an extremely important difference between the two literary species comes out very clearly. Goethe says: "Their big essential difference lies ... in the epic poet's recitation of an event as belonging *entirely to the past* and the dramatist's representation of an event as belonging *entirely to the present.*"

It is clear that these two kinds of relationship to a given theme are most closely connected with the public character of recitation. The presentness of something already contains in itself a direct relationship with the hearer. To witness something depicted and conceived as happening in the present, one has to be present in person, whereas to learn about something entirely past neither the physical immediacy of communication nor therefore a public is at all necessary. Thus we see that although Goethe, starting from the classical tradition, still construes epic recitation as public in character, the *accidental* nature of this character—that is, the fact that it is not irrevocably tied to the form of epic—also emerges clearly from his remarks.

Further important differences between epic and dramatic form follow from this antithesis. We shall mention only some of the most important. The immediate effect of drama, the necessity for each phase of action and character development to be understood and experienced immediately and simultaneously with the events they represent, for there to be no time in which the spectator may ponder, pause or go back over what has happened etc. creates a greater strictness of form for both author and recipient. Schiller sums up this difference clearly in his reply to Goethe's essay: "The action of drama moves before me, I myself move round the action of epic which seems as it were to stand still." Schiller goes on to stress the greater freedom of the reader of epic in comparison with the spectator of drama.

There goes with this difference the definite and limited range of drama in contrast to the almost limitless extension and variability of epic. Since drama has this framework in which to create the impression of a totality, it follows that all the features appearing in characters and action must be immediately intelligible, clear and effective, while at the same time their meaning must be highly condensed. Drama cannot treat the various elements and motifs, which are objectively linked with one another, in separation, by means of some artistic division of labour. Of course, these elements are objectively linked in epic, too, but the novelist may interpolate scenes and stories etc. which do not carry the action directly forward, which for example, tell of the past in order to elucidate something in the present or future. In drama proper the action must move forward with each phrase of the dialogue. Even the recounting of a past event must have the function of spurring on the action. Therefore each statement of a proper drama always concentrates within itself a whole series of functions.

Dramatic portrayal makes man much more emphatically the centre of things than epic, in particular man as a social-moral being. Drama portrays character and action exclusively through dialogue; it is only concerned artistically with what is viable in terms of dialogue. In epic, on the other hand, an enormous part is played by the physical being of men, by the natural world surrounding them, by the things which form their environment etc.; man is represented via the inter-action of all these, his social-moral features forming only a part, though a decisively important part, of this whole. Hence the atmosphere in drama is much more spiritual than in epic. This does not mean that characters and relationships are idealistically stylized, but simply that anything which is not a directly social-moral feature of a specific individual can only be present as a precondition or outward cause of a social-moral collision, that both the surrounding natural world of man, as well as his self-made environment may figure only as background or as a means for linking characters, and this only in the barest outlines. (The failure to recognize the inner laws of drama has produced in recent years a whole range of sophisticated, barren productions which have sought to make up for the lack of drama in the theatre by using epic substitutes.)

All these factors of dramatic concentration are most evident in the time taken by dramatic events: it must be the same as it would be in reality. While in epic a long stretch of time can be accounted for in a few words, and conversely, the epic writer may be justified in making quite a brief event last for longer than it would in reality. The celebrated demand for "unity of time" has, I believe, its real roots here. Of course, the arguments upon which this demand was based were mostly wrong and artificial, but many of its opponents, too, missed the real problem. Manzoni fought against the unities of *tragédie classique* in the name of a real historical drama still to be created, but he also contended, quite rightly, simply for the right of the dramatist to insert whatever intervening period he liked *between* scenes represented in their real time.

All these differences between drama and epic appear in a condensed form in the statement of Goethe's, quoted earlier, on the symbolic nature of dramatic characters and the unity of physical immediacy with typical significance in each representational moment of drama. The unity of these two factors is, of course, to be found in epic, too, but there it is much looser. In drama this unity must be constantly realized, whereas in epic it is sufficient if it asserts itself gradually as a tendency in the course of the action as a whole. Here, too, we can perceive clearly the formal consequences of drama's public character.

There are, however, two misconceptions to be disposed of here. We have connected the direct and immediate effect of drama with the problem of public character. But is not this immediacy the essential characteristic of every art? Of course it is. Belinsky quite rightly put the necessity of direct representation and immediate effect at the centre of his theory of art. But the immediacy of the public character of drama, which we have stressed, is something special, something characteristic only of drama *within* the *general* immediacy of all literature. These special features of public immediacy in drama emerge even more sharply and emphatically in the course of historical development. With the growing social division of labour and the complication of social relations in class societies, a division between the public and private occurs in life itself. Literature as the reflection of life cannot help reproducing this process. But this does not only affect the themes of literature which deal with the human problems arising out of this development. The forms of literature, too, as generalized forms reflecting constant and recurring features of life, which grow more pronounced with time, cannot remain untouched by this process.

During the process, however, drama and epic take entirely opposite directions. Epic, as the reflection of the extensive totality of life, of the "totality of objects", has to adapt itself to this process. The novel, as the "bourgeois epic", arises precisely as the product of the artisic consistency with which all inferences have been drawn, in terms of form as well, from the changes in life. (The divided artistic character of the so-called "literary epic" is due, among other things, to the retention of certain formal elements of the old epic at a time when the reality corresponding to them was already dead, to the fact that these elements were applied to subjects alien to them and hence used formalistically, because they belonged to specific types of reflection of a past period of human development).

Drama is quite different. Dramatic form stands or falls with the direct public character specific to it. It must therefore either disappear from life or, in unfavourable circumstances, attempt to give portrayal in its own way to the public elements still present in social life, but it will have to struggle with unfavourable material and as it were against the current. These problems became particularly acute at the turn of the eighteenth to nineteenth centuries and they are extremely closely connected with the endeavours of the time to create a great historical drama. The important playwrights of this period experienced deeply both sides of the dilemma confronting them, both the unfavourableness of the life of their time (a feeling which affects the portrayal of historical material as well) and the necessities of dramatic form.

The discussions round what seems a purely formal principle—whether the ancient chorus could be used in modern drama—show perhaps in the most plastic fashion the social factors which became decisive for drama. In the preface to his tragedy *The Bride of Messina* Schiller speaks very clearly of this problem. Of the use of the chorus in ancient tragedy, he says: "It found the chorus in nature and used it because it found it. The actions and destinies of the heroes and kings are already public in themselves and were so even more in simple, primitive times." The position for the modern writer, according to Schiller, is quite different. Life in present-day society has become abstract and private. "The poet must resurrect the palaces, he must bring the courts out into the open, he must set up the gods again, he must restore all that is immediate and which has been abolished by the artificial arrangements of real life. . ." It was precisely to this end that Schiller introduced the chorus into *The Bride of Messina*.

We are not interested here in repeating the well-known fact that Schiller's use of the chorus produced an artificial formal experiment and his weakest play. We are concerned here with the general problem. Schiller sensed, very rightly, that the presence of the chorus in Greek tragedy sprang spontaneously out of the social-historical conditions of Greek life, and that the key question for the modern dramatist was to portray all events in such a way, to raise all manifestations of life to such a level that they could sustain the presence of the chorus.

As soon as the stage's fourth wall became no more than the transparent screen of Lesage's *Diable Boiteux*, drama ceased to be really dramatic. The spectator of drama is not accidentally present at any accidental private incident of life, he does not eavesdrop on the private lives of his fellows through an enlarged key-hole; what he is offered must be a public event in terms of inmost content and form. The difficult task of modern playwrights is to find such material in life and to give it the kind of radical dramatic overhaul that will enable it to sustain a public character consistently in this sense. And the modern playwright must combat here not only the material of modern society in an outward sense, he must simultaneously combat his own attitude to life born of this same society. Extremely typical of this attitude are Grillparzer's remarks on the chorus: "Familiar disadvantages of the chorus. Its constant presence is generally a nuisance where secrets are concerned. The chorus gave the dramas of the ancients a public character. Well so much the worse, perhaps! For my part I should not like an institution which compelled me to give up all feelings and situations which could not admit a public character."

Long before so-called "intimate theatre" (*Kammerspiel*) came into existence Grillparzer expresses the attitude which underlay it. He does so frankly and honestly as befits a writer of stature. But he does not notice—and still less do his later successors, much smaller fry—that it is precisely the increasing predominance of this attitude which turns drama into an artefact, makes it the object of fruitless, formalist experiments; that it is precisely this development which severs the living contact between drama and the people.

We have been interested here not in the problem of the chorus itself, but in the problems behind the chorus. The actual experiments with the chorus are very problematic, not only Schiller's, but Manzoni's too. This problem, however, shows how difficult it is to portray life publicly in modern drama. The great modern playwrights from Shakespeare to Pushkin tried to solve the problem by means of crowd scenes, and undoubtedly the natural and healthy solution is to be found here. Of course, the principles behind the classical chorus and the modern crowd scene are quite different, and we cannot possibly give this problem the analysis it deserves here. We shall point out just one essential: the classical chorus is omnipresent, while the crowd scenes are no more than isolated factors of the drama. The most important scenes between the protagonists often take place in the absence of these witnesses. But this certainly does not mean that such scenes have no relation to the crowd present in the play. In Shakespeare there is often a very active relationship of this kind. One has only to think of the lively influence of popular sentiments upon Brutus and Portia or Brutus and Cassius. The new wave of historical drama draws these relations closer together. Thus, while Schiller only introduces his tragedy with Wallenstein's camp, in the form of a prologue, yet in terms of inner drama it is much more than a prologue. And in the post-Scott period of drama these relations grew even closer. Again, to take one very typical example. we shall mention Büchner's *Danton's Death* and the interaction there between the crowd scenes and the scenes from Danton's "private life". These scenes follow one another as it were in question-and-answer form, the question raised in one scene being answered in the next, and so on.

We come now to the second group of possible misconceptions regarding the immediacy specific to drama. As we know, this immediacy is that of public character. It would seem to follow, therefore, that those sides of modern life (and history), which are public directly and of necessity, should provide the most suitable themes for drama—namely, political life as such. Yet it would be a mistake to think that political life as it stands can provide material immediately suitable for drama. We have seen that to accept without a fight the trends which make many important individual and social manifestations of life private, means the self-destruction of drama in the form of "intimate theatre". But this "making private" is only one side of a process, whose other and inseparable side is the increasing abstraction, the seemingly ever greater separateness and autonomy of political life. Thus, if politics is to provide fruitful material for drama, the playwright must break through this division, the seeming division between *citoyen* and *bourgeois* pointed out by Marx; he must disclose the social foundations of politics by portraying living human destinies, individual destinies which concentrate in their individual uniqueness the typical, representative features of these connections. In the seventeenth century one had the hollow pathos of the "Crown and State" drama (*Haupt and Staatsaktion*), in the nineteenth the empty and declamatory "tendency drama" etc.

On this subject, too, Schiller had some instructive things to say. While working on *Wallenstein*, he wrote to Körner: "The material is ... most unpliable for such a purpose... basically it is a state drama and when it comes to turning it into poetry it exhibits all the unfortunate characteristics of a political theme: the object is invisible and abstract, the means *petty* and *numerous*, the action scattered, the pace timid, the purpose far too cold and dry (to be of benefit to the poet), for it is not spurred to consummate itself and so achieve the greatness of poetry—the plan fails in the end only as a result of clumsiness. The basis upon which Wallenstein builds his enterprise is the army, for me therefore a limitless expanse which I am unable to visualize and can only imagine by means of indescribable art. Thus I am able to show neither the object upon which he bases himself, nor which causes his downfall; for these are the same—the mood of the army, the court, the Emperor".

We find this analysis unusually instructive. Above all it shows that even political material, in its immediate form, is limitless, profuse and scattered and can only properly be portrayed by epic means. Dramatic stylization here means singling out those few factors which inwardly combine the political, its social basis and the human passions which give expression to this basis. It means concentrating them in an immediate and tangible form (we recall the "link in the chain") which does not, however, reduce the profusion of conflicting social tendencies evoking the political collision. A "stylization" in the latter sense, that is, a truncation or curtailment of the "totality of movements", would distort the material in terms of content and flatten the dramatic collision. However, more than a simple selection of a few factors is required here; the limitless and scattered profusion of factors must be concentrated round those which really represent all the factors, all the driving forces of the political-historical collision.

Particularly interesting and instructive are those remarks of Schiller where he talks about the "dry purpose" of his play and how this should be overcome poetically. He is quite right theoretically in saying that the "dry purpose" should be pressed to its logical conclusion. Which means that where such a collision is represented in an extreme and concentrated form by a particular character, he must bring out precisely the social-human foundations of the "dry purpose" and that the consistent pursuit of this path, the disclosure of its specific determinants, will remove the unfavourable qualities of the material. Schiller's own practice shows how little such material can be mastered by the addition of "human ingredients". They stay put as ingredients and supplements, and the "dryness" of the political connections continues despite them. On the other hand nothing can live in drama which does not translate into sensuously-immediate, human terms. However correct the interpretation of a political conflict in terms of content, however subtly contrived a historical collision in terms of historical philosophy, they will both be lifeless if there is not this direct translation. And from the point of view of the destruction of dramatic form, it hardly matters whether this lifelessness, produced by a purely intellectual presentation of political-historical connections, is expressed propagandistically or mystically. The most recent development in drama is again an oscillation between these false extremes.

Shakespeare showed titanically how great historical collisions could be translated into human terms and imbued with dramatic life. In this context, it may be of some interest to mention the objection raised by Hegel to *Macbeth*. Hegel found that Shakespeare's source spoke of Macbeth's rightful claim to the Scottish throne, and regretted that Shakespeare had dropped this motif. We think that it is quite superfluous to the problem of the disintegration of feudal society and the internecine strife which it inevitably produces. In his cycle of chronicle plays Shakespeare gives example after example to show the entirely arbitrary use of such claims in the class struggle between monarchy and feudalism. In his concrete representation of these English struggles he assigns these motifs the episodic role they deserve. *Macbeth*, however, gives a concentrated portrayal of the human quintessence of Macbeth's rise and fall. Shakespeare shows the human qualities which inevitably arise in just this social-historical context, and does so with marvellous fidelity and expressiveness. And he is quite right to portray this human essence (socially and historically conditioned) and not to clutter up the clear outlines of his work with trivial motifs. To have acted on Hegel's suggestion would have led to a play of the Hebbel type and not to Shakespeare's.

Yet, in general, Hegel recognized the necessities of drama, both as regards historical content and dramatic form, more clearly than most theoreticians. He warns repeatedly against two extremes in characterization: on the one hand, against allowing a character to lose individuality in the expression of abstract historical forces, on the other against lapsing into merely private human psychology. In demanding "pathos" from dramatic characters and in attempting to distinguish pathos from passion, he is on the right road to describing the specific nature of characters in drama. He calls pathos "a force in the soul which is justified in itself, an essential part of reason" and cites the "sacred sisterly love" of Antigone and the fact that Orestes does not kill his mother in a violent fit of emotion, but that "the pathos which impels him to the deed is well weighed and fully considered". This does not mean, of course, that the heroes of tragedy should be men without passion. Antigone and Orestes have their passions, too. The emphasis on pathos here means that what is decisive is the direct coincidence of the great historical theme, embodied in the concrete task, with the particular personality and passion of the dramatic hero. In this sense the hero of a historical play must be a "world-historical individual". And it is this very character of his pathos, the very quality of his passion which is neither abstractly general nor individually pathological, which enables the concentration of personality upon pathos to find a direct response among the masses. The concrete universality, rationality and immediacy of this pathos allows the hero to set kindred feelings into motion, directly and personally, in each individual of the mass.

4. The Portrayal of Collision in Epic and Drama

Our comparison of novel and drama shows that the novel's manner of portrayal is *closer* to life, or rather to the normal appearance of life, than that of drama. But, as we have said, the so-called distance of drama is not that of formalist "stylization", but rather the artistic reflection of particular facts of life. In the same way, the novel's closeness to life differs from the mere copying of empirical reality; naturalism is not the innate style of the novel. The span of the hugest novel is limited. If one were to take the *Comédie Humaine* as a single novel, it would give only an infinitesimal fraction, even in breadth, of the incommensurable reality of its time. An adequate quantitative, artistic reflection of the infinity of life is quite out of the question. The naturalist writers set themselves a Sysiphus-like task, for not only do they lose the totality of an artistically reflected world by producing simply an extract, an inwardly incomplete fragment, but not even the greatest naturalistic accumulation of detail can possibly reproduce adequately the infinity of qualities and relations possessed by one single object of reality. And the novel does not in any case set itself the task of reproducing faithfully a mere extract from life; but, by representing a limited section of reality, however richly portrayed, it aims to evoke the totality of the process of social development.

The formal problems of the novel thus arise out of the fact that any reflection of objective reality is necessarily relative. The novel has the task of evoking directly the full span of life, the complexity and intricacy of its developments, the incommensurability of its detail. Hence the problem of the "totality of objects" as the representational aim of large epic, which we have already raised a number of times, should be understood in a very broad sense; i.e. this whole includes not simply the dead objects through which men's social life manifests itself, but also the various customs, institutions, habits, usages etc. characteristic of a certain phase of human society and of the direction it is taking. Society is the principal subject of the novel, that is, man's social life in its ceaseless interaction with surrounding nature, which forms the basis of social activity, and with the different social institutions or customs which mediate the relations between individuals in social life. We recall that in drama these various factors may be portrayed only in a very abbreviated and allusive form, only insofar as they provide suitable points of departure for the social-moral actions of men. The proportions in the novel are quite different. The world of the novel is not only a point of departure, but a thoroughly concrete, complex and intricate world inclusive of all the details of human behaviour and conduct in society.

It is clear, however, that if this world is to evoke a totality, if a restricted circle of people and a restricted group of "objects" are to be portrayed in such a way that the reader has the immediate impression of an entire society in movement, then some form of artistic concentration is again necessary and any straightforward copying of reality must be resolutely abandoned. Accordingly, the novel, like drama, must give central place throughout to all that is typical in characters, circumstances, scenes etc. The only difference is that the content and form of what is typical here will be differently constituted in either case. The relation of the uniquely individual to the typical is treated in a slacker, looser and more complex fashion in the novel. While the dramatic character must be directly and immediately typical, without of course losing his individuality, the typical quality of a character in a novel is very often only a tendency which asserts itself gradually, which emerges to the surface only by degrees out of the whole, out of the complex interaction of human beings, human relations, institutions, things etc. The novel, like drama, must represent the struggle of different classes, strata, parties and trends. But its representation of them is much less concentrated and economical. In drama everything must serve to support the basic possible attitudes and concentrate upon *one* central collision. Hence dramatically, a single basic trend of human conduct can by its very nature have only one representative; any doubling, as we have seen, would be artistic tautology. (This must not, of course, be understood schematically. When Goethe in his analysis of *Hamlet* points out Shakespeare's subtlety in representing the servile, characterless courtier in the pair Rosenkranz and Guildenstern, he is not contradicting the general law of dramatic stylization. Rosenkranz and Guildenstern always appear together and, from the standpoint of the drama's structure, constitute only *one* figure.)

The novel, on the other hand, gives us not the concentrated essence of some particular trend, but, on the contrary, the way in which the trend arises, dies away etc. For this reason, the way in which the character of a novel is typical, the manner in which he represents social trends, is much more complex. The novel aims at showing the various facets of a social trend, the different ways in which it asserts itself etc. What, therefore, would be tautology in drama, is in the novel an indispensable form for crystallizing the really typical.

It follows from this that the relation of the individual to the social group to which he belongs and which he represents is a much more complex one than in drama. This complication of the relation between individual and class, however, is again not a product of the development of literature; on the contrary, the entire development of literary forms, and here in particular the novel, is nothing more than a reflection of social development itself. Marx has given a very precise picture of this changed relationship between individual and class under capitalism. He says: "... in the course of historical development and precisely because social relations within the division of labour are inevitably rendered independent, there emerges a difference in the life of each individual between what is personal and what is subsumed under any particular branch of labour and its relevant conditions ... In the estate (in the tribe still more) this is as yet hidden, e.g. a nobleman always remains a nobleman, a commoner a commoner, whatever his other circumstances, a quality which is inseparable from his individuality. The difference between the personal individual and the class individual, the accidental character of the individual's conditions of life makes its appearance only with the appearance of the class which is itself a product of the bourgeoisie. Competition and the struggle of individuals amongst themselves first produce and develop this accidental character as such. Hence, in imagination the individuals under the rule of the bourgeoisie are freer than before, because their conditions of life are more accidental for them; in reality, they are naturally more unfree, because much more subsumed under material power." This is shown most clearly in transitional figures. While the dramatic collision separates the actors into two combatant camps, in the novel it is not only permissible, but altogether necessary, that the characters should be neutral or indifferent towards the central questions.

It is obvious that this development of the relationships between individual and society is highly unfavourable for dramatic portrayal. On the other hand it forms the very life element of the novel. It is not by accident that the special characteristics of the novel emerged only after these social relations between individual and class had developed. Only the thoroughly crude ahistoricism of vulgar sociology could be totally blind to these connections and subsume the Greek or Persian "novel" under the same genre as the specific modern form of the "bourgeois epic".

However, this close connection between the novel's form and the specific structure of capitalist society on no account means that the novel can simply reflect this reality as it immediately and empirically presents itself. The naturalists for their part have fallen victim to this error. But the classicist champions of the old, traditional forms have understood the artistic problems of the new situation no better, their criterion has simply been a contrary one. Thus, Paul Ernst, for example, the theoretical leader of neo-classicism in Germany, calls the novel "semi-art".

Our previous remarks have been sufficient to show that such a conception of the novel and its relation to the reality it reflects is fundamentally false. In analysing the so-called distance of drama, we showed it to be a specific kind of artistic reflection of very concrete facts of life. Similarly, we must now mention a few important, general facts of life which constitute the basis of form in the novel. Our argument here has, of course, an opposite aim. There, we had to show that the apparent stylization was a genuine reflection of life, here we must show that the novel depends for its apparent closeness to life just as imperatively as drama upon a recasting of its material, though by different means and to different ends.

Let us begin at the point where the contrast between novel and drama is most obvious, the problem of collision. A collision in a novel does not have to be represented in its highest and sharpest form and then violently resolved. What must be shown rather is the complexity, multiplicity, intricacy and "cunning" (Lenin) of those trends which produce, solve or abate such conflicts in social life. And this brings us to a very important fact of actual life.

If tragic collision is a necessary form of social life, it is so only under very definite conditions and circumstances. It is also a fact of social life that conflicts abate or peter out, achieve no clear and definite resolution, either in the lives of individuals or in society as a whole. This is so in a twofold respect: first, there are definite phases in the growth of society where the mutual blunting of contradictions is the typical form in which social antagonisms are decided; secondly, even in periods when antagonisms are at their sharpest in the lives of individuals, not all conflicts acquire that final edge which leads on to the tragic. Now since the subject of the novel is the total span of social life, a fully carried-through collision can only be a marginal case existing alongside many others. In some circumstances there is no need for it to take place at all, but if it is included, then only as a link within a system of many links. The particular circumstances, the specific clashes which produce the collision will be shown, but precisely as particular circumstances alongside others, and they certainly will not have to unfold in perfect purity.

If there is a parallel plot in tragedy, it complements and underlines the main collision. Think of the already mentioned parallel between the fates of Lear and Gloster. In the novel it is quite different. Tolstoy, for example, has several plots to parallel the tragic fate of Anna Karenina. The pairs Kitty-Levin, Darya-Oblonsky are only the big central complements to Anna and Vronsky; there are many others, more episodic, parallel plots besides. In both cases the plots complement and illuminate one another, but in quite different directions. In Lear the fate of Gloster underlines the tragic necessity of what happens to the principal hero. In *Anna Karenina* the parallel plots stress that the heroine's fate, while typical and necessary, is yet an extremely individual one. Obviously her fate reveals the inner contradictions of modern bourgeois marriage in the most powerful terms. But what is also shown is first, that these contradictions do not always necessarily take this particular path, thus that they may have an altogether different content and form, and, secondly, that similar kinds of conflict will only lead to Anna's tragic fate in very specific social and individual conditions.

We see here that these complementing parallels and contrasts are much more closely related in drama than in the novel. All that is needed in the novel to justify a complementary plot is a mere affinity with the basic social-human problem, however remote it may seem. In drama, this general resemblance will not do; the problem in the two cases must be visibly related in content, tendency and form.

This difference may be seen perhaps still more clearly by looking at the way contrasting characters are handled in drama and novel. Think of such contrasting groups as Hamlet-Laertes-Fortinbras in Shakespeare or Egmont-Oranien-Alba in Goethe. And compare the relations of these figures, their mutual elucidation with, say, the mutual complementing of the principal characters in Balzac's *Père Goriot*. Balzac himself points out in a theoretical piece that Goriot and Vautrin are complementary parallel figures; the novel itself emphasizes the complementing "pedagogic" influence of the Vicom-tesse de Beauséant and Vautrin on Rastignac; at the same time Rastignac, du Marzey, de Trailles form a series of parallels and con-trasts which are complemented by Vautrin, Nucingen, Tailleffer etc. as a group. The important thing about this confrontation is that it is not necessarily a character's chief quality or what is essential to its destiny that gives it this function; the factors which produce such complements or contrasts may themselves be quite accidental, epi-sodic and unimportant; they become appropriate and effective in a particular, all-round context.

This all links up with the specific character of the novel mentioned at the outset, namely that the conflict is not given "in itself", but through its broad objective social connections, as part of some large social development. We can learn a lot here by comparing the com-position of *King Lear* and *Père Goriot*, particularly as Balzac's novel was obviously very strongly influenced by Shakespeare. Above all, Goriot's "Lear" fate is itself an episode in the novel, even though a very important one. Otto Ludwig's remark, which we quoted earlier in a different context, that if *King Lear* were turned into a novel Edgar would be the main hero, is realized here with certain modifica-tions. For Rastignac's destiny also raises the problem of the relation between parents and children, and the naïvely egoistic matter-of-courseness with which Rastignac exploits his family has a certain limited similarity with the behaviour of Goriot's daughters to their father. The most important compositional difference, however, is that the family relations here are pushed right into the background. Balzac only alludes to this side of Rastignac; what is important for him is the development which Rastignac himself undergoes as he be-comes involved with the most varied people and in the most varied human relationships. And it is interesting to observe how it is pre-cisely the novel's greater breadth, the fact that its principal aim is the broad and gradual development of character (as opposed to the dram-atic explosion of qualities already present in a character), that gives a greater concentration and a new emphasis to the typical, in a way which necessarily would have been quite alien to Shakespeare.

Otto Ludwig's remark about Edgar as the hero of a Lear novel is extremely shrewd. However, the genius of what Balzac did in practice gives it greater depth and breadth. For Rastignac is not simply a kind of Edgar, but an inferior variety of the same, who, under the influence of circumstances, *develops* into a weaker, more pliant, less scrupulous, less extreme form of Edgar. Or, rather, he is such, if we see this novel developing *in this direction* as a whole. The novel is as familiar as drama with the unity and contrast of extremes and sometimes brings them to a head in similar ways. But it can also present this unity and contrast quite differently, for example where the interaction of the extremes produces a new development, a new direction, unexpected on the surface. The most significant feature of the really great novels is precisely the portrayal of such directions. It is not a particular condition of society or, at least it is only apparently a condition which is portrayed. The most important thing is to show how the *direction* of a social tendency becomes visible in the small, imperceptible capillary movements of individual life.

There is a tangible and important fact of life to be seen here underlying the form of the novel. Drama has portrayed the great convulsions, the tragic breakdowns of a world. At the end of each of Shakespeare's great tragedies a whole world collapses, and we find ourselves at the dawn of an entirely new epoch. The great novels of world literature, in particular those of the nineteenth century, portray not so much the collapse of a society as its process of disintegration, each one embracing a phase of this process. Not even in the most dramatic of novels is it at all necessary to allude to the social collapse as such. To fulfil the aims of the novel all that is required is to show convincingly and powerfully the irresistible course of social-historical development. The essential aim of the novel is the representation of the way society moves.

For certain classes and in certain conditions this movement may of course be an upward one. But even in such a case, the consistent epic writer will only show the direction of this movement; there is not the slightest need for him to depict ultimate victory or even a decisive triumph. Think of the classical example of Gorky's *Mother*, and compare the irresistible drive of this masterpiece, which portrays the later victory inherently, with the dramatic sense of doom of the old bourgeois world in Gorky's great play *Yegor Bulichov*.

We have now, I believe, said sufficient to show that a limited number of characters and destinies—however numerous compared with the economy of drama—must be very specially selected and grouped if they are to give a clear focus to any such direction. Naturally, these directions are present "in themselves" in the lives of actual people. But the dramatic collision is also present "in itself" in the collisions of life. The artistic adaptation of life, the artistic form of reflecting reality is in both cases a matter of turning this "in itself" into a "for us", though by different means. This is present in the novel's material to as great and as slight an extent as it is in the drama's. The novel, too, must translate social-historical laws directly into characters and destinies which appear uniquely individual. The unity of appearance and essence in art, the complete emergence of essence into pure appearance requires no less a rejection of the immediate and crude empirical world when appearance and essence seem too close to one another, as in the novel's material, than when they are visibly far apart. The difficulties which have to be overcome in the novel are different from those of drama, but no less great.

The difference in the facts of life reflected by each of the genres appears most clearly in the different handling of the action. In his essay on epic and drama, from which we have already quoted, Goethe also dealt with the principles behind this question. He analyses the different motifs governing action, finding some that are common to both epic and drama and others that form particular characteristics of either of the two genres. These motifs are, according to Goethe: "1. *Progressive ones*, which further the action; such are used primarily by drama. 2. *Retrogressive ones*, which distance the action from its goal; such are used almost exclusively by the epic poem."

To understand Goethe's last statement it should be specially pointed out that he distinguishes exactly between retrogressive and *retarding* motifs. Retarding factors for Goethe are those "which hold up the pace or increase the distance; such are used by both kinds of literature to the greatest advantage". One might think that there is only a quantitative difference between retarding and retrogressive motifs; if the retarding motif is made into the dominant one, it will become *eo ipso* retrogressive. Such an objection is not altogether wrong, but it overlooks what is qualitatively new in this apparently only quantitative development. The question is relatively simple and obvious in drama : the hero storms towards his goal, vehemently combating all obstacles in his path; the action is a ceaseless encounter between progressive and retarding motifs. In large epic, however, the scheme of the action is quite the opposite: precisely the motifs which distance the hero from his goal triumph, and this affects not only the outward circumstances; these motifs become a moving force in the hero himself. Think of the great Homeric epics. What motifs govern the action of the *Iliad*? Chiefly, the anger of Achilles and the events which result therefrom, motifs then which without exception push the goal, which is the subject of the *Iliad*, namely the capture of Troy, further and further into the distance. What governs the action of the *Odyssey*? The anger of Poseidon, who endeavours to frustrate the epic goal of the poem, namely the homecoming of Odysseus.

Of course, this retrogressive movement by no means succeeds without struggle. There is not only the hero himself, but also a group of fellow actors bent on realizing the epic goal and they struggle ceaselessly against this movement away from it. Were it not for this struggle, the whole of epic would subside into mere circumstantial description. However, this particular kind of action and its predominance are most closely connected with the artistic aim of large epic, with the particular character of the facts of life expressed by these forms.

It is obvious first of all that the "totality of objects" can only spread itself out within a story of this kind. Dramatic action moves rapidly forwards, and its halts, brought about by retarding motifs, are simply specific and prominent nodal points on the way to the utmost extreme, the collision. But to portray the whole environment of an action, including nature and society, as stages along this path, as important events and happenings, and to show all this in movement, the action must be based on retrogressive motifs. It is not by chance that as early as the *Odyssey* we have what was to become so important a motif for later epic, namely the journey or wandering and its obstacles. However it is clear that a simple account of a journey will never produce an epic poem, but merely circumstantial description. It is only because Odysseus's "journey" is a ceaseless struggle with a stronger power that every step along this path acquires an exciting significance: not a single circumstance depicted is mere circumstance, but a real event, the result of an action, the driving cause of a further encounter between the contending forces.

Here then is a form of action which alone is suited to solve the basic stylistic problem of epic, namely to translate into human activity that great series of natural circumstances, human institutions, manners, customs etc., which taken together form the "totality of objects". Dramatic action storms its way through such "circumstances"; they simply provide the occasions against which man reveals the social-moral moving forces within him. Thus there is no specific creative difficulty for drama here. Since epic, however, must both render this world of "things" and "circumstances" in their most extended fullness and yet all the time translate them into the activity of men, it needs a story which will lead its characters through this entire world in the course of an unending struggle. Only by means of endless battlefields, reasons for fighting, prizes for fighting etc. is the mechanical circumstantiality of "things" artistically overcome; the extended world of man appears in unceasing, living movement. Referring to Odysseus we mentioned the superiority of his antagonist. This factor is again of decisive importance for the manner of portrayal peculiar to epic. Both drama and large epic, to give a faithful image of human life, must reflect correctly the dialectics of freedom and necessity. Both, therefore, must present man and his actions as bound by the circumstances of his activity, by the social-historical basis of his deeds. At the same time, however, both must portray the role of human initiative, of the individual human deed within the course of social events.

In the dramatic collision individual initiative occupies the foreground. The circumstances which, as the result of a complex necessity, give rise to this initiative are indicated only in their general outlines. It is only in the collision and its consequence that the human deed is shown to be restricted and limited, to be socially and historically determined. In large epic, however, the element of necessity is present and prevalent throughout. The retrogressive motif is only an expression of those general objective forces which are necessarily stronger than the will and resolve of the individual. Thus, whereas drama concentrates the correct dialectics of freedom and necessity in a heroic catastrophe, epic gives a broadly unfolded, entangled picture of the varied struggles—great and small, some successful, some ending in defeat—of its characters, and it is through the totality of these that the necessity of social development is expressed. Both great forms, therefore, reflect the same dialectics of life. They place their emphasis, however, on different sides of the same relationship. This difference is only an expression of those different facts of life which both forms express and of which we have already spoken in detail.

These connections make it clear that the personal initiative of the characters is much more important in drama than in epic. Even in classical drama, where a much stricter necessity prevails, this is the case. Let us take Sophocles' *Oedipus Rex*, a play which has for long served as the model of fatalistic "dramas of destiny". How is it really constructed? Certainly, Oedipus is "called to account" at the end for his past life; certainly, the main theme of the play is the revelation of events long past. But the path which leads to this is determined by the vigorous and tireless initiative of Oedipus himself. True, he is oppressed by the past, but he himself, by his own efforts sets the stone rolling which crushes him. The "novelization" of many modern plays is most strikingly revealed by comparison with this classical model. This is particularly the case with Schiller's plays of the Weimar period. His *Maria Stuart*, for example, is almost exclusively the object of struggle between opposing historical forces, embodied in minor figures. Her position in the play already betrays strong epic tendencies.

We have seen that in classical epic, too, the driving force of the action is not the epic hero, but the forces of necessity embodied in the gods. The greatness of the epic hero emerged only in his heroic, or tenacious and cunning, resistance to these forces. This character of large epic becomes more marked in the novel. The predominance of the retrogressive motif acquires an even greater significance. For the subject of epic is a struggle of national character and thus, necessarily, has a clear and definite aim. The retrogressive motif dominates the story in the form of an uninterrupted chain of obstacles which resist the realization of this aim.

The new relationship between individual and society, between individual and class, creates a new situation for the modern novel. It is only very conditionally and in special cases that individual action has a direct and social aim. Indeed, as the novel develops, more and more important works arise which neither have nor can have any concrete aim at all. This is true already of *Don Quixote* where the hero's aim is no more than a general one to revive chivalry and seek adventure. But this cannot possibly be called an aim in the same sense as Odysseus's intention to return home. It is the same with important novels like *Tom Jones*, *Wilhelm Meister* etc. In *Wilhelm Meister*, indeed, the peculiarity of the new novel is clearly stated in the conclusion : the hero realizes that he has achieved something quite different from what he set out to achieve on his wanderings. This expresses clearly, in terms of social content, the enhanced function of the retrogressive motif. As the force of social circumstances proves stronger than the intention of the hero and emerges triumphant from the struggle, so the socially necessary asserts itself : the characters act according to their individual inclinations and passions, but the result of their actions is something quite different from what they intended.

Naturally, here again there is no Chinese wall between epic and novel. On the one hand, there are important modern novels which contain a very definite aim; although even when this aim is achieved social necessity triumphs. Thus again the wisdom of *Wilhelm Meister's* final words applies, whereas the national aim of the old epic could be adequately realized, even though great obstacles had to be overcome. Think, say, of Tolstoy's *Resurrection*, where Nekhlyudov wishes to free Maslova; he succeeds, but the achieved aim appears inwardly and outwardly quite different from the imagined one.

These gradations are more important with respect to the historical novel. Since the social reality which it depicts is closer to the world of epic than to that of the modern novel, it is obvious that some of its motifs may bear a strong affinity to the old epic. We have already remarked upon the epic qualities in Scott, Cooper and Gogol. But here, too, there is an important difference. The old epos showed a historical phase of mankind in full flower. For the modern historical novel this period belongs to a distant past, it is a human order which has perished, and is seen in terms of the tragic necessity of its decline. For this reason necessity is a far less straightforward, much more complex thing than in the old epos; here the old order interacts with other, more advanced social formations. General epic aims may remain, but they have already assumed a sectional character within the total picture of society; thus, they have lost their pure epic character.

The second important instance of a connection between epic and novel relates to the art of socialism. Within capitalist society the class struggle of the proletariat gives birth to aims which directly unite the individual and the social. These aims can never, of course be adquately realized in capitalist society, but epic literature can show their straight and unmistakeable movement towards future fulfilment. Since an analysis of the formal problems which this involves lies outside the scope of this study, let us simply mention Gorky's *Mother*.

In both great forms, then, social-historical necessity must triumph over the will and passions of individuals. But the nature of this struggle and of the victory are entirely different in drama and the novel. Primarily because drama and the novel each reflect a separate side of the life process. We have seen how in the novel necessity manifests itself in an extended, intricate fashion, asserting itself gradually through a series of accidents. In drama, the same necessity is portrayed in the form of the inevitable outcome of a great social collision. For this reason the hero has a definite aim in modern drama, too, or at least this is so in tendency. The tragic hero storms with fateful determination towards his goal, and the accomplishment, failure or collapse of his aim etc. will reveal the necessary character of the dramatic collision.

This analysis of the difference between novel and drama again takes us back to our earlier definition. The heroes of drama are "world-historical individuals" (in the correct sense, of course, in which this concept applies to drama, as suggested by Hebbel). The central figure of the novel, on the other hand, belongs of equal necessity to the "maintaining individuals". (This, too, in the broad, dialectical sense in which we have used the term, namely that the self-reproduction of society, its tendencies of gradual development upwards or downwards, also belong to the concept of "maintenance".) The "world-historical individual" can only figure as a minor character in the novel because of the complexity and intricacy of the whole social-historical process. The proper hero here is life itself; the retrogressive motifs, which express necessary tendencies of development, have as their hidden nucleus the general driving forces of history. The historical greatness of such characters is expressed in their complex interaction, their manifold connection with the diverse private destinies of social life, in whose totality the trends of popular destiny are revealed. In drama these historical forces are represented directly through the protagonists. Since the hero of drama unites in his personality the essential social-moral determinants of the forces which produce the collision, he is necessarily—in the broad sense used above—a "world-historical individual". Drama paints the great historical explosions and eruptions of the historical process. Its hero represents the shining peak of these great crises. The novel portrays more what happens before and after these crises, showing the broad interaction between popular basis and visible peak.

This stressing of different, though equally valid, factors of social life has far-reaching consequences for the relation of both genres to historical reality. Drama concentrates its portrayal of the basic laws of development round the great historical collision. The depiction of the times, of specific historical factors is in drama only a means of giving the collision itself a clear and concrete expression. The historical character of drama thus concentrates round the historical character of the collision itself in its pure form. Whatever will not be absorbed directly and completely by the collision will spoil or even ruin the flow of the drama.

This, of course, does not mean that the collision has a "supra-historical" or abstract "universal-human" character, as was to some extent assumed by the Enlightenment and as many reactionary modern theorists of drama proclaim. Hebbel still saw clearly that even the pure form of the collision, if correctly grasped, is in its deepest essence historical. "The question is," says Hebbel, "what is the relation of drama to history, and to what extent must it be historical? I think, *insofar as it is already this in itself* (my italics G.L.) and insofar as art may count as the highest form of historical writing, for it is quite unable to represent the most glorious and significant processes of life without at the same time revealing the decisive historical crises, which evoke and condition them, the loosening up or gradual consolidation of the world's religious and political forms as the chief guides and bearers of all culture, in a word: the atmosphere of the ages." These remarks of Hebbel, though exaggerating certain idealist tendencies of Hegel, go to the heart of the historical character of drama in the right way. Hebbel is also on the right path when in subsequent remarks he rules out of bounds to drama the co-called period details describing individual historical facts etc. In drama, historical authenticity means the inner historical truth of the collision.

For the novel, on the other hand, the collison is only a part of that total world which it is its task to portray. The novel's aim is to represent a particular social reality at a particular time, with all the colour and specific atmosphere of that time. Everything else, both collisions and the "world-historical individuals" who figure in them, are no more than means to this end. Since the novel portrays the "totality of objects", it must penetrate into the small details of everyday life, into the concrete time of the action, it must bring out what is specific to this time through the complex interaction of all these details. Therefore the general historicity of the central collision, which constitutes the historical character of drama, does not suffice for the novel. It must be historically authentic in root and branch.

Let us briefly summarize these conclusions: the novel is more historical than drama. This means that the historical penetration of all the manifestations of life must go much deeper in the novel than in drama. The novel counters the general historicism of the essence of a collision with the concrete historicism of all the details.

It follows from this that the possibility of "necessary anachronism" is much greater in drama than in the novel. In representing the quintessential moments of a historically authentic collision, it may suffice if the historical essence of the collision has been grasped in a deep and genuinely historical manner. Thereby the intellectually heightened speech necessary to drama may further transcend the real horizon of the time, while still preserving the necessary faithfulness to history —that is, if it does not do harm to the essential historical content of the collision, but on the contrary intensifies it.

The limits of "necessary anachronism" in the novel, on the other hand, are much narrower. We have already pointed out that the novel cannot do without this anachronism. But since historical necessity in the novel is not simply general and quintessential but a highly complex and cunning process, this process as such must there take a central place. As a result the scope of "necessary anachronism" is much more restricted than in drama. Of course, the broad portrayal of popular life with all its externals also plays a big part. But the development of the modern novel shows how undecisive a part is played by authenticity of detail. The detail may be of the most conscientious, antiquarian exactness—and the novel as a whole may yet be a crying unhistorical anachronism from beginning to end. This does not mean that authenticity of detail plays no part. On the contrary, it is very important. But it acquires its importance as the sensous mediator of this specific quality, this peculiar process by which historical necessity asserts itself at a particular time, in a particular place and within certain class relations etc.

This seems to have landed us with a paradoxical conclusion. We said that the possibility of "necessary anachronism" was much greater in drama, yet at the same time showed that drama uses authentic historical heroes more frequently than the novel. Our previous remarks surely show clearly enough why the novel must be faithful to history despite its invented hero and imagined plot. The question of the playwright's faithfulness to history, on the other hand, whether he is tied or not tied to the real historical lineaments of his heroes, has dominated all theoretical discussions on history as a subject of literature. As we shall be dealing with this question at length in the next section, we shall not enter into the dialectics of the problem here.

In the meantime let us mention one important factor which will throw light on the formal side of this question. The main distinction we drew between drama and large epic was that drama is by nature something which takes place in the present, while epic, also by nature, presents itself as something already past, a happening which is all over.

This affects historical subjects in the following way: in a novel there need be no paradoxical relationship between the historical character of an event and its manner of representation. Although everything we experience in a historical novel must concern us directly, if it is to have artistic effect, nevertheless we experience it all as our *prehistory*. Whereas in historical drama what "concerns us" has something of a paradox about it. We have to experience a happening of long ago as if it is actually taking place in the present and has direct reference to us. If mere antiquarian interest, mere curiosity can ruin the effect of a historical novel, then the experience of mere prehistory will not evoke the immediate and sweeping impact of drama. Thus, while the essence of a collision must remain historically authentic, historical drama must bring out those features in men and their destinies which will make a spectator, separated from these events by centuries, feel himself a direct participant of them. The "tua res agitur" ("it concerns you") of drama has a meaning qualitatively different from that of the novel. Thus drama draws out those features in all men which in the course of history have been relatively the most permanent, general and regulative. Drama, as Otto Ludwig once said, has an essentially "anthropological" character.

5 A Sketch of the Development of Historicism in Drama and Dramaturgy.

Now we are able to see clearly and provide an answer to the historical question posed at the beginning of this chapter: How was it that when historical consciousness had barely developed or hardly existed at all, that when the historical novel was no more than caricature both of the novel and of history, it was yet possible to have great historical dramas? We are referring here primarily, of course, to

Shakespeare and a number of his contempories. But not only to them, for some of the tragedies of Corneille or Racine, of Calderon or Lope de Vega are undoubtedly historical tragedies which have a tremendous import and effect. Today it is a well-known fact already that this wave of great drama, and *historical* drama along with it, arose out of the crises and break-up of the feudal system. It is also well-known—and immediately verifiable for anyone who reads Shakespeare's chronicle plays attentively—that the most notable writers of the period had deep insights into the important collisions of this great transitional age. In Shakespeare, especially, a whole set of the inner contradictions of feudalism, pointing inevitably to its dissolution, emerge with the greatest clarity.

However, what interested these writers—and Shakespeare above all—was not so much the complex, actual historical causality responsible for the decline of feudalism, as the human collisions which sprang necessarily and typically from the contradictions of this decline, as the forceful, interesting historical types among the older, declining human stock of feudalism and the new type of hero, the humanist noble or ruler. Shakespeare's cycle of historical plays, in particular, is full of collisions of this kind. With brilliant clarity and discernment he views the welter of contradiction which had filled the uneven but fatal path of feudal crisis over centuries. Shakespeare never simplifies this process down to a mechanical contrast between the "old" and the "new". He sees the triumphant humanist character of the rising new world, but also sees it causing the breakdown of a patriarchal society humanly and morally better in many respects and more closely bound to the interests of the people. Shakespeare sees the triumph of humanism, but also foresees the rule of money in this advancing new world, the oppression and exploitation of masses, a world of rampant egoism and ruthless greed. In particular, the types representing the social-moral, human-moral decay of feudalism are portrayed in his historical plays with incomparable power and realism and sharply opposed to the old, inwardly still unproblematic and uncorrupted, nobility. (Shakespeare feels a keen, personal sympathy for this latter type, at times idealizes him, but as a great, clear-sighted poet regards his doom as inevitable.) His clear eye for the social-moral features which emerge from this violent historical crisis allows Shakespeare to create historical dramas of great historical authenticity and fidelity, even though he has not yet experienced history as history in the sense of the nineteenth century, in the sense of the conception which we have analysed in the work of Scott.

This, of course, has nothing to do with the innumerable, small factual anachronisms in Shakespeare. Historical authenticity, in the sense of costume, objects etc., is always treated by Shakespeare with the sovereign licence of a great dramatist, who knows instinctively how immaterial such small features are as long as the big collision is right. Therefore, Shakespeare states every conflict, even those of English history with which is most familiar, in terms of typical-human opposites; and these are historical only insofar as Shakespeare fully and directly assimilates into each individual type the most characteristic and central features of a social crisis. Characterizations as of Richard the Second or Richard the Third, contrasts in character as between Henry the Fifth and Percy Hotspur always have this marvellously observed, social-historical basis. But their dramatic effect is essentially social-moral, human-morals "anthropological"; in all these cases Shakespeare is portraying the most general, regulative features of such social collisions and contradictions.

In this way Shakespeare concentrates the decisive human relations round these historical collisions with a force unparalleled before and after him. With the great tragedian's disregard for so-called probability (which Pushkin always fought passionately in his theoretical writings) Shakespeare always allows the human point to emerge from the historical struggles of his time, but he both concentrates and generalizes it to such a degree that the opposites often acquire an antique clarity and sharpness. There is the sense of a classical chorus when, in the third part of Henry the Sixth, Shakespeare brings onto the battlefield a son who has killed his father and a father who has killed his son, and the son says:

> From London by the king was I press'd forth;
> My father, being the Earl of Warwick's man,
> Came on the part of York, press'd by his master;
> And I, who at his hands receiv'd my life,
> Have by my hands of life bereaved him.

Then, later in the scene:

> SON
> Was ever son so rued a father's death?
> FATHER
> Was ever father so bemoan'd his son?
> KING HENRY
> Much is your sorrow; mine ten times so much.
> Was ever king so griev'd for subjects' woe?

Similar features can be pointed out at all the great moments of these plays. Shakespeare always looks for these magnificent human confrontations in history and finds them in the real historical struggle of the War of the Roses. He is historically faithful and authentic because the human features absorb the most essential elements of this great historical crisis. Let us point to just one example, Richard the Third's wooing of Anne. The immediate content of this scene is a human-moral one, no more than the measuring of two human wills. But this very character of the scene bears tremendous historical witness to the magnificent energy and thoroughly amoral cynicism of the most significant figure produced by this period of dissolution, namely the last tragic protagonist of the civil war of the nobles.

It was not by chance that Shakespeare, at the height of his powers, should have abandoned historical subjects in the narrow sense. Yet he remained true to history in the sense in which he experienced it, and produced even more magnificent canvases of this historical transition than in his chronicle plays. For in the great tragedies of his maturity (*Hamlet*, *Macbeth*, *Lear* etc.) he used the legendary anecdotal material of the old chronicles in order to concentrate certain social-moral problems of this transition crisis even more powerfully than was possible when tied to the events of English history. These great tragedies breathe the same historical spirit as the historical plays in the narrower sense, except that they retain no more of external events, of the (from a dramatic point of view) accidental ups and downs of the social struggles of real history, than is indispensable to the crystallization of the central human-moral problem. For this reason the great tragic figures of Shakespeare's maturity are the most colossal historical types of this transition crisis. Precisely because Shakespeare was able to proceed here with greater dramatic concentration and a more "anthropological" kind of characterization than in the "histories", these great tragedies are historically more profound and true in Shakespeare's sense than the latter.

It would be quite wrong to view Shakespeare's adaptation of legendary material as a form of "modernization" in the modern sense. There are important critics who consider that the Roman plays, written concurrently with the great tragedies, really portray English events and English characters and simply use the ancient world as costume. (At times we find similar statements even in Goethe.) But in judging these plays what matters is precisely the generalizing nature of Shakespeare's characterization, the extraordinary breadth and depth of his insight into the various currents forming the crisis of his period. And the classical world is a living social-moral force in this period; it is not felt as a distant past to which one has to reach back. Thus when Shakespeare portrays Brutus, say, he can see the stoic features of aristocratic republicanism in living evidence about him in his own time. (Think, for example, of the friend of Montaigne's youth, Etienne de la Boëtie.) Since Shakespeare was familiar with this type and his deepest social-human characteristics, he was able to adapt from Plutarch's history those features which the two periods had in common, historically and "anthropologically". Thus, he does not simply inject the spirit of his period into the ancient world, but rather brings to life those tragic events of antiquity which were based on historical-moral experiences inwardly similar to those of his own time; so that the generalized form of the drama reveals the features which the two ages hold objectively in common.

For this reason, the Roman plays belong stylistically alongside the great tragedies of Shakespeare's maturity. In them he concentrates the most general tendencies of crisis in his epoch round some important collision which has typical universality and depth. In them, the first real historical drama reached its climax—and this historical drama owed its existence to the first transition crisis of the rising new society.

The second wave of historical drama, as we have already shown, sets in with the German Enlightenment. We pointed out the social-historical reasons for this strengthening of historical feeling in Germany. The development begins with Goethe's Götz von Berlichingen, outwardly a continuation of Shakespeare's "histories". Outwardly, because Goethe lacks the great dramatic sweep of Shakespeare. On the other hand, Goethe tends towards faithfulness of detail in a way that was quite alien to Shakespeare. A strong epic element, a historical "totality of objects" was introduced into drama. But any further extension of this trend was rendered impossible by the poverty of German historical themes, as Goethe himself later admitted. The immediate continuation of this form of drama leads to the empty theatricality of plays about chivalry. Götz von Berlichingen is, in a wide historical sense, much more a precursor of Scott's novels than a milestone in the development of historical drama.

Nevertheless, a new flowering of historical drama occurs both in Goethe himself and in Schiller. Its basis is the time of crisis preparatory to the French Revolution and the Revolution itself. As a result of the inner dialectics of this crisis this drama is more markedly and consciously historical than Shakespeare's. The factors which it reveals of the historical reality of a period are not simply those which are inseparably linked with the human-moral features of the characters and are wholly absorbed by them, they are also the very concrete social-historical features of a particular phase of development. The representation of the crises leading to the Netherlands revolution in Egmont and to the Thirty Years' war in Wallenstein evince definite historical characteristics of this kind to a much greater degree than the historical plays of Shakespeare. And it is not a matter now of amassing the interesting historical features of an epoch in an epic way, as it was in Götz, but of imparting as deeply as possible to the characters themselves, to their particular mode of behaviour and to the particular turns of the action, the specifically historical peculiarity of a definite historical situation.

These historical portraits are particularly deep and correct in *Egmont*. The departure from the epic trend of *Götz* is linked with the attempt to bring the new historical drama closer to the type of drama created by Shakespeare in his maturity. Goethe and Schiller aspire to the heights of human generalization at which Shakespeare's collisions are enacted in these late plays. Nevertheless, they wish to portray a very concrete, historically real crisis of development. Thus it is intended that the style of *Macbeth, Lear etc.* should become the dominant style of historical drama. (We may disregard certain classicist experiments in this shortened summary.)

These tendencies undoubtedly enhance the historicism of drama. But it is also undoubtedly a more divided and problematic historicism than Shakespeare's. For both Goethe and Schiller approached their historical material in a self-contradictory way, which in Schiller's case in particular led to serious discordances of style. In the first place, both inherited the Enlightenment tendency to portray the "universally human" in their works. Many polemic and revolutionary Enlightenment aims are contained in this tendency; the "universally human" is consciously counterposed to the particularism of estate society. And however the outlook of Goethe and Schiller may change, this tendency is never extinguished: for them the human essence of man is something which can never be fully penetrated and accounted for by his social-historical appearance. Secondly, however, and as a result of the very development of Enlightenment ideology, the historicism in them is enormously strengthened at the end of the eighteenth century. It is not even necessary to mention Schiller's special historical studies, for even earlier he tended to make his subjects historically concrete, and in the case of Goethe this tendency corresponds to his general realist aims.

The attempt to apply the style of mature Shakespeare to historical drama so conceived is essentially an attempt to seek an artistic balance between these contradictory tendencies. We have already pointed out in another context Goethe's solution to this problem and its historical position in the development of literature as a whole. Schiller does not succeed in achieving a unified picture. Although he studies in great detail the historical character of the epochs he deals with, often reproducing them in captivating and historically authentic pictures, particularly in his later period, many of his characters nevertheless, on becoming "universally human", forsake historical reality and become the poet's "mouthpieces", as Marx called them, direct effluences of his idealist humanism.

A new and higher stage of historicism in drama was brought about by Scott's historical novel. Admittedly, this stage has initially only a few outstanding, individual works to show for itself—the plays of Manzoni and, above all, Pushkin's *Boris Godunov*. Pushkin as we have seen, realizes very clearly that the arrival of Scott indicates a new period in historical drama even by comparison with Goethe. And he feels with great certainty that the only way this new period can express itself is by drawing consciously near to Shakespeare; that its new character will be the need, when trying to unite the historically concrete with its social-moral generalization, to work out historical necessity and "anthropological" laws more tangibly, in a consciously historical spirit.

In this Pushkin diverges from the stylistic aims of Goethe and Schiller; his stylistic model is once again Shakespeare's "histories", but unlike the young Goethe, instead of making drama more epic, he makes it more inwardly dramatic. This he does chiefly by stressing general historical necessity much more strongly than Shakespeare himself. Admittedly in this tendency Pushkin concords with the aims of Goethe and Schiller in their Weimar period. But he surpasses them both, especially Schiller, by avoiding any formalist abstraction in his rendering of necessity which he allows to grow organically out of his portrayal of popular life. (We recall our earlier statements on the chorus in tragedy.) Pushkin thereby creates a framework of historical necessity so strict that it is able to withstand the truly Shakespearean explosiveness of some of his scenes—particularly where a great historical personality reaches the crucial moment of his life. The boldness, concreteness, truthfulness of passion and the dramatic-human generalization of the scene in which the False Dimitri confesses to Marina, with its abrupt turn-about at the end, are to be found nowhere else but in Shakespeare.

A singular feature of the new stage of historicism is that the deeper concretization of historical material enables Pushkin (and Manzoni) to make the attitudes of their heroes to social-political problems deeply human, to give them direct human-moral, dramatic expression. Goethe and Schiller, on the other hand, were compelled to build motifs of love and friendship into their historical plays so that a space could be created in which the really human passions could live themselves out to the full. (Think, above all, of Max Piccolomini in *Wallenstein*.) The relative withdrawal of such motifs in Pushkin, Manzoni as well as in the great German playwright, Georg Büchner, is highly characteristic of this phase of development; not least of all, these elements could provide a new starting-point in our development today.

But here we must mention two factors which have since been obscured. First of all, the retreat of "private" human motifs in no way means that they are altogether excluded. They are only reduced to the dramatically indispensable, they are presented in a highly concentrated form and only insofar as they are absolutely necessary for characterizing the great historical personalities in their relation to the problems of popular life. Hence Dimitri, Boris Godunov, Carmagnola or Danton are portrayed as historical heroes in whose personal lives just those features are underlined and explained which have made them the concrete, "world-historical individuals" they are, which cause their tragic rise and fall. Thus, in contrast to later drama this manner of portrayal never treats political-historical necessity in a naked, fetishized, mystified or merely propagandistic fashion. The dramatic greatness of this period, above all of Pushkin, lies in its successful translation of social-historical driving forces into the interplay of contending, concrete individuals.

Secondly, the manner in which Pushkin and his really great contemporaries individualize has nothing of the merely individual about it, it never gets bogged down in historical-social details. The fragments of Pushkin's preface to his play show clearly how consciously he raised the problem of the human generalization of his characters. For example, he points out features which his Pretender has in common with Henry IV and gives similar, searching indications of his intentions with regard to Marina, Shuisky and so on. And it was in generalizing his characters and their tragic destinies that he was so outstandingly successful. True, this tendency was lost on the pettier kind of realism following Pushkin's period, and so his great beginning was without succession.

In Germany, Georg Büchner's ambitious attempt met a similar fate. Drama in the succeeding period degenerates either into psychologistic refinement of the dramatic hero's "private" passions or into a mystification of historical necessities. Admittedly, the important historical dramatists, especially in Germany, do endeavour to make an adequate dramatic translation of the spirit of the ages, but despite often profound understanding for these problems they always slip into some form of modernization. (This "problematic" may be seen at its clearest in the outstanding theoretician of tragedy and highly gifted tragedian, Friedrich Hebbel.)

We have seen that the necessity of "world-historical individuals" as the heroes of historical drama makes the problem of faithfulness to historical facts a very early one. Since the majority of these "world-historical individuals" are obviously well-known historical figures and since dramatic form necessarily requires a radical transformation of any given historical material, the question inevitably arose in the theory of drama as to where a playwright's freedom vis-à-vis his material begins and how far it may go without cancelling a play's historical character.

Tragédie classique still takes a fairly empirical attitude towards this question. It naïvely violates the past on its own terms. Corneille held the view that while the basic features of historical or legendary events were binding on the poet, he was free to invent the connections between them. Their concrete treatment of these questions, however, shows very clearly how little the French dramatists understood the classical subject-matter they favoured. Whereas the material Shakespeare takes from the past always has a living and objective affinity with the problems of the great historical crises of his own day, the subject-matter of *tragédie classique* is, from this point of view, often indiscriminate and arbitrary. It aims to portray great examples of tragic necessity. It thinks it can find these in classical history and legend. But it lacks the premises for comprehending the real foundations of these actions. Hence, it gives its characters a psychological make-up quite alien to the original material, so that the observation of the facts becomes a mere formality.

It will perhaps suffice to quote one characteristic example. Corneille, in his theoretical treatise on tragedy, analyses the manner in which the *Oresteia* could be brought "up to date". It is interesting that he should take exception to the decisive social-historical motif of the trilogy, namely Orestes' murder of his mother, i.e. the motif in which the struggle between mother-right and father-right appears as a world-historical crisis. The solution Corneille suggests is that while Orestes has to kill his mother *de facto*, since this is what the legend says, his intention should be only to kill his mother's seducer, Aegisthes, and the murder of his mother should be the result simply of an unfortunate accident in the struggle. One sees here how the conception of faithfulness to historical material becomes a caricature. And this attitude is by no means confined to Corneille. According to Condorcet, Voltaire boasted that his adaptation of the very same theme had made Clytemnestra more "touching" and Electra "less barbaric" than they were in the originals.

Such statements show very clearly the unhistorical, indeed anti-historical spirit of this period. An unbridgeable gulf appears to separate this anti-historicism from the great historical conception we find in Shakespeare's drama. The contrast is self-evident and is reflected, too, in the way *tragédie classique* portrays more familiar subjects. But these theoretical formulations would probably sound less naïvely crude, if the Elizabethan playwrights had made similarly abstract pronouncements about their attitude to history. Shakespeare's dramatic practice towers above the general theoretical appreciation of history in his time. This superiority has its real roots in the living links between Shakespeare's art and the people; he was besieged by the major, general problems of his time and they demanded portrayal.

Tragédie classique, on the other hand, was an art of the court and therefore much more under the influence of theoretical currents which had ceased to appreciate these problems of popular life and hence any analogous events in history which might have a direct bearing on them. Pushkin very rightly points out in his remarks on drama that the popular playwright has much greater freedom of movement in regard to both theme and public than the court playwright, who, whether in fact or imagination, writes for a public socially and culturally superior to himself.

Yet despite this problematic conception of the relation of drama to history, which became something of a caricature, these writers did seek the really dramatic, a direct contact with their age, the direct, public character of drama. Thus, however forcibly they modernized historical themes an element of real drama remains. Admittedly, often in a perverse and distorted form, because of the problematic social basis of their entire drama. At the same time, even this ahistorical distortion should not be seen as uniform all the way through. It depends very much upon the inner connection of the given concrete theme with the burning problems of the present. In this respect the classical myths certainly constitute an extreme case of incomprehension. But where the play has a feudal theme, which forms a bridge to the present, as in *Le Cid*, or where classical history raises problems with a certain natural affinity to contemporary problems, as in Shakespeare's classical plays (e.g. Corneille's *Cinna* or, still more, Racine's portrayal of Nero), a fairly high degree of dramatic historicism may still be attained. An examination of these gradations and certainly of their causes would take us outside the limits of this study.

However, despite all such countervailing tendencies, the principal trend of these dramas is ahistorical or supra-historical. For this reason the rise of historical feeling during the eighteenth century inevitably aggravated the "problematic". The problem of historical authenticity and faithfulness for Voltaire is only faithfulness towards historical facts. And since he takes over the principles of drama of his predecessors almost unaltered, the contradictions are more patent than even in Corneille or Racine.

How sharp the contrast was in the eyes of the Enlighteners between the demands of drama and those of historical authenticity may perhaps be most clearly shown in the pronouncements of Hénault. He was one of the few Frenchmen of his time to be influenced by Shakespeare in a major and positive way. *Henry VI*, particularly, earned his enthusiasm, and he attempted to emulate the breadth and variety of Shakespeare's picture of the age in a series of prose scenes on the reign and fortunes of François II. He raises the problem, however, from the historical side. Describing the impression which

Shakespeare's play has made on him, he asks: "Why is our history not written in this way? and why is it that nobody has thought of this idea?" And from this standpoint he criticizes the cursory, unplastic, lifeless manner of representation of the historians of the times: "Tragedy has an opposite and as serious a shortcoming for anybody who would be instructed, but which nevertheless it rightly treats as a law: that it should represent only an important happening and, like painting, restrict itself to a single moment: for our interest grows cold if the imagination wanders over several different moments. Thus, history's presentation of a long and exact series of facts is cold by comparison with tragedy; while tragedy's presentation of a single event, though powerful, is factually bare in comparison with history. Could not something useful and agreeable arise out of their combination?"

We see that in this theory historicism and drama are still antinomous and sharply opposed to one another. In spite of his enthusiasm, Hénault is largely blind to Shakespeare's *dramatic historicism*. Yet, despite the rigid and undialectical nature of the antithesis, it marks an enormous step forward in the clarification of the problem.

The dialectical connection between history and tragedy is first grasped as a problem, in however approximate a fashion, in the writings of Lessing. This is his great achievement and to this he owes his special position in the history of aesthetics during the Enlightenment. In the writings of Lessing the Enlightenment's new conception of the relationship between drama and history finds its highest formulation. We saw that Lessing's attitude appears at first to be thoroughly anti-historical, since he views history as a mere "repertory of names". However, a closer analysis shows that it is not quite as simple as this. The essence of Lessing's conception may be summed up as follows: "the poet must hold characters more sacred than facts". Hence he formulates the question as follows: "*How far may the poet stray from historical truth?* In all that does not concern the characters, as far as he likes. He must hold *only the characters sacred* and may be allowed to add only what will strengthen them, show them in their best light; the least essential alteration would eliminate the cause of why they hold these names and not others. And nothing is more offensive than something for which we cannot find a cause."

Lessing thus puts the question, above all, more decisively, openly and honestly than the theorists of French classicism. As a great theorist of the theatre he understands that man must be at the centre of drama, that only a person with whom we can directly and wholeheartedly sympathize throughout the entire compass of his destiny and unique psychology can become the hero of a play. Thus, despite the apparently anti-historical formulation of his question, despite many anti-historical tendencies in his outlook. Lessing already poses the question much more historically. He no longer allows playwrights to devise a "path" which will connect uncomprehended historical facts. He demands that they should approach the figures of the past as whole and indivisible characters, that from among them they should choose as their heroes only such as can be made intelligible to the present throughout the entire range of their destinies. This is a great step forward in the theoretical clarification of the question. Admittedly, historical material is still something accidental for Lessing, since history does not yet appear as a process leading up to the present, since the suitability of historical characters which Lessing demands does not yet depend so necessarily on the inner historical nature of the clash of social forces underlying the collision.

Nevertheless, it cannot be denied that there are other tendencies in Lessing which show a dawning appreciation for these connections. To be sure, they are due more to his deep understanding of the special nature of dramatic form than to a real historical sense. But Lessing is entirely in the right when he resolutely rejects any appeal to historical authenticity or lack of authenticity in the assessment of an historical play. This he does for the sake of the necessities of dramatic form. "That has really happened? so be it: there will be a good reason for it in the eternal infinite connection of all things. In the latter there is wisdom and goodness, which, in the few links which the poet takes out, seem to us blind fate and cruelty. From these few links he should make a whole which is fully rounded, where one thing is fully explained by another, where no difficulty arises as a result of which we become dissatisfied with this one plan and must seek satisfaction outside in the general plan of things..." Lessing thus defends the freedom of the dramatist against the merely factual correctness of historical data in the name of the self-contained totality of drama, with which he links the demand that this totality should be an adequate image of the general laws of the historical process. He demands therefore the freedom to diverge from individual facts in the name of a deeper fidelity to the spirit of the whole. This is already a profound demonstration of the relation of drama to reality.

In his concrete analysis Lessing goes still further. He recognizes that there are many cases where historical reality already provides in a pure form the tragedy which the playwright seeks. In such cases he requires the playwright to surrender himself to the inner dialectic of the material and to elicit the laws of its movement with the greatest possible faithfulness. In reproaching late Corneille he concentrates on the latter's inability to recognize the great, tragic course of real history and his having to resort, therefore, to trivial inventions which deform and debase this great line of events already present in reality.

In this spirit Lessing defends the material of Corneille's *Rodogune* against Corneille himself. "What more does it need. . . to provide the material of a tragedy? With the genius, nothing, with the bungler, everything. Only such events can engage the attention of the genius as are grounded in one another, only chains of causes and effects. To trace the latter back to the former, to weigh the former against the latter, everywhere to exclude chance, to allow everything that occurs to occur in such a way that it could not occur differently: this, this is his task, if he works in the field of history, transforming the useless treasures of the memory into nourishment for the mind." The "wit" of the French classicists on the other hand was merely interested in analogies, it joined incompatibles and therefore found the most powerful historical subjects unfruitful, so that they had to be supplemented and "embellished" with trivial love intrigues.

Already here an extremely deep relationship between the dramatist and the life process is being demanded. What Lessing's theory still lacks is the realization that this life process is already historical in itself. It was left to the classical period of literature and philosophy to understand this theoretically, however much individual formulations still inevitably suffer from the perverseness of philosophic idealism. Our earlier quotation from Hebbel clearly shows what this step forward meant.

But this new understanding won through only very gradually, in the course of difficult struggles, and did not achieve real clarity, even on the question of drama until after Scott. We saw earlier that in many respects Lessing's unhistorical tendencies still held good theoretically for Goethe. Our few references to Goethe's literary practice also explain why this had to be so. Indeed, the earlier traditions prevailed so strongly in this period that even as fierce an opponent of classicist drama as Manzoni, who with great resoluteness and originality opposed it with historical drama, divided the figures of his historical plays into "historical" and "imaginary", i.e. invented by himself. Goethe was quite right to combat this conception with arguments drawn from the *Hamburg Dramaturgy* and even convinced Manzoni of the incorrectness of his position.

The decisive turning-point in this question is marked by Goethe's and Hegel's theory of "necessary anachronism" with which we are already acquainted. Belinsky drew all the inferences of this theory in its application to historical drama with unusual radicalness. "The division of tragedy into historical and non-historical has no meaning whatsoever: the heroes of both represent equally the realization of the eternal substantial forces of the human soul." One should not pay too much attention to Belinsky's Hegelian formulation. The general spirit of his essays shows a deep understanding for the concrete problems of the historical process. Thus, in the remarks following this general thesis, where Belinsky deals with individual problems of historical drama, using classical examples, he does so entirely in the spirit of the new and great historicism of this period. He defends Schiller's conception of King Philip in *Don Carlos*, which he thinks consciously diverges from the historical King Philip, against Alfieri's Philip, who is more faithful to the historical model. Similarly, he defends Goethe's conception of Egmont against the objections which chiefly Schiller raised, namely that Goethe had turned Egmont from a married man with a large family into a radiant, captivating youth with no ties at all. And he backs up his remarks by quoting Goethe's arguments against Manzoni.

Does this make Belinsky a defender of historical arbitrariness in drama? Or is it not the new and deeper understanding of the dramatic treatment of history which he is voicing? We believe the latter to be the case. For what have Goethe and Schiller altered in the characters of their heroes? Have they made their heroes unhistorical? Have they removed the specifically historical character of the tragic collisions they portray? We think not. Schiller certainly did this in some cases, but not in the case with which Belinsky is dealing. His conception of King Philip is of the human tragedy, the inner personal breakdown of the absolute monarch, a breakdown which is caused by the inevitable working-out of the typical social-human determinants of despotism and by these alone, not by any malignity indwelling in the king *qua* human being. Is such a collision not historical? It is in the deepest sense of the word, and remains such even if neither the Spanish King Philip nor any other absolute monarch ever in fact experienced such a tragedy. For the historical and human necessity of this tragedy are produced by historical development itself. If it was never experienced—and of this we cannot be certain—then it is only because the individuals who found themselves in this position were not of sufficient human stature to endure such a tragedy.

Admittedly, there is an element of "necessary anachronism" in the loftiness and pathos of this portrayal, an understanding of the inner "problematic" of absolute monarchy, which only became a conscious "problematic" during the Enlightenment. But it is not Schiller's own invention. If one looks, say, at the prince in Lessing's *Emilia Galotti*, it is obvious that it was not this great Enlightener's intention, either, to fight absolute monarchy merely from the outside; he showed in addition how this system, condemned to death and revolutionary destruction by history, ruined its own representatives humanly and morally of historical-social necessity: in lesser instances allowing them simply to degenerate, in greater, leading them on to tragic collisions

and tragic self-laceration. In *Don Carlos* Schiller portrays a monumental instance of the latter kind. Thus Belinsky was wholly in the
right in defending the historical justification of such a play, which
he felt to be more profoundly tragic than Alfieri's historical fidelity,
The superiority of the great German Enlighteners over their predecessors resembles *mutatis mutandis* the superiority of Maxim Gorky's
presentation of the inner tragedies of the best representatives of the
capitalist class over the black-and-white portraits of the agitator
(agitka) playwrights. *Mutatis mutandis* Gorky's *Yegor Bulichev*
provides an historical analogy for the rightness, which Belinsky defended, of young Schiller to state his problem in the way he did.

Belinsky is even more obviously right in the case of Goethe. The
alteration of Egmont's outer circumstances, his family relations etc.
does not affect the historical nature of the collision, which Goethe
presents, at all. Goethe portrays the special character of those aristocrats who, like Egmont and Oranien, have been placed at the head of
the national liberation movement by the circumstances of their time.
This he does with rare historical fidelity, so much so that he is able
to disclose, with true genius, the connection between Egmont's inde-
cisive behaviour and the material basis of his existence. By altering
the material circumstances and psychology of his hero, by involving
him in his love-relationship with Klärchen, Goethe is able to portray
in far more dramatic and plastic a fashion the popular character of
Egmont and of his relations to the people than would have been
possible without this relationship. The kind of Egmont Schiller wished
for would only have had contact with the mass in the popular scenes
in the narrow sense, and the great upsurge at the end of the tragedy
where Klärchen grows into a popular heroine, expressing the coming
triumphant revolt of the people, would have been entirely lost.

Let us sum up. The standpoint of historicism which Goethe and
Hegel, Pushkin and Belinsky uphold centres upon this: that the
writer's historical fidelity consists in the faithful artistic reproduction
of the great collisions, the great crises and turning-points of history.
To express this *historical* conception in an adequate artistic form the
writer may treat individual facts with as much licence as he likes, for
mere fidelity to the individual facts of history without this connection
is utterly valueless. "Truth of passions, verisimilitude of feelings in
imagined circumstances—that is what our mind demands of the
dramatic writer," says Pushkin.

This distinction between real historical fidelity to the whole and
the pseudo-historicism of the mere authenticity of individual facts
naturally applies to the novel as much as to drama. The only difference, as we have repeatedly shown in detail, is that this whole in the
novel is the reflection of other facts of life. What matters in the novel

is fidelity in the reproduction of the material foundations of the life of a given period, its manners and the feelings and thoughts deriving from these. This means, as we have also seen, that the novel is much more closely bound to the specifically historical, individual moments of a period, than is drama. But this never means being tied to any particular historical facts. On the contrary, the novelist must be at liberty to treat these as he likes, if he is to reproduce the much more complex and ramifying totality with historical faithfulness. From the standpoint of the historical novel, too, it is always a matter of chance whether an actual, historical fact, character or story will lend itself to the particular method by which a great novelist conveys his historical faithfulness.

If we take exact cognizance of these circumstances, we see that the writer's relation to historical reality—be he playwright or novelist—can be no different in principle from his relation to reality as a whole. The practice of all great writers teaches us that it is a matter of chance whether the immediate material which life offers them is suitable or not for revealing adequately the laws of life. Balzac, for example, describes how the model for d'Esgrignons (*Cabinet des Antiques*) was in fact condemned in reality and not rescued, like his hero. Another and similar case of which he knew underwent a much less dramatic development, but for the manners of the provinces it was more characteristic. "Thus out of the beginning of one fact and the end of another there emerged this whole. This mode of procedure is necessary for the historian of manners: his task consists in uniting analogous facts into one single picture; is he not compelled to adhere more to the spirit than to the letter of events?"

Even had Balzac not called himself a historian of manners here—and he does so not figuratively, but in a deeply justified sense, it would be no less obvious that his reflections apply as much to the historical novel as to the novel on a contemporary theme. There is no ground whatsoever for supposing that, because events are past, their inner structure and the necessarily accidental character of individual phenomena are thereby rendered invalid. Nor is the fact that they are to be found handed down in memoirs, chronicles, letters and so on any guarantee that this kind of selection will necessarily preserve the essentials of the particular accidents which give artistic life to an underlying reality.

The deeper and more genuinely historical a writer's knowledge of a period, the more freely will he be able to move about inside his subject and the less tied will he feel to individual historical data. Scott's extraordinary genius lay in the fact that he gave the historical novel just such themes as would allow for this "free movement", and so cleared the way for its development; whereas the earlier traditions of his so-called predecessors had obstructed all such freedom of movement, preventing even a genuine talent from developing. Naturally a special difficulty is involved in the treatment of specifically historical subject-matter. Every really original writer who portrays a new outlook upon a certain field has to contend with the prejudices of his readers. But the image which the public has of any familiar historical figure need not necessarily be a false one. Indeed, with the growth of a real historical sense and of real historical knowledge it becomes more and more accurate. But even this correct image may in certain circumstances be a hindrance to the writer who wishes to reproduce the spirit of an age faithfully and authentically. It would require a particularly happy accident for all the well-known and attested actions of a familiar historical figure to correspond to the purposes of literature. (For the sake of simplicity we are assuming both that the historical image is an accurate one and that the playwright or novelist who deals with history is really aiming at historical truth.)

In many cases quite insoluble problems occur. We have seen the freedom with which great playwrights of the classical age refashioned well-known historical figures and yet adhered faithfully to history in the large sense. Balzac admires again and again the shrewdness with which Scott avoids such dangers, not only in making the protagonists of history minor figures—this corresponds to the inner laws of the historical novel, but also in choosing wherever possible unknown and unattested episodes from the lives of these figures. This avoidance is not a compromise; for the possibility of radically refashioning an historically very familiar figure is, for reasons we already know, more difficult in the novel than in drama. The fact that the novel is closer to life and necessarily includes more detail leaves less possibility for the kind of generalized raising of a character to the level of the typical that we have observed and traced in drama.

We repeat, a writer's relation to history is not something special and isolated, it is an important component of his relation to the whole of reality and especially society. Surveying all the problems which occur in novel and drama as a result of the writer's relation to historical reality, we see that there is not a single essential problem which is unique to history. This of course does not mean that the writer's relation to history can be mechanically equated with his relation to contemporary society. On the contrary, there is a very complex interaction between his relation to the present and his relation to history. But a closer theoretical and historical examination of this connection would show that the writer's relation to the social problems of the present is decisive in this interaction. This we have been able to observe both in the rise of the historical novel as well as in the peculiar, uneven development of historical drama and its theory.

These observations, however, have a much broader theoretical foundation, namely the whole question of whether the past is knowable. This question always depends upon the extent to which the present is known, the extent to which the contemporary situation can clearly reveal the particular trends which have objectively led to the present; and, subjectively, it depends on how and to what extent the social structure of the present, its level of development, the character of its class struggles etc. further, inhibit or prevent knowledge of past development. Marx states very clearly the objective connection which exists here: "The anatomy of man is a key to the anatomy of the ape. The indications of something higher in the subordinate animal species, however, can only be understood when what is higher is itself known. Bourgeois economy provides the key to the classical world etc. But by no means in the manner of the economists who blur all historical distinctions and see the bourgeois social form in all social forms. One can understand tribute and tithe etc. when one knows about ground rent, one must not, however, identify them."

Marx comes out very sharply against the modernizing of history in these remarks. In other places he shows how such false notions of the past arise of historical necessity from the social problems of the present. Thus, in refuting false conceptions of the past, he is simultaneously providing fresh historical confirmation of his conception, quoted here, that the knowledge of history is an objective process. These connections are of the utmost importance for us, for we have seen what a high level had to be reached in the epic handling of contemporary social problems, what deep insight was required of writers into the problems of their own day, before a genuinely historical novel could arise.

If one eschews both the petty-philological and the mechanical-sociological attitude towards the development of the historical novel, one sees that its classical form arises out of the great social novel and then, enriched by a conscious historical attitude, flows back into the latter. On the one hand, the development of the social novel first makes possible the historical novel; on the other, the historical novel transforms the social novel into a genuine history of the present, an authentic history of manners, something which the novel of the eighteenth century was already striving for in the works of its most eminent representatives. Thus, we cannot separate the historical novel in the narrower sense from the fortunes of the novel in general, for neither the deepest problems involved in portraying reality nor the historical laws of development of the genre will allow us to do so. (The course of development of historical drama is different, for reasons which we have shown, but it depends no less upon these fundamental issues.) Hence, the question of the historical novel as an independent genre only ever arises if for some reason or other the proper and adequate connection with a correct understanding of the present is lacking, if it is either *not yet* or *no longer* present. Thus, quite contrary to what so many moderns think, the historical novel does not become an independent genre as a result of its special faithfulness to the past. It becomes such when the objective or subjective conditions for historical faithfulness in the large sense are either not yet or no longer present. When this happens a number of highly complicated and highly metaphysical "criteria" are concocted to give this separation a theoretical justification. (The significance of these connections both in theory and practice can, naturally, only be brought fully to light when we deal with the post-1848 novel. Thus, a detailed analysis of these problems will have to wait until the following chapters.)

If one treats the Marxist problem of genre seriously, acknowledging a genre only where one sees a peculiar artistic reflection of peculiar facts of life, there is not a single fundamental problem one can adduce to justify the creation of a specific genre of historical subject-matter either in the novel or in drama. Naturally, a preoccupation with history will always produce its individual and special tasks. But none of these specific problems is or can be of sufficient weight to justify a really independent genre of historical literature.

CHAPTER THREE

The Crisis of Bourgeois Realism

FOR THE countries of Western and Central Europe the Revolution of 1848 means a decisive alteration in class groupings and in class attitudes to all important questions of social life, to the perspectives of social development. The June battle of the Paris proletariat in 1848 constitutes a turning-point in history on an international scale. Despite Chartism, despite sporadic uprisings in France during the "bourgeois monarchy", despite the rising of the German weavers in 1844, here for the first time a decisive battle is carried out by force of arms between proletariat and bourgeoisie, here for the first time the proletariat enters upon the world-historical stage as an armed mass, resolved upon the final struggle; during these days the bourgeoisie for the first time fights for the naked continuance of its economic and political rule. One has only to trace closely the history of events in Germany in 1848 to see the significant turn which the proletarian uprising and defeat in Paris gave to the development of the bourgeois revolution in Germany. Of course, anti-democratic tendencies as well as a disposition to turn bourgeois-democratic revolutionary trends into a rotten compromise with the feudal-absolutist régime were already present before then in German middle-class circles. Immediately after the March days they became much more pronounced. Nevertheless it is the June battle of the Paris proletariat which produces a decisive change in the bourgeois camp, accelerating to an extraordinary degree the inner process of differentiation which is to transform revolutionary democracy into compromising liberalism.

This change affects all spheres of bourgeois ideology. It would be altogether superficial and wrong to suppose that, when a class turns its back so radically upon its earlier political aims and ideals, the spheres of ideology, the fates of science and art can remain untouched. Marx repeatedly showed in great detail how significant the class struggles between bourgeoisie and proletariat were for the classical social science of bourgeois development, political economy. And today, particularly in the light of the recently published works of Marx and Engels of the pre-1848 period, if we follow attentively the process of dissolution of Hegelian philosophy, we can see that the philosophical struggles of the various trends and nuances within Hegelianism were in essence nothing but partisan struggles of the period preparatory to the coming bourgeois-democratic Revolution of 1848. It is only in the light of these connections that it becomes clear why Hegelian philosophy, which from the middle twenties had dominated the entire intellectual life of Germany, "suddenly" disappeared after the defeat of the Revolution as a result of the betrayal by the German bourgeoisie of its own earlier bourgeois revolutionary aims. Hegel, earlier the central figure in Germany's intellectual life, was "suddenly" forgotten, became a "dead dog".

In his analyses of the Revolution of 1848, Marx writes at great length about this change, about its causes and consequences. He also provides formulations of extraordinary intellectual depth, summing up this change and its effect upon all spheres of bourgeois ideological activity. "The bourgeoisie", writes Marx, "had a true insight into the fact that all the weapons which it had forged against feudalism turned their points against itself, that all the means of education which it had produced rebelled against its own civilization, that all the gods which it had created had fallen away from it. It understood that all the so-called liberties and organs of progress attacked and menaced its class rule at its social foundation and its political summit simultaneously, and had therefore become *socialistic*."

We can only examine this change briefly here with respect to its effects on historical feeling and on the sense and understanding of history; only in relation to those aspects, therefore, which are of immediate and vital importance to our problem.

1. *Changes in the Conception of History after the Revolution of 1848.*

Here, as in our introductory remarks to this work, we are concerned not with an internal affair of history *qua* science, not with a scholars' dispute over method, but with the mass experience of history itself, with an experience shared by the widest circles of bourgeois society, by those even who were not in the least interested in the science of history or aware that a change had taken place within it. In the same way the awakening of a more conscious sense of history had influenced the experience and ideas of the broadest masses without their necessarily knowing that their new feeling for the historical connections of life had produced a Thierry in historical science and a Hegel in philosophy etc.

The nature of this relationship must therefore be specially emphasized so that, when we speak of a change in the conception of history among authors of historical novels, it is not thought that we mean that their writing was necessarily directly affected by the changes in historical science. We can of course find influences of this kind. Flaubert, for instance, was not only acquainted with Taine, Renan etc. through their works, but also knew them very well personally. The influence of Jakob Burckhardt on Conrad Ferdinand Meyer is well known; the immediate influence of Nietzsche's conception of history on writers perhaps extends even further, and so on. However it is not this philologically demonstrable influence which is important, but rather the *common character of the reactions to reality* which in history and literature produce analogous subjects and forms of historical consciousness. These reactions have their roots in the briefly sketched change in the entire political and intellectual life of the middle class. If individual historians or philosophers achieved a notable influence in these questions, this influence is not a primary cause, but itself a consequence of the new ideological tendencies among both writers and readers, produced by the social-historical development. If then, in the following, we cite a number of leading ideologists of this new attitude to history, we regard them as representatives of general social currents which they have simply formulated in the most effective literary manner.

There is, however, one more introductory remark to be made. In the pre-1848 period the bourgeoisie was also the ideological leader of social development. Its new, historical defence of progress blazes the trail for the whole ideological development of this period. The proletariat's conception of history matures upon this basis, extending the last great phase of bourgeois ideology by means of criticism and struggle and by overcoming its limitations. The important forerunners of socialism who did not absorb these ideas were, in this respect, mystical or retrograde. This situation is very radically altered by the change which 1848 brings about.

The division of every people into "two nations" took place—in tendency, at least—in the field of ideology, too. The class struggles of the first half of the nineteenth century had already led, on the eve of the 1848 Revolution, to the scientific formulation of Marxism. The latter contained all progressive views on history in a "sublated" form, that is in the threefold Hegelian sense of the word: they were not only criticized and annulled, but also preserved and raised to a higher level.

The fact that in this period we find strong influences of general bourgeois ideology in both the working-class movement and the democratic currents allied to it, does not contradict the fundamental fact of the "two nations". The working-class movement does not develop in a vacuum, but surrounded by all the ideologies of decline of bourgeois decadence, and the "historic mission" of opportunism within the working-class movement consists here in "mediating", in smoothing out the sharp division and guiding it onto a bourgeois path. But all these complex inter-relations should not obscure the fundamental fact that the ideologies of the bourgeoisie analysed here are no longer the leading ideologies of a whole epoch, but simply class ideologies in a much narrower sense.

The central problem in which the change of attitude to history is manifested is that of *progress*. We saw that the most notable writers and thinkers of the period before 1848 made their most important step forward by giving an historical formulation to the idea of progress: they advanced to a concept of the contradictory character of human progress, even if it was only relatively correct and never complete. However, the events of the class struggle presented to the ideologists of the bourgeoisie so threatening a prospect for the future of their society and class, that the disinterested courage with which the contradictions of progress had been disclosed and declared was bound to disappear. How closely the attitude to progress connects with the future perspective of bourgeois society, can best be studied by glancing at the intelligent opponents of the idea of progress in the pre-1848 period. The latter still stated their ideas fairly uninhibitedly, since the social dangers to which they alluded and which determined their thinking were not yet so menacingly immediate as to provoke apologetic falsifications. Such is the way, for example, the Romantic reactionary, Théophile Gautier, writes about this question even in the thirties. He derides all ideas of progress as shallow and foolish; he treats Fourier's utopias with irony, but at the same time adds that if progress is at all possible, then only by this means; everything else is a bitter mockery, a spiritless harlequinade: "The phalanstery is truly an advance on the abbey of Thelème."

In these circumstances the idea of progress undergoes a regression. Classical economics, which in its day had boldly admitted certain contradictions in captitalist economy, changes into the smooth and mendacious harmony of vulgar economics. The fall of Hegelian philosophy in Germany means the disappearance of the idea of the contradictory character of progress. So far as an ideology of progress continues to prevail—it is for a long time still the leading ideology of the liberal bourgeoisie—every element of contradiction is extinguished from it, history is conceived as a smooth straightforward evolution. On a European scale and for a long period this is increasingly the central idea of the new science of sociology, which replaces the attempts to master the contradictions of historical progress dialectically.

Admittedly, this change is bound up with a renunciation of the high-flown idealism of Hegelian philosophy and, here and there, even with an at least partial return to the ideology of the Enlightenment and mechanical materialism (e.g. in Germany in the 50's and 60's). But it is precisely the weakest and most unhistorical tendencies of the Enlightenment which are revived, quite apart from the fact that certain currents of thought, which in the middle of the eighteenth century contained seeds of the right conception, in this renewed form inevitably became obstacles to the adequate scientific comprehension of history.

Let us illustrate this with two examples which are of the greatest importance for the conception of history in this period. It was a great and important historical advance when the Enlighteners of the eighteenth century started to investigate the natural conditions surrounding social development and attempted to apply the categories and results of the natural sciences directly to the knowledge of society. Naturally, this gave rise to much that was perverse and unhistorical, but in the struggle with the traditional theological conception of history it signified a very considerable advance at the time. It was quite different in the second half of the nineteenth century. If historians or sociologists now attempted to make Darwinism, for example, the immediate basis of an understanding of historical development, this could only lead to a perversion and distortion of historical connections. Darwinism becomes an abstract phrase and the old reactionary Malthus normally appears as its sociological "core". In the course of later development the rhetorical application of Darwinism to history becomes a straightforward apology for the brutal dominion of capital. Capitalist competition is swollen into a metaphysical history-dissolving mystique by the "eternal law" of the struggle for existence. The most telling historical conception of this kind is the philosophy of Nietzsche, which makes a composite mythology out of Darwinism and the Greek contest, Agon.

The other, just as characteristic, example is that of race. As is well-known, the problem of race plays an important part both in the historical explanations of the Enlightenment and in the historical works of Thierry and his school later on—here particularly. Now when Taine makes the idea of race the centrepiece of his sociology (not to mention such out-and-out reactionaries as Gobineau), this appears at first sight a continuation of these tendencies. But this is deceptive, because for Thierry the problem of race which he never fully analysed belonged to his central conception of history as the history of class struggles. The counterposing of the Saxons and Normans in England and of the Franks and Gauls in France forms no more than a transition to the analysis of the class struggles between the rising "third estate" and the nobility in the history of the Middle Ages and modern times. Thierry did not succeed in unravelling the complicated tangle of national and class antagonisms during the rise of the modern nations, but his theory of the struggle of races was the first step towards a coherent and scientific history of progress. With Taine the tendency is in the opposite direction. Under the guise of pseudo-scientific terminology race is turned into a thoroughly unhistorical and anti-historical mythical entity. History is negated in a reactionary fashion and disolved partly into an ahistorical system of sociological "laws", partly into a mystified philosophy of history, in essence just as ahistorical.

We are naturally unable to enumerate here, even remotely, the different, often conflicting trends into which the historicism of the earlier period disintegrated. In part, this development takes the form of an open denial of history. We need just mention the philosophy of Schopenhauer, which in this period was ousting the teachings of Hegel in Germany, and which gradually continued its triumphant march throughout every country in Europe. But this abstract and radical denial of history in any shape could not long maintain its dominant position. Parallel tendencies arose which sought to stabilize anti-historicism in a historical form. Ranke's conception of history, like Schopenhauer's philosophy, was formed before 1848. But it only became an important and dominant trend after the defeat of the bourgeois revolution. Ranke's conception pretends to be a truly historical one and takes arms against Hegelian philosophy on account of its constructive character. But if we look at the real core of the polemic, we find that Ranke and his school are denying the idea of a contradictory process of human advance. According to their conception history has no direction, no summits and no depressions: "All epochs of history are equally near to God." Thus, there is perpetual movement, but it has no direction: history is a collection and reproduction of interesting facts about the past.

Since history, to an ever increasing extent, is no longer conceived as the prehistory of the present, or, if it is, then in a superficial, unilinear, evolutionary way, the endeavours of the earlier period to grasp the stages of the historical process in their real individuality, as they really were objectively, lose their living interest. Where it is not the "uniqueness" of earlier events that is presented, history is *modernized*. This means that the historian proceeds from the belief that the fundamental structure of the past is economically and ideologically the same as that of the present. Thus, in order to understand the present all one has to do is to attribute the thoughts, feelings and motives of present-day men to the past. In this way, conceptions of history like those of Mommsen, Pöhlmann etc. arise. The very influential art-historical theories of Riegl and his followers, though they have different points of departure, rest on the same assumptions. As a result history is dissolved into a collection of curiosities and oddities. If a historian refuses to apply these methods in full, then he must stop at a mere description of these curiosities; he remains a raconteur of historical anecdotes. If he consistently modernizes, then history really does become a collection of curiosities. Thus, for example, if capitalism and socialism really did exist in ancient history in the modern sense, then the conduct of the ancient exploiters and exploited would indeed be the most curious, quirkish and anecdotal affair imaginable.

This tendency to modernize, and, closely connected therewith, to mystify history, which in the age of imperialism reached its apex in conceptions like those of Spengler, is intimately bound up with the philosophical change in bourgeois ideology after 1848. Both Hegel's objective idealism as well as the writings of the great historians of the time were permeated through and through with the conviction that objective reality, and therewith history, was knowable. Thus, the important representatives of this period approached history in a materialist fashion, however unconscious and hence incomplete their materialism; that is, they attempted to uncover the real driving forces of history as they objectively worked and to explain history from them. This now ceases right along the line. Vulgarized bourgeois economics can no longer act as an auxiliary to history: during this development economics itself turns into an analysis of economic notions rather than the objective facts of production (theory of marginal utility). The single original methodological feature of the new science of sociology is that it separates knowledge of the "laws" of social behaviour from economics and renders them independent. Philosophy, which in varying ways turns towards subjective idealism, comes increasingly to regard "facts of consciousness" as the only starting-point for a scientific method. In this way the modernization of history gains a broad ideological basis. It seems that the only possible way of "understanding" the past lies in projecting our way of seeing things, in starting out from our own notions.

All these tendencies which hitherto we have observed mainly among currents more or less acknowledging progress are intensified among the heirs to the Romantic critique of capitalism. Criticism of the capitalist division of labour, of capitalism's lack of culture etc. enters increasingly into the service of the most reactionary classes, the most reactionary wing of the ruling classes. Marx and Engels, as early as 1850, give an interesting critique of this change in the case of two outstanding representatives of the pre-1848 period. They show how Guizot, out of fear of a proletarian revolution, nullifies all the achievements of the French school of historians, how a vulgar evolutionism cancels out all concrete differences and problems of development in English and French history. Then, in a discussion of Carlyle's latest works, they show how the latter's earlier criticism of capitalism, which contained revolutionary elements, has become an ideology of the most naked and brutal reaction.

Later developments clearly proved the correctness of Marx's analysis. Whereas earlier the Romantic critique of capitalism, despite its reactionary glorification of the Middle Ages, had in many respects been a democratic and, occasionally, even rebellious protest against the oligarchic rule of the big capitalists, as in the case of Cobbett and young Carlyle himself, it now developed more and more in the direction of clear hostility to democracy and combated the democratic elements still present in capitalism and even in imperialism with ever increasing determination. The fight against capitalism's lack of culture becomes a fight against democracy, against "massification", in favour of a new reactionary dictatorship of the "strong", the élite etc. It suffices to think of such sociologists as Pareto or Michels. This anti-democratic development produces its own philosophic-cum-psychological science, whose sole purpose is to unmask the activity of the masses "scientifically" as being from the outset unreasonable, irrational and senseless (Nietzsche, Le Bon etc.)

For literature during the transition period the views of Taine, Burckhardt and Nietzsche were of especial importance. We shall select only a few aspects of Burckhardt's methodology and conception of history which will serve to illuminate from the ideological side those tendencies which appear in literature. We may disregard those aspects of his conception which are already contained in our general picture, for example the denial of progress; this can now be taken as known.

Burckhardt starts from a deliberate and conscious subjective attitude to history: "One cannot avoid a good measure of subjective arbitrariness in one's choice of subjects. We are 'unscientific'." There exist, according to Burckhardt, bare transmitted facts which only the individual subjectivity has the power of bringing to life. According to his theory a very important role is played by historical anecdotes in this animation of history. They form "an imagined history, which tells us what was expected of men and what is characteristic of them". (The reader will surely recall here the programme of the Romantic, Vigny.)

The most important consequences of this conception is its separation of history's great men from history's lawful course, its isolation of them and raising them into myth. Burckhardt states this idea repeatedly and with emphasis: "Greatness is what we are not... Real greatness is a *mystery*, its effect is magic" etc. These views of Burckhardt have become extremely widespread and popular as a result of his great historical portrayals, particularly of the Renaissance. This is a natural and inevitable consequence of the ideological retreat from the earlier period's conception of progress.

Of course, Burckhardt himself is no simple apologist for the glory of the capitalist "strong man". On the contrary, as far as the present is concerned, he is tormented by the gravest doubts and caught in a ceaseless dilemma. This characteristic division in Burckhardt is also the expression of the general tendency of the period. Burckhardt approaches his glorified great men with mingled admiration and dread. Through his means the Renaissance man of violence becomes the ideal model of a "cultured" capitalism which has overcome every manifestation of democracy. He himself, however, regards these men, who combine "deep depravity with noblest harmony", with a feeling that "balances between admiration and horror".

This introduces a double and contradictory subjectivism into historical obervation which simulates a kind of dialectic in its dividedness, but which, in reality, only mirrors the disunity of the observer's standpoint and has nothing to do with history itself. That is, historical figures are separated from the real driving forces of their epoch, and their deeds, thus rendered incomprehensible, acquire a decorative magnificence by virtue of their very incomprehensibility. This decorative portrayal is further intensified by the special emphasis and central place given to the brutal excesses of history.

Such a figure then having emerged, who is "beyond Good and Evil", Burckhardt the historian approaches him with a present day moral yardstick, with the withdrawn and refined ethics of the late capitalist intellectual. Wherever possible, he introduces his own conflicts into the past. So that the apparent dialectic of morality and beauty, which thus arises, is not an inner contradiction of the thing itself, but a mirror of the incapacity of such subjectivity to grasp the movement of historical reality in a unified way.

What in Burckhardt existed only in seed, blossoms into a system with Nietzsche. Here again, we can only refer to a few aspects of decisive importance to our problem. Nietzsche's extraordinary influence rests not least on the seriousness with which he took the agnosticism and subjectivism of his time and the extreme boldness with which he came to grips with them. He declares openly and plainly "that it is not possible to live with truth". From this standpoint he pronounces the essence of art to be: "an interested, in the highest degree, and *ruthlessly* interested adjustment of things, a fundamental falsification, an exclusion precisely of the merely ascertaining, cognizing, *objective* sense ... Pleasure in conquest by the injection *a meaning*."

This already is the philosophy of the lie as the necessary mode of reaction of a living human being to reality.

Where history is concerned Nietzsche, if anything, puts this even more emphatically. He takes arms against academic history writing, against its isolation from life. However, the relation which he establishes between historical science and life is that of the conscious distortion of history, above all the conscious omission of unpleasant facts unfavourable to "life". Nietzsche relates history to life by invoking the following fact of life: "All action requires the ability to forget."

This already is a cynical philosophy of apologetics. What the university professors in the pay of the bourgeoisie, cowardly hiding behind the mask of objectivity, conceal with embarrassment, Nietzsche here pronounces openly and unashamedly. The historical necessity for the bourgeoisie of his time to falsify the facts of history, increasingly to omit them appears to Nietzsche a "profound", "eternal", "biological" truth of life.

What is extremely characteristic for the ideological development of this whole period is the way Nietzsche presents this philosophical justification of the apologetic falsification of history. Hence we quote it here: "What such a nature does not master, it may soon forget; it is no longer there, the horizon is closed and whole, and there is nothing to recall that beyond there are still men, passions, doctrines and purposes. And this is an universal law; everything that lives can only become healthy, strong and fruitful within a horizon; can it not draw a horizon round itself or, on the other hand, is it too self-centred to enclose its own outlook within a foreign horizon, then it must sink wearily or over-hastily towards a timely end."

The philosophy of historical solopism is stated here, perhaps for the first time, in its most radical form. The theory itself is, admittedly, already present in the culture and race conception of earlier and contemporary sociology. But it is not until Nietzsche that it is generalized in such a cynical fashion. What it says in effect is that each unit, be it individual, race or nation can experience no more than itself. History exists only as a mirror of this ego, only as something to suit the special life needs of the latter. History is a chaos, in itself is of no concern to us, but to which everyone may attribute a "meaning" which suits him, according to his needs.

In this early work Nietzsche also classifies three possible ways of approaching history: the monumental, the antiquarian and the critical method. All three methods are defined in a similar "biological" way, i.e. none of them aims at knowledge of objective reality, but only at adapting and grouping suitable historical facts in accordance with the life requirements of a certain type. (Here we have the schema of the unhistorical conception of society and history for a whole period: Nietzsche's schema corresponds equally to Spengler's procedure, to the "sociology of knowledge" and to Menshevist vulgar sociology.)

It is unnecessary to say much more about the different forms in which this subjectivism vis-à-vis history developed. We have quoted Burckhardt and Nietzsche as representatives of broad currents in this question. But as a concluding example let us recall Croce's conception of history in order to show quite clearly that this tendency continues undiminished through the whole period and that so-called tendencies towards objective idealism—Croce is a neo-Hegelian— do not affect this main trend. "All true history is history of the present", says Croce. This, however, should not be interpreted as connecting history with the objective problems of the present; it is not a conception according to which the present can only be comprehended objectively through its prehistory. No, for Croce, too, history is something subjective, an experience. He elaborates his thesis in the following way: he quotes a few examples of subjects treated by history and says: "At the moment not one of these moves me: and hence for me, at this moment, these chronicles are not histories, but at the most titles of history books. They are histories, or will be such, for those who have thought or will think about them, and for me they were such when I thought about them and used them for my intellectual requirements, and they will be such again if I think of them again." This theory of history has only to be turned into verse to produce a poem by Hoffmannsthal or Henri de Régnier.

In all these theories one sees the convulsive attempts of the ideologists of this period to turn their gaze away from the real facts and tendencies of history, deny them recognition and at the same time to find an illuminating, up-to-date explanation in the "eternal essence of life". History as a total process disappears; in its place there remains a chaos to be ordered as one likes. This chaos is approached from consciously subjective viewpoints. Only the great men of history provide firm holds in this chaos; they are always rescuing mankind in a mysterious way from downfall. The comedy of this situation (or at best tragi-comedy) can only really be judged if one looks a little more closely at the real historical "saviours" of this period—Napoleon III and Bismarck. Burckhardt and Nietzsche, of course, have too much intelligence and good taste to admire blindly these "great men" of their time as really great men, in the same way as the large mass of the class they represented. But their attitude to great men in general is in fact the same as that of the Parisian philistine to his "badinguet" or the German beer-drinker to his "iron chancellor". Burckhardt's and Nietzsche's intellectual superiority comes to this: dissatisfied with the real Bismarck, they conjure up out of a mythical history greater and, above all, aesthetically more refined Bismarcks for their own purposes.

The historical-political categories which assist them in these constructions (abstract power, "Realpolitik" etc.) bear entirely the stamp of the actions of the pseudo-great men of their own period. The fact that Burckhardt constantly makes moralizing reservations, that he sees all power as inherently evil, does not, as we have seen, importantly alter the fundamental principles of this approach; indeed it only increases the contradictions of the latter, approximating it to the on-the-one-hand/on-the-other-hand attitude of the petty bourgeois, whose intellectual level he normally transcends.

What then can art take from a past conceived in this way? This past appears, more so even than the present, as a gigantic irridescent chaos. Nothing is really objectively and organically connected with the objective character of the present; and for this reason a freely roaming subjectivity can fasten where and how it likes. And since history has been deprived of its real inner greatness—the dialectic of contradictory development, which has been abstracted intellectually —all that remains for the artists of this period is a pictorial and decorative grandeur. History becomes a collection of exotic anecdotes. At the same time and again, inevitably, as real historical relations are less and less understood, wild, sensual, indeed bestial features come to occupy the foreground. In all art of this period depicting the present, inability to understand the great problems of the age is accompanied by brutality in the presentation of physical processes, veiled by biological mysticism (Zola as against Balzac and Stendhal). This is also true, as we shall see, of the portrayal of history.

It is very interesting from this point of view to hear the judgments of the leading critics of this period on the classical type of the historical novel. Taine, who in his history of English literature describes the world of Shakespeare as a fascinating madhouse, full of witty and passionate lunatics, complains above all of the lack of brutality in Scott. "Walter Scott stops at the threshold of the soul and the entrance-hall of history; in the Rennaissance and the Middle Ages he selects only what is proper and pleasing, omitting the naïve language, the unbridled sensuality, the bestial savagery ..." This view is faithfully echoed by his pupil, George Brandes. Walter Scott, he says, "presented earlier times with such a strong diminution of their brutal elements that historical truth suffers very greatly". This attitude determines the judgment of the most progressive literature of this time on the classical period of the historical novel. Zola regards Balzac's preoccupation with Scott as an incomprehensible fad. Brandes sums up his judgment by saying that Scott's works slip from the hands of the educated; they "are snapped up by those simply after some light reading or they are preserved and bound by the educated to be revered as birthday and confirmation presents for their sons and daughters, nephews and nieces".

The writers themselves, despite their loss of contact with the not-so-distant classical period of the historical novel—an historically inevitable loss, as we shall soon see—mark the literary summit of this period. Their conception of history, with all its subjective arbitrariness, is nevertheless an honest protest against the ugliness and sordid triviality of their capitalist present. The past is stylized and idealized into the gigantic and barbaric out of romantic protest. (In the following section we start off with a detailed examination of the chief example of this trend, Flaubert's *Salammbô*.)

However problematic this literary trend, it nevertheless towers above the deadly boring historical novel of apologetics for the present, apologetics for that "Realpolitik" which led to the shameful capitulation of the German bourgeoisie before the "Bonapartist monarchy" of the Hohenzollerns and Bismarck. Since we are analyzing types of development in terms of world literature, we can only just mention Gustav Freytag's *Ahnen* (*Forefathers*) as the best literary product of this trend.

This kind of literature still has a certain significance as regards content, even though it is the content of liberal compromise. But the severance of the present from history creates an historical novel which drops to the level of light entertainment. Its themes are indiscriminate and unrelated and it is full of an adventurous or emptily antiquarian, an exciting or mythical exoticism. Aldous Huxley wittily ridicules this "magic of history" which from Ebers to Maurois is the stock-in-trade of historical light reading. He says that among the "cultivated" history provides a kind of family remembrance, a subject of family conversation. "All the more or less picturesque figures of history are our cultural uncles, our cultural aunts", if one does not know them, one is an outsider, one does not belong to the "family".

But both in history and in the history of literature, these family remembrances are very short-lived. An exotic subject crops up, sets the cultured afire for a year or two; after five years the whole hubbub is forgotten; after ten years it is only the diligent literary scholars who will remember that there was ever a famous historical novelist called Felix Dahn. Our method of approach must ignore these mass graves of former celebrities.

2.   *Making Private, Modernization and Exoticism.*

Flaubert's *Salammbô* is the great representative work of this new phase of development in the historical novel. It combines all the high artistic qualities of Flaubert's style. Stylistically, it is the paradigm of

Flaubert's artistic aims; which is why it shows so much more clearly than the writings of the mediocre and untalented writers of this period the unresolved contradictions, the irremovable inner "problematic" of the new historical novel.

Flaubert formulated his aims programmatically. He says that he wished to apply the procedure and method of the modern novel to antiquity. And this programme was fully acknowledged by the important representatives of the new trend of naturalism. Zola's criticism of *Salammbô* is essentially a realization of this statement by Flaubert. Zola admittedly, finds fault with a number of details, but accepts that Flaubert has applied the methods of the new realism correctly to historical material.

Outwardly *Salammbô* has not had the outstanding success of *Madame Bovary*. Nevertheless its echo has been quite strong. The leading French critic of the period, Sainte-Beuve, devoted a whole series of articles to it. Flaubert himself considered this critique so important that in a letter to Sainte-Beuve, published later, he took up all his critic's points in detail. This controversy illuminates so sharply the new problems which had arisen in this new phase of the historical novel that we must deal at length with the main arguments of the polemic.

Sainte-Beuve's basic critical position is deprecatory, despite his respect for Flaubert's literary personality. What makes this depreciation so interesting for us is that the critic himself takes up a similar philosophical and literary position in many respects to the Flaubert he criticizes. The difference is that the older Sainte-Beuve is still somewhat bound to the traditions of the earlier period; he is more flexible and willing to compromise than Flaubert, particularly in artistic questions. Flaubert pursued his path to its logical conclusion with the radical disregard of a deeply convinced and important writer. Sainte-Beuve's criticism, therefore, of Flaubert's creative method is certainly not that of the Scott-Balzac period, as we shall see. Indeed in this period Sainte-Beuve proposed and even realized artistic views which in many respects approached those of Flaubert and sharply contrasted with those of Balzac.

Flaubert keenly felt this affinity between his own basic position and that of his critic. Thus, in his letter to Sainte-Beuve, the author of *Port Royal*, he presents his critic with the following *argumentum ad hominem*: "One last question, master, an improper question: why do you find Schahabarim almost comic and your good fellows of Port Royal so serious? For me M. Singlin is funereal beside my elephants ... And it is precisely because they (the characters of Port Royal, G.L.) are very distant from me that I admire your talent in trying to make them intelligible to me. For I believe and wish to live in Port

Royal even less than I do in Carthage. Port Royal, too, was exclusive, unnatural, forced, all of a piece and yet true. Why do you not want two truths to exist, two contrary excesses, two different monstrosities?"

It is interesting to compare Flaubert's praise for Sainte-Beuve here with Balzac's entirely negative judgment on Port-Royal. Balzac and Flaubert are fairly close to one another in their judgment of the world which Sainte-Beuve, as an historian with artistic pretentions, presents. Both see the fragmented, eccentric, bagatelle nature of Sainte-Beuve's picture of history. But while Balzac passionately rejects such a conception of history, Flaubert regards it with an interested and sceptical curiosity. And there is no question here of simple politeness on the part of Flaubert towards the famous critic. His discussion in his correspondence of the Goncourts' historical pictures of the eighteenth century, for example, clearly proves the sincerity of these remarks, for there these Sainte-Beuve tendencies are pushed to the extreme. What comes out in all these cases is the new feeling of the leading ideologists towards history.

Of course, Flaubert's position in this process is not an average one. His literary greatness is expressed in the fact that the general tendency of the time appears in his work with an honest, passionate consistency. While in most other writers of the time, a negative attitude towards the contemporary prose of bourgeois life was simply a matter of aesthetic amusement or, frequently, of reactionary feeling, in Flaubert it is an intense disgust, a vehement hatred.

This disgust and hatred are behind Flaubert's interest in history: "I am weary of ugly things and sordid surroundings. Bovary has disgusted me with bourgeois morals for some time to come. I am going to live, for several years perhaps, inside a subject of splendour, far from the modern world of which I am heartily sick". And in another letter, also written while he was at work on Salammbô: "When one reads Salammbô, one will not, I hope, think of the Author. Few will guess how sad one had to be in order to resuscitate Carthage! There's a Thebaid to which disgust with modern life has driven me."

Thus Flaubert set himself a consistent programme: to reawaken a vanished world of no concern to us. It was precisely because of his deep hatred for modern society that he sought, passionately and paradoxically, a world which would in no way resemble it, which would have no connection with it, direct or indirect. Of course, this lack of connection—or rather the illusion of such—is at the same time the subjective factor which connects Flaubert's exotic historical subject matter with the everyday life of the present. For one must not forget that he tried to plan and execute his social novels, too, as a bystander, a non-participant. The letters he wrote while working on them testify to this again and again. And similarly one has to see that in both cases the programmatic non-partisanship, the famous "impassibilité" turns out to be an illusion : Flaubert reveals his attitude to both Emma Bovary and Salammbô through the atmosphere he creates. The only difference one can really discover in the treatment of the two themes is that the author is not in fact very emotionally involved with the masses of protectors and enemies of Carthage, while the everyday world of the contemporary novels kindles unceasing hatred and love in him. (It would be too superficial altogether to overlook this factor; it is enough to think of Dussardin in *L'Education Sentimentale*.) This all explains why Flaubert could think it possible to use the same artistic means for both *Salammbô* and *Madame Bovary*. At the same time, however, it also explains the completely different artistic results : the artistic fruitfulness of genuine hatred and love, however hidden and suppressed in the one case, the transformation of disinterestedness into sterile exoticism in the other.

In the attempt to solve this task artistically the contradictions in Flaubert's position come out very plainly. Flaubert wishes to portray this world realistically, using the artistic means which he himself had discovered a few years earlier for *Madame Bovary* and there brought to perfection. But now it is not the grey everyday reality of French provincial life to which this realism of minutely observed and exactly described detail is to be applied; instead it is the alien and distant, incomprehensible but picturesque, decorative, grandiose, gorgeous, cruel and exotic world of Carthage which is to arise before us. This explains Flaubert's desperate struggle to evoke a graphic picture of old Carthage by means of exact study and exact production of archaeological detail.

Sainte-Beuve has a strong sense of the artistic discrepancy which results from this aim. He is always pointing out how the description of objects in Flaubert, the dead environment of men, overwhelms the portrayal of the men themselves : he criticizes the fact that, though all these details are correctly and brilliantly described in Flaubert, they do not add up to a whole, not even in relation to the dead objects. Flaubert describes doors, locks etc., all the components of a house, but the architect who builds the whole is nowhere to be seen. Sainte-Beuve sums up this criticism as follows : "the political side, the character of the persons, the genius of the people, the aspects whereby the particular history of this seafaring and, in its own way, civilizing people is of concern to history in general and of interest to the great current of civilization, are sacrificed here or subordinated to the exorbitant, descriptive side, to a dilettantism which, unable to apply itself to anything but rare ruins, is compelled to exaggerate them".

That these remarks hit a central defect in *Salammbô* is shown by

Flaubert's despairing letters written while at work on the book. Thus he writes to a friend: "I am now full of doubts about the whole, about the general plan; I think there are too many soldiers. That is History, I know quite well. But if a novel is as tedious as a scientific potboiler, then Good Night, there's an end to Art . . . I am beginning the seige of Carthage now. I am lost among the machines of war, the balista and the scorpions, and I understand nothing of it, neither I nor anyone else."

But what can a world thus re-awakened mean to us? Granted that Flaubert successfully solved all the problems which he raised artistically—has a world so represented any real living significance for us? Flaubert's paradoxes with regard to subjects which do not concern us, and which are artistic because they do not concern us, are very characteristic of the author's moods, but they also have their objective aesthetic consequences which are already known to us. Sainte-Beuve denies that the world of *Salammbô* has this significance for us. He uses an interesting argument, which shows that something of the old tradition of the historical novel is still alive in him. He doubts whether one can treat antiquity artistically, whether it can be made the theme of a really living historical novel. "One can reconstruct antiquity, but one cannot bring it back to life." And he refers specifically to the living, continuous relation between Scott's themes and the present, to the many living links which make it possible for us to experience even the distant Middle Ages.

But his chief objection to the theme of *Salammbô* is not confined to this general doubt. Flaubert's subject, he says, occupies a special, remote, unrelated position even among the themes of antiquity. "What do I care about the duel between Tunis and Carthage? Speak to me of the duel between Carthage and Rome, that's a different matter! There I am attentive, there I am involved. In the bitter struggle between Rome and Carthage the whole of future civilization is at stake; our own depends on it. . ."

To this decisive objection Flaubert has no concrete answer. "Perhaps you are right in your considerations of the historical novel as applied to antiquity, and it is very possible that I have failed."

But he has nothing more concrete to say about this question and, while rejecting the artistic significance of archaeological authenticity, simply speaks of the immanent connections within the historical world he has so selected and portrayed. And he maintains that he is right or wrong according to whether he has been successful or not with regard to this immanent harmony.

Apart from which he defends his subject-matter and portrayal in a more lyrical and biographical vein. "I believe even," he says, "that I have been less hard on humanity in *Salammbô* than in *Madame*

Bovary. The curiosity, the love which made me seek out vanished religions and peoples has something moral and sympathetic about it, so it seems to me."

The comparison between *Salammbô* and *Madame Bovary* does not derive from Flaubert himself; it occurs already in Sainte-Beuve's critique. Sainte-Beuve analyses the figure of *Salammbô*: "She talks to her nurse, confides to her her vague anxieties, her stifled sense of unease, her listlessness ... She looks for, dreams of, calls to something unknown. It is the situation of more than one daughter of Eve, Carthaginian or otherwise; to some extent it is that of *Madame Bovary* at the beginning, when life has become too tedious for her and she goes off on her own to the beech-grove of Banneville... Well, poor Salammbô experiences in her own way the same feeling of vague yearning and oppressive desire. The author has only transposed, with great art, and *mythologised* this muffled lament of the heart and the senses." In another connection he compares Flaubert's general attitude to his historical characters with Chateaubriand's manner of portrayal. He says that Flaubert's Salammbô is less a sister of Hannibal than of Chateaubriand's Gallic maiden, Velléda.

The reproach of *modernization* is clearly contained in these comparisons, although Sainte-Beuve does not make an issue out of this question and often shows a great deal of tolerance towards modernization. Nor has Flaubert's protest anything to do with the general methodological problem of modernization. This he takes to be self-evident. His disagreement is only with the concrete comparisons which Sainte-Beuve makes. "As for my heroine, I do not defend her. According to you she resembles ... Velléda, Mme. Bovary. Not at all! Velléda is active, intelligent, European, Mme. Bovary is stirred by multiple passions; Salammbô, on the contrary, is rooted in a fixed idea. She is a maniac, a kind of Saint Theresa. What does it matter? I am not sure of her reality, for neither I, you, nor anyone, neither ancient nor modern can know the oriental woman, because it is impossible to associate with her."

Thus Flaubert is protesting only against the concrete form of modernization which Sainte-Beuve has attributed to the figure of Salammbô. The modernization itself he grants as self-evident; for it is really quite immaterial whether one attributes to Hannibal's sister the psychology of a French *petite bourgeoise* of the nineteenth century or of a Spanish nun of the seventeenth. To which must be added that Flaubert is, of course, also modernizing the psychology of Saint Theresa.

This is not a minor aspect of the work and influence of Flaubert. He chooses an historical subject whose inner social-historical nature is of no concern to him and to which he can only lend the appearance of reality in an external, decorative, picturesque manner by means of the conscientious application of archaeology. But at some point he is forced to established a contact with both himself and the reader, and this he does by modernizing the psychology of his characters. The proud and bitter paradox which contends that the novel has nothing at all to do with the present, is simply a defensive paradox contending against the trivialities of his age. We see from Flaubert's explanations which we have already quoted that *Salammbô* was more than just an artistic experiment. It is for this reason that the modernization of the characters acquires central importance; it is the only source of movement and life in this frozen, lunar landscape of archaeological precision.

Naturally it is a ghostly illusion of life. And an illusion which dissolves the hyper-objective reality of the objects. In describing the individual objects of an historical *milieu* Flaubert is much more exact and plastic than any other writer before him. But these objects have nothing to do with the inner life of the characters. When Scott describes a medieval town or the habitat of a Scottish clan, these material things are part and parcel of the lives and fortunes of people whose whole psychology belongs to the same level of historical development and is a product of the same social-historical ensemble as these material things. This is how the older epic writers produced their "totality of objects". In Flaubert there is no such connection between the outside world and the psychology of the principal characters. And the effect of this lack of connection is to degrade the archaeological exactness of the outer world: it becomes a world of historically exact *costumes and decorations*, no more than a pictorial frame within which a purely modern story is unfolded.

The actual influence of Salammbô is in fact also connected with this modernization. Artists have admired the accomplishment of Flaubert's descriptions. But the effect of Salammbô herself was to provide a heightened image, a decorative symbol, of the hysterical longings and torments of middle-class girls in large cities. History simply provided a decorative, monumental setting for this hysteria, which in the present spends itself in petty and ugly scenes, and which thus acquired a tragic aura quite out of keeping with its real character. The effect is powerful but it shows that Flaubert, because of his embitterment with the shallow prose of his time, had become objectively untruthful and distorted the real proportions of life. The artistic superiority of his bourgeois novels lies precisely in the fact that in them the proportions between emotion and event, between desire and its translation into deeds correspond to the real, social-historical character of emotion and desire. In *Salammbô* the emotions, in themselves quite unmonumental, are falsely and distortedly monumentalized and hence inwardly unequal to such artistic heightening. The way in which the figure of Salammbô was regarded as a symbol during the obvious decline of Royalism and the psychological reaction which set in against Zola's naturalism, is best shown by the analysis which Paul Bourget gives of her: "It is a constant law in his (Flaubert's G.L.) eyes that human effort must end abortively, first of all because external circumstances run counter to one's dreams, secondly because even favourable circumstances cannot prevent the soul from devouring itself in the gratification of its chimera. Our desire floats before us like the veil of Tanit, the embroidered *Zaïmph*, before Salammbô. While she cannot seize it, the girl languishes in despair. As soon as she touches it, she must die."

This modernizing determines the structure of the plot. Its basis is formed by two motifs which are only very externally connected: a "crown and state" conflict between Carthage and the rebellious mercenaries, and the love episode of Salammbô herself. Their involvement with one another is quite external and inevitably remains so. Salammbô is as much a stranger to the interests of her homeland, to the life-and-death struggle of her native city, as Madame Bovary is to the medical practice of her husband. But while in the bourgeois novel this indifference can be made the vehicle of a plot with Emma Bovary at the centre precisely because she is a stranger to provincial daily life, here instead we have a "crown and state" story, outwardly grandiose and requiring therefore extensive preparation, with which Salammbô's destiny has no organic connection. The links are all either pure accidents or external pretexts. But in the presentation of the story the external pretext must inevitably suppress and stifle the main theme. External occasions take up the major part of the novel; the main theme is reduced to a small episode.

This lack of relation between the human tragedy, which is what kindles the reader's interest, and the political action clearly shows the change already undergone by historical feeling in this age. The political plot is not only lifeless because it is cluttered up with descriptions of inessential objects, but because it has no discernible connection with any concrete form of popular life that we may experience. The mercenaries in this novel are the same kind of wild, irrational, chaotic mass as the inhabitants of Carthage. True we are told in exhaustive detail how the quarrel arises, namely the fact that the mercenaries have not been paid, and by what circumstances this quarrel grows into a war; yet we have not the least idea of the real social-historical and human driving force which causes these clashes to take place in the way they do. These remain an irrational, historical fact despite Flaubert's detailed portrayal. And since the human motives do not spring organically out of a concrete social-historical basis, but are given to isolated figures in a modernized form, they only confuse the total picture still further, reduce still further the social reality of the entire story.

This comes out at its crudest in the love episode of Mâtho. Sainte-Beuve, in his analysis of this love-maddened mercenary, rightly recalls the so-called historical novels of the seventeenth century, in which Alexander the Great, Cyrus or Genserich appeared as love-stricken heroes. "But Mâtho in love, this African Goliath, who behaves so wildly and childishly in sight of Salammbô, seems just as false to me; he is as outside nature as he is outside history."

And Sainte-Beuve rightly remarks on the feature peculiar to Flaubert here, what is new in this distortion of history as compared with the seventeenth century: whereas the lovers of the old novels had been sweet and sentimental, Mâtho has a bestially savage character. In short, those brutal and animal features are emphasized and placed at the centre, which occur later in Zola as characteristics of the life of modern workers and peasants. Thus Flaubert's portrayal is "prophetic". Not however, in the sense in which Balzac's works were prophetic, anticipating the actual, future development of social types, but merely in a literary-historical sense, anticipating the later distortion of modern life in the works of the Naturalists.

Flaubert's defence against this criticism of Sainte-Beuve is extremely interesting, illuminating yet another aspect of his method of approach to history. This is how he defends himself against the charge of modernization in the figure of Mâtho: "Mâtho *prowls like a madman* round Carthage. Madness is the right word. Wasn't love, as conceived by the ancients, a madness, a curse, an illness sent by the gods?"

This defence bases itself apparently on historical evidence. But only apparently; for Flaubert never examines the real nature of love within the social life of antiquity, the connection of its different psychological forms with other forms of ancient life. His starting point is an analysis of the isolated *idea* of love, as we find it in certain ancient tragedies. Flaubert is right when he says for instance that the love of Phaedra in Euripides' *Hippolytus* is presented as a sudden passion, innocently visited upon her by the Gods. But it is an entirely unhistorical modernization of ancient life to take merely the subjective side of such tragic conflicts and then to blow this up into a "psychological peculiarity" of the whole of antiquity. Obviously, in certain cases individual love and passion did irrupt "suddenly" into people's lives and cause great tragic collisions. It is also true that these collisions were far more unusual in ancient life than in the period of development from the Middle Ages until modern times, when similar problems occurred, though in a different form in keeping with the changed social circumstances. The special manifestation of passion in the portrayals of the ancients is connected in the closest possible way with the special forms of the break-up of gentile society in antiquity. But this is the final ideological result of a particular development. If this result is then torn out of its social-historical context, if its subjective-psychological side is isolated from the causes which produce it, if therefore the artist's point of departure is not existence but an isolated idea, then whatever one's apparent historical evidence one's only approach to this idea is via modernization. Only in Flaubert's imagination does Mâtho embody ancient love. In reality, he is a prophetic model of the decadent drunkards and madmen of Zola.

This connection between approaching history from the standpoint of an idea and portraying it as a compound of outward exoticism and inner modernity is so important for the whole artistic development of the second half of the nineteenth century that we may be allowed to illustrate it by a further example. Richard Wagner, whose points of similarity with Flaubert Nietzsche disclosed with spiteful shrewdness, discovers the brother-and-sister love of Siegmund and Sieglinde in the Edda. This is an unusually interesting, exotic phenomenon, and is made "intelligible" by a lavish display of decorative pomp and modern psychology. Marx in few words revealed Wagner's falsification of the social-historical connections. Engels, in his *Origin of the Family*, quotes this letter of Marx: "Was it ever possible that brother embraced sister as a bride?" To these "lewd gods" of Wagner who, quite in the modern manner, spice their love intrigues with a little incest, Marx replied: "In primitive times the sister *was* the wife, and that was moral." Wagner's example shows even more clearly than Flaubert's, how, by starting from an isolated idea rather than from actual existence, one inevitably ends up by misrepresenting and distorting history. What remains are the outward, soulless facts of history (here love between brother and sister) which are injected with an entirely modern sensibility, and the old story, the old occurrence serves only to give picturesqueness to this modern sensibility, to add to it a decorative grandeur which, as we have seen, it does not deserve.

This question, has, however, still another side which is of exceptional importance for modern developments. As we have seen, the inner emptiness of social-historical events, left by the rift between the outward happenings and the modernized psychology of the characters, gives rise to the exotic historical *milieu*. The historical event, emptied in this subjectivist manner of its inner greatness has to acquire a pseudo-monumentality by other means. For it is precisely the longing to escape from the triviality of modern bourgeois life which produces these historical themes.

One of the most important means of producing this pseudo-

monumentality is the emphasis on brutality. We have already seen
how the most significant and influential critics of the period, Taine
and Brandes, lament the absence of such brutality in Scott. Sainte-
Beuve, belonging to an older generation, notes its presence and predominance in Salammbô with great unease: "he cultivates atrocity.
The man is good, excellent, the book is cruel. He believes that it is a
proof of strength to appear inhuman in his books."

For anyone who knows Salammbô it is hardly necessary to quote
examples. I shall simply mention the great contrast during the siege
of Carthage: while Carthage's supply of water is cut off and the whole
city is dying of thirst, the most terrible hunger rages in the camp of the
mercenaries. Flaubert takes delight in giving detailed and cruel
pictures of the sufferings of the masses in and around Carthage. There
is never any humanity in this suffering; it is simply horrible, senseless
torment. No single member of the masses is individually characterized,
the suffering yields no single conflict or action which might humanly
interest or grip us.

Here we may see the sharp opposition between the old and the new
representation of history. The writers of the classical period of the
historical novel were only interested in the cruel and terrible happenings of previous history insofar as they were necessary expressions of
definite forms of class struggle (e.g. the cruelty of the Chouans in
Balzac) and also because they gave birth of a similar necessity to great
human passions and conflicts etc. (the heroism of the Republican
officers during the Chouans' massacre of them in the same novel).
The placing of the cruel processes of social development in a necessary
and intelligible connection and the relationship between these and
the human greatness of the combatants take from the events their
cruelty and brutality. Which does not mean that the cruelty and
brutality are in any way ironed out or mitigated—the reproach which
Taine and Brandes levelled at Scott; they are simply given their rightful place inside the total context.

Flaubert begins a development where the inhumanity of subject-
matter and presentation, where atrocity and brutality become ends
in themselves. These features acquire their central position owing to
the weak presentation of what is the chief issue—the social development of man; indeed for the same reason they assume even more
importance than even this position warrants. Since real greatness is
everywhere replaced by extensiveness—the decorative splendour of
the contrasts replaces the social-human connections—inhumanity,
cruelty, atrocity and brutality become substitutes for the lost greatness of real history. At the same time they spring from the morbid
longing of modern man to escape from the suffocating narrowness of
everyday life, a longing which he projects into this pseudo-monumen-

tality. Disgust with small and petty office intrigues produces the ideal image of the mass poisoner, Cesare Borgia.

Flaubert felt deeply hurt by Sainte-Beuve's accusation. But his objections to the critic do not exceed a feeling of injury. And this is not accidental. For the extraordinarily sensitive and highly moral Flaubert has against his will become the initiator of the inhuman in modern literature. The development of capitalism not only levels and trivializes, it also brutalizes.

This brutalization of feeling manifests itself in literature to an ever increasing extent, most clearly of all in the description and portrayal of love, where the physical-sexual side gains growing ascendancy over the passion itself. Think how the greatest portrayers of love—Shakespeare, Goethe and Balzac—confined themselves to the merest intimations in their description of the physical act itself. The interest shown by modern literature in this aspect of love on the one hand derives from the increasing brutalization of the real emotions of love, which occurs in life itself, and on the other has the consequence that writers are forced to search for more and more exquisite, abnormal, perverse etc. themes in order to escape monotony.

Flaubert himself, in this respect, stands at the beginning of this development. And it is very characteristic both for him as well as for the entire development of the historical novel during the crisis of decline of bourgeois realism that these tendencies are much more pronounced in his historical novels than in his pictures of modern society. In both, hatred and disgust for the pettiness, triviality and meanness of modern bourgeois life are expressed with equal force, yet very differently in keeping with the difference of subject-matter. In his contemporary novels Flaubert concentrates his ironic attack on the portrayal of everyday bourgeois life and average bourgeois man. As an outstanding realist artist he thus achieves an infinitely nuanced picture of that dismal greyness which is a real aspect of this everyday life. Precisely his naturalist tendencies restrain Flaubert from any eccentricity in his treatment of the inhuman forms of capitalist life. But his historical novel, as we have seen, he considered a liberation from the fetters of this monotonous flatness. All that his naturalist conscience had forced him to renounce in his picture of contemporary reality found a place here. In terms of form—the colourfulness, the decorative monumentality of an exotic *mileu*; in terms of content— eccentric passions in their fullest extent and uniqueness. And it is here that we clearly see the social, moral and ideological limitations of this great and sincere artist : while he sincerely hates the capitalist present, his hatred has no roots in the great popular and democratic traditions either of the past or present and therefore has no future perspective. His hatred does not historically transcend its object. Thus if, in the historical novels the suppressed passions break open their fetters, it is the eccentric-individualist side of capitalist man which comes to the fore, that inhumanity which everyday life hypocritically seeks to conceal and subdue. The later decadents already portray this side of capitalist inhumanity with boastful cynicism. In Flaubert it appears in the Bengal illumination of a romantic-historical monumentality. Thus the sides which Flaubert here reveals of the new manner of portraying life do not become widespread until later and he himself was not yet aware of them as such general tendencies.

But the contradiction between Flaubert's ascetic disgust with modern life and these inhuman excesses of a riotous and demented imagination does not alter the fact that he appears here as one of the most important precursors of dehumanization in modern literature. This inhumanity is not, of course, in every instance a simple and straightforward capitulation to the dehumanizing tendencies of capitalism, which is the simple and most general case, in literature as in life. The important personalities of this crisis of decline, Flaubert, Baudelaire, Zola and even Nietzsche, suffer from this development and savagely oppose it; yet the manner of their opposition leads to an intensification in literature of capitalist dehumanization in life.

This modernizing of feelings, ideas and thoughts, combined with archaeological faithfulness towards things and customs of no concern to us, which can therefore only appear exotic, is the sole basis on which the question of *language* in the historical novel can be correctly and concretely raised theoretically. It is customary to-day to treat linguistic problems separately from general aesthetic questions, questions of concrete genres etc. All that this produces, however, are abstract "principles" and (equally abstract) subjective judgments of taste. Thus if we now proceed to the problems of language in the work of the first important writer to modernize and exoticize history then we must view them as the final artistic consequence of those tendencies we have seen at work previously in the break-up of the classical historical novel as a whole.

It is obviously that linguistically the problem of "necessary anachronism" plays a decisive role. The sheer fact that all epic is an account of something *past* establishes a close linguistic relation to the present. For it is a present-day storyteller who speaks to present-day readers of Carthage or the Renaissance, of the English Middle Ages or Imperial Rome. It follows therefore that archaism must be ruled out of the general linguistic tone of the historical novel as a superfluous artificiality. The point is to bring a past period *near* to a present-day reader. And it is a universal law of great narrative art that this results from plastically presented events; that in order to understand the psychology of people in distant ages we must understand and feel ourselves close to their social and natural conditions of life, their customs etc.

It is certainly more difficult to do this with history than with the present. The epic task, however, is fundamentally the same. An important epic writer—say Gottfried Keller, Romain Rolland or Gorky—recounting his childhood, would never think of using baby language in order to convey his early attempts at orientation in life, his first childish gropings and babblings. Artistic truth consists in correctly rendering the feelings, ideas and thoughts of a child in a language in which all this can be readily understood by the adult reader. In principle there is no more reason why a medieval person should be better and more truthfully portrayed by the use of archaic language than a child by linguistic imitation of its first babblings. For this reason the linguistic means of the historical novel are *in principle* no different from those of the contemporary novel.

The Flaubertian attitude to history inevitably leads to a disintegration of epic language. This is true even for as great a stylist as Flaubert himself. Flaubert is too important an artist, and much too great an artist of the word to wish to evoke historical authenticity by means of a consistent archaic tone. Lesser contemporaries, however, readily yield to this very tempting pseudo-historical language form. Thus, Meinhold in Germany cleverly imitated the old chronicles of the Thirty Years' War in his *Bernsteinhexe* (*The Amber Witch*) so that the reader should think he is reading not a narrative about the past, but the notes of a contemporary, a "genuine document".

It is, of course, natural for epic, particularly historical epic, to make the event narrated appear real and factual. But it is a naturalistic mistake to think that this authenticity can be brought about by imitating the old language. This is of as little help as external archaeological authenticity if the essential social-human relations are not brought close to the reader. And the achievement of the latter renders the naturalist authenticity superfluous in either case. Hebbel, who praised the *Bernsteinhexe* as a whole, with correct arguments, and attributed great artistic sensibility to its author in other respects, says of the so-called authenticity of language in the novel: "The real language of the hero has as much place in the novel and in literature in general as his real boot in a painting."

This authenticity is in any case pointless unless the characters belong to the same linguistic area, and this alone shows the naturalist character of any argument favouring the use of archaic language. Pushkin ridicules such theories of "probability" in poetry and asks ironically how, according to such a theory, is a Philoctetes in French drama supposed to rejoice at the sounds of his long missed native Greek. Hebbel, in his criticism of Meinhold from which we have just quoted, expressed a similar thought: "If Meinhold were right, then in novel and drama an old German would have to speak old German, a Greek Greek, a Roman Roman, and Troilus and Cressida, Julius Ceasar and Coriolanus could not have been written, at least not by Shakespeare." Hebbel shows that the *Bernsteinhexe* exercises its artistic effect despite rather than because of its archaic language.

It is important to stress the naturalist character of this use of archaic language. For again it is not a problem peculiar to the historical novel (or drama), but merely a specific naturalist degeneration which replaces real characterization by picturesque bagatelles. If Gerhart Hauptmann in his play *Florian Geyer* was incapable of portraying the basic class antagonisms inside the camp of the rebellious peasants, if, therefore, Götz, Wendel, Hippler, Karlstatt, Bubenleben, Jacob Kohl etc. acquire no political and historical physiognomy, then how much use was the "authentic" language of the time? Goethe, on the other hand, is able without this "authenticity" of language to give a moving portrayal of the division among the knights in the destinies of Götz and Weislingen. Hauptmann is a particularly instructive example. He has an unusually sensitive ear for different idioms and dialects; he is nearly always successful when he can characterize in this way. But this very ability proves itself to be a secondary thing, for the liveliness of his characters varies enormously in spite of it, depending upon principles of portrayal far transcending the faithful linguistic reproduction of the intonation of a given person, time and place.

We have deliberately quoted dramatic examples here, because in drama, the form of "the present" (Gegenwärtighkeit—Goethe), there would appear to be a stronger compulsion to let a character speak his "real" (i.e. archaized) language than in epic, where a present-day storyteller speaks *about* figures of the past, and for whom he also provides the formal linguistic means of expression. We can see from this how especially absurd is the use of archaic language in the historical novel. It is of *past human beings* that the deeds, emotions, ideas and thoughts are communicated to us. The characters must be genuine both in content and form; but the language is necessarily not theirs, it is the narrator's own.

In drama it is different. However, the conclusion which naturalism draws from this difference is just as fallacious and possibly more dangerous. Quite apart from the absurd consequences which Pushkin and Hebbel pointed out, the fact that dramatic action, characters and dialogue have the form of the present means that they must be present for the spectator, *for us*. Thus the language of drama must be more immediately, more directly intelligible than that of narrative. The greater scope which is both possible and necessary for "necessary anachronism" in historical drama (which we have discussed at length in the previous section) also determines the language of drama.

But as with epic, the rejection of archaism does not mean modernization. The limits of "necessary anachronism" in drama are likewise set by the historical authenticity of the deeds, thoughts, emotions and ideas of men. Thus, while Shakespeare's Brutus or Caesar stay within this limit, Shaw's comedy *Caesar and Cleopatra* is, albeit brilliantly, modernized through and through.

In Flaubert this question is not nearly as acute as in the later naturalists. Yet Sainte-Beuve can already ridicule a whole series of "authentic" details—the use of dogs' milk and flies' feet as cosmetics and similar curiosities. But these are not accidental in Flaubert, nor simply an attempt to produce a striking effect; this would be quite foreign to so serious and sincere an artist of the word. They derive, in his case too, from naturalist principles. The principle of the photographic authenticity of description and dialogue etc. can lead to nothing else. The ever more furious ransacking of technical dictionaries which goes on in the contemporary novel in order on the one hand to reproduce each object with professional accuracy and on the other to render it in an appropriate specialist jargon must in the historical novel lead to archaeologism. In neither case does the writer wish his objects to be universally understood as the material basis, the material mediator of human actions. They appear before the reader, rather, on the one hand, strange and unfamiliar (the stranger, the more interesting) and on the other in the jargon of the initiated, which even the experts of neighbouring fields cannot be expected to understand.

In debates on the historical novel modernization of language often appears as an *antinomous opposite* of archaism. In fact they are *connected* tendencies, mutually conditioning and complementing one another. The need to modernize language likewise springs from an unhistorical or anti-historical conception of the feelings, ideas and thoughts of men. The livelier the concrete historical approach to the being and consciousness of a past epoch, as in the classical historical novel, the more natural it is to avoid the phraseology of an emotional and intellectual world which is foreign to the past period, which does not make the feelings, ideas and thoughts of *past human beings intelligible to us*, but attributes our feelings etc. to them.

While introjection is the psychological basis of naturalism, its social-historical basis is that of analogy. We have heard Flaubert's own words as to Salammbô and her modern models in his controversy with Sainte-Beuve. We see the same modernization all along the line. Sainte-Beuve, for example, complains of Flaubert's portrayal of the Council meeting in Carthage. Flaubert replies: "You ask me where

I got such an idea of the council of Carthage? But from all the analogous *milieux* of the time of the Revolution, from the convention to the American Parliament, where until recently they still exchanged blows with sticks and shot at one another with revolvers, which sticks and revolvers were carried (like daggers) in coat sleeves. And my Carthaginians have more propriety than the Americans, since there was no public present."

It is obvious that with such a conception of social basis and psychology the modernization of language is *unavoidable*. The conception itself is modernized by means of analogy; the Council of Carthage is an American parliament minus gallery, Salammbô a Saint Theresa under oriental conditions etc. It is only consistent that the feelings, ideas and thoughts which have been introjected into the characters should also receive a modernized language.

In *Salammbô* all the tendencies of decline in the historical novel appear in concentrated form: the decorative monumentalization, the devitalizing, dehumanizing and at the same time making private of history. History becomes a large, imposing scene for purely private, intimate and subjective happenings. These two false extremes belong closely together and appear, independently of Flaubert, in the work of the representative exponent of the historical novel in this period, Conrad Ferdinand Meyer, in a different combination.

The naturalist development itself, particularly in its transition to a lyrical subjectivism and impressionism, underlines the tendency to make history private. Historical novels appear where some hard thinking is required on the part of the reader before he can establish that their stories do not occur in the present. Maupassant's novel *Une Vie*, in itself a fine and interesting work, is the paradigm of this trend. Maupassant with great psychological realism gives us the story of a marriage, the disillusionment of a wife, the collapse of her entire life. For some curious reason, however, he sets the novel in the first half of the nineteenth century, so that it begins in the Restoration period and its action takes up the following few decades.

Maupassant, as an important writer, captures the purely external aspects of the time he depicts. But the essential action of the novel is quite "timeless"; the Restoration, the July Revolution, the July Monarchy etc., events which objectively must make an extremely deep impression upon the daily life of an aristocratic *milieu*, play practically no part at all in Maupassant. The way in which the private story has been set within a definite time is purely external. The purely private character of the action deprives it of an historical character.

The same trend if more markedly present in Jacobsen's very interesting novel, *Frau Marie Grubbe*. Jacobsen calls his book *Interiors from the Seventeenth Century*, thus underlining programmatically his tendency towards circumstantial description. He does not omit the historical background as consistently as Maupassant; wars, sieges etc. are described, the chronological connection of the private story with the history of Denmark is traceable step by step. But only the chronological connection. The wars are waged and the peaces concluded, yet the reader neither understands nor is interested in them. The central action has nothing to do with these events.

We find here the same characteristic as in *Salammbô*; since the novel bases itself not on popular problems, but on the psychological problems of an upper stratum *unconnected* with general social-historical problems, all possible ties between historical events and private destinies are severed. Jacobsen, like Flaubert, takes a lonely person as his heroine. The chain of disappointments which she experiences in her search for the "hero" forms the action of the novel. A typical modern problem. The source which enabled the writer to set his story in the seventeenth century is quite immaterial; as a *typical* destiny Marie Grubbe's story has its place in Jacobsen's own time, the second half of the nineteenth century. Since the main part of the story rests upon a modernized sensibility, it is understandable that the historical *milieu* and events can again form no more than a decorative scene. The more authentic the details of the historical environment, the more authentic the individual minor figures and scenes etc., the greater must be the discrepancy between these and the psychological tragedy of the heroine, the more eccentric must her destiny become in these surroundings.

Here, as in Maupassant, a real problem of contemporary life is portrayed. But, even more than Maupassant, it is severed from social life and depicted purely in terms of its psychological causes and effects. Hence in both cases the historical background becomes purely arbitrary. In both cases the historical setting produces a weakened and eccentic version of what ought to be a portrayal of the present.

This tendency to make history private is a general characteristic of the nascent decline of great realism. It is true, naturally, of the contemporary novel as well, even where important contemporary events have a direct bearing on the action. The change in the relation of such events to the private experiences of the main characters not only alters their function in the action itself, but also their appearance in the whole structure of the novel's world. The classical historical novel—and following it the great realistic contemporary novel—chooses central figures who despite their "middle of the road" personalities, which we have analysed at length, are nevertheless suited to stand at the meeting-point of great social-historical collisions. The historical crises are direct components of the individual destinies of the main characters and accordingly form an integral part of the action itself. In this way the individual and the social-historical are inseparably connected in regard to both characterization and action.

This manner of portrayal is simply the artistic expression of that genuine historicism—the conception of history as the destiny of the people—which motivated the classics. The more this historicism breaks down, the more everything social appears simply as *"milieu"*, as picturesque atmosphere or immobile background etc., against which supposedly purely private histories are unfolded. Generalization takes the form both of making the main figures "sociological" average men and of inserting "symbols" from outside into the characterization and action. Obviously the greater the social events, the more visible their historical interest, the more inevitable is this kind of portrayal. The portrayal of the outbreak of the Franco-Prussian war in Zola's *Nana* and of the historical events in *Marie Grubbe* are fundamentally no different in their general conception, however much they may differ technically and stylistically.

There is perhaps even more to be learned in this respect from the important English realists of the transition period, for Maupassant and Jacobsen belong already to a more advanced stage of this development. We wish briefly to take the example of Thackeray. Thackeray is an outstanding critical realist. He has deep ties with the best traditions of English literature, with the great social canvases of the eighteenth century, which he treated at length in several interesting critical studies. Consciously, he has no interest in separating the historical from the social-critical novel, that is in turning the historical novel into a genre of its own, which was generally the objective result of this development. However, he does not base himself on the classical form of the historical novel, that is on Scott; instead, he attempts to apply the traditions of the eighteenth century social novel to a new type of historical novel. We have said before that eighteenth century historical events were included in the English realist novel particularly in Fielding and Smollett, however only insofar as they came into direct contact with the personal lives of the heroes; thus from the standpoint of the general conception and artistic tendencies of this period, only episodically and never really affecting the chief problems of the novels.

Thackeray, then, consciously takes over this manner of portrayal in his historical novels, but his outlook and artistic aim are quite different from those of the eighteenth century realists. *The approach of the latter towards historicism* grew in a natural way out of their social-critical, realist tendencies. It was one of the many steps towards that realistic conception of history, of social and natural life, which reached its apex in Scott or Pushkin. In the case of Thackeray this *return* to the style and structure of the novels of the eighteenth century stems from a quite different ideological cause, from a deep and bitter disillusionment with the nature of politics, with the relations between social and political life in his own time. This disillusionment expresses itself satirically. By resuming the style of the eighteenth century Thackeray wishes to expose contemporary apologetics.

He, therefore, sees the dilemma in the portrayal of historical events as a choice between public pathos and private manners, the glorification of the one or the realistic depiction of the other. Thus when his hero, Henry Esmond, telling his own story—at the turn of the seventeenth to eighteenth centuries—polemically counters the official histories with the novels of Fielding, when in a discussion with Addison he defends the rights of realism in describing war against poetic embellishment, his language—the language of the memoir—captures the tone of the period beautifully, yet at the same time it expresses Thackeray's own artistic convictions. The basis of this style is the exposure of false heroism, in particular the reputed heroism fostered by historical legend. Esmond speaks of this, too, very vividly and finely: "What spectacle is more august than that of a great king in exile? Who is more worthy of respect than a brave man in misfortune? Mr. Addison has painted such a figure in his noble piece of *Cato*. But suppose fugitive Cato fuddling himself at the tavern with a wench on his knee, a dozen faithful and tipsy companions of defeat, and a landlord calling out for his bill; and the dignity of misfortune is straightway lost." Thackeray requires this exposure in order to strip history of its periwig, in order to deny that English and French history took place only at the courts of Windsor and Versailles.

Of course, it is Esmond who says all this and not Thackeray himself, and the novel is not meant to be an objective picture of the time, but simply the hero's autobiography. But apart from the fact that this relationship between private manners and historical events is very similar, say, to that in *Vanity Fair*, with a writer as important and conscious as Thackeray the composition of *Henry Esmond* cannot be accidental. The memoir is an appropriate form for Thackeray's exposure of pseudo-greatness. Everything can be seen from the proximity of everyday private life and, shown in this microscopic way, the false pathos of the artificial, self-imagined hero collapses. And this is what is intended. The hero has seen Louis XIV in old age. Louis, says Esmond, was perhaps a hero for a book, for a statue, for a mural, "but what more than a man for Madame Maintenon, or the barber who shaved him, or Monsieur Fagon, his surgeon?" Proximity destroys the alleged greatness of Marlborough, the Stuart Pretender and many others. And when every great man swindle of history has been exposed, there remains just the honesty of simply, slightly above average men capable of real sacrifice like the hero himself.

This picture is remarkably consistent. But is it a real picture of the time, as Thackeray intended? Thackeray's answer to his own dilemma is right enough. But the dilemma itself is narrow and wrong. There is a third way: what, in fact, the classical historical novel does. Admittedly, the epoch following the "Glorious Revolution" and ending with the establishment of the House of Hanover on the throne of England is certainly not one of the most heroic of periods; especially as regards the behaviour and activity of the supporters of Stuart Restoration. But we recall that Scott, too, had portrayed these Stuart restoration attempts (in *Waverley* and, for a later period, in *Rob Roy* and *Redgauntlet*), and had neither idealized nor indeed spared either the dynasty or its followers. Nevertheless, the picture of history he produced was grand, dramatic and rife with deep conflict in every phase. The secret of these grand dimensions is easily discoverable. Scott gives a broad and *objective* picture both of the historical forces which lead to the Stuart rebellions and of those which inevitably foredoom them. At the centre of this picture are the Scottish clans, driven to desperation by economic and social circumstances and misled by adventurers. The fate of the Pretender himself is tragi-comic in Scott, the fate of his English adherents either comic or pathetic. The latter are dissatisfied with the Hanoverian régime, yet keep quiet because they are too cowardly and irresolute to act, because they do not dare jeopardize their material well-being; because the growth of capitalism in England has levelled out the former distinctions between feudal and capitalist land-ownership. But since the background to the action is the real suffering and real heroism (however untimely and misguided) of a people, the events lose all their trivial, mean and haphazard qualities, all that is purely individual and private about them.

Thackeray, however, does not see the people. He reduces his story to the intrigues of the upper classes. Of course, he knows perfectly well that these trivialities are confined to the class he describes and tell us nothing of the real historical process. It is not by chance that every so often the Cromwell age, the heroic period of the English people, casts its shadow in discussions. But this period seems to have wholly disappeared, and the life which is described is given over entirely to trivial and private goings-on. The people's attitude to what happens is never revealed. Yet it was at this time that those who had fought the battles of the Civil War, above all the middle farmers, yeomanry and city plebeians were undergoing economic and moral ruin as a result of the tempestuous development of capitalism. Only much later did the new heroes, the Luddites and Chartists, arise from the soil made fertile by their blood. Of this tragedy, which is the real basis of the tragi-comedies and comedies occurring "on top" Thackeray sees nothing.

But he thereby dispels historical objectivity, and the more compellingly he motivates his characters psychologically, the subtler this private psychology, the more haphazard it all appears in an historical perspective. The psychology is not wrong, on the contrary it very subtly shows the accidental nature of the political standpoints of the characters. But this accidentality can only appear truly false, if placed within an objective class context where it becomes a factor of historical necessity. Scott's Waverley also joins the Stuart Rebellion by accident; but he is simply there as a foil to those for whom the revolt is a social-historical necessity. The perspective in which Thackeray shows Marlborough, however, is purely private. His hero, he says, has become a bitter enemy rather than an enthusiastic follower of Marlborough simply because of bad treatment at a levée. The resulting caricature is such that Thackeray himself feels compelled to counter his own subjectivism with supplementary corrections and notes to his memoirs. But these corrections lessen the one-sidedness only theoretically, they cannot give the figure of Marlborough any objective-historical relief.

This subjectivism degrades all the historical figures who appear in the novel. We see only the "all-too-human" side of Swift, so that we should have to regard him as a petty intriguer and careerist, if we did not have a different picture of him from *his own* works. But even characters whom Esmond describes with obvious sympathy, such as Steele and Addison, the well-known writers of the epoch, are objectively degraded, because their personalites reveal no more than the normal, sociable habits of everyday private life. What made them into important representatives of the epoch, into ideologists of big social changes is excluded from the story by Thackeray's general conception. The influence of their journal *The Spectator*, which extended over the whole of educated bourgeois Europe, is sufficiently well-known in both history and the history of literature, as well as the fact that it was largely due to the use of everyday events as a basis for arguing and demonstrating the new, triumphant morality of the rising bourgeoisie. *The Spectator* turns up in *Henry Esmond*, too; the hero uses his personal friendship with the editors in order to ridicule the frivolous coquetry of the woman with whom he is in love and so exert a beneficial moral influence upon her. No doubt such articles did appear in the journal. But to reduce its historical role to private episodes of this kind means, objectively, the distortion of history, its degradation to the level of the trivial and the private.

Thackeray undoubtedly suffered as a result of this discrepancy. In another historical novel (*The Virginians*) he gives voice to his dissatisfaction. He argues that it is not possible for the present-day writer to show his characters in the context of their professional lives, their actual work etc. The writer has to confine himself to the passions

—love or jealousy—on the one hand and to outward forms of social life (in the superficial "worldly" sense) on the other. Thackeray herewith states very tersely the decisive failing of the period of the nascent decline of realism—though without understanding the real social causes and their artistic consequences. He does not see this failing as the result of a narrowed-down and one-sided conception of man, of the fact that characters have come adrift from the main currents of popular life and hence from the really important problems and forces of the age.

The classic realist writers were able to portray these sides of human life poetically and plastically, because in their works all social forces still took the form of human relationships. An important reversal such as the threatened bankruptcy of old Osbaldiston in Rob Roy enables Scott to draw from the social-human drama of the situation the various commercial practices of the Glasgow merchants without any ponderous descriptions of milieu. In Tolstoy, the different attitudes to professional army life on the part of Andrei Bolkonsky, Nikolai Rostov, Boris Drubetskoy, Berg etc., the differing views on agriculture and serfdom on the part of old and young Bolkonsky are organic integral components of the story, and of the human and psychological development of these characters.

As attitudes towards society and history become more amd more private, so such vividly seen connections vanish. Professional life appears dead; everything human is submerged under the desert sands of capitalist prose. The later naturalists—even Zola—seize upon the prose and place it at the centre of literature, but they only fix and perpetuate its withered features, limiting their picture to a description of the "thing-like" milieu. What Thackeray, with the right instinct, though from a false situation, declared unportrayable, they leave as it is, replacing portrayals by mere descriptions—supposedly scientific, and brilliant in detail—of things and thing-relationships.

Thackeray is too conscious a realist, too strongly tied to the traditions of true realism for him to take this naturalist way out. Hence he escapes back beyond the classical and for him unattainable form of the historical novel to an artificial renewal of the style of the English Enlightenment. This archaism, however, can only lead to problematic results, as it does elsewhere. The quest for a style leads to stylization, bringing the weaknesses in Thackeray's general conception of social life garishly to the surface, stressing them much more strongly than he would consciously intend. His only wish is to expose false greatness, pseudo-heroism, yet the effect of his stylization, as we have seen, is to show every historical figure, whatever his importance, in a disparaging and sometimes thoroughly destructive light. He wishes to counter this with the genuine, inner nobility of simple morality, but his stylization turns his positive characters into tedious, insufferable paragons of virtue. True, the literary traditions of the eighteenth century lend cohesion to his works and this has a beneficial effect at a time when naturalism is beginning to break up narrative form. Still, this cohesion is only a stylistic one, it does not touch the depths of the portrayal; hence at most it can only cover up the "problematic" which arises from the making private of history, but not solve it.

3. The Naturalism of the Plebeian Opposition

The force of the tendencies unfavourable to literature is felt most strikingly where writers consciously fight against them, yet in practice fall under their sway. We saw that by restricting itself *exclusively* to the faithful reproduction of immediate reality naturalism robbed literature of its power to give a living and dynamic picture of the essential driving forces of history. The historical novel, even of such important writers as Flaubert and Maupassant, degenerates into a collection of episodes. There is no connection between the exclusively private individual experiences of characters and historical events. The characters cease to be really historical; the historical events become external and exotic, a merely decorative backdrop.

All these artistically unfavourable tendencies spring from the general social and political development of the bourgeoisie after the Revolution of 1848. But here again, the connection between the general tendencies of the time and questions of literary form must not be conceived in too straightforward, too direct a manner. The effect of these tendencies is to deprive the historical novel of its popular character. Writers no longer have the power (and often not the will) to experience history as the history of the people, as a process of development in which the people play the chief role actively and passively, in action and in suffering.

Where the immediate concern of writers is the bourgeoisie, their conception of history—as in the case of Flaubert—is decorative and exotic: they attempt to produce a counter-image of the grey, desolate, hated and despised prose of everyday bourgeois life. History shimmering colourfully in its distance, remoteness and otherness has the task of fulfilling the intense longing for escape from this present world of dreariness.

It is different with writers whose bonds are still with the people, who take the sufferings of the people under the fearful pressure from "on top" as the starting-point for their outlook and artistic portrayal.

They react to the prevailing world of bourgeois prose with a similar mistrust, contempt and hatred. Yet it is not a refined aesthetic and ethical disillusionment which determines their work, but the rancour and indignation of the broad masses of the people whose real desires remained unfulfilled by the bourgeois revolutions from 1789 to 1848.

All students of the naturalist movement in literature know that the part played in it by the early socialist consciousness of the proletariat was largely negative. The ever more pronounced and undeniable fact of the "two nations" has a very two-edged effect upon literature. Where the spirit of revolutionary democracy lives on in society or where socialism takes hold of important writers, new and major forms of realism may emerge. But in Western Europe after the 1848 Revolution the writer is alienated from comprehensive social problems and his vision limited to one or other of the "two nations". We have already seen and shall continue to see the disadvantageous results of narrowing one's subject matter to what happens "on top".

But a similar narrowing and a similar impoverishment of literature occurs when the writer—again with naturalist immediacy—concerns himself exclusively with the "bottom" of society. We can see this best in the historical novels of Erckmann-Chatrian. The well-known Russian critic, Pisarev, rightly saw them as a new type of historical novel. However, in his democratically justified joy at his discovery and in his equally democratically justified polemic against the historical novels of his contempories, he overlooked the limitations of Erckmann-Chatrian and their manner of portrayal. He writes of them: "Our authors are not interested in how and why this or that historical event came about, *but* in the impression it produced upon the masses, how it was understood by the masses, how they reacted to it." (My italics, G.L.)

We have stressed the word "but" in order to draw the reader's attention to Pisarev's over-sharp antithesis. True, he immediately adds that there is a "living interaction" between the outer side of history (great events, wars, peace treaties etc.) and its inner side (the life of the masses). But there is still something external about this interaction in his analysis—an interaction of factors, which have almost nothing in common. Hence in dealing with the works of Erckmann-Chatrian, he fails to see that as far as this interaction is present in them at all, it is an external one.

It would be wrong to deny the relative justification of looking at historical reality in this way. Indeed, *immediately* but only immediately, the history of class societies must reflect itself in this way in the eyes of the oppressed and exploited masses. Wars are waged in the interests of the exploiters—and in them the exploited masses are bled, materially ruined and crippled. Laws are but a system for strengthening a particular kind of exploitation. This is true even for bourgeois democracy, even for the democracy which inscribed "liberty, equality and fraternity" upon its banners and realized the most complete formal freedom before the law. For the law, as Anatole France wrote, with the mordant irony of disillusion, forbids the rich and the poor with equal severity to sleep under bridges.

However, does this immediate, and in its immediacy relatively justified, picture correspond to the objective truth of the historical process? Are the oppressed masses *equally* indifferent and hostile to all the events and institutions of the history of class society? This, of course, not even Pisarev maintains. He emphatically declares: "But not always and not everywhere has there prevailed such a complete absence of attitude on the part of those below towards great historical events. Not always, nor everywhere has the mass remained blind and deaf to those teachings, which workaday life, with its deprivation and bitterness, constantly offers to those who are capable of seeing and hearing." And he praises as the literary virtue of Erckmann-Chatrian the fact that they select those moments of class life where the masses draw conclusions from these experiences, where they awake "to face up sternly and clearly to what prevents them from leading a happier and more decent life".

To the extent that Erckmann-Chatrian concern themselves with these periods of popular life, Pisarev's praise is apt. However, the limitations of this outlook, which he as a critic does not sufficiently recognize, makes themselves felt in many respects. First of all, there is objectively not such a rigid antithesis in the different periods of human development between the completely passive indifference or the active awakening of the masses as might appear at first sight. Certainly the development of society is an uneven process, but it is one which, despite all fluctuations—sometimes centuries long—does move forward. And the masses can never, objectively, be indifferent to the individual stages of this journey, even when what is emerging has no visible popular movement for or against it. The contradictory character of progress in class society manifests itself above all in the contrary effects which individual moments and stages can exercise simultaneously upon the life of the masses. Anatole France's wittily malicious criticism of bourgeois equality does not erase the fact that equality before the law, with all its class limitations, was an extraordinary historical step forward in comparison with estate justice, even from the standpoint of the masses, even seen from below. (The convinced democrat, Pisarev and Anatole France, too, would have been the last to have doubted this.) Consequently, the masses who laid down their lives for this equality were entirely in the right—despite the justness of France's criticism.

To the objective many-sidedness of the individual stages of development there must correspond an even richer and more differentiated
many-sidedness of response in the lives of the masses. For these reactions may from a social-historical standpoint be either right or wrong.
And because the echo of the great events is necessarily more immediate
among the politically less developed masses, the path of false reactions of the most varied kind is the unavoidable path towards a
standpoint which really corresponds to popular interests.

The classical historical novelists were great, precisely because they
did justice to this richness of popular life. Scott describes the most
varied class struggles (reactionary Royalist insurrections, Puritan
struggles against Stuart reaction, class struggles of the nobility against
the rise of absolutism etc.), but he always shows in addition the richly
articulated variety of response to these struggles on the part of the
popular masses. In Scott, too, the popular characters are fully aware
of the gulf which separates the "top" from the "bottom" of society.
But these really are two comprehensive worlds, comprehensive also in
the sense that they embrace the entire lives of many-sided characters.
Thus their interactions produce clashes etc. whose totality really does
comprehend the entire social range of the class struggles of an age.

And only this differentiated, rich, manifold completeness can give
a true and correct picture of popular life in the critical periods of
human development. Erckmann-Chatrian, however, cut out the
"upper" world completely, and Pisarev praises them for this. They
write about the French Revolution, he says, and we see neither Danton
nor Robespierre, they write about the Napoleonic Wars without
Napoleon. This is true. But is it really an advantage?

In the foregoing we spoke at great length about the role of the
leading and representative figures of history in the classical historical
novel. We saw and shall see even more clearly by means of negative
examples as we analyse modern developments that Scott's or Pushkin's practice of making them minor characters rests upon a profound
historical rightness and truthfulness to life, namely the concrete
possibility of portraying popular life to its fullest historical extent. If
Erckmann-Chatrian omit Danton and Robespierre from their picture
of the French Revolution, they naturally have a right to do so. But
only if they are able to depict those currents in French popular life of
the Revolutionary period, of which Danton and Robespierre were in
fact the clearest, most distinct and comprehensive representatives, as
convincingly and plastically without Danton and Robespierre.
Otherwise the picture of popular life remains fragmentary; it lacks
its highest conscious expression, its real political and social summit.

This problem, which in itself is perhaps not insoluble artistically,
Erckmann-Chatrian did not even pose, let alone solve. On the contrary

by entirely omitting the main protagonists from their picture, they express an outlook to which Pisarev gave a more conscious expression —the opposition of inner and outer history (mere interaction)—than it has in Erckmann-Chatrian themselves. This change of historical outlook also develops as a result of the 1848 Revolution. It expresses that general disillusion with the results of the bourgeois revolutions which begins after the great French Revolution, but which only now becomes a really powerful current. Among bourgeois-liberal historians and writers it takes the form of "cultural history", i.e. the conception that wars, peace treaties, the overthrow of states etc. are only the outward and unimportant part of history; whereas the really decisive factor, that which really changes things, the "inner" part of history is made up of art, science, technology, religion, morality and world-view. The changes in these spheres is what determines the real path of humanity, whereas "outer" history, political history, only describes the surface splashing of the waves.

Among the disappointed plebeians, however, particularly among those writers and thinkers for whom the proletariat has already begun to take its place as an integral part of the people, this change expresses itself quite differently, indeed in an opposite way, although the historical-social causes are the same. Here, too, there is mistrust for "large-scale politics" and "external history". However the counter-image here is not the nebulous idealist concept of culture, but the real, immediate, material, economic life of the people themselves. This mistrust for politics may be observed in the entire pre-Marxist history of the rise of socialism, from Saint Simon to Proudhon. And it would be wrong not to see the many new points of view which this turning-away from politics, this search for a key to the "secret history" of humanity brought with it; very important germs and beginnings of the materialist outlook on history come to light here—in the work of the great utopians—for the first time.

Very soon, however, the break occurs, and the negative and limiting motifs become predominant—in Proudhon, for example. The mistrust for politics leads increasingly to a levelling and impoverishing of the picture of social life, indeed even to a distortion of economic life itself. The appeal to the immediate, material existence of the people, which had been the starting-point of a really enriched picture of the social world, is transformed into its opposite, if it remains in this immediacy.

For the historical novel, too, and for literature in general, such is the fate of the point of view of "below", applied in this one-sided and limited way. The mistrust for *everything* that happens "above" becomes an abstract mistrust, it freezes in this abstraction and impoverishes the historical reality depicted. The consequence of this over-nearness to the immediate, concrete life of the people is the shrinking or even disappearance of their highest and most heroic qualities. The abstract contempt for "external" history gives historical events a grey everyday character, reduces them to a level of simple spontaneity.

We were able to observe similar ideological features in Leo Tolstoy, who in the major part of his work was a worthy and original successor to the classics, enlarging their richness of life. But Tolstoy, as a result of the peculiar development of Russia, belongs to the preparatory period of a democratic revolution; he is, whatever his conscious opposition, a contemporary and strongly influenced contemporary of revolutionary democracy in literature. Hence in his work he is able to break through the narrow limits of his conscious outlook.

Let us think of Tolstoy's depiction of war. No writer in the world's literature has such mistrust as Tolstoy, particularly as regards this question, for all that occurs "on top". His presentation of the "upper" world, the general staffs, the court, the interior of the country etc. reflects the mistrust and hatred of the simple peasant and soldier. Nevertheless, Tolstoy does depict this "upper" world and simply by so doing gives the mistrust and hatred of the people a concrete, visible object. And this difference is not just external and schematic. For the very existence of the hated object introduces a degree of differentiation, heightening and passion into the depiction of popular reactions to this "upper" world.

But further, Tolstoy not only differentiates more by means of this manner of portrayal, he produces a quite different kind of articulation. This is by no means a purely artistic problem of expression; on the contrary, it proceeds from the heightening, enriching and concretizing of the social and historical picture. Tolstoy draws with masterly skill the awakening of national feelings among the people during the campaign of 1812. Previously the popular masses had been dumb cannon fodder for the predatory aims of Tsarism. Accordingly the aims and fortunes of war were not of the slightest interest to them. Patriotic utterances arose from stupidity, boasting or in response to inspiration from "above". When the Russian army retreats to Moscow, and especially when Moscow has been captured and burned, the objective historical situation changes, and popular attitudes change with it. Tolstoy depicts these changes with his usual richness, never failing to point out that large sections of popular life under Tsarist rule remain both objectively and subjectively untouched by their country's fate. But the turning-point is nevertheless there. And Tolstoy gives it a clear and plastic expression by showing how Kutuzov, borne along by the trust of the people, is appointed Commander-in-Chief against the will of the Tsar and the court; how, in spite of all the intrigues of the world "above", he is able not only to keep his post, but also to carry through at least the main line of his strategy. As soon as the popular defensive war is over, however, and a new Tsarist war of conquest takes its place, Kutuzov collapses, outwardly as well as inwardly. His mission to defend the country, as the representative of popular will, is at an end; the conduct of the new war is once again taken over by the courtiers and intriguers of before. The cessation of popular activity takes on a clear and visible shape in Kutuzov's resignation.

This concreteness is lacking in the novels of Erckmann-Chatrian. Let us take their *History of a Conscript of the Year 1813*. War for the people here is simply war, without any concrete political content. We hear nothing of the complex contradictions of the period which apply in particular to the German spheres of Napoleonic rule in which the story takes place. Admittedly, we learn that the Leipzig populace, for example, previously friendly to the French, has now turned against them. But we are told no more of this change of attitude than any quite unpolitical, average recruit might chance to hear during a chance visit to an inn.

The limitation of the naturalistic and one-sided manner of representation, which confines itself to immediate reactions in the life of an average person, is plainly visible. In previous essays (*The Intellectual Physiognomy of Literary Characters* and *Narration or Description*), I have examined this general limitation of naturalism in detail. To this must be added now, with regard to the specific problems of the historical novel, simply that the naturalist manner of portrayal inevitably blunts both popular movements and popular attitudes; it deprives the one of historical objectivity and the other of consciousness. As a result, all the good observation and portrayal of life in its immediacy is turned into an abstraction; the war of 1813 could be any war. The experiences of the Pfalzburg peasants under Napoleonic rule could be the experiences of any peasants under whatever régime. Just as specifically social attitudes are extinguished by the merely immediate authenticity of naturalist *milieu* pictures, so historical concreteness is dissolved by the naturalism of Erckmann-Chatrian into the abstract contemplation of an exclusive world "below".

The contrast between Tolstoy's and Erckmann-Chatrian's manner of composition therefore provides fresh confirmation of the rightness of the classical structure of the historical novel, especially as their historical conception of the role of the masses is in some respects similar. The problem here again is that of the world-historical personality as minor figure. We said earlier that it would be possible in the abstract to depict the French Revolution without Danton and Robespierre. That is correct. The only question is, however, would not the writer who tried to embody the political and social principles of Danton and Robespierre find himself faced with a more difficult, less soluble task than the writer who followed in the tradition of the historical novel? In Danton and Robespierre the latter has a ready possibility and yardstick for raising the popular movements he portrays to their intellectual and politically conscious summits. Just as the "world-historical individual" as a central character stands in the way of a concrete historical and human portrayal of actual popular movements, so, as a minor character, he assists the writer in conducting them to their concrete historical summits.

This connection is all the more true in the case of Erckmann-Chatrian, because their method is the result of a conscious aim, which is not just artistic; their conception of true popular character excludes the "world-historical individual" from the historical novel even as a minor figure. And here the inner connection between literary natur-alism and abstract-plebian mistrust for the world "above" appears quite plainly. In a political respect this mistrust is as much a theory of mere spontaneity as in the literary sphere it is the method of natural-ism.

Marat's deep and truly revolutionary mistrust for the "statesmen" of his time, for the traitors to the democratic revolution is most closely bound up with the plebeian movements of his time and constitutes one of their highest summits, but it is by no means their immediate product. It was—to use Lenin's phrase in *What is to be Done?*—brought to the plebeian masses "from without". Marat as a disciple of the Enlightenment, in particular of Rousseau, was able to lend a clear expression to the political and social desires of the French plebeians and to bring these desires nearer to realization within the concrete context of the inter-relations of all classes in society; he was able to clarify and articulate the dark, but instinctively correct, mistrust of the masses for everything that took place "on top", so that it became concrete *political* mistrust for the *actual* traitors to the revolution.

The proletariat, by virtue of its position in the process of produc-tion, is more organized and conscious than any other exploited class in history. Nevertheless, the definition which Lenin gave applies to the workers as well : "The workers can acquire political class conscious-ness *only from without*, that is, only outside of the economic struggle, outside of the sphere of relations between workers and employers. The sphere from which alone it is possible to obtain this knowledge is the sphere of relationships between *all* classes and the state and the govern-ment—the sphere of the inter-relations between all *classes.*"

That the popular movements of pre-proletarian times proceed at a qualitatively lower social and conscious level than the proletarian class struggles does not invalidate the general applicability of Lenin's definition. Nor the fact, say, that the consciousness, which Marat was able to give the popular movements of his time, was clouded by historically unavoidable illusions—this simply warns us to be concrete

in applying the definition to particular historical cases. Lenin's definition applies generally to the origins and nature of political consciousness among oppressed classes.

One of the things the "world-historical individual" in the sense of
the classical historical novel exemplifies, if he is really a leader or
representative of genuine popular movements, is Lenin's "from without". It is no accident therefore that writers, who experienced and
portrayed only the disillusion of the masses as a result of the social
collapse of popular interests in the bourgeois revolutions, and not the
new upsurge of popular revolution which came with the developing
consciousness of the proletariat, should have abandoned these traditions and sought their appropriate literary expression in naturalism.
They sink politically into a glorification of mere spontaneity, and it is
this political-historical weakness which constitutes the point at which
naturalism, the form into which great bourgeois realism declines,
becomes irresistibly attractive to them.

We have dealt with Erckmann-Chatrian at such length less for their
artistic than for their symptomatic significance. Also, because the
spontaneous and exclusive emphasis on the viewpoint of "below"
(additionally supported by the authority of Pisarev) can easily lead
one into believing that here is the true, "proletarian" "socialist" form
of the historical novel. This misconception, too, belongs with the great
range of problems which socialist realism has to face in passing beyond
all the various naturalist traditions which at first obstruct or hinder
its real and full development.

The fundamental importance of this criticism of naturalism, even
when it serves to express not just plebeian, but plebeian-revolutionary
experiences of history, may be seen perhaps still more clearly in the
most important work of this trend, de Coster's *Ulenspiegel*. This novel
is on an altogether different artistic level from the sincerity and
worthiness of Erckmann-Chatrian. To criticize its ideological, historical and literary limitations one has to come to terms with as
deservedly great an authority as Romain Rolland.

Romain Rolland rightly recognizes the uniqueness of this very
important novel: de Coster in voicing the national-revolutionary
traditions of the Belgian people far surpasses all his contemporaries,
artistically and humanly; his work is a unique phenomenon in the
whole of Western European literature of the mid-nineteenth century.

It might appear then that our inclusion of de Coster in the naturalist current is an injustice. After all, de Coster calls his book a legend
and not only uses many motifs of the Eulenspiegel saga, but introduces
a whole series of events and anecdotes from the old "popular book"
into his novel. Thus he has no wish whatever—so it appears at first
sight, and this is undoubtedly de Coster's conscious intention—to give

a slavishly photographic picture of the liberation struggles of the Netherlands people; on the contrary his aim is to bring out the general human quintessence of their democratic rebellion against the political, religious and human powers of darkness and oppression, against absolute tyranny, Catholicism etc. Given this aim, de Coster is fully justified in calling his book a legend.

However, this antithesis to naturalism is not as sharp as it appears. If we look at his story a little more closely, we soon see that he is by no means averse to such tendencies. Indeed his attempt to seize directly the most general, anthropological laws of human life was one of the chief aims of the important founders and leaders of naturalism. Despite all Zola's ideological concessions to the fashionable dogma of agnosticism, for example, he is nevertheless profoundly sure of having found the most important and decisive laws of existence as a whole in the immediately verifiable influence of the *milieu* and heredity upon human destinies. Which is why he considers naturalism to be the modern and "scientifically" correct method of writing, because he thinks that it is specially capable of revealing and depicting directly the operation of these general laws.

Thus a denial of general connections and laws is certainly not characteristic of naturalism. This occurs as a general trend only at a much more advanced stage of literary decadence, very often in opposition to naturalism. What is decisive, rather, is the naturalistic, that is, immediate and therefore abstract attitude to these general laws. Thus, what Hegel laid down generally in his criticism of all immediate knowledge, applies *mutatis mutandis* to artistic truth as conceived by naturalism: "Its peculiarity (i.e. of immediate knowledge, G.L.) is this: the content of *immediate* knowledge is only truth when taken in *isolation*, when mediation is excluded." This exclusion of mediations may be easily studied in literature by comparing the relationship between man and society in Balzac and Zola.

Universality without mediation is necessarily *abstract*. We could observe this abstraction in Erckmann-Chatrian though they kept strictly to an exact rendering of immediate reality. Their exclusion of historical determinants (mediations), which in the everyday life of the average person are not, as a rule, readily perceptible, but which interacting in their totality with immediate everyday existence form the concrete, essential features of an historical situation, transformed naturalist authenticity into abstraction.

Still more striking is this transformation when important naturalist writers directly confront the big questions of life and history. The literary form of abstration here is the *symbol*. One need only think of works like Flaubert's *Temptation of St. Antony* to see this relationship clearly. From the literary point of view, it is the lack of transition between the purely empirical, naturalist observations, the small individual features of life and the abstract-general which is most characteristic; or the thoughtless way in which these details, in themselves neither deep nor significant, are made into bearers of abstract-general connections and identified with them.

This fundamentally inorganic combination of the crude-empirical with the abstract-general, of the naturalistic with the symbolic is characteristic of de Coster's manner of composition, too. Admittedly, his subject differs profoundly in spirit from Flaubert's. And this difference, indeed contrast, in attitudes has far-reaching thematic and artistic consequences. While Flaubert looks for the decorative and exotic in history, while for him it is the sharp contrast to the prose of the present, the unrelatedness to the present which is the decisive artistic motif, de Coster's aim is popular, national and democratic. Hence in his presentation of history he seeks to awake popular traditions to new life. His harking back to the old popular book about Eulenspiegel is in no sense a flight from the present into the distant past. On the contrary, it aims to bridge the heroic, revolutionary past of the Belgian people with the present.

The bridge, however, is never created. The relationship with the present is abstract, because the representation of the heroic past is abstract: in part naturalistic and episodic-anecdotal, in part symbolist and legendary-heroic. De Coster's aim is to bring the heroic past as close as possible to the present by raising it into a "legend", to elevate the terrors of the age of oppression, the simple, joyful heroism of the people to a universally human and thereby contemporary level. His principal heroes are intended to embody, as it were, the permanent, ever-present forces of the Belgian people, as potent in the present as in the past.

This is why de Coster goes back to the hero of the popular book and its naïve, rough, realistic style—not because of any artistic yearning for the remote. But the result he achieves comes very close in many respects, objectively, to the artistic aims of the leading naturalists. The main reason is that his popular hero, who is historical despite his transfiguration into a legendary figure, does not develop organically out of the hero of the chap-book. The latter is not heroic at all and quite unconnected with the Netherlands war of liberation. Eulenspiegel himself is an authentic figure of the declining Middle Ages, pleasure-seeking, cunning, yet upright; a naïve and sturdy embodiment of the native intelligence, slyness and practical wisdom of the peasantry of the time. The loose and anecdotal portrayal of the old Eulenspiegel figure is therefore by no means accidental; it is the natural and appropriate artistic expression of the primitive form of crystallization which the type had so far assumed, and inevitably assumed, at the time. De Coster wishes both to preserve these rough and naïve characteristics of the original Eulenspiegel as they are and at the same time to evolve from them those of a Netherlands popular hero. But this is impossible, for national-democratic heroism is a quality quite absent from the old figure. Of course, this need not have prevented de Coster from turning Eulenspiegel into a hero of this kind. But then he would have had to transform the figure completely, as for instance Goethe did with Faust: i.e. by giving a new meaning to traditional motifs which would lend themselves to the new conception and by omitting those which would not.

De Coster did not do this. His attitude to the old literary tradition is much the same as that of the naturalists to their documents; he wants to preserve the empirical facts and merge them into his own generalizations. This however, was not possible. Even Romain Rolland, a fervent admirer of this work, says of the first part: "And yet the master storyteller still hesitates to tell the story himself... He feels bound to intersperse the first part of his Legend with raw and rancid-smelling slices of the old farce. These venerable jokes which have gone the rounds have the effect on us of ghosts who are seeking their ruins and have strayed into a new house. Their cast-off garments do not always suit the supple and nervous figure of the son of Claes."

To this need only be added, we believe, that the same division runs through the entire work, though not quite so crudely.

This applies first to the style. De Coster's model is the fragmentary, anecdotal style of the old chap-book with its loose construction; and what he adds to the story from himself he invests in the same literary form. This new context, however, turns the naïve and earthy realism of the old texts into a stylized naturalism. Naturalism, because the characterization does not take place on the basis of inner development, but of representative anecdotes. Stylization, because the naïve earthiness of the sixteenth century inevitably assumes a *recherché*, exotic manner coming from a present-day narrator. The connection between naturalism and archaism, which we mentioned earlier on, shows itself again to be the case here, and particularly forcefully so, because de Coster was quite averse to the aesthetic affectations of archaism. But facts have their own, relentless logic.

Still more important is, for the very same reason, the lack of a real, concrete, historical basis to de Coster's hero. Because the basis given to him by de Coster is that of the old chap-book, full of life in itself, Eulenspiegel has no historically concrete, material and spiritual foundation. De Coster's picture of popular life—again, in itself, very lively, colourful, often moving—has an entirely abstract character seen historically; he draws the joyful, innocent people as such, ground down by the dark torturers of reaction. And even de Coster's plebeian hatred for the vacillating and treacherous noble leaders of the liberation struggle is abstractly general, like the feelings of the mass characters in Erckmann-Chatrian. William of Orange's sudden emergence as a real leader, as a real hero-figure is entirely unmotivated. The concrete class struggles, which formed the social content of the Sea Beggars' rising, are missing; yet it is only through and as a result of them that one can understand William of Orange's simultaneous connection with, and opposition to, the plebeians of this period. De Coster, however, leaves all these concrete mediations out. The section taken from and modelled on the old saga is too close to the ground, too local, too anecdotal, too animal-like and natural to reveal this differentiation among the combatants; the "legend" itself is again too generalizing, too heroic, too simplifyingly "monumental" to show concrete historical outlines, limitations and contradictions.

Romain Rolland in his criticism very rightly emphasizes de Coster's powerful, hate-inspired attack upon Catholicism. "But," he continues, "if Rome has everything to lose here, Geneva gains nothing. If, of the two faiths, the Catholic appears ridiculous, the other, the Reformed, does not appear at all. We are indeed told that the rebels have rallied to it. But where does one see a single great Christian amongst them?"

Rolland intends this as praise. He quotes Ulenspiegel's statement that in order to save Flanders he had turned to the God of the Earth and the Heaven, but had received no answer. Katheline, who in the course of the novel is executed as a witch, replies: "The great God could not hear you; you ought to have spoken first to the spirits of the elemental world."

And Romain Rolland adds: "The elemental world: here are the true Gods. With them alone de Coster's heroes communicate. And the only faith in the work—but a torrential one—is faith in Nature."

Romain Rolland in his understandable enthusiasm for many fine aspects of Ulenspiegel overlooks two important ones here. First, that the absence of Protestanism in de Coster's work is the most visible symptom of its anti-historicism. Protestantism, particularly in the liberation struggle of the Netherlands, was with its various currents and sects, practically the only concrete ideological form in which the national and social antagonisms of the time could be fought. De Coster, by ignoring this or by simply acknowledging it abstractly and declaratively but not incorporating it artistically, evades historical concretization, evades an historically differentiated picture of the age. Or rather, because he has in mind only an abstract-general and not an historical-concrete picture of this liberation struggle, he is unable to decipher in social and human terms and hence portray artistically either the role of Protestantism in the Netherlands Revolution or the differences inside the Reformed camp. The fact that Catholicism was the object of general popular hatred makes its representation somewhat more possible despite de Coster's abstract historical conception. Although again it is more the contemporary literary echo of the popular hatred that he reproduces than the actual, concrete reactionary role which Catholicism itself played at the time.

Secondly, Romain Rolland—to our mind—overlooks the modern naturalist motifs in de Coster's cult of nature and the elemental spirits. He is right in saying that de Coster's finest and most moving scenes arise out of this feeling for nature (for instance, the figure and fate of Katheline, though here again the modern naturalist synthesis of pathology and mysticism is specially visible). But only certain individual episodes and scenes are on such a level. And many even of the best scenes bear a naturalist stamp; on the one hand, the one-sided cult of animal life, of gluttony, drunkenness and fornication, on the other, the predilection for brutality, so characteristic of modern naturalism.

Torture, burnings at the stake and other bestial kinds of execution are described extensively and in detail. De Coster surpasses even Flaubert in this respect.

At the same time we must not overlook the difference in feeling and outlook which motivates the cruelty here. Romain Rolland rightly says: "Holy vengeance becomes a monomania, whose frenzied tenacity hallucinates." De Coster allows the reader to believe that the fishmonger, who has delivered Ulenspiegel's father Claes over to his executioners, has drowned. "But he reappears a long time afterwards. De Coster reserves him for a second death. And this, his real death, is made to last! For those whom Ulenspiegel hates death is never too slow. They must die by slow degrees. They have to suffer. . . One is stifled by this delight in torture, by this sad tormenting cruelty. The avenger himself derives no pleasure from it."

We see that the cruelty here has an opposite cause to that in Flaubert (and, as we shall soon see, in Conrad Ferdinand Meyer). Here it is the explosive excesses of popular hatred and revenge, the stored-up anger of the bestially oppressed. There is genuine plebeian feeling behind De Coster's cruelty. Its closest neighbour in naturalism is the eruption of mass cruelty in Zola's *Germinal*. But it is more genuinely and more directly plebeian, which makes it even more explosively cruel.

However, the difference of cause does not remove the similarity of effect. All the less because this escape of plebeian hatred into avenging cruelty is deeply connected with the social roots of de Coster's naturalism. Precisely because de Coster's view of the popular movements in the Netherlands liberation struggle is not concrete—he does

not see them in their origins, social ramifications and inner antagonisms, but simply as an abstract and monumentalized popular uprising—he must, if his writing is to achieve human vividness and
artistic clarity, resort to the depiction of animal joys or blind cruelty.

If the classics of the historical novel avoided these animal frenzies
of pleasure and torment—and were suitably reprimanded by all the
Taines and Brandes for doing so—it was because their portrayals
could live fully in the world of historical "mediations", in the world
of those determinants which show that people in their highest
moments are yet children of their age. The pleasures of gluttony,
drunkenness and fornication and the distress of the physically tortured
undergo little change in history. But the spiritual uprise of a Jeanie
Deans in Scott or the unshakeable constancy of Lorenzo and Lucia in
Manzoni are linked by countless bonds, often not immediately perceptible, to the here-and-now of a definite historical period. And for this
reason their human influence has a broader, deeper, more lasting and
concrete radius than has this abstract immediacy of the purely
elemental.

We think, therefore, that Romain Rolland underestimates the division in de Coster's work. He does so because of the understandable
enthusiasm which de Coster's attempt, the attempt of a modern writer
to create a national epic, inspires in him. He sees in de Coster a path
leading from the initial dualism which Rolland himself shrewdly
established, to the epic. "The individual has become a type. The type
becomes a symbol; he no longer grows old, he no longer has a body,
and he says so: 'I am no longer body, but Spirit . . . The spirit of
Flanders . . . I shall never die.' . . ."

He is the genius of the Netherlands. And he departs from the book
singing his sixth song, "*but no-one knows where he will sing his last*".

This patriotism, this unshakeable faith in the eternity of plebeian
Flanders is really impressive, really moving, everyone will share
Romain Rolland's enthusiasm. But the literary expression of this
faith remains lyrical, the merely subjective emotion of the author; it
does not serve as the basis of an objective and richly articulated
historical world, complete in itself; it does not become epic. From an
epic point of view the emotions remain abstract, precisely because
they are merely lyrical.

There were several attempts in the nineteenth century to make an
abstractly seen world appear epic by charging it with a high lyrical
pathos. This is true of some of the most important representatives of
naturalism. But the lyrical pathos of de Coster is no more a substitute
for the lack of historical concreteness than is Zola's for the lack of
social concreteness.

4. *Conrad Ferdinand Meyer and the New Type of Historical Novel.*

The real representative of the historical novel in this period is Conrad Ferdinand Meyer, who along with Gottfried Keller—likewise a native of Switzerland—is one of the most important realistic narrative writers of the period following 1848. Both, however differently, have stronger ties with the classical traditions of narrative art than most of their German contemporaries and hence surpass them far in respect of a realism which comes to grips with essentials. But Meyer already shows marked features in both his outlook and art of the decline of realism. Yet this did not prevent his exercising a powerful influence far beyond the German speaking world. On the contrary, precisely because he appeared to combine a classical containment of form with a modern hypertrophy of sensibility and subjectivism, an objectivity of historical tone with a wholesale modernization of characters' emotions, and did so with artistry—he became the true classic of the modern historical novel.

In Meyer the conflicting tendencies of the new phase of development cohere in a new form. Yet his essential problems are strikingly similar in many respects to those of Flaubert. This is particularly interesting because the concrete historical situation of the two writers and hence their concrete attitudes to historical problems are so very different. Flaubert's decisive historical experience is the Revolution of 1848 (in *L'Education Sentimentale* one can clearly see its effect on him). Conrad Ferdinand Meyer's great historical experience, on the other hand, is the dawning of German unity, its struggle and realization. The fact that Meyer is the living contemporary of this conclusion to the bourgeois-democratic struggles for German unity, and particularly the contemporary of their capitulation to the "Bonapartist monarchy" of the Hohenzollerns under Bismarck's leadership, this makes his historical subject-matter less arbitrary than Flaubert's. Admittedly the decorative contrast between a "grandiose" past and a trivial present plays an important part in his work, too, and determines his predilection for the Renaissance. But even so, considerable importance is attached to struggles for national unification and national unity (*Jürg Jenatsch, The Temptation of Pescara,* etc.)

However, the treatment of these themes suffers disastrously from the central position of Bismark in this period, which affected even Meyer. Meyer speaks quite openly on the subject, particularly in reference to Jürg Jenatsch. He complains in a letter that his hero's resemblance to Bismarck is "not palpable enough"; in another place:

"and how petty, despite murder and killing, is the confederate (Jenatsch—G.L.) compared with the prince". This Bismarck adulation is very closely connected with the fact that Meyer, like the German liberal middle class in general, after the 1848 Revolution no longer regards the establishment of national unity and the defence of national independence as the cause of the people to be carried out by the people themselves under the leadership of "world-historical individuals", but as a historical destiny whose executive organ is some enigmatic, lonely "hero" or "genius". Pescara especially is portrayed in this way—a lonely figure who decides in lonely ruminations whether Italy is to be freed from foreign domination and of course decides negatively: "Does Italy deserve freedom at this hour and is she of sufficient worth, as constituted, to receive and preserve it? I think not," says Pescara. But this statement is simply an expression of his secluded personality, it does not relate in the novel itself to any popular movement which has such an aim; he says this only among the higher circle of diplomats and generals etc.

Naturally, one cannot make a simple comparison between the Swiss patrician and the vulgar-liberal supporters of Bismarck in Germany. Meyer's superiority to them, however, is chiefly one of taste, moral feeling and psychological sensitivity, not of political vision or of deeper solidarity with the people. Thus Meyer's remoulding of the problems of his age, once he has projected them into history, is purely a matter of aesthetic feeling and taste; he turns the fatalistic geniuses, the supposed makers of history into decorative and superb decadents. His aesthetic and moral superiority to his German contemporaries simply means that he introduces moral problems and scruples into the Bismarck conception of history as a question of naked power. (We recall the similar position of Jacob Burckhardt.)

The abstract ideology of power and the mystical and fatalistic mission of "great men" remains unchanged and uncriticized in Meyer. He says in his novel on Pescara: "He believes in power alone and in the single duty of great men to attain to their full stature through the means and tasks of the age." As a result the tasks themselves shrink more and more into power intrigues within the upper stratum and the real historical problems, whose executive organs these men were in reality, fade increasingly from sight. It is very characteristic of Meyer's development that in *Jürg Jenatsch* there was still some rudimentary connection with real popular aims even though it was expressed, à la Bismarck, solely through the "genius" of the hero. In *Pescara* such connections have disappeared and the other historical novels are even further away from the historical life of the people; in them the dualism between questions of power and subjective moral rumination becomes even more the exclusive preoccupation.

This conception of heroes is linked in Meyer with a fatalistic view of the unknowability of the paths of history, with a mystique of "great men" as the executors of the fatalistic will of an unknowable divinity. In his youthful and lyrical-historical work on the fortunes of Ulrich von Hutten he states this view quite clearly:

"Wir ziehn ! Die Trommel schlägt ! Die Fahne weht !
Nicht weiss ich, welchen Weg die Heerfahrt geht.

Genug, dass ihn der Herr des Krieges weiss—
Sein Plan und Losung ! *Unser* Kampf und Schweiss."

("We're off! The drum strikes up! The flag is flying!
I do not know the way the expedition goes.

Enough that the Lord of war knows it—
His plan and battle-cry ! *Our* struggle and sweat.")

The unknowability of the ways and ends of the historical process is exactly countered by the unknowability of the individuals acting in history. They are not temporarily isolated, as a result of definite objective or subjective circumstances, but fundamentally lonely.

This loneliness is connected in Meyer, as in almost all the important writers of this period, very deeply with his general outlook, with his belief that man and his destiny are fundamentally unknowable. The inevitable result of the loss of interaction between man and society, of blindness to the fact that if man is formed by society, then this is also a process of his own inner life, is to make the words and deeds of men appear to the writer as impenetrable masks, behind which the most varied motives may be at work. Meyer has stated this feeling clearly several times, most plastically in the *Novelle*, *The Monk's Wedding*. Dante tells a story in which the Hohenstaufen Emperor, Frederick II and his Chancellor, Petrus de Vines, appear episodically. To the question of the listening tyrant of Verona, Cangrande, as to whether he, Dante, really believes that Frederick was the author of the piece *Of the Three Impostors*, Dante replies "non liquet" (it is not clear); and to the question as to whether he believes in the Chancellor's treachery he replies in a similar fashion. Cangrande then reproaches him for having shown Frederick guilty and Petrus asserting his innocence in the *Divine Comedy*: "You do not believe in the guilt and you condemn. You believe in the guilt and you exonerate." The real Dante certainly had no such doubts. It is only Meyer who makes of him an agnostic in his attitude to people. In this way the decorative robes of the Renaissance conceal the most modern agnosticism and nihilism.

There is apparent self-criticism on Meyer's part in Cangrande's reproaches to Dante. Yet at best it is but one side of his conception.

For Meyer feels that Dante has every right to portray history and people, whom he admits he cannot really penetrate, in an autocratic manner, according to his own lights; the more so, as this loneliness and unknowability is in Meyer's eyes a *merit*: the greater a person's stature, the greater his loneliness and unknowability.

This sentiment becomes more and more pronounced in the course of Meyer's development and, as a result, his heroes, too, acquire more and more of this enigmatic loneliness, they become more and more eccentric in their attitudes to the events of history in which they are the heroes. Already in *The Saint* Meyer turns the struggle of crown and church in medieval England into a psychological problem of Thomas Beckett. The tendency is still more pronounced in *Pescara*. What appears to be a highly dramatic action, the question namely of whether General Pescara will renounce the Spaniards and fight for the unification of Italy is no more than the illusion of a conflict. Pescara wanders through the novel, an enigmatic sphinx whose far-sighted plans nobody understands. And why? Because Pescara has no such plans. He is dangerously ill and knows that he soon must die, that he can never again take part in any great enterprise. He says himself: "For no choice ever appeared before me, I stood outside of things ... The knot of my existence is inextricable, it (that is death, G.L.) will cut it apart."

Here we see in a different form a similar problem to the one we observed in Flaubert: the combination of a desire for great deeds with a personal and social inability to accomplish them in reality is projected into the past, in the hope that this social impotence may lose its modern pettiness in the ostentatious attire of the Renaissance. However, this projection into an illusory monumentality—a monumentality merely of picturesque gestures, hiding the decadent, tormented broodings of the modern bourgeois—produces in the general tone of the writing notes as false and feelings and experiences as distorted as in Flaubert.

Here also is the real source of Meyer's modernization of history. Meyer, like Flaubert, always gives an accurate picture of the externals of historical life, except that he is more concentrated, decorative and less prone to naturalistic detail. Brandes's criticism of Scott's naïve handling of contemporary plastic arts in his historical novels could never be levelled against Meyer. Yet the *innermost conflicts* of his heroes do not grow out of the real historical conditions of the given period, out of the popular life of the period. Instead they are specifically modern conflicts of passion and conscience in an individual artificially isolated by capitalist life, just as Flaubert's conflicts were conflicts of desire and fulfilment in present-day bourgeois society. For this reason the psychology of Meyer's heroes—despite the fine gradations and picturesque portrayals of historical attire—is through-out the same or almost so; it is immaterial which country or which age is chosen as the arena of the historical plot.

Meyer was quite aware of this "problematic" in his art. In a letter he writes of his aims and attitude in regard to the form of the historical novel: "I use the form of the historical *Novelle* simply and solely to express my experiences and my personal feelings, I prefer it to the 'period novel', because it gives me a better mask and puts the reader at a greater distance. Thus within a very objective and highly artistic form I am essentially very individual and subjective." This subjec-tivity appears chiefly in the fact that the heroes are spectators rather than executors of their own deeds, that their real interest is the moral-metaphysical scruples and broodings which have as their object the "questions of power" in the foreground of the story.

Because of this attitude Meyer follows on from Vigny rather than from Scott in the historical novel. But he makes history even less historical. Vigny and similar Romantic historical novelists see the historical process incorrectly, standing on its head. But they never-theless see some kind of historical process, even if it is of their own false construction. And their "great men" act within this historical process. In Meyer, apart from certain attempts and survivals, the historical process itself has disappeared, and with it man disappears as the real actor in world history. It is very interesting to see that in Meyer's original plan for *Pescara* the fatal illness was absent. He says in a conversation: "I could have done it differently, and that would have had its attractions, too: Pescara's wound was not mortal; he is tempted, fights the temptation, overcomes and repudiates it. And then afterwards seeing the gratitude of the House of Habsburg, he regrets having done so. He can also then fall in the battle outside Milan." One observes how, even in this plan, the psychological-moral element prevails over the historical-political motifs. And it is no acci-dent that Meyer in subsequent work on the material takes it further in this direction, giving his hero an irrational, biological "depth". In so doing Meyer produces on the one hand the fatalistic-melancholic groundnote of the novel, on the other the enigmatic loneliness of his hero. He himself says on one occasion: "One does not know what Pescara would have done without his wound."

Thus by having only protagonists of history at the centre of his novels and almost totally neglecting the people and their lives, the real broad forces of history, Meyer has reached a much more advanced stage of the liquidation of history than the earlier Romantics. History has become something purely irrational for him. The great men are eccentric and lonely figures caught up within meaningless events which never touch them at the centre. History is a complex of decorative *tableaux*, great pathetic moments, in which this loneliness and eccentricity gives vent to itself with a lyrical psychological force that is often very moving. Meyer is an important writer because he does not conceal his "problematic" with art; the modern bourgeois incapacity of his heroes breaks through the historical costume again and again. But this very artistic honesty and uprightness is what shatters the fine structure of his works. Again and again his history is unmasked as mere costumery.

Yet from a formal point of view the structure of Meyer's works is of a very high quality, outwardly well-nigh perfect. His exploitation of the decorative possibilities does not, as in Flaubert, lead to excessive description. Meyer, on the contrary, is unusually economical in his descriptions. He concentrates his action round the pathos and drama of a few scenes and his description of surrounding objects is always subject to the psychological problems of the characters. His model is the strict compactness of the old *Novelle*. But this compactness serves for him a double purpose: at once to mask decoratively and unmask lyrically the subjective projection of present-day feelings into history. His plots are constructed with the deliberate aim of stressing the enigma of his heroes. The form of a story within a story serves to make events, conceived as incomprehensible and irrational in themselves, actually appear so, and in particular to underline the impenetrable enigma of the main characters.

Meyer already belongs quite consciously with those modern writers for whom the charm of storytelling lies no longer in the elucidation of an apparently incomprehensible event, in the elucidation of deeper connections of life which comprehend the apparently incomprehensible, but in the mystery itself, in portraying the irrational "unfathomable depth" of human existence. Meyer, for example, lets a simple archer, who naturally understands nothing of the deeper connections, recount the fortunes of Thomas Beckett. He tells of events which were "astounding and inconceivable" not only for distant observers but also for the participants.

Meyer hopes by this strict composition to avoid the modern writer's submergence in psychological analysis. But his way out is illusory, for the psychologism of the moderns had nothing to do with analysis as a form of expression, it springs from the writer's orientation on the inner spiritual life of his characters, which he believes to be independent of the total coherence of life and to move according to its own laws. Meyer's decorative concentration is thus no less psychologistic than the writings of those of his contemporaries who were open adherents of psychological analysis. Simply that with him the discrepancy between the decorative outward spectacle of history and the modern psychology of the characters is sharper.

This discrepancy is further underlined by the fact that Meyer, like Flaubert, inclines to see the greatness of vanished ages in the brutal excesses of the people of the past. Gottfried Keller, his great democratic contemporary, who had a high regard for Meyer's honest artistic aims, continually jibes in his letters at this passionate weakness of the humanly very sensitive writer for cruelty and brutality in his stories.

All these features, as with Flaubert, express opposition to the triviality of bourgeois life. But because of the different social historical circumstances they do so in quite a different way. Flaubert's rejection of modern bourgeois life has very romantic sources and modes of expression, yet it is full of a passionate radicalism. Meyer has much more the weary melancholy of the liberal bourgeois, who watches with repudiation and bewilderment the evolution of his own class amid the vehement advances of capitalism while at the same time timidly admiring the power that is manifested therein.

Meyer's portrayal of historical protagonists is interesting and important because it shows so vividly how the once democratic aims of the bourgeois class are transformed, even in the case of honest and highly gifted writers, into a compromising liberalism. Meyer cherishes a great admiration for the men and theories of the Renaissance. But the fiery wine of this admiration is always mixed with a goodly measure of liberal water. We have already seen the overdone moral-psychological reflections which are mixed up with the question of "power in itself". This mixture appears again and again in Meyer's novels as a longing for the "beyond Good and Evil" world of the Renaissance mingled with liberal reservations and extenuations. Thus in the Pescara novel, for example: "Caesar Borgia, he tried with pure Evil. But. . . Evil must be used only in small portions and with caution, otherwise it kills." Or as Pescara himself says—in a very Bismarckian way—of Macchiavelli: "There are political principles which are meaningful to intelligent minds and prudent hands, but which become corrupt and wicked as soon as a rude mouth utters or a criminal pen inscribes them." So we see that Meyer's enthusiasm for the Renaissance is not based upon the recognition and acknowledgment of a great and unsurpassed period of progress, as it was with Goethe or Stendhal, Heine or Engels. His contemporary, Burckhardt, played a decisive part in popularizing the Renaissance. Yet despite important individual discoveries, he is already waging an ideological rearguard action: correct insights are frequently obscured by infusions of liberal "problematic". In Meyer this tendency is more marked as is his form-alist-decorative conception of the Renaissance.

This "problematic" leads on to the liberal hero-cult of Bismarck. For while the principle of "beyond Good and Evil" is permissible to the "man of destiny", woe betide should it become the property of the people. Behind Meyer's conception of history lies his admiration for Bismarckian *Realpolitik*, for the superior skulduggery of the upper-most spheres of society, for a form of politics which in the eyes of the liberal ideologists has become an "art", an "end-in-itself".

Thus the virtual disappearance of popular life in these novels, the fact that it is only an artificially isolated upper stratum which acts in the foreground, is only apparently an artistic problem. In Vigny this expressed a reactionary-Romantic opposition to the progressive, popular character of Scott's conception of history. In Meyer, who personally was not nearly so openly reactionary as Vigny, it shows the triumph of the National Liberalism into which the liberalism of the German speaking world had turned. The Swiss, Meyer, is sufficiently independent socially and sufficiently honest, personally and artistically, not to succumb entirely to the apologist excesses of the German national-liberal bourgeoisie. He creates works of art superior in every respect to contemporary productions in Germany, yet for precisely this reason the effect of national liberalism and its estrangement from the people on the historical novel is in his case all the more important and fatal.

In most of Meyer's works this estrangement is expressed directly: the historical events take place exclusively "above"; the inscrutable course of history manifests itself in the power-political deeds and moral scruples of individuals who are completely isolated and uncom-prehended even within the upper stratum. If the people are shown at all, then it is simply as an amorphous, spontaneous, blind and savage mass, usually as wax in the hands of the lonely hero (Jürg Jenatsch). Popular figures which are given any independence and individuality express in the main only blind devotion to (archer in *The Saint*) or blind enthusiasm for (Leubelfing in *Gustav Adolf's Page*) the great historical hero.

But when Meyer, very exceptionally, gives us a popular story, even in the form of an episode, the contrast between his character-ization and that of the classical period of the historical novel comes out with particular clarity. In the Novelle, *Plautus in the Convent* (*Plautus im Nonnenkloster*), the story is told of a brave and deter-mined peasant girl, Gertrude, rigorously bound by the Catholic Faith of her time. She has taken a vow to become a nun which she wishes to fulfil despite the resistance of her whole being, despite her love for a youth whom she would like to marry. When the novices are received into the convent "miracles" are made to occur: the novice is expected to carry a heavy cross (with a crown of thorns on her head). Only if she does not collapse under its weight will she be accepted as a nun. According to superstition the holy Virgin assists; in actual fact the novice is given quite a light cross, outwardly similar to the heavy one. Poggio, the narrator of this story, succeeds through various circumstances of the main plot to reveal this deception to the girl. Gertrude now chooses the really heavy cross in order to test in fact whether the holy Virgin really wants her to become a nun. After heroic efforts she collapses, and now she is able to become the happy wife of her loved one.

But how does Poggio—and with him surely C. F. Meyer—react to this? Poggio relates: "This she did and calmly descended from step to step radiant with joy, once more the simple peasant girl, who, now that her modest human wish had been granted and she could return to everyday life, would no doubt quickly and happily forget the moving spectacle which she had afforded the crowd in her despair. For a brief while the peasant girl had stood before me, and I with my excited senses had seen her as the embodiment of a higher being, a demonic creature, truth jubilantly destroying illusion. But what is truth asked Pilate?"

We have quoted this passage in full, because if one compares the story of Gertrude with that of Goethe's Dorothea or Scott's Jeannie Deans the contrast between the two periods is vividly apparent. At the same time the comparison reveals the social and human foundations of this new type of historical novel. We have to limit ourselves here to the most essential features of the contrast. First of all, the bravery of Meyer's peasant girl has something eccentric and decorative about it. We do not see its significant human qualities; instead we have one short, unique act which shows physical strain on the one hand and pictorial effect (cross and crown of thorns) on the other. Secondly, Meyer views the moment of heroism in isolation from life, indeed as a complete antithesis to life. The return to everyday life is not, as in Goethe and Scott, a broad epic destiny, it does not suggest the slumbering presence of similar forces in countless ordinary people which, for personal or historical reasons, have simply never been released or tested. For Meyer it is determined by the antithesis between the "demonic" and the "everyday", so that the return to everyday life in fact nullifies the "heroic moment", whereas in Goethe and Scott the heroism is "sublated" (aufgehoben) in the dialectical, two-fold sense.

Meyer proves himself to be an important artist amid the onset of decline by portraying a completely normal heroine and not, as Huysmans, Wilde or d'Annunzio would have done, a really "demonic" and hysterical creature. But he is already sufficiently contaminated by decadence to treat his own rightness of view with a certain sceptical melancholy.

This type of sensibility reveals the spirit of the new times. Meyer's heroes stand spiritually and morally on tiptoe in order to appear to others and particularly to themselves greater than they are, in order to convince others and themselves that the height which they have attained or at least dreamed of attaining at individual moments of their lives is theirs at all times. The decorative historical costume serves to conceal this tiptoe posture.

It is clear that this inner weakness, coupled with the morbid longing for greatness, is due to the divorce from popular life. The everyday life of the people appears as dull, degrading prose, nothing more. No longer is an organic connection seen between this life and an historical upsurge. The hero, as Burkchardt says, is "what we are not".

The German bourgeoisie became national-liberal; it betrayed the bourgeois-democratic Revolution of 1848 and later, with ever fewer reservations, chose the Bismarck way to German unity. In German literature of the time this path of development takes the form ideo-logically of pure apologia and artistically of the wholesale decline of classical traditions and the most superficial assimilation of a second-class West European realism.

Whatever Meyer's superiority aesthetically and ethically to these German bourgeois, who from 1848 to 1870 turned from democrats into national-liberals, and however complex the connections between the development of his art and this social-historical development, he nevertheless mirrors this process in the most intimate, spiritual and artistic problems of his life's work. His Renaissance figures reflect liberal timidity and faint-heartedness. His "lonely" heroes bear typical traits of the decline of German democracy.

5. The General Tendencies of Decadence and the Establishment of the Historical Novel as a Special Genre.

In the works of Conrad Ferdinand Meyer the historical novel establishes itself as a special genre. This is his decisive significance for literary development. True, Flaubert also stressed the special character of the historical novel and wished to "apply" the methods of the new realism to the historical field which he regarded as a special sphere. But Meyer is the only really important writer of this transitional period who concentrates his entire life's work on the historical novel and evolves a special method for dealing with it. It is clear from prev-ious remarks how large the difference was between this approach to history and that of the old historical novel. Scott gave expression to a new, historical attitude on the part of society which arose from life itself. His historical themes emerged organically, by themselves as it were, from the development, spread and deepening of historical feeling. They simply give expression to this feeling—the feeling that a real understanding for the problems of contemporary society can only grow out of an understanding of the society's prehistory and formative history. Hence Scott's historical novel, as the artistic expression of an historicized attitude to life, of a growing historical understanding for the problems of contemporary society, necessarily led, as we have seen, to a higher form of the contemporary novel in Balzac and again in Tolstoy.

In this period the situation is quite different. We have heard both Flaubert's and Meyer's explanations for their decision to treat historical subjects. We saw that in both cases their motives arose not from an understanding of the connection between history and the present, but on the contrary, from a repudiation of the present, which though understandable and justifiable on human-moral, humanist-aesthetic grounds, in their case is no more than a subjectivist, aesthetic-moral repudiation. The representation of historical subjects is simply a question of costume and decoration, simply a means for expressing their subjectivity more fully than—according to them—a contemporary subject would permit.

We do not wish to dwell here on the self-deception to which the literary spokesmen of this attitude fall victim in regard to their own work; we shall speak about this later. What is important is that this approach to historical subjects expresses on the one hand a general attitude of the whole epoch and on the other *impoverishes* the world portrayed. For what was it that attracted Scott and his important followers to historical subjects? The realization that those problems whose importance they observed in contemporary society took a different and specific form in the past; that history, therefore, as the objective prehistory of the present, is something which is not alien and incomprehensible to the human spirit.

For the modern writers, however, it is precisely the strangeness of history which is attractive. The well-known positivist sociologist and aesthetician, Guyau, spoke of this relationship very clearly and definitely. He said: "There are various ways of escaping the *trivial*, of embellishing reality for ourselves without falsifying it; and these ways constitute a kind of idealism which is also available to naturalism. They consist above all in the distancing of things or events, whether in time or in space... Art is intended to exercise the transforming, embellishing function of memory." It is very interesting that Guyau makes no difference between the temporal or spatial distancing of the artistic subject. What is essential for him is the embellishing effect of the picturesque, the unfamiliar, the exotic which occurs. Now if one looks, for example, at French literature of this time, one sees a real orgy of exotic themes. Alongside the Orient, Greece, the Middle Ages (Leconte de Lisle's poems), we find decadent Rome (Bouilhet), Carthage, Egypt, Judea (Flaubert), primeval times (Bouilhet), Spain, Russia (Gautier), South America (Leconte de Lisle, Hérédia); in the same period the brothers Goncourt introduce the vogue of the Japanese etc. In Germany one has the analogy of Meyer's Renaissance, Hebbel's and Richard Wagner's varied, but predominantly exotic, subject-matter and among smaller fry Eber's Egypt and Dahn's tribal migrations etc.

A literary current of this kind, embracing writers of the most varied trends and importance, has deep roots in the life of the present. Romanticism had made its protest against the ugliness of capitalist life by escaping to the Middle Ages. But this protest still had a fairly clear though reactionary political and social content. The writers protesting now—in the form of exotic subjects—have no such reactionary illusions, or only exceptionally. Their chief experience, particularly in the case of French writers, writing in conditions of more advanced capitalism and sharper class struggle than the Germans, is a universal disgust, an infinite disillusionment with life which has no visible goal. If they long to get away, "away" is more important than "where". The past is no longer the objective pre-history of men's social development, but the innocent and forever lost beauty of childhood, to which a squandered life is passionately but fruitlessly drawn in desperate, unrealizable yearning. This sentiment is expressed most fully in the following stanza from Baudelaire's *Moesta et Errabunda*:

> Emporte-moi, wagon ! enlève-moi, frégate :
> Loin ! Loin ! ici la boue est faite de nos pleurs !...
>
> —Mais le vert paradis des amours enfantines !...
>
> L'innocent paradis, plein de plaisirs furtifs,
> Est-il déjà plus loin que l'Inde et que la Chine?
> Peut-on le rappeler avec des cris plaintifs,
> Et l'animer encor d'une voix argentine,
> L'innocent paradis, plein de plaisirs furtifs?

Distance then, is no longer something historically concrete, not even in the reactionary-utopian sense of the earlier Romantics. Distance is simply negation of the present, difference of life in the abstract, something forever lost, which is impregnated with memory and desire to give it poetic substance. Its poetic sources are thus purely subjective. And the aim of the archaeological exactitude and nervous precision with which the detail of a spatially or temporarily remote, exotic world is explored is, as we have seen particularly in Flaubert's case, not to investigate the social-historical character of such a world, but to achieve pictorial effect. True the exactitude is supposed to guarantee the objective-artistic reality of the portrayed world, but since the inner life of this world depends solely upon the subjective, very modern and very European longing and despair of the writer, the archaeological exactitude can provide no more than stage decorations for the enactment of human destinies which have inwardly nothing in common with the exotic objects so exactly described. And this applies to the most important writers.

But however anti-bourgeois this longing and despair in their immediate content, they are profoundly bourgeois at heart. They express the feelings of the best representatives of the bourgeois class at the time, who were yet unable to rise above the onsetting decline of their class. Despite the sharp opposition for instance of Flaubert or Baudelaire to the bourgeoisie of their time, despite the violent repudiation with which their works were received, the socially identical factor which connects them with their class nevertheless predominates. This is why in time their works overcame the indignant repudiation of their contemporaries and they themselves were acknowledged as writers who had given expression to essential themes of their age.

The apparent contradiction here exists only for vulgar sociology. Marx himself defined this relation between writer and class very clearly and precisely : "Just as little must one imagine that the democratic representatives are indeed all shopkeepers or enthusiastic champions of shopkeepers. According to their education and their individual position they may be as far apart as heaven from earth. What makes them representatives of the petty bourgeoisie is the fact that in their minds they do not get beyond the limits which the latter do not get beyond in life, that they are consequently driven, theoretically, to the same problems and solutions to which material interest and social position drive the latter practically. This is, in general, the relationship between the political and literary representatives of a class and the class they represent."

This relationship between the important representatives of historical (exotic) writing in this period and their class comes out particularly in the way real historical greatness is replaced by cruelty and brutality. We have already dealt with this problem : we pointed out the paradox whereby lofty and sensitive writers, in both an aesthetic and moral respect, like Flaubert and Meyer, were driven to such cruelty and brutality in their writing. We also showed the inevitability of this change, following on the loss of an inner relationship with history, its close connection with the general attitude of the period of decline which no longer saw historical action in terms of the deeds and sufferings of the people themselves, nor "world-historical individuals" as the representatives of popular movements. We need now only mention briefly the relationship between these attitudes and the unconscious experiences of broad bourgeois and petty bourgeois masses for us to realize that while these writers may have towered humanly and intellectually above the mass of their contemporaries, they in fact only gave artistic expression to the latter's hidden, warped and disavowed feelings. Baudelaire again expressed the attitude of the average bourgeois or petty bourgeois of this period, who equated greatness with brutal excess, in an exceptionally clear and significant form (in *To the Reader*):

> Si le viol, le poison, le poignard, l'incendie,
> N'ont pas encor brodé de leurs plaisants dessins
> Le canevas banal de nos piteux destins,
> C'est que notre âme, hélas! n'est pas assez hardie.

In his foreward to *Les Fleurs du Mal* Théophile Gautier gives an extremely interesting and characteristic exposition of this passage. He speaks of the great modern monster of boredom, "which in its bourgeois cowardice dreams insipidly of the savagery and debauchery of the Romans, of the bureaucrat Nero and the shopkeeper Heliogabalus".

Some important modern writers, already more aware of these connections, have actually portrayed the living relationship between ideologies of this kind and the material foundations of bourgeois life. Think of Heinrich Mann's unforgettable Professor Unrat or Heinrich Mann's *Untertan* which bring out the common features of the megalomaniac imperialist bourgeois of the Wilhelmine period and the decorative monumentality of Wagnerian art, where Wagner's Lohengrin appears as the inner ideal of the capitalist Hessling.

This relationship enables us to understand the special position of historical material within the general trend towards the exotic. We have heard the arguments which for Meyer determined the superiority of the historical novel over one with a contemporary subject. Meyer's biographer and critic, F. Baumgarten, has commented very interestingly on Meyer's attitude to historic material, in many respects defining more clearly both Meyer's conception as well as Guyau's general theory of the exotic. Baumgarten says of the writer who deals with the present: "His material is without destiny, it requires the forming hand of the writer to become a destiny. The *historical writer* already has a destiny in his model, one formed by the interaction of character and environment." Baumgarten has no understanding of the historical connections which gave rise to his or Meyer's outlook. In the forces which the historical novel is supposed to portray he sees (in a Rickert-cum-Meinecke form) only ideas, something simply imported by us into the historic material. Because of this subjectivism his contrast between history and the present remains rigid and exclusive. A present-day character cannot be portrayed "because the forms of construction, which only a closed historical process can render visible, cannot be recognized, known and established for the present".

We have quoted this commentary at length because in it incomprehension of the present the essential unknowability of the present appears as the basis for treating historical subjects. The past, history, therefore, has no organic connection with the present; in this respect, too, it is rather the latter's rigid opposite pole. The present is obscure, the past reveals clear outlines. That these outlines do not in fact belong to the past as such, but are importations of the subject (or, as the philosophers would have it, "the cognitive subject"), does not affect this opposition in any way, since according to thinkers and writers of this kind any such application of categories of thought to the present is in practice impossible. The prevalent philosophical attitude that the outside world is unknowable receives a heightened and qualitatively new emphasis when extended to the knowability of the present. The philosophic and artistic idealization of an attitude of helplessness, of a refusal to confront basic problems, of a reduction of the essential to a level with the inessential etc. deeply affects all problems of portrayal.

The extent and permanence of these subjectivizing trends may be seen most clearly if we look at the remarks of the important anti-Fascist writer and militant humanist, Lion Feuchtwanger, at the Paris Congress for the Defence of Culture. Feuchtwanger in the main—as we shall see in the next chapter—stands quite apart from the purely descriptive writing of the period we have just analysed, and, in a certain sense, even contrasts with it. Nevertheless, his theoretical arguments in favour of the historical novel betray the influence of the leading reactionary philosophers of the period of decline, particularly Nietzsche, but also Croce, and are full of the same subjectivism with regard to historical subject-matter.

Feuchtwanger compares contemporary and historical subjects from the point of view of their ability to express the writer's ideas. He says: "If I feel drawn to array a contemporary subject in historical costume, negative and positive causes come into play. Sometimes I am unable to distil certain sections of my plot as I would wish: left in contemporary costume, they remain raw material, report, reflection, idea, they do not form a picture. Or if I use a contemporary *milieu*, I am aware of a missing conclusion. Things are still in flux; whether and to what extent a contemporary development may be assumed complete must always remain arbitrary, every supposed full-stop will be accidental. In portraying contemporary circumstances I am discomforted by a lack of perspective; it is a scent which evaporates because you cannot close the bottle. In addition our very hectic age very rapidly turns all that is present into history, so that if to-day's *milieu* will in any case be historical in five years' time, then why should I not just as well choose a *milieu* which lies as far back as I please, if I want to express a theme which I hope will still be alive in five years' time?"

Thus Feuchtwanger repeats many of the arguments which we have met in the writings of the important theorists and writers of this period. It is common to all these theorists that both history and the present are conceived as dead complexes of facts, which have no living movement, no spirit or soul of their own, but which are inspirited from outside, by the writer. On the other hand, the writers' own experiences do not appear to them to be tied down to any time. They believe that the spatial and temporal manifestations of human feelings and ideas are simply a matter of externals and costume, while the feelings and ideas themselves lie outside the historical process and hence may be transferred forwards or backwards to any age without serious alteration. The choice of historical subjects on the basis of this attitude is, say, in the case of Conrad Ferdinand Meyer purely a question of tasteful artistic selection: those periods of history are chosen in which the decorative embodiment of these feelings can be most adequately adapted to the subjective intentions of the writer.

Dead facts and, in connection with them, subjective arbitrariness in their treatment determine the artistic principles of the historical novel in the period of decline of bourgeois realism. Naturally, all false theories of the historical novel arise upon this basis and find support in the practice of the important writers of this period of decline. The difference from the classical type of historical novel is either, as in the case of Taine and Brandes, a reason for repudiating the latter or this difference is completely blurred over. This is the basis, too, of the vulgar sociological theories of the literary treatment of history, which are founded on history's objective strangeness and incomprehensibility for us and therefore view the artistic treatment of history purely in terms of "introjections" (in the sense of Mach and Avenarius).

In the debate on the historical novel in the Soviet Union in 1934 a number of vulgar sociological conceptions were put forward, the essence of which was to separate history entirely from the present. One trend regarded the historical novel as a "science of rudiments", hence saw in history nothing that might have a living influence upon the present. This conception, which entirely corresponds to the aesthetics of vulgar sociology, namely the conception that classless society has nothing more to do with the literary products of preceding periods, turned the historical novel into an *omnium gatherum* of "rudiments", which may be grouped and "animated" by the writer as he pleases. The other trend drew up two types of historical novel, which together exactly mirror the duality of dead facts and subjective introjection. The first is the historical novel proper in which the idea of a past epoch is immanent. Should this perfect immanence be lacking, then what we get, according to this "theory", is a "contemporary novel" on a historical theme, i.e. pure introjection. In the first case we have once again a history which does not concern us; in the second, we have our own ideas and feelings arrayed in a costume which has nothing in common with the given historical events of the past. Both "theories", therefore, are bastards of bourgeois decadence and vulgar sociology. In these cases we are dealing with theories which arose when revolutionary democracy degenerated into national liberalism and which where then smuggled into Marxism by vulgar sociology as achievements of progress. One need only think of the uncritical glorification with which the literary theories of Taine have been treated by vulgar sociology.

What is most important for us here is this transformation of revolutionary and progressive bourgeois democracy into cowardly, compromising and ever more reactionary liberalism. For we have been able to see, when analysing writers as important, sincere and outstanding as Flaubert and C.F. Meyer, that the central question of the crisis of realism in the historical novel consists in the same kind of withdrawal, artistically, from popular life and its living forces as took place politically and socially among the bourgeoisie itself in this period. And in the case of honest, democratic writers like Erckmann-Chatrian and also of the much more important de Coster we were able to see how these social and spiritual currents of the age limited and drove to abstraction their plebeian sentiments, in part impoverishing, in part stylizing their literary expression.

The great bourgeois culture of the eighteenth century, whose realism experienced a last flowering in the first half of the eighteenth century, had its social basis in the fact that the bourgeoisie was objectively still the leader of all progressive forces of society aiming at the destruction and liquidation of feudalism. The pathos of this historic vocation gave the important ideological representatives of the class the courage and élan to raise all the problems posed by popular life, to immerse themselves deeply therein and, by grasping the forces and conflicts at work there, to represent the cause of human progress in literature even where this raising and solving of problems contradicted the narrower interests of the bourgeoisie.

With the turn to liberalism this bond is severed. Liberalism is from now on the ideology of the narrow and limited class interests of the bourgeoisie. This narrowing holds true even in cases where the content of what is represented appears to have remained the same. For it is one thing if the great representatives of bourgeois economics championed the rights of capitalist economy as an historical advance over guild restrictions, territorialism etc., and quite another what the vulgar free traders of Manchester propagated in the second half of the nineteenth century.

The narrowness which this divorce from the people produces is linked with an ever increasing hypocrisy on the part of the political representatives of the bourgeoisie of this period and its ideological hacks in the spheres of economics, philosophy etc. To all outward appearances the bourgeoisie still figures as the leader of progress, as the representative and pioneer of the entire nation. But since the interests represented are in fact the narrow and egoistic class interests of the bourgeoisie, this kind of "extension" can only be achieved by means of hypocrisy, hushing-up, lies and demagogy. To which must be added that the liberal turn-away from the people is rooted in a fear of the proletariat and of proletarian revolution. Alienation from the people constantly changes into hostility towards the people. And in closest connection with this development liberalism tends increasingly, and in cowardly fashion, to compromise with and capitulate to the surviving forces of feudal absolutism. The ideology of this capitulation finds its expression in the theory of *Realpolitik*, a theory which, to an ever greater extent, not only liquidates ideologically the old glorious revolutionary traditions of the bourgeoisie, but derides them for abstractness, "immaturity" and "childishness" (treatment of 1848 by liberal German historiography).

We have repeatedly pointed out the enormous distance separating important writers like Flaubert or Meyer from the liberal bourgeoisie and its intelligentsia (not to mention the plebeian-democratic writers). Indeed, no writer in this period depicted the baseness, stupidity and corruption of the bourgeois class with more trenchant satire than Flaubert. And in the case of both Flaubert and Meyer their withdrawal into history is a protest against this baseness and triviality, against this stupidity and depravity of the bourgeois class of their time.

But because this opposition is abstract Flaubert and Meyer remain prisoners of their period, with its limitation and narrowing of the social-historical horizon. True, the weapon of satire, the passionate romantic contrast between past and present prevents these writers from becoming apologists of the liberal bourgeoisie, gives their work significance and interest but it does not help them to escape the curse of alienation from the people. However much they may repudiate or criticize the ideological consequences of this historical situation—and so they do—the social-historical facts themselves, whose ideological consequences they combat, are inevitably reflected in the content and form of their works.

Their artistic problems, themes and method remain determined by this alienation from the people. The fact that in the historical novels of this period, even in the most important, the relations of the individual to public life are either quite apolitically private or confined to the *Realpolitik* of intrigue within the upper stratum of society, is a clear reflection of those basic changes in bourgeois social life, the political expression of which was liberalism. Even Flaubert's most passionate contempt for the liberal bourgeoisie of his time cannot undo his artistic connection with the decline of the bourgeois class.

Thus the new historical novel *as a genre in its own right* is born of the weaknesses of a nascent decline, of the inability of even the most important writers of this period to recognize the real social roots of this development and to combat them genuinely and centrally. We have shown in individual analysis that all the particular artistic weaknesses of this type of historical novel derive from this fundamental weakness. It would be wrong, however, to think that these weaknesses were confined to the historical novel. We have already shown how Flaubert's substitution of atrocities and brutalities for the real summits of social life "prophetically" anticipates the social novel of Zola. In reality, of course, what lies behind this very general literary current, which engulfs even the humanly most refined writers, is a general demoralization and brutalization of human feeling which becomes predominant with the final victory in society of the bourgeoisie. Similarly, the transference of social themes to the world "above" is not confined to the historical novel, although it occurs here earlier and more decisively than elsewhere. When Edmond de Goncourt goes over to painting the upper social classes he proclaims this as a higher phase of naturalism. And in the currents superseding naturalism this trend becomes predominant. Naturally, the fact that an historical trend is general does not mean, either in this or any other case, that it is exclusive, and certainly not that it has a uniform effect upon the work of all writers active in this period. Nevertheless, given the deep roots of these literary tendencies in the social body of advanced capitalism and especially of imperialism, the struggle against the social tendencies must go very far before a successful artistic struggle can be waged against their literary manifestations. (That such a struggle is possible is shown by international literature in such figures as Gottfried Keller, Anatole France, Romain Rolland and many others.)

We see therefore that not a single question of the historical novel can be treated in isolation without thoroughly distorting the historical and social continuity of literary development. What right then has one to speak of the historical novel as a genre in its own right? The genre theory of later bourgeois aesthetics which splits up the novel into various "sub-genres"—adventure novel, detective novel, psychological novel, peasant novel, historical novel etc. and which vulgar sociology has taken over as an "achievement" has nothing to offer scientifically. In the formalist approach to genre all the great traditions of the revolutionary period have completely vanished. This soulless and ossified, this thoroughly bureaucratic classification is meant as a substitute for the living dialectics of history.

Of course each of these ossified categories has a real social content behind it. But in each case the content is that of an increasingly reactionary ideology. And only Menshevist vulgar sociology is so "naïve" as not to notice the social character of this content and to concentrate solely upon the "scientific achievements". We cannot possibly deal in full here with the theory of genre. It suffices to mention one example. When the psychological novel was created a genre in its own right, its important representatives, above all Paul Bourget, clearly stated the tendency which led to the founding of this new genre. For, of course, so intelligent and cultivated a reactionary as Bourget knew quite well that the earlier novelists had been notable psychologists. What he was after, however, was to achieve an idealist and reactionary separation of the psychological from the objective determinants of social life, to establish the psychological as a self-contained and independent sphere of human life. This separation is consolidated by allowing "conservative" instincts supremacy over "destructive". Above all, this psychologism is intended by Bourget to make the flight from the (abstractly presented) contradictions of contemporary life into religion appear convincing. The opportunities for sophistry multiply. It is no longer necessary to present the church and religion through their social determinants, with their political aims etc., as Balzac and Stendhal did, or even Flaubert and Zola. The question of religion now becomes a "purely inward" question: Rome is no more than a picturesque background (Cosmopolis).

The psychological novel is in line with the vulgarization and conceptual freezing of social life by sociology, particularly Taine's. "Status", social position becomes a metaphysical given: it need not be investigated itself; it is unalterable. Only the psychological reactions are to be shown; each case of non-harmonization with the "status" appears as an illness. This is the new interpretation which Bourget gives of Madame Bovary and Le Rouge et le Noir: "It has not been sufficiently remarked that the essence of Madame Bovary, as of Stendhal's Rouge et le Noir, is: the study of a spiritual illness produced by a displacement of environment. Emma is a peasant girl who has received the education of a bourgeoise. Julien is a peasant lad who has received the education of a *bourgeois*. This vision of a colossal social fact dominates the two books." Thus, as a result of separating off the psychological, all social criticism disappears. Stendhal and Flaubert proclaim the "deep" psychological and social "truth" : the cobbler must stick to his last !

We have seen that the social reason for creating the historical novel a genre or sub-genre in its own right is similar: the separation of the present from the past, the abstract opposition of the one to the other. Of course, these intentions cannot really create new genres. In our previous remarks, particularly when comparing historical novel and historical drama, we went to some length to show that every genre was a peculiar reflection of reality, that genres could only arise as reflections of typical and general facts of life that regularly occur and which could not be adequately reflected in the forms hitherto available.

A specific form, a genre must be based upon a specific truth of life. When drama divides off into tragedy and comedy (we shall disregard the intermediary stages), the cause lies in the facts of life which these forms reflect and *dramatically* reflect. For no such separation of genres occurs in epic. Even bourgeois and pseudo-Marxist vulgar sociology have not got round to inventing the sub-genre of the tragic novel. Tragedy and comedy have a different relationship to reality and for this reason a different method of organizing action and characterization etc. The same applies to the novel and short story. It is not a question of extent. The difference in extent is simply the result of a difference in aim, and there are sometimes border-line cases where a long short story is more extensive than a short novel. It is always the case of a specific form reflecting specific facts of life. The difference of range between novel and short story is only *one* means among many for expressing the different facts of life portrayed by both genres. The real distinguishing mark of the short story is that it does not aim to portray life as a totality. For this reason its form is appropriate to very specific connections of life, e.g. the role of chance.

Conrad Ferdinand Meyer, as a highly conscious artist, clearly felt that the irrationalism of his conception of history required the form of the *Novelle* (the German form of long short story—trs.), and therefore called his works *Novellen* rather than novels. The final Pescara motif, the fact that he is physically incapacitated from acting or deciding because of his fatal illness, is a typical *Novelle* motif. But Meyer nevertheless did want to present a total picture of the problems of the age and so his works broke through the strict and narrow framework of the *Novelle*. On the basis of *Novelle* motifs there arose irrationalist, fragmentary novels.

If then we look at the problem of genre seriously, our question must be: which facts of life underlie the historical novel and how do they differ from those which give rise to the genre of the novel in general? I believe that when the question is put in this way, there can only be one answer—none. An analysis of the work of the important realists will show that there is not a single, fundamental problem of structure, characterization etc. in their historical novels which is lacking in their other novels, and *vice versa*. Compare, for example, Dickens's *Barnaby Rudge* with his social novels, *War and Peace* with *Anna Karenina* etc. The ultimate principles are in either case the same. And they flow from a similar aim: the portrayal of a total context of social life, be it present or past, in narrative form. Even special problems of theme, as seem to belong specifically to the historical novel, as, for example, Scott's portrayal of the survivals of gentile society are not exclusive to it. From the *Oberhof* episode in Immermann's *Münchhausen* right through to the first part of Fadeev's *Udegs* we find problems of this kind repeatedly in novels dealing with the present. One could go through all the problems of content and form in the novel without lighting upon a single question of importance which applied to the historical novel alone. The classical historical novel arose out of the social novel and, having enriched and raised it to a higher level, passed back into it. The higher the level of both historical and social novel in the classical period, the less there are really decisive differences of style between them.

The new historical novel, on the other hand, sprang from the weaknesses of the modern novel and by becoming a "genre in its own right" reproduced these weaknesses on a greater scale. There is, of course, a fact of life behind this difference of scale, too. But the difference is due not only to an objective fact of life, it is also and especially due to an exaggeration of the general false ideology of the period.

The special character of the historical novel in this period may be stated as follows: the false intentions of the writer are less easily corrected by life in the historical novel than in the novel which deals with the present. In the historical novel the false theories, literary prejudices etc. of the author cannot be, or are much less easily, corrected by a wealth of living material such as is contained in contemporary themes. What Engels described as the "triumph of realism" in Balzac—the triumph of an honest and complete reflection of the real facts and connections of life over the social, political or individual prejudices of a writer, is much more difficult in the new historical novel than in the contemporary social novel.

We dealt very briefly with two important realist writers of this period, Maupassant and Jacobsen. Maupassant approaches *Bel Ami* in the same way as he does *Une Vie*, Jacobsen *Niels Lhyne* in the same way as *Marie Grubbe*. In *Bel Ami* and *Niels Lhyne*, despite the general "problematic" of the new realism, social reality is richly nuanced. In both cases there occurs a "triumph of realism". Why? Because it was impossible for Maupassant and Jacobsen, as talented and honest observers of life, to pay no attention to the big social problems of their time when portraying a character in the present. It may have been the inner psychological development of the hero or heroine which primarily interested them, but whatever their conscious intentions the social life of the present flowed into their novels from every side, filling them with a rich and articulated life.

This happened much less readily in the historical novel. Feuchtwanger in the remarks we quoted was quite right to say that a subject removed in time can be more easily managed than the material of the present. His only mistake is to see this as an advantage and not a disadvantage. For the post-1848 writer historical material is less resistant, the subjective aim of the writer may be more easily imposed upon it. Hence that abstractness, that subjectivist arbitrariness, that almost dreamlike "timelessness" which we have seen in Maupassant's and Jacobsen's historical novels and which sets them off very much to their disadvantage from the more powerful and more clearly outlined social novels of the two authors.

Even with a writer of Dickens's rank the weaknesses of his petty bourgeois humanism and idealism are more obvious and obtrusive in his historical novel on the French Revolution (*Tale of Two Cities*) than in his social novels. The between-the-classes position of the young Marquis Saint Evremonde—his disgust with the cruel methods used for maintaining feudal exploitation and his solution of this conflict by escape into bourgeois private life—does not receive its due weight in the composition of the story. Dickens, by giving pre-eminence to the purely moral aspects of causes and effects, weakens the connection between the problems of the characters' lives and the events of the French Revolution. The latter becomes a romantic background. The turbulence of the times is used as a pretext for revealing human-moral qualities. But neither the fate of Manette and his daughter, nor of Darnay-Evremonde, and least of all of Sidney Carton, grows organically out of the age and its social events. Here again any social novel of Dickens, say *Little Dorrit* or *Dombey and Son*, will show how much more closely and organically these relations are portrayed than in *A Tale of Two Cities*.

Yet Dickens's historical novel is still relatively grounded on classical traditions. *Barnaby Rudge*, where the historical events are more episodic, preserves entirely the concrete manner of portrayal of the contemporary novels. But the limitations of Dickens's social criticism, his sometimes abstract-moral attitude towards concrete social-moral phenomena inevitably come out much more strongly here. What otherwise was only an occasional blurring of line becomes here an essential defect in the entire composition. For in the historical novel this tendency of Dickens must necessarily take on the character of modern privateness in regard to history. The historical basis in *Barnaby Rudge* is much more of a background than in *A Tale of Two Cities*. It provides purely accidental circumstances for "purely human" tragedies, and this discrepancy emphasizes what is otherwise only a slight and latent tendency in Dickens to separate the "purely human" and "purely moral" from their social basis and to make them, to a certain degree, autonomous. In Dickens's best novels on the present this tendency is corrected by reality itself, by its impact upon the writer's openness and receptivity. In the historical novel this kind of correction is inevitably weaker. That this is so with as great a writer as Dickens, a classic of the novel who is affected only peripherally by the decline, serves as a particularly vivid illustration of our argument.

The pliancy of historical material, which Feuchtwanger praises, is in fact a trap for the modern writer. For his greatness as a writer will depend upon the conflict between his subjective intentions and the honesty and ability with which he reproduces objective reality. The more, and the more easily, his subjective intentions prevail, the weaker, poorer and thinner will be his work.

Of course historical reality is also objective reality despite the influential modern "cognitive theories" of history. But the writers of the post-1848 period no longer have any immediate social sense of continuity with the prehistory of their own society. Their relationship to history—the social causes of which we already know—is very indirect, relying mainly on the modern and modernizing historians and philosophers of history (e.g. Mommsen's influence on Shaw).

This influence is unavoidable because of the break in social experience between past and present, and is much larger than is normally assumed. Modern writers take from the historiography and historical philosophy of their time not only the facts, but the theory that these facts may be freely and arbitrarily interpreted, the theory that historical development is unknowable and that therefore it is necessary to "introject" one's own subjective problems into the "amorphousness" of history, the theory which proceeds from the anti-democratic hero-cult and posits the lonely "great man" as the focus of history, which sees the mass both as raw material in the hands of "great men" and as a blindly raging, natural force etc.

Obviously historical facts which have been channelled through such an organized system of prejudice and preconception can offer the writer no controlling or fruitful resistance. In a few exceptional cases this is achieved by the facts of life themselves. But where history and life are opposed, where the wretchedness of contemporary life is abandoned for the gorgeous splendour of the past, the subjectivism and distortion are only increased. And the consequences are not lessened by the fact that the cause of this flight is, as in Flaubert, an ardent opposition to, and hatred for, the bourgeois present.

Thus the modern historical novel inevitably contains in a heightened form all the weaknesses of the decline in general; it lacks those important qualities of realism which the great writers of the epoch wrested from contemporary life despite the false tendencies of the time. In this sense, but only in this sense, could one speak of the historical novel in the time we are examining as a separate genre. One has simply to compare the descending line of the historical novel with that of the contemporary novel. The severed-from-life, autonomous, reified character of the *milieu* is not only cruder in the former (this is true already of the Romantic historical novel, particularly marked in the case of Bulwer Lytton), but very soon reaches proportions which the contemporary novel can equal only in its worst representatives. The reason is obvious. Even the driest and most tedious description of *milieu* is, in some way or another, very deviously, still connected with real life. "*Milieu*" in the historical novel, however, inevitably degenerates into a deadening preponderance of antiquarianism. This can take quite vulgar forms as in the once so popular novels of Dahn and Ebers. It can also take a refined, precious, nuanced and decorative form, from both a scholarly and stylistic point of view, as in Walter Pater's *Marius the Epicurean*. The difference, however, is by no means as fundamental as it appears at first sight. The characters are schemas in both. Here they are simply supplied with cleverly formulated ideas and refined emotional attributes; historical reality is no more the living development of a people in a concrete age than it is in Ebers or Dahn, it remains the same lifeless stage, though its colours are more subtly selected and combined. The differences, which are undoubtedly there, only emerge, if one disregards the fact that one is dealing with works of art and looks upon them as essays. Then of course Ebers appears as a vulgar popularizer of a superficial and banal egyptology, while in Pater we have an over-refined, decadent conception of late antiquity.

This judgment does not mean that we are abstracting them from the general development of the modern novel. It simply means that we have in Ebers or Dahn an anticipation of the flattest and most soulless naturalism in German literature, while in Pater we have the aesthetic precursor of the symbolist immobility which seizes an over-refined impressionism. Think of works like Rodenbach's *Bruges-la-morte* in which—though the outward form and technique are very different—an over-refined emotional experience is coupled with an over-stylized background just as organically as history and human destiny in Pater.

This path, which leads indirectly but surely into imperialist decadence, cannot be described one-sidely, either from the aesthetic or from the ideological-moral standpoint. From both standpoints it is a question of a primary alienation of bourgeois ideologists from the progressiveness of history, from a recognition of the progressive tendencies and perspectives in the present. The ideologist is reduced to a dreary philistinism. The great democratic-revolutionary Russian philosopher and critic, Chernyshevsky, already recognized this motif in E.Th. A. Hoffmann's criticism of philistinism, and the parallel we have just drawn between Ebers-Dahn on the one hand and Walter Pater on the other finds its justification in the pronouncement of another important democratic writer, Gottfried Keller, for whom the drunken philistine was not a jot better than the sober one. Perhaps the most typical textbook example of this common identity is Adalbert Stifter, who combined the most conscious "philosophical deepening" of the most narrow-minded philistinism with an alleged literary mastery of the loftiest and most detached kind. Since of Stifter's writing only his late work *Witiko*, concerns our theme, the following remarks refer principally to it.

Witiko exhibits the two sides we have seen in the similar but more important cases of Flaubert, Maupassant, Jacobsen etc.: on the one hand, the unity of philosophical and aesthetic principles in a writer's work, whether he is writing about the present or the past—*Witiko* in this respect applies the results and illustrates the principles of his educational novel *Der Nachsommer* (*An Indian Summer*). On the other hand, the less resistant historical material allows his narrow-minded and reactionary outlook much more licence than a contemporary subject. For this reason *Witiko* provides a synthesis of all Stifter's philistine and retrograde features; and in such a pure form that even Gundolf is compelled to speak about the "dreariness" of this work and range it historically alongside Freytag, Ebers, Dahn, Piloty and Makart.

At the same time Gundolf, like the entire George school, above all Bertram, is influenced by Nietzsche's enthusiasm for Stifter which was what started this literary fashion. True, Nietzsche's praise concerns mainly *Nachsommer*, and Gundolf, too, tries to show the positive sides, the deeper causes and lovable aspects of Stifter's limitations in this work; though, apart from the general contrast we have pointed out between contemporary and historical subjects, very wrongly. At least as far as a real contrast in aesthetic value is concerned. Admittedly *Nachsommer*, as a story of developments, has a

THE CRISIS OF BOURGEOIS REALISM

certain, inner, illusory kind of movement, although this is almost submerged in an ocean of material description. Witiko on the other hand has as its hero the model youth of the period prior to the March Revolution, the realized ideal of the largely miscarried "educational work" of Metternich. The epic movement here is purely external: battles, parades, receptions etc., which owing to their purely material and descriptive presentation thoroughly justify Gundolf's reproach of dreariness. Bertram, however, calls Witiko the "high late work" of Stifter, a "Homeric Walter Scott novel". This appraisal clearly manifests the firm intention of near-Fascist and Fascist German literary history and criticism to systematize Nietzsche's impulse and turn Stifter into a classic of German reaction. Thus Gundolf's somewhat cautious appraisal becomes a rearguard action. The Fascist literary historian, Linden, calls Nachsommer and Witiko "educational novels of an eternally valid kind". The Fascist critic, Fechter, extends Bertram's Homeric principle and discovers in Witiko the greatness of "Germanic freedom", of the Icelandic saga. Stifter (the motives and consequences are quite clear) is made a forerunner of Hans Grimm, who, in Fechter's words, "created the first German political novel after Stifter's Witiko".

This praise is not of the besmirching or slanderous variety which the Fascists bestow on Hölderlin or Büchner. Here, as with Nietzsche, they have claimed a genuine and legitimate inheritance. Obviously not in the sense of any direct relationship between Stifter and the "national-Socialist outlook". There is no question of this; his aesthetically reified quietism seems, on the contrary, to be the complete antithesis of the dynamic of "heroic realism". But here, too, the sharp contrast is illusory. We recall simply that it was the Fascist development in German literary history which enacted Biedermeier as a period in order to remove all that was progressive and, above all, revolutionary from pre-1848 German literature, to glorify the reactionary stagnation and obscurantist philistinism of this period as the true essence of Germany.

Stifter is the born classic of such tendencies. It is well known that for Stifter the Revolution of 1848 meant the collapse of a world, the end of a culture and a civilization. The defeat of the Revolution and the suppression of all nations by the Habsburgs laid the basis for his two large novels. Gundolf is not altogether wrong in characterizing this period in his work as follows: "From a writer of naïve idylls he became after 1849 a writer of intentional ones and the moral clarity with which he was able to see and point things out, he now used, so to speak, as a weapon against the evil will and folly of a forsaken humanity." One sees from this, too, that the aesthetic grounds on which Gundolf attacks Witiko are only of secondary importance; he, too, regards Stifter as the "political" poet of *Biedermeier*, seeing his apolitical outlook and method as his special form of "politics". The fact that these tendencies only become conscious ones after the defeat of the 1848 Revolution only reinforces the point.

Witiko contains these tendencies in concentration; so that whatever one's appraisal of it aesthetically, in comparison with Stifter's other works it constitutes the ideological summit of his literary career. Bertram's appraisal which we quoted shows the thorough ignorance and misunderstanding of Scott characteristic of the decline. In historical conception Stifter is indeed his opposite pole and follows on from his opponents, the reactionary Romantics. It would not be difficult to show this in the general structure and the individual details of *Witiko*. We shall mention only a few essentials. When Scott depicts the Middle Ages, his chief aim is to portray the struggle of progressive and reactionary tendencies, particularly those which lead beyond the Middle Ages, cause the break-up of feudalism and assure the victory of modern bourgeois society. (It will suffice if we think of the opposition between Louis XI and Charles of Burgundy in *Quentin Durward*.) Stifter, on the other hand, glorifies the most reactionary developments in the Middle Ages, for instance Barbarossa's struggle with the Italian cities, in particular Milan. What even moderately progressive writers like Hebbel recognized, namely that the politics of the Hohenstaufens was responsible for Germany's ruin, Stifter will not see. Thus in an intellectual and artistic form he continues the tradition of his pre-1848 protector, Metternich.

This tendency comes out still more clearly in his apotheosis of feudal institutions. Stifter carries on here from reactionary Romanticism. The difference is chiefly a stylistic one, but it has of course its ideological grounds. The Romantics created their model Middle Ages in a polemical spirit, from Novalis's essay *Christianity or Europe* to Arnim or Fouqué. With Stifter there is no clear polemic against the present; feudalism in *Witiko* and the present in *Nachsommer* are equally natural and organic social orders: Stifter thus goes much further than the most reactionary Romantic in his conception that "essential" man is the same under any authority—as long as it is not a revolutionary one. Whether he knew Schopenhauer or not, it is Schopenhauer's brand of reactionary Romanticism that he is continuing. His unpolemical style aptly expresses this retrograde development. This is what Bertram calls a "Homeric" intensification of Scott; obviously, he regards the absence of any plebeian or bourgeois opposition to feudalism (the citizens of Milan are for Stifter rebels and criminals) as an advance. And in the sense of *Biedermeierism*, of course, it is an advance. In the sense, however, of true knowledge and genuine portrayal of history, it is the opposite; Scott's Robin Hood in *Ivanhoe* or Henry Gow in

The Fair Maid of Perth show what a realistic presentation of the Middle Ages can accomplish.

Hebbel in his brilliant review of *Nachsommer* picked out the essentials of Stifter; the misproportion of the trivial to the significant, of surface to depth in favour of the former in each case. However removed Sifter may be from naturalism in a formal-stylistic sense, he thereby becomes its spiritual and aesthetic forebear. Hebbel also recognizes another tendency in Stifter which anticipates still more important and dangerous tendencies in the imperialist period: the inhumanity which as yet still wears the cloak of humanism. Hebbel says: "It was left to Adalbert Stifter to lose sight of man completely." If Stifter is celebrated by Nietzsche, the George school and finally Fascism itself as a genuine modern successor to Goethe, as a renewer of his legacy, it is a clear parallel to the attempts of Gundolf, Spengler, Klages etc. to turn Goethe, following Nietzsche's example, into an exponent of the irrationalist "life philosophy". These two tendencies may in many details reveal big differences or even contrasts; nevertheless they form the common poles of the reactionary, imperialist falsification of Goethe. From different angles but in equal measure they remove from Goethe's life-work all its social and historical progressiveness; in content they are as complementary as Gottfried Keller's sober and drunken philistine.

Stifter is a transitional figure insofar as his philistine detachment has much in common with the tedious academic classicism of the second half of the last century. Nevertheless, the features in his work which point towards the decadence of the future are the predominant ones; they determine Stifter's present-day position in literary history.

If one needs convincing of this relationship between naturalism, philistinism and decadence, one has a particularly blatant example of it in Merezhkovsky, a typical decadent of the imperialist age who belongs with the drunken philistines. With him the historical novel really does become an organ of reactionary demagogy and hostility towards the people. If one looks a little closely at the false profundity of these novels, one discovers remarkably naturalistic features beneath the mystical veil. For example, Merezhkovsky describes how Alexei falls into a fit of rage: "Alexei's pale convulsed face with its blazing eyes suddenly assumed a fearful and as it were supernatural, phantom-like resemblance to Peter's. It was one of those fits of rage into which the Tsarevich fell from time to time and during which he was capable of any crime." It must be obvious to any reader that this is simply a feeble and mystically flavoured caricature of Zola's hereditary catastrophe. In the same way one could quote other passages from this and similar decadent, reactionary historical portrayals of the imperialist period to show how they exaggerate and caricature the weaker sides of naturalism, symbolism etc. But these distortions will no more found a separate genre than the empty exoticism which is produced by estrangement from the present. Historical novels of the latter type simply provide an inferior form of light-reading. Behind the decadence or the banal degeneracy one can always glimpse the general decline of the epoch. And the merely quantitative increase of false tendencies cannot possibly lay the basis for a separate genre.

CHAPTER FOUR

The Historical Novel of Democratic Humanism

WITH THE imperialist period the main trend in both historical attitudes and literary theory and practice is the further disintegration of realism. In the previous chapter we compared a number of writers (Croce, Merezhkovsky) in whose works this increasing disintegration was clearly visible. Since we are confining ourselves here to the over-all and typical forms of the historical novel, we shall not deal with representatives of extreme decadence. It will suffice to say that what for the important writers of the transitional period was the difficult "problematic" of realistic, historical portrayal, now blossoms forth into a decadent play with forms—the conscious violation of history.

We have already seen that the disintegration proceeds in a twofold and seemingly contrary fashion. On the one hand there is an ever greater disbelief in the possibility of knowing social reality and hence also history. This disbelief necessarily turns into mysticism, as we have seen in the case of the great figures of the transitional period. These mystical tendencies increase as imperialism develops, reaching their peak in the barbaric Fascist falsification and mythicization of history. On the other hand, the presentation of history is one of maximum exactness with regard to individual, isolated facts, torn from their proper context. (Fascism occupies a special position in this development, since it also falsifies the isolated facts of history in the crudest and most brutal fashion.)

The subjectively honest writers of the imperialist period consider themselves faithful to history—naturally, within the limits of their outlook, that is whether they believe that objective knowledge of history is possible—but this faithfulness is restricted to the observation of isolated facts. In the case of Flaubert it took the form of decorative archaeologism. There develops in the imperialist period a new cult of "facts". This is to be seen in the naturalism of the pre-war period and later in the *neue Sachlichkeit* (new objectivity). However, mysticism, mystical biology and psychology are not excluded from these trends, indeed they are favoured to an ever increasing extent.

The wave of historical *belles lettres* which swept over literature after the First World War is also connected with these trends. A great deal of historical writing appears which is neither scholarship nor art. This hybrid is accurately described by the witty and satirical remarks of Huxley which we quoted above. The basis of these *belles lettres* is a synthesis of mystical psychology and isolated "facts" which found its justification at the time in the very widespread exaggeration of the term "art". The older traditions of art lay buried, one no longer saw art as a specific way of reflecting the essential features of objective reality, thus the "artistic principle" could be arbitrarily applied to all spheres—especially as science and philosophy were taking an increasingly agnostic attitude towards objective reality. This conscious subjectivism was now identified with art. Hence the theories of Oscar Wilde or later Alfred Kerr on the so-called art of criticism.

In the post-war period these theories were applied to a new sphere —the art of *montage*. Born of the nihilist theory and practice of the various Dadaist trends the theory of *montage* "consolidated" itself in this period of "relative stabilization" and became a deliberate surrogate for art: a special creative originality was supposed to manifest itself in the sticking together of disconnected facts. The art of *montage* reached on the one hand the utmost limit of naturalism, because it abandoned even the superficial linguistic-cum-atmospheric elaboration of the empirical world of the older naturalism; on the other, it reached the utmost limit of formalism, since the way in which details were linked no longer had anything to do with the objective inner dialectic of characters' lives—they are manipulated "originally" from outside. Such was the philosophical justification of this historical serial literature and *reportage* which posed as a special kind of historical art. The theory of *montage* and the proclamation of *reportage* as a special kind of art exercised a particularly strong influence upon these *belles lettres*.

The only importance these historical *belles lettres* have for us is that the would-be "genre" of historical biography has attracted writers of intellectual and artistic distinction among whom it has wrought much confusion and harm. We shall discuss the question of the so-called biographical method in the historical novel later on. Here we shall simply quote a few remarks from Maurois' preface to his Shelley biography in order to illustrate the principles behind this *pot-pourri* of novel and history which objectively is neither novel nor history.

"The aim in this book has been to produce a novelist's work rather than a historian's or critic's. Of course, the facts are true and not a phrase or thought has been attributed to Shelley which are not to be found in the memoirs of his friends, in his letters and in his poems; but we have tried to order these true elements so as to give the impression of progressive discovery, natural growth, which seems to be the proper sphere of the novel. Therefore the reader should not look for erudition here, nor for revelations, and if he has not the taste for sentimental educations, let him not open this little work."

Later we shall see more clearly that this combination of sticking to the facts and dressing them up in *belles lettres* is rooted in the writer's divorce from popular life. What seems to be the inexhaustible inventiveness of the great realist writers—and the historical novel is a quite special case of this—is explained by the freedom with which they handle their material: they know the types thrown up by popular life sufficiently well for them to give rein to their imagination and yet not depart from the truth of the typical; they are sufficiently familiar with popular life to be able to devise situations in which the deepest truths emerge more clearly and luminously than in everyday life itself.

The "cult of facts" is a miserable surrogate for this intimacy with the people's historical life. And for this surrogate to dress itself up in *belles lettres* and to pass off a smooth or mannered prose as epic art only aggravates the situation, for it increases the public's confusion.

1. *General Characteristics of the Humanist Literature of Protest in the Imperialist Period.*

What interests here are the revolts against, and resistance to, this decline of literature. The epoch of imperialism is not only the period of the decay of capitalism, it is also that of the greatest transformation in human history—the proletarian revolution, the decisive struggle between capitalism and socialism. But it would be extremely superficial and narrowing if one were to reduce the camps of revolutionary progress and barbaric reaction simply and mechanically to a rigid antithesis between proletariat and bourgeoisie. Lenin showed in his fundamental analysis of the imperialist age how deeply the parasitic tendencies of imperialism penetrate into the working-class movement itself, how they create a labour aristocracy and bureaucracy—hence a social basis for Menshevism, for the influence of bourgeois, imperialist ideology upon the working-class movement. On the other hand, Lenin also pointed out that in all spheres of life there also existed a petty-bourgeois democratic opposition to imperialism, to its anti-democratic tendencies. The ideology of this opposition is naturally confused and often shot through with reactionary tendencies: as an ideology which wishes to return from the period of monopoly capitalism to that of free trade, it is, like any desire to turn back the wheel of history, necessarily reactionary.

But such observations by no means exhaust the problem, least of all if we are concentrating our attention on the field of literature. The contradictory character of democratic protest against imperialist capitalism is complicated by the contradictory position of the whole struggle for democracy in this period. The general tendency of imperialism is naturally anti-democratic: this includes not only the open anti-democracy of monopoly capitalism and the parties it immediately influences, but also the growing anti-democratic tendencies in liberalism and the latter's influence upon the opportunistic wing of the working-class parties and trade unions. These anti-democratic tendencies call forth a broad sociological, psychological and philosophical anti-democratic propaganda literature. At the same time, however, the revolutionary working-class parties produce a critique of bourgeois democracy from the left; the insufficiently democratic, merely formal character of bourgeois democracy is disclosed.

The opposition movements against imperialism are affected by this double influence. They always run the danger of swinging over from a left to a right-wing criticism of bourgeois democracy, i.e. from dissatisfaction with *bourgeois* democracy to opposition to *democracy in general*. If one, for instance, follows the careers of thinkers like Sorel or important writers like Bernard Shaw, one sees in both cases —admittedly, in a very different way—zigzag movements of this kind from one extreme to the other. Even in Romain Rolland's critique of the present in his important youthful work *Jean Christophe* one finds time and again, amidst the vehement and wonderfully outspoken democratic protest against the age, sporadic elements of a critique of democracy from the right.

The complex intricacy of motives, however, should not cloud one's view of the essentials. Every writer is the son of his age. The contradictory tendencies of the age—the decay of the imperialist period and the democratic protest of the working masses, literary decadence and the yearning for popular roots—affect the writer in a contradictory and criss-cross fashion. It is true, as Marx and Engels observed, that in critical periods of class struggle many of the best ideological representatives of the ruling class separate themselves from it, but this too is a very complicated and contradictory process. Thus it is very difficult for the writer really to free himself from the currents and fluctuations of his time and, within them, from those of his class. This liberation, this strengthening of democratic tendencies was greatly hindered by the ideological weakness of the left wing of central and Western European social democracy. Whereas the Bolsheviks in Russia succeeded in working out a strategy and tactics in the writings of Lenin, which achieved a revolutionary combination between consistent struggle for the liberation of the proletariat and struggle for democracy, this aspect was precisely one of the weakest points of radical opposition in social democracy elsewhere, and this weakness was inherited by the young Communist parties. The bravery and determination of a democratic opposition based on the petty bourgeoisie will depend always upon a consistent and revolutionary attitude on the part of the working-class parties. And it was precisely here that the radical wing of central and Western European social democracy failed. To quote just one example: the Dreyfus campaign in France. The democratic protest which was roused here was of the highest importance for French literature. Writers like Zola and Anatole France became extremely political as a result of this protest movement. And there is no question but that this activity of theirs, especially in the case of France, gave a considerable impetus to their literary work. But the fact remains that the real support for the Dreyfus campaign came from the right wing of French social democracy, while the left took up a stand of sectarian neutrality. It requires no lengthy analysis to show that the impetus given to such writers as Zola and France by their participation in the democratic protest movement against growing imperialist reaction would have been much greater and deeper had they found real ideological support in a revolutionary Marxist working-class party.

Therefore, in a historical examination of these currents, one must keep firmly to the main issues and regard the confusion of individual writers over many ideological and political questions as their tribute to the age. This includes—to mention only a few essential points—on the one hand the inability of many important writers to draw a clear dividing-line between their really democratic aims and the rotten and compromising liberalism of their class. (Even in such important works as Heinrich Mann's Untertan (The Subject) this blurring of frontiers shows itself in the form of an embellishment of the weaknesses of German liberalism.) On the other hand, very many writers fall victim to the reactionary romantic critique of democracy. The great influence of Nietsche upon the most important opposition writers of the imperialist period has its roots in this confusion. In the Latin countries this influence is strengthened by the influence of the syndicalist opposition to the opportunism of social democracy.

In terms of outlook the complexity of the situation is expressed in the fact that while writers reproduce reality realistically, consciously they make far-reaching concessions to the sceptical, agnostic theories of the bourgeois class of their time. Naturally, the interaction between a writer's outlook and his work must not be interpreted in any direct and simple fashion. Nevertheless, in most cases the writer's outlook does have some effect upon his work, upon the quality of his realism and the extent to which he trusts his own imagination in reproducing reality realistically etc.

Any analysis is complicated by the fact that the writer's agnosticism or scepticism is not a static condition; it must always be carefully examined from the point of view of whence it comes and where it is leading. Lenin in his analysis of the literary career of Alexander Herzen pointed very acutely to two kinds of scepticism, whose difference is vital to our present study. He points on the one hand to a scepticism which provides an ideological accompaniment and support for the transition of the bourgeois class from revolutionary democracy to a rotten and treacherous liberalism; and on the other hand to a scepticism which is critical of bourgeois society and takes the direction of socialism. The latter was Herzen's case. If, keeping Lenin's distinction in mind, one looks more closely at the important writers of democratic protest in the imperialist period, while one finds in many writers an intricate and complex mixture of both forms of scepticism, in the really great writers there is a preponderance of the second variety. This is particularly visible in the development of Anatole France.

This democratic protest movement plays an extremely important part in determining the literary handling of history. Indeed, it and it alone has created a new type of historical novel which, chiefly in the literature of the German anti-Fascist emigration, has become a central problem of letters in our day. Hitherto the historical novels of important writers had played little more than an episodic role in the life-work of their authors. Nevertheless, it is necessary to mention, if only hastily, these forerunners of the literature of our time. First of all, there is the late period of Victor Hugo, whose 1793 is perhaps the first important historical work to attempt to interpret the history of the past in the new spirit of protesting humanism and by so doing took a different path from the historical novels of Hugo's older and younger contemporaries, which we have already analysed, and in many respects a different path from the novels of Victor Hugo himself. Not that Hugo had broken with all his earlier Romantic traditions. In a certain sense 1793 is a last echo of the Romantic historical novel. Hugo's old manner of substituting large decorative and rhetorical contrasts for the lack of inner movement is still present. But between his Romantic novels in the textbook sense and 1793 Hugo had after all written Les Misérables and, however stylized and Romantic popular life appears in this work, it nevertheless gives quite a different picture of the people from any other work of any other Romantic (including the younger Hugo).

These tendencies are intensified in his late work. The very fact that, at a time when it is considered particularly modern to slander the French Revolution—both in scholarship (Taine) and in literature (the Goncourts), Victor Hugo writes a glorification of it, shows how these tendencies work against the general current. They are strengthened by the fact that the object of Hugo's enthusiasm is 1793, the year of the Terror, and not merely 1789. Here, despite all Hugo's vacillations, which Lafargue criticized—and in many ways rightly—are the tendencies which point to the future, to a revival of revolutionary democracy. This we see above all in Hugo's tragic conflicts which are real ones, sprung of the soil of the Revolution. Admittedly, his portrayal is often more rhetorical than realistic. And this rhetoric is not simply a survival of the Romantic period: it clearly expresses the limits of his humanist conception, the metaphysical abstractness of his humanism. This abstractness determines the final conflicts which lead the heroes to their tragic doom. The real, human and historical collisions of the aristocrat and the priest, who have allied themselves with the Revolution, are turned into ingenious conflicts of duty based on this abstract humanism.

In the imperialist period a similar fresh and independent position is occupied by the historical novels of Anatole France. Even in France, particularly in his youth, a certain subjective arbitrariness is detectable in his treatment of history, but it is miles removed from the tendencies, say, of Flaubert or Meyer, indeed, quite opposed to them. In the historical figures of Anatole France the humanist and militant kind of scepticism acquires a clearer and more rounded portrayal than in the work of many of France's followers. France is the first example of a return to the outlook of the Enlightenment on the part of democratic opposition writers. Within the social and ideological conditions of the imperialist period this return is the nearest and clearest path for bourgeois ideologists who wish to take a firm stand against the reactionary tendencies of their time. Later it will be the path of Heinrich Mann and Lion Feuchtwanger. The difficulties and contradictions which spring from an attempt to judge and portray the problems of our time from the standpoint of the Enlightenment we shall analyse later on. Here let us simply state that France's Enlightenment is less the abstract and closed outlook that it is with his followers (struggle between reason and unreason in the case of Feuchtwanger) and more a defensive, superior scepticism towards both the openly reactionary tendencies of his time and (which is his distinctive note) the limits and questionableness of bourgeois democracy. It is this spirit which gave rise to that historically genuine, radiantly humanist, unforgettable figure—the Abbé Jerome Coignard. In the same spirit France's scepticism strikes at medieval and modern historical legends of all kinds. And it is a much more historical spirit than is the case with most other writers of the time. (Think of Shaw's deliberate modernization of history—with the exception of St. Joan—although this too was part of the fight against historical legend.) And the principle of humanity is far less abstract in the works of Anatole France than is generally the case with the assimilation of Enlightenment ideology in our time. For France's reception of the epicurean materialism of the eighteenth century is a very personal one; his triumphant humanity never disavows flesh and blood. On the contrary it is a principle which unmasks every kind of inflated aesthetic. For the same reason France will have no truck with the reactionary historical legend which identifies materialism with egoism. Thus Brotteaux, in his novel on the Revolution *The Gods Athirst*, is not only true-to-life as a human being, he is also based on a genuine understanding of the historical contradictions of this period.

The critique of bourgeois democracy itself does not belong specially to the literature of the imperialist period. The most varied Romantic anti-capitalist and even reactionary trends put this criticism to the fore, both in theory and in literature. The special character of Anatole France lies in the fact that he never posed this question in a romantic manner, not even in his youth. And in his last period, after the experiences of the Dreyfus campaign, this critique takes a resolute step beyond bourgeois democracy towards the socialist future.

For this reason his return to the problems of the French Revolution is something quite new in the literature of the imperialist period. The Soviet critic, Fradkin, in his parallel between 1793 and *The Gods Athirst*, brilliantly and correctly underlined the decisive difference between the two works. Victor Hugo is essentially in agreement with the political and social aims of the Jacobins; on the other hand he sees their tragic "problematic" in their method—the Terror. Anatole France, for his part, has no objection to the method of terror as such; he sees, however, an insoluble contradictoriness in the social aims of the Jacobins: the "liberty, equality and fraternity" which had been fought for with such heroism and sacrifice by the best of them leads to increasing misery for the liberated working masses, as long as the economic basis of capitalism remains unshaken. The heroism of the Jacobins, which comes out plastically in France, thus appears as a tragic "problematic". However, there is not a single moment of hopelessness within the social content of this tragedy, nor any "eternal" dilemma, as in Victor Hugo, but an unspoken, and for this reason so much the clearer, perspective of the future. And because France sees this great crisis of transition in this way, he can allow the enemies of the Revolution an objectivity which makes true human beings of them, without in the least diminishing his own partisanship.

It is obvious that any forward-pointing, transitional literature that might appear in Germany could not possibly have anything like the historical farsightedness and progressiveness of Anatole France. Nevertheless, we think it necessary to mention a few major examples, however sketchily, since we have dealt in relative detail with the chief representatives of the decline in the historical novel and do not wish to suggest that there was no counter-movement during this period in Germany.

Such a movement begins already soon after the defeat of the '48 Revolution. Its chief figure is Wilhelm Raabe. In the life-work of this writer, too, historical themes play only an episodic role. (I have analysed the basic questions of his literary career in *German Realists of the Nineteenth Century*.) Raabe's historical vision shows great merits and obvious limits. Perhaps his most positive quality is his passionate indignation at German wretchedness which he attacks in his contemporary novels in terms of the degrading philistinism of the German petty states. With this there goes a healthy plebeian sense which makes him seek and portray the causes of corruption predominantly "above" and the possibilities of renewal predominantly "below". But when we see that this, applied to history, produces an idealization of the medieval independent cities, we also see the limitations which prevent Raabe from portraying the past in a way which would equal his critical presentation of the present; the more so as Raabe is much more aware of, differentiates much more between the "above" and "below" of the present than of the past, where his idealization of (often very dubious) city splendours clouds his vision.

His critical sense of humour becomes really fruitful where he re-discovers in the past his central theme—the fight against German wretchedness. The best example is the story *Die Gänse von Bützow* (*The Geese of Bützow*). Raabe shows the philistine wretchedness of a small German town by means of a double contrast: on the one hand, the distant background of the French Revolution and the great wars it produces; on the other, the high cultural level of the intellectual stratum which laid the basis for German classicism. These general contrasts produce a whole series of very concrete and vivid contrasts in the characters, situations and the language itself. The language is that of a schoolmaster well acquainted with the whole of contemporary literature telling the story in the first person. His use of language discloses continuously the contradiction between the fearful pettiness of characters and events and the loftiness of ideas, feelings, quotations and language; it creates in the best sense an ironic atmosphere. In addition the petty tyrannical authorities of the small town and the cowardly or pettily intriguing opposition movement of the inhabitants are constantly haunted by the heroic deeds and personalities of the French Revolution: the petty fear of the rulers and the cowardly and hesitant resistance of the oppressed, ceaselessly admiring their own "temerity" with simultaneous pride and alarm, continually conjure up these shades. The "revolt" of the small town against a senseless and

unjust ordinance concerning the rights of geese on the roads underlines these contrasts still more.

The irony and self-irony of this story do not cause any Romantic
disintegration of form, but create an at once differentiated and
harmonized picture of the times; they express the variety and unity
in the contradictions of this period of German development and thereby, indirectly, an attitude to the present. The irony and self-irony are
not aimed at the French Revolution, which is what reactionary
histories of literature usually suggest; on the contrary, they are used
to criticize the petty and servile behaviour of the German middle and
lower middle classes, which appear all the more wretched by being
contrasted with great, world-historical events and the intellectual
heights of their own culture. Thus, as a call for self-criticism and
self-transformation in a Germany where the later sell-out and over-
bearingness of the Bismarck period could already be anticipated (the
story was written on the eve of the Austro-Prussian War), it is a forerunner of later humanism. This basic tendency emerges when the
first person narrator quotes Mirabeau's famous words on Prussia
"pourriture avant maturité" in a concluding letter which is placed
in a well-prepared and unmistakable position. The story itself does
not take place in Prussia.

Almost two decades later this motif becomes the central idea of a
small historical masterpiece, Theodor Fontane's *Schach von Wuthenow*. In Fontane, too, historical subjects are only episodic by comparison with contemporary themes. Admittedly, his initial ballad
period is historically oriented; and his first novel is a large historical
one *Vor dem Sturm* (*Before the Storm*). Nevertheless, the real novelty
of his art, despite the originality of a number of details, is still to come.
This is shown in the idea of the work. Fontane, like Willibald Alexis
before him in *Isegrimm*, chooses von Marwitz, a not uninteresting
reactionary eccentric, as his central figure. But by doing so he prevents
himself from portraying the really progressive tendencies of the wars
of liberation, both as represented by Scharnhorst and Gneisenau and
by the insurrectionary plebeians, for whom Raabe had shown great
understanding.

The story *Schach von Wuthenow*, however reveals the true and
mature Fontane. Here the glorifier of Prussia, old and new, begins with
deadly accuracy to criticize Prussian man and Prussian "bearing".
The latter is revealed as a petrified moral norm, a life principle which
forms and kills. This criticism reaches its peak in *Irrungen, Wirrungen*
(*Wanderings and Confusions*) and *Effi Briest*. (The problems of
Fontane's development, particularly this fruitful contradiction, I have
treated at length in my book *German Realists of the Nineteenth
Century*.)

In a certain sense Fontane's historical début is more forceful or at any rate more clearly defined than the perhaps richer human portrayals of his later social novels. Here, as an exception proving the rule, our frequent opposition of historical and social subject-matter is reversed: this time it is the historical subject which shows a greater resistance to the views, inclinations and temperament of the writer than the contemporary subject. It is not difficult to explain this contradiction and exception. In his works on the present Fontane shows the at once inflexible and brittle character of Prussian "bearing", its fundamental inhumanity, but he can only reveal its consequences by means of purely private and personal examples—however typical they may be. He would need to have a passionate desire to change society in order to interpret the historical consequences of Prussian "bearing" even in the form of a future perspective. And nothing was further from the personality of the old Fontane than passion of this kind; although many of his letters show that insight as such was not lacking.

Schach von Wuthenow, however, takes place on the eve of the battle of June. The effect of this is to link the atmosphere of the approaching catastrophe with the subject of the story in an inseparable and organic manner. Fontane's mastery shows itself in two ways. First, the whole inner conflict of Schach is morally a typical pre-Jena phenomenon in the ruling circle of Prussia and appears as such to the reader. Secondly, the entire course of the action—and the circumstances, conversations, contrasting types etc., which seem only loosely connected with it—give forth unobtrusive variations on the following theme: *why had* the battle of Jena to lead to a catastrophe for Frederick the Great's Prussia? There is no question of any subjective connection between Raabe and Fontane; objectively, however, it is certainly no accident that Raabe's story ends with Mirabeau's words on Prussia (pourriture avant maturité), while the same sentiment forms the prologue to Fontane's story. This spiritual affinity links both writers despite their difference of outlook and style and makes them both precursors of the militant humanism of the imperialist period.

It cannot possibly be our task to trace a step-by-step development of this new type of historical novel. To illustrate its general tendency let us simply point to Ricarda Huch. Also because most of her historical novels (not her early social ones) already show clear tendencies in the direction of historical *belletrism* which we shall be criticizing later on. We must concentrate, however, on the historical novel of militant, anti-Fascist humanism. This is made easier for us by the fact that all the tendencies we have discussed meet here in concentration, so that an analysis and critique of this literature is as much an analysis and critique of the typical forms of the historical novel in our time, as earlier our analyses of Scott or Flaubert took into account the typical features of the respective periods of the historical novel.

Since the present historical novel reflects the main anti-barbaric tendencies possible under dying capitalism, it also reveals the growing ideological influence which the socialist humanism of the Soviet Union has exercised upon the best intellectuals of the West. This influence intertwines naturally with an ever more incisive critique of Fascist barbarism, and gives to the latter a brighter and more hopeful perspective upon the future of humanity. To assess the extent of this influence, it will perhaps suffice if we refer to the two kinds of scepticism mentioned earlier. We stressed the positive sides of Anatole France's scepticism, and they must always be stressed. Yet in the historical novel of today, most clearly of all in Heinrich Mann, but also in Feuchtwanger and others, there is a quite different spirit at large in the approach to mankind's future. And one would have to be blind not to see that in this decisive artistic and ideological question of perspective, the influence of socialism in the Soviet Union is of exceptional importance.

The humanist protest against the barbarism of the imperialist age declares itself more clearly and militantly, the more openly imperialist barbarism reveals itself—at its most brutal in Fascism. With the advance of Fascism, in the struggle against it, the humanism of the democratic opposition becomes ever more broadly political and social; its important representatives take an ever higher critical stance towards their age. While this happens, the democratic opposition of course, undergoes shifts within its own ranks. The sharpening of antagonisms frightens a section of fellow-combatants away, sometimes driving them into the camp of the enemies of human progress. But the main trend is visible in the ideological and artistic growth of such strong personalities as Romain Rolland or Heinrich and Thomas Mann.

The victory of Hitler Fascism in Germany is a turning-point not only for Germany, but above all for the oppositional humanism of the important *German* writers. The formation of the popular front against Fascism is not only politically an event of worldwide significance, it also marks the beginning of a new period in German outlook and literature. In the most important representatives of the humanist opposition one can observe an extraordinary clarification of outlook; they view the events of the present and the paths that have led to them with a searching historical vision. It would be petty, narrow and sectarian to want to measure this social and ideological growth in German literature by the extent to which its important representatives consciously approach Marxism, as an outlook, and Communism, as a political programme. The main effect of the popular front, ideologically and politically, is one of fermentation; it causes writers to develop in an organic sense. As a result of Hitler's domination, the popular front in France and the revolutionary liberation struggle of the Spanish people, the spirit of *revolutionary democracy* has been rekindled among a number of important writers, who have for the whole of their lives opposed—more or less consciously, more or less resolutely —the dominant reactionary trends of their countries.

This process is of the utmost political significance, particularly for Germany, and at the same time one of extraordinary complexity and difficulty in German literature and thought. For among the civilized countries Germany is the one with the weakest revolutionary-democratic traditions. Heinrich Mann has put this very clearly in an article on the question: "The Revolution will come. The Germans so far have not made one, the word does not conjure up familiar images for them. Even the workers, however bravely and intelligently they struggle, are content to leave the last part of the struggle in obscurity, even it would seem to themselves." The more farsighted and honest writers are persuaded by their bitter experience with the liberal bourgeoisie and its intelligentsia inside Germany (think, simply, of what happened to Gerhart Hauptmann under Fascism) and with the recurrent shifts among bourgeois and petty bourgeois popular fronters that liberalism must be criticized from the standpoint of revolutionary democracy—that is, the standpoint of resolute defence and consolidation of the popular front.

This criticism must also be a self-criticism in the widest sense, and in most cases this is so in a more or less conscious fashion. Compare Heinrich Mann's following remarks taken from the same essay with those we have just quoted and the line of this criticism and self-criticism will be clear: "Liberalism and a restricted kind of humanitarianism helped us to tolerate capitalism while the system was still possible, brightened it up for us so that we could still afford flights of conscience and human love."

In such remarks Heinrich Mann raises the problems of revolutionary democracy for today in a very decisive manner. For of equal importance as this appeal to the revolutionary-democratic instincts of all whom monopoly capital oppresses, exploits and deprives of their rights, materially and culturally, is the fact that this revolutionary-democratic revival is proceeding today under quite special conditions. For this reason Diaz was quite right to speak of a democracy of a completely new type, whose realization is the goal of the Spanish popular front. The popular front in all countries is fighting for this kind of new democracy. And if before we repudiated the petty and narrow-minded demand that the significance of the great anti-Fascist writers should be measured by the extent to which they approached Marxism, this does not mean that a coming-to-grips with the problem of socialism is not an important touchstone for the genuineness and sincerity of revolutionary democracy in our day.

And not only in our day. The complexity and difficulty of the development of revolutionary democracy in the nineteenth century is closely bound up with the fact that after the rising of Baboeuf, after the risings of the weavers of Lyons and Silesia, after the Chartist movement etc., nobody could any longer be a consistent revolutionary democrat, unless he took a positive attitude to the question of the emancipation of the proletariat. (This was still possible for the Jacobins.) However weak revolutionary-democratic traditions have been in Germany, the political and above all literary history of the German nineteenth century offers interesting and significant examples of revolutionary democrats who have come to grips with the problem of socialism and such figures have always given an affirmative answer to the great question of the epoch. So Georg Büchner, Heinrich Heine and Johann Jacobi. This is the path which the important anti-Fascist writers of the German popular front take; these traditions echo in their writings.

And this, of course, is not an exclusively German problem. If in France one follows the development of the leader and hero of the armed barricade struggles, Blanqui, or thinks of the development of such writers as Zola or Anatole France, one sees everywhere the same problem and the same *direction* (not the same content) in the attempts to solve it. Still clearer is this connection between revolutionary democracy and socialism in Russian development from 1840 to 1880. One only needs to think of figures like Belinsky and Herzen, Chernyshevsky, Dobrolyubov and Saltykov-Schedrine to see this connection quite clearly.

This coming-to-grips is not just theoretical but a struggle with real problems of life. The reality of Hitler Fascism, the reality of the Spanish Revolution, the reality of socialism in the Soviet Union, the reality of the heroic struggle of the German workers: these are the great facts against which revolutionary democracy strengthens itself in the best German writers, from which it forms a tradition which it seeks to apply to all spheres of German life. Socialism in this context appears as a central problem of popular life: as the question of the material and cultural well-being of the broad mass of workers. It is not necessary to be a supporter of socialism, let alone of Marxism, in order to experience these problems and know them to be central. Thomas Mann, for example, wrote in the twenties: "I said that all would be well with Germany and it would find its proper feet, once

Karl Marx had read Friedrich Hölderlin—a meeting by the way which is now on the point of realization. I forgot to add that a one-sided acquaintance would necessarily remain unfruitful."

Of course the model of the Soviet Union plays a big part in all this. And a mastery of these problems will help every important and honest thinker to assimilate Marxism. But Marxism, from a typical point of view is at best the conclusion, certainly not the beginning of this path. The primary thing is an honest and consistent coming-to-grips with the really burning problems of popular life in the present. And the world-historical actuality of socialism today is manifested in the fact that every honest intellectual who takes the problems of the popular front and the liberation of his people from the real or threatened yoke of Fascism seriously must come up against the problem of socialism in practice as soon as he examines any question concretely. Zola went through this experience during the last period of his life. But at that time life itself did not pose the question as urgently as it does today, thus Zola could give himself up to Utopian reveries, to a watered-down revival of Utopian socialism.

The burning urgency today of all the problems of socialism underlines the enormous practical-political significance of this revival of revolutionary democracy. For the urgency of socialism means that its problems spring from the living experiences of the working masses, and its task is to fulfil the requirements of the transitional period which correspond to the immediate wishes and experience of the working masses. The unity of revolutionary democracy with all sections of the working people, its sensitivity towards their present stage of growth, both subjectively and objectively, is one of the most important factors in the present-day period of transition. This must be all the more strongly emphasized, given the pseudo-radical passion in many circles of Social Democracy for Utopian "planned economies" and given, too, the use of the slogan of the immediate realization of socialism by anarchist muddleheads and Trotskyist nuisances in order to break up the popular front and thereby hinder the actual revolutionary struggle against Fascism which will reach its peak in socialism only as an ultimate end. The Communist Parties of Europe were bolshevized by incorporating the living traditions of revolutionary democracy. One of the basic differences between the Bolsheviks and the left Social Democrats in non-Russian Europe before the First World War was the fact that the Bolsheviks really "sublated" the traditions of revolutionary democracy in their theory and practice (in the sense, too, of preserving and raising it to a higher level), while left opposition movements in the West either abandoned these traditions or allowed them to degenerate into vulgar democracy.

One could thus briefly summarize the history of the German anti-

Fascist emigré writers in the following way, accepting that a brief summary inevitably simplifies: starting off generally as liberal intellectuals, some with democratic inclinations, they have developed radically under the influence of the gigantic events of the past four years in the direction of revolutionary democracy. This is the first such movement since the period preparatory to the 1848 Revolution when revolutionary democracy began to crystallize itself in Germany under the leadership of Marx. In this respect the change in political outlook on the part of the German emigration anticipates a turning-point in the destiny of the German people.

This path to revolutionary democracy is naturally very uneven and contradictory. The great difficulties, inward and outward, which the unfolding of revolution involves, inevitably frighten many intellectuals and writers away; their liberal attitudes metaphysically harden and assume an ideological halo. In German literature the recent historical works of Stefan Zweig show this kind of stubborn halting at liberal humanism which is characteristic of a large section of Western intelligentsia in the pre-Hitler period.

In his book on Erasmus of Rotterdam, Zweig makes humanism and revolution into mutually exclusive opposites: "But humanism by its very nature is never revolutionary ..." In this way Zweig pseudo-philosophically fixates the false humanism of the liberal German bourgeoisie. The really great traditions of European humanism were, on the contrary, always revolutionary. The best section of the European intelligentsia saw the realization of the ideals of humanism in the French Revolution, that "glorious dawn" of which the old, tired and disappointed Hegel still spoke with emotion and enthusiasm. It was not before the German bourgeoisie submitted to Bismarckian Bonapartism that there came to predominate in universities and schools that empty, formalist classicism and humanism, which concealed itself timidly from the people and popular movements, which emptied humanism of all revolutionary-democratic content and therewith degraded it to a wearisome, bourgeois and liberal respectability.

To be sure, Stefan Zweig, despite the huge pretentions with which he, objectively, renews this fundamentally reactionary pseudo-humanism in his recent works, is an honest and farseeing writer who towers above this type of mediocre liberal academicism. In particular, he sometimes sees very clearly the limitations of the humanist type whom he has consistently glorified in recent times, and his mistake lies primarily in his inability to draw the right conclusions from his clear insights. Thus, on the one hand, he draws Erasmus of Rotterdam as a model type of humanist. On the other, he clearly sees the limitations of this type: "But ... what moves the masses at the deepest level, this they neither know nor wish to know."

Here Zweig states an important connection clearly and well, precisely the connection which forms the point of departure for the self-criticism of the more important and consistent humanist anti-Fascists and for their further ideological and political development. But Zweig, unlike the latter, above all Heinrich Mann, does not bravely draw the conclusion that the old and favoured humanist type, whom he has drawn with such love in the figure of Erasmus, is not only condemned to defeat by his alienation from the problems of popular life, but as far as the basic questions of humanism are concerned is more limited, restricted and therefore on a lower level than those who have the courage and ability to derive their ideas from living contact with popular life.

This contact is not confined simply to present-day humanism, it is true of humanism originally. Thus Zweig's choice of Erasmus as the model type of humanist is a distortion of the historical picture; for he disregards the militant type of humanist who was deeply involved in the problems of popular life. Engels in his enthusiastic analysis of the great men of this period puts forward Leonardo da Vinci and Dürer as the great types. And even though he erased the name of Erasmus from his manuscript yet his concluding remarks fit the type of Zweig's Erasmus very well. "Scholars of the book," he says, "are the exceptions: either people of the second or third rank or cautious philistines who do not wish to scorch their fingers."

In Zweig's work we find a very characteristic mixture of two heterogeneous currents: on the one hand modern anti-popular prejudices masked by "science" (people as the "irrational" mass) and on the other the resuscitated Enlightenment. We have already pointed out, and shall subsequently come back to it again and again, that the renewal of Enlightenment philosophy was not only socially necessary, but also progressive. If the anti-Fascist intellectuals oppose "reason" to the barbarically irrationalist, demagogic intoxicants of Fascist propaganda, then this is right and forward-pointing.

But this principle only remains right and progressive as long as it is not metaphysically exaggerated, for then it absorbs the modern prejudices which spring from the decline of bourgeois ideology. Chief among these is the attitude that the people, the mass represents the principle of irrationality, of the merely instinctive in contrast to reason. With such a conception of the people humanism destroys its best anti-Fascist weapons. For Fascism's point of departure is precisely this "irrationality" of the mass, and it uses its ruthless demagogy to draw all the inferences from this conception. Thus, if one really wants to unmask the hostility of Fascism towards the people, one must concentrate on the fallaciousness and mendacity of this argument; one must protect the creative energies of the people from Fascist slander; one must show how every great idea and act of mankind has sprung from popular life. Should humanist reason be metaphysically and exclusively opposed to the irrationality of the people, it inevitably becomes an ideology of renunciation. Humanism is made to retreat from the arena where the destiny of mankind is being decided.

This ideology of renunciation is expressed in Stefan Zweig's book on Erasmus where reason and "fanaticism" are mutually and exclusively opposed. The latter is seen as the "spiritual enemy of Reason". Now obviously the struggle against fanaticism and for tolerance has always stood at the centre of the humanist ideology both in the Renaissance and particularly in the Enlightenment. But it would be historically wrong to overlook the social content of this antithesis in the Enlightenment itself: the Enlighteners understood by fanaticism the religious fanaticism of the defenders of the Middle Ages and of medieval social and ideological survivals; tolerance meant for them the securing of a free field of battle against the powers of Feudalism. But it would be an exaggeration, to say the least, to describe the Enlighteners as tolerant (in the Erasmus-Zweig sense) in their demand for tolerance. It suffices to think of Voltaire's "écrasez l'infâme!" The political-social demand for tolerance obviously does not exclude a fanatical championship of the humanist standpoint. And Stefan Zweig is under an enormous delusion if he thinks that Voltaire, Diderot or Lessing lived, thought and behaved according to his psychological-metaphysical antinomy—reason or fanaticism.

Zweig's rigid antithesis, which comes out in his idealization of Erasmus's historically necessary weaknesses, lead straight to liberal compromise. Zweig sums up Erasmus's views, with which he entirely sympathizes, as follows: "He believed that almost all conflicts between men and peoples could be solved without violence through *mutual willingness to yield*, because they all lay within the domain of the human; almost every antagonism could be fought out *by means of comparison*, were it not for those who were always ready to stretch the warlike bow too far." (My italics, G.L.) These views belong to the stock of abstract pacifism. Yet they acquire extraordinary political and ideological importance from the fact that they are pronounced by a leading anti-Fascist humanist at the time of the Hitler dictatorship in Germany and the heroic liberation struggle in Spain.

These views are rooted in ignorance and mistrust of the people, and in a false and abstract aristocracy of the spirit to which this gives rise. Undoubtedly tendencies of this kind—e.g., aristocracy of the intellect—are to be found among Renaissance and Enlightenment humanists, particularly the former. But in the first place these tendencies were not dominant. In the second place they spring of historical necessity from the weaknesses of the popular movements upon which the political social and ideological demands of humanism had to base themselves at the time. But today huge popular masses are engaged in the fight for humanist ideals, so that to produce a humanist strategy and tactics from an earlier historical situation, from the glorious pioneering periods of democratic revolution, is to stand the real relationship on its head and to turn the real content of Enlightenment humanism into its opposite. To reproduce certain aspects of humanism according to the letter is to sin heavily today against the real spirit of humanism. Naturally, every view of Zweig's can be backed up by definite quotations. But these quotations belong spiritually to the historical situation of the great humanists which we have outlined. And when Zweig states "that never can an ideal which takes into account only the general good" fully satisfy broad popular masses, he is slapping the most authentic humanist traditions in the face.

The decisive step in the development of anti-Fascist humanism is the conquest of such views. There is no point today in quoting statements made in the first years after Hitler's usurpation of power to show how strong liberal prejudices were even then. It is much more important and necessary to point to the extraordinarily long path which Germany's anti-Fascist intelligentsia has traversed since then. It has regained confidence—and this is the main thing—in a fundamental renewal of Germany through the forces of the German people. Heinrich Mann, in this respect again, is the most progressive and determined leader of anti-Fascist writing. He traces with a clairvoyant attention the human, the heroic, the significant cultural and humanist qualities which the revolutionary anti-Fascist struggle of the German people reveals more and more clearly from day to day. We can quote only one example here: Heinrich Mann shows how the heroic behaviour of the German anti-Fascists produces a new type of German and a new type of language. "Edgar André, a Hamburg dock worker, displayed in face of death, in his last fight, the same admirable qualities that other Germans of his kind are displaying today. He is the German in new and glorious figure. This does not happen easily, it has had to be won through heavy trials: the strength of conviction together with the loftiness and purity of expression. Here one has the cadence of the hero and the victor over death. The words are preserved for times when the victorious people will look back upon his great examples. For only genuine knowledge and selfless devotion can introduce such a cadence into a man's speech and such courage into his heart." Here is the clear voice of the newly awakened revolutionary democracy of Germany. Words like these in the writing of the German emigration spring from the soul of the fighting German people.

This big and important development in the anti-Fascist emigration made the historical novel the centre of interest for German literature. (The fact that certain anti-Fascist writers, in particular Feucht-wanger, wrote historical novels before the Hitler period, does not really alter the position as we have analysed it here; these are currents which join the mainstream of development.) The central position which historical subject-matter begins to occupy in the novel is in no way accidental; it is connected with the most important conditions of the anti-Fascist struggle. The demagogy of Fascism has very cleverly used a number of mistakes on the part of all left-wing parties and trends. Above all their narrowness—the narrow manner in which they appeal to the whole man with all his capacities and aspirations, and, in connection with this, their narrow attitude to German history and the links between the problems of the German people today and their historical development.

Dimitroff made some fundamental observations on both aspects of this question in his speeches to the 7th World Congress of the Comintern. He said: "Fascism not only arouses deeply rooted pre-judices in the masses, it also speculates with the best feelings of the masses, with their sense of justice and occasionally with their revolu-tionary traditions." And in close connection with this question Dimi-troff comes to speak of the problem of history: "The Fascists ransack the entire *history* of every people in order to pose as successors and continuators of all that is 'sublime and heroic' in its past, and use everything that has humiliated or offended the national feelings of a people as a weapon against the enemies of Fascism. In Germany hundreds of books are published which pursue a single aim—to falsify the history of the German people in a Fascist manner ... In these books the greatest men in the the German people's past are presented as Fascists and the great peasant movements as direct precursors of the Fascist movement."

These remarks demarcate a considerable area of the battlefield between Fascism and anti-Fascism, and provide a correct theoretical guide to the struggle. They explain why the problem of history, and in particular its treatment in literature, is brought more and more into the centre of the anti-Fascist struggle. If the anti-Fascist literature of Germany resuscitates the great figures of humanist development, if Cervantes, Henry IV and Montaigne, Josephus Flavius, Erasmus of Rotterdam, etc., come to life in the books of the German anti-Fascist writers, this is obviously a humanist declaration of war against Fascist barbarism. The subject-matter of the anti-Fascist writers is of a militant kind, born of the political and social demands of the present. This may be seen still more clearly in historical novels which hark back to the period of the great peasant uprisings. And even remoter subjects reveal this closeness to, and conditioning by, the present. Heinrich Mann portraying the formation of the French nation remains just as German and just as topical as Schiller in *The Maid of Orleans*. In certain of the German anti-Fascist historical novels the subject is simply a thin veil covering a satirical portrait of Hitler Fascism (e.g., *The False Nero*).

This very general description of the German anti-Fascist historical novel should make clear its difference from the novel of the period dealt with in the previous chapter. The chief defect of the latter—its lack of connection between past and present—is apparently overcome here. True a contrast is made between past and present here as well, but it is no longer a decorative antithesis between picturesque poetry and grey prose. The antithesis here has a political and social aim: knowledge of the great struggles of the past, familiarity with the great forefighters of progress will inspire men in the present with aims and ideals, courage and consolation amid the brutal terrors of Fascism. The past will show the way mankind has gone and the direction in which it is moving.

It is striking, though not accidental, that German history plays a subordinate role among the themes of German anti-Fascist humanism. The decisive reason for this is the deliberate internationalism of the anti-Fascist writers. The principal theme of Feuchtwanger's novels is precisely the struggle between narrow nationalism and militant internationalism. Heinrich Mann's internationalism has similar roots, but they are more deeply and organically embedded in the actual development of Germany. Heinrich Mann, as an essayist and publicist, has always pointed out the contrast between the political development of France and Germany and held up the more democratic development of France as a model for the progressive bourgeoisie of Germany. Old democratic traditions of German history manifest themselves here—perhaps unbeknown to Heinrich Mann. From Börne and Heine onwards up to the *German-French Yearbooks* this contrast was one of the central ideological issues round which the democratic forces of Germany gathered in the struggle of 1848. And in Engels's letter where he criticizes Franz Mehring's *Lessing Legend* he points out the topicality and instructiveness of this contrast between the grand line of French political development and the forever disjointed, stick-in-the-mud, petty character of German history. Heinrich Mann's novel *Henri IV* follows on from his publicist writing and pursues the same aim of popularizing French democracy for the German intelligentsia; in the history of German revolutionary democracy this novel constitutes a modern revival of the great ideological struggles of the thirties and forties of the previous century.

But of course this is not the only motif. A large part is played by the lack in German history of really significant democratic-revolutionary events. And this lack is felt doubly strongly by today's anti-Fascist writers, because their aim is to produce a monumental, all-national effect, something that will be readily understood in large outlines. For this reason they feel drawn to subjects where the struggle for humanist ideals is expressed in a monumentally concentrated and grandiose manner. This tendency is combined with an attempt to find deterrent historical counterparts of the Hitler régime, which can in this way be pathetically or satirically unmasked. Feuchtwanger's novel on Nero is not alone in this respect; Heinrich Mann's Duke de Guise shows the same tendency.

These are important positive features. The alienation of the historical novel from the life of the present is effectively overcome by such tendencies. It would, however, be superficial not to see the *transitional character* of this literature : in our previous remarks we have indicated the path taken by an often very hesitant liberalism in the Weimar period to today's revolutionary democracy. Obviously, literature cannot just reflect what has been reached, the end-result, without at the same time giving expression to the complicated path with its fluctuations, relapses and unevennesses.

In addition, it must be specially emphasized that the complete journey necessarily takes place at a *slower* rate in an ideological-literary context than in the directly political. The great events of our time press writers into taking up positions with dramatic suddenness, and many of the best of them mature very rapidly as a result of the extraordinary responsibility which devolves on them, the extraordinary demands which the times make on them. And it is inevitable that this development should be an uneven one. A step forward in the direction of revolutionary democracy cannot possibly bring about an immediate revision of all the philosophic and aesthetic views associated with a writer's previous political state. Moreover, such important works as the historical novels of the anti-Fascist writers cannot possibly be produced from one day to the next. Thus, in their original conceptions they still bear the marks of phases of development which the writers themselves have already overcome, and an adequate expression of their more recent phases of development will only emerge in their future works. (We shall examine these different stages of development later, when we compare the first and second volume of Feuchtwanger's Josephus novel.)

This transitional character is felt chiefly in the fact that revolutionary democracy often remains no more than a demand and is not concretely portrayed. Present is a desire for close unity with the people—recognition of the people in a political, and popular life in a creative respect, but not as yet the concrete portrayal of popular life itself as the basis of history. We shall deal with this question in detail when we come to analyse the individual important historical novels of this period. Here we must just briefly point out that this transitional character, this still incomplete conquest of the estrangement of modern bourgeois literature from the people has a deep effect upon the artistic character of these works.

It is true that the literary principles of bourgeois decadence penetrate into the works of even important anti-Fascists, or remain still active in them. We mention only one, though, to our mind, decisive, point: namely the boldness of literary invention, the ability to dispose freely of historical facts, characters and situations, without thereby departing from historical truth—indeed, in order to bring out the specific features, the particular characteristcs of an historical epoch. A close familiarity with the life of the people is the precondition for real literary invention. In later bourgeois literature the writer's alienation from the people is mirrored, as we have seen, in two ways: on the one hand, in his anxious clinging to the facts of contemporary (or historical) life; on the other, in his conception of artistic invention which he sees not as the highest literary form of a correct reflection of objective reality but as something purely subjective which draws him arbitrarily away from the sole truth of the factual. (It is immaterial for our present considerations whether the individual writer or trend affirms or rejects this subjectively conceived imagination.)

Alfred Döblin, in an essay on the historical novel, sums up this false dilemma very vividly: "The present-day novel, not only the historical, is subject to two currents—the one derives from the fairytale, the other from the report. Their source is not the ether of aesthetics, but the reality of our life. Within ourselves we incline towards both currents to a greater or less extent. But we are not deluding ourselves if we say: the active progressive circles are taking today to the report, while the serene and satisfied go over to the fairytale." On this basis Döblin formulates the dilemma of the contemporary and historical novel: "The novel is caught up in a struggle between the two tendencies: fairy-tale constructions with a maximum of elaboration and a minimum of material and—novel constructions with a maximum of material and a minimum of elaboration."

These remarks of Döblin—whether one agrees with them or not—are of great typical significance for the present position of the historical novel. Döblin endeavours to break down theoretically the wall dividing historical novel and life. From this standpoint he rightly attacks the decadent-bourgeois theory of the historical novel as a genre in its own right: "There is no difference in principle between an ordinary and an historical novel," and he criticizes, again quite rightly, the fashionable historical *belles lettres* of today which are "neither fish nor fowl". He says of the author of such works: "He produces neither a decently documented picture of history, nor an historical novel. One's taste naturally revolts against this simultaneous botching and distortion of historical material."

Döblin would thus appear to have got through to a real theory of the historical novel. What prevents him is the false and subjectivist modern conception of the nature and function of the artistic imagination. He rightly objects to the many falsifications of history on the part of writers, he rightly pleads for a genuine and truthful conception of history. But according to Döblin's conception this very honesty, this endeavour to give a truthful reproduction of reality cannot be reconciled with poetry in the traditional sense. "The moment the novel acquires the new function we have mentioned of a special form of discovery and presentation of reality, it is difficult to call the author poet or writer, he is rather a *special kind of scientist*." This science, however, is confined to the ascertaining of facts. Döblin dismisses the imagination, the creative faculty as something purely subjective, not only in art, but in science, too. "If we look at the writing of history, we see that *only chronology is honest*. Once dates are ordered the manoeuvre begins. To put it bluntly: *one makes use of history*." Before we examine this last and extremely important pronouncement of Döblin's, we must briefly show how he accepts all the literary consequences which follow from this theory. He says of the contemporary novel: "It is unable to compete with photography and the newspapers. Its technical means are not sufficient." Here Döblin succumbs to the widespread naturalist prejudice which sees photography (and the newspaper) as being truer to life than the embodiment of reality in artistic images.

More important, however, is the theory which sharply opposes faithfulness to facts to participation in social struggle. Döblin himself is far too active a writer and combines far too many militant aims with his own writing for him to be satisfied with such a conclusion. He himself speaks of the "partisanship of the active person", and in a positive sense. How does this agree with his theory and practice? It agrees with his practice insofar as writers who wish to be active simply brush aside their theoretical prejudices during their practical activity. This would solve the question if they really did and could manage simply to lay these prejudices aside. Then it would matter very little what kind of theory they might proclaim outside their work, in theoretical articles.

Unfortunately, it is not as simple as this. For what Döblin says here epistemologically about the relation of science and art to reality is not an ingenious theory, but a fairly faithful mirror of the general attitude of most writers in the period just behind us. A truthful conception of reality and active participation in events constitute for most writers an insoluble dilemma. How is this dilemma to be solved? Obviously through life itself, through a writer's connection with the life of the people. The writer who is deeply familiar with the tendencies at work in popular life, who experiences them as if they were his own, will feel himself to be simply the executive organ of these tendencies, his rendering of reality will appear to him as simply a reproduction of these tendencies themselves, even should he render every individual fact differently from the way he found it. "French society should be the historian, I but its secretary," says Balzac.

The objectivity of a great writer depends upon an objective and, at the same time, living involvement with the major tendencies of social development. And the "partisanship of the active"? This too, grows organically out of the struggle of historical forces in the objective reality of human society. It is a modern fetishism to think that the tendencies operating in history possess a form and objectivity wholly independent of and separate from men. They are, for all their objectivity, for all their independence of human consciousness, simply the living concentrations of human endeavours, arising from the same social-economic causes and oriented towards the same social-historical goals. For people who have close and living ties with this reality correct insight and practical activity form a unity and not an antithesis. Lenin rightly objected to Struve who wished to smuggle the bourgeois concept of dead "scientific objectivity" into the revolutionary working-class movement: "On the other hand, materialism includes so to speak the element of partisanship within itself, since it is obliged at every assessment of an event to represent the standpoint of a certain social group directly and openly."

Lenin is only saying with the scientific clarity of dialectical materialism what all important representatives of revolutionary democracy—be they practical politicians, writers or thinkers—have always done in practice. The difference between the Marxist and the non- or pre-Marxist revolutionary democrat consists in the fact that the latter is not conscious of the social and epistemological connections which underly the unity of his theory and practice and that he fulfils this unity generally on the basis of a "false consciousness", often full of illusions. But the history of literature proves that if a writer is deeply rooted in popular life, if his writing stems from this intimacy with the most important questions of popular life, he can, even with a "false consciousness", plumb the real depths of historical truth. So Walter Scott, so Balzac, so Leo Tolstoy. And the objectivity of the artistic imagination is associated with this "partisanship of the active man" in the most intimate way. It becomes objective by continually altering the immediate "facts" of life so that the great objective laws, the really decisive tendencies of historical development may achieve expression.

A further indication of the transitional character of the humanist historical novel today is its relatively accidental choice of theme. We mentioned earlier the objective historical causes for this. But it is one thing to see the social and historical cause of a phenomenon, and another to view it as an adequate expression of an historically correct trend. The transitional character comes out very clearly in this particular respect, but it assumes very complicated forms. One must be careful not to confuse the accidental choice of historical subject here with that of the previous period. Admittedly Feuchtwanger's theory is, as we have seen, closely connected with the theories of bourgeois decadence in regard to the subjectivization of history; and Feuchtwanger bases himself in some detail on Nietzsche and Croce. But it would be quite wrong to equate Feuchtwanger's historical subjectivism with that of Flaubert's, Jacobsen's or Conrad Ferdinand Meyer's. The historical-political content of Feuchtwanger's work is firmly opposed to theirs. And it is this political content which leads Feuchtwanger to choose his themes more organically and which brings him progressively nearer to achieving this. His first historical novels largely correspond to his "costume theory" of history, as we shall later see. Yet the theme of Josephus Flavius already implies an altogether higher degree of historical objectivity. For although Feucht-wanger often modernizes the struggle between nationalism and inter-nationalism, the antagonism itself belongs to the historical material and Feuchtwanger develops it from the material in despite of his own theory; he does not introduce a subjective antithesis. The sharp con-trast between the historical novel of the humanists of our day and the historical novel of bourgeois decline is clearly visible here.

But there is still a long way to go before the haphazardness of theme is fully overcome. We have already said that the anti-Fascist novel rarely chooses German history as its subject. This is undoubtedly a weakness of the anti-Fascist struggle itself. Dimitroff very rightly pointed to the extreme political and propagandist significance of the Fascist falsification of German history. The weakness of left opposi-tion movements in Germany has for long consisted in an abstract and negative attitude to the great national problems of German history. This was already apparent in the attitude of important revo-lutionaries like Johann Jacobi and Wilhelm Liebknecht towards the national side of Bismarck's wars which, whatever else they did, achieved German unity. A situation arose in the German working-class movement which was later to prove disastrous: Marx's and Engel's correct attitude remained unknown and instead the broad

THE HISTORICAL NOVEL OF DEMOCRATIC HUMANISM 277

masses were treated to Lasalle's and Schweitzer's ideological capitulation to Bismarck's *Realpolitik* successes on the one hand and to Liebknecht's abstract, provincial-moralizing oppositional theories on the other. And the later opposition movements which arise in Germany against imperialism, chauvinism, reaction, etc., suffer in almost every case from this abstract-moralizing one-sidedness, this disinclination to examine the problems of German history concretely and to fight the propaganda of reaction with the weapons of a truly patriotic ideology, historically and artistically. It is to the undying credit of Franz Mehring that he, almost alone, engaged concretely and vigorously in this struggle.

The experiences of the struggle against Fascism should lead the democratic left to criticize its own previous practice. (The German Communist Party, where Rosa Luxemburg traditions on the national question as on others, were kept alive well into the Weimar period, is of course equally guilty for this state of affairs.) The task is not simply to unmask Fascist falsifications of history, it goes far beyond that; it is to restore the traditions of revolutionary democracy in Germany, historically and artistically, to show that the ideas of revolutionary democracy were not an "import" from the West, but grew up out of the class struggles of Germany and that the greatness of the greatest Germans has always been intimately linked with the destiny of these ideas. Thus, the great task of anti-Fascist writing is to bring the ideas of revolutionary democracy and militant humanism near to the people by showing that these ideas are necessary and organic products of German development itself. It is obvious that precisely the historical novel can and surely will play an enormous part in this anti-Fascist struggle. But it has not yet acquired this significance.

Admittedly, the literary traditions of Germany run counter to this demand. It is striking how small a part German historical subjects have played in Germany's otherwise very significant historical literature (particularly the drama). But one must not forget that the position of a Schiller or Georg Büchner can in no circumstances be compared with that of an anti-Fascist emigré of today. At that time live mass movements were only to be found abroad. It was therefore understandable and correct that the German public should be confronted with foreign subjects which dealt with problems related to their own. Today, however, the anti-Fascist emigration is the far-off voice of the liberation struggle of millions of German workers. Hence, whether German history is portrayed and propagated in a revolutionary or in a reactionary manner is today a veritable *hic Rhodus, hic salta.*

By conquering German history German revolutionary democracy acquires a concrete national character and a leading national role.

The great task of the day is to demonstrate historically and artistically that revolutionary democracy is Germany's only path of salvation. But if the broadest masses are to understand this, the Fascist demagogic theory of the "Western import character" of progressive and revolutionary ideas in Germany must be demolished by positive examples.

Let us give one example. The central problem of Feuchtwanger's Josephus Flavius novel is essentially a very German problem. The struggle between the problems of nationalism and internationalism plays an enormous part in actual German history even before the rise of a revolutionary working-class movement. The French Revolution has already placed this question and the tragic conflict it involves on the agenda. Think of Georg Forster and the Jacobins of Mainz. Forster's fate was admittedly an extreme one, but anyone who knows the history of this period in Germany will realize that the very extremity of his case was typical of a general tragedy of the time. Similarly, any live and concrete approach to the Josephus Flavius problem which takes in human types as well as social-political significances must demonstrate similar connections. But the broad masses of Germany, and even of the German intelligentsia, are more or less ignorant of these connections. Hence it is unavoidable if important works such as Feuchtwanger's novel, which may be humanly moving and raise very profound and topical political questions, nevertheless hang in the air from a national-historical point of view. The direct and immediately graspable connection with the national life of the present, which was present in Scott or Balzac or Tolstoy, is lacking and *must* be lacking in these circumstances. And in this way the anti-Fascist emigration presents an undefended flank to the national demagogy of Fascism.

A third factor illustrating the transitional character of the anti-Fascist historical novel is its striving after historical monumentality. It, too, starts out from the heroes of history and, unlike the classical type of historical novel, does not allow them to grow out of the concrete historical basis of popular life. But here again, despite the apparent resemblance to the previous period of the historical novel, we must underline the difference. This striving after monumentality is, as we have emphasized, not decorative or picturesque. It springs from the militant-Enlightener traditions of the important humanists of our day. By reducing the great struggles of history to a contest between reason and unreason, progress and reaction, they render them intelligible to themselves and to their readers. We repeat: this vigorous and militant defence of the traditions of human progress, which assumes the mantle of the Renaissance and the Enlightenment, produces an important change in the history of literature. After the fruitless scepticism, the indignant or, later, even comfortably resigned compromise with capitalist reality—that is, after the literary decadence, here is the first call to battle in defence of human culture.

But as a result of the all-too-rapid, all-too-abstract reduction of concrete historical class struggles to problems of reason versus unreason much of the connection with real popular life is lost. The living significance of such great abstract summaries as the theories of the Enlighteners rests precisely on the fact that they were summaries of real popular problems, popular sufferings and hopes. They could at any time be translated back out of this abstract form into the concrete language of social-historical problems; they never lost their link with these problems. In intention no doubt this link is present in the literature of the anti-Fascist emigration. Nevertheless, this filing-down to an abstract struggle of principles does at times produce a remoteness from life in the concrete portrayal which blurs the real antagonism and sometimes distorts the most ardent intentions of the author. Feuchtwanger, in his essay on the historical novel, formulates this antithesis in an extremely dangerous manner, so that his formulation, as against his actual work, admits an unpopular, aristocratic note. "Both historian and novelist see history as the struggle of a tiny minority, capable and determined to judge, against the enormous, compact majority of the 'blind'—those who are incapable of judgment and led only by instinct." This is a theoretical justification of Zweig's Erasmus, but not of Feuchtwanger's own Josephus novels.

But even Heinrich Mann at times—and they are not insignificant —allows the concrete struggle between concrete historical forces to evaporate into this kind of abstraction. Mann at one point says of his Henri IV: "But he knows that, as a species, Man does not want this, and it is Man that he will meet everywhere, to the very end. There are neither Protestants, Catholics, Spaniards nor Frenchmen: there is a species, Man. And what Man wants is the darkness of brute force, the bondage of the earth; sinful riot and unclean ecstasy. These will be his eternal opponents, while he is forever the emissary of reason and human happiness." Here, the great social-historical antagonisms which determine the content of mankind's struggle for progress evaporate into an almost anthropological abstraction. And if these antagonisms have no concrete social-historical character, but are eternal opposites of two types of man, then what is to guarantee that victory of humanity and reason whose best and most eloquent champion is precisely Heinrich Mann.

This attitude determines certain essential features of composition. Since Henri IV is presented as the eternal emissary of reason and humanity it is natural that he should occupy the central position in the novel. His character, problems, historical importance and political-human physiognomy do not grow concretely out of the definite antagonisms of a definite phase in the life of the French people. On the contrary the problems of French popular life appear to be no more than a—in a certain sense accidental—sphere in which these eternal ideals may be realized.

Of course, Heinrich Mann's *Henri IV* is not constructed throughout on this principle. If it were, it could not be a work of art which breathed real life. It, too, has a transitional character: a concrete historical conception of the problem of popular life at a particular stage of historical development conflicts with an abstractly monumentalized, eternalizing conception of an exaggerated Enlightenment kind.

From a literary-historical point of view the influence of Victor Hugo can be felt here in Heinrich Mann. This is important and noteworthy, because Victor Hugo's development led him away from Romanticism and made him into a forerunner of the humanist revolt against the growing barbarism of capitalism. In this development Victor Hugo takes over much of the ideology of the Enlightenment; artistically, however, he retains many Romantic and profoundly anti-historical attitudes. Here then we may see a link between Heinrich Mann and the past, which does not, however, take us back to the classical type of historical novel, but on the contrary to its Romantic antipode.

Heinrich Mann has himself spoken of Hugo's relation to modern literature in a review of the novel *1793*; he comes out here in favour of Hugo as against Anatole France. Today, no doubt, Heinrich Mann would consider this essay an already dated phase in his development (it appeared in book form in 1931). However, its approach is so important for the artistic and ideological genesis of *Henri IV* that we must quote its essential passages. Heinrich Mann discusses the big scene in Hugo between Danton, Robespierre and Marat: "Each one could be determined socially and clinically. This should be of particular concern to us; we have *The Gods Athirst*. Nothing would remain then but more or less sick creatures artificially inflated by their age which puts them and their kind on show. But this would be a belittling insight. Anyone can see into the dubious nature of human greatness at times, and no writer who has lasted was ever a bad connoisseur of life. A magnifying insight, however, prefers to see a character in a more-than-real, exaggerated form, whatever his roots. Hallucinations, near-manic depressions, here they take on unquestionable personality and destiny. Isn't this our experience? We should realize that only in this way can history escape the clinics. Only in this way can we look at life and not be depressed."

Again, we have to do here with a typical modern dilemma. Heinrich Mann's choice between pathology and abstract monumentalization between "belittling" and "magnifying" insights, arises because writers' social-historical attitudes have been severed from popular life. Heinrich Mann is unjust towards Anatole France. France's depiction of men at close quarters in his novel on the Revolution is something quite different from a "belittling insight". France is expressing his disappointment with bourgeois democracy at its point of highest realization. It is an artistic portrayal of the human contradictions which occur precisely at this tragic level. We are not saying that France completely solved this problem, but Mann's criticism, instead of touching the real limitations of France's writing, picks upon those features which France has in common, though only superficially, with the rest of the late bourgeois literature of disillusion. This literature really does propagate a pathological, a "belittling" attitude to man.

But is Heinrich Mann's antinomy of belittling or magnifying insights really unavoidable? Is there not a third way? We believe that *Henri IV* itself clearly shows that there is. Mann's conception of humanity as something that is real and triumphant starts from the same premise as we find in all really important realistic writers. The premise, namely, that the really great features of humanity are present in life itself, in the objective reality of society, in man, and are only reproduced by the writer in a concentrated artistic form.

Heinrich Mann's magnificent words on Edgar André show that he was fully alive to this *tertium*. The colossal events following Hitler's seizure of power sharpened his awareness of this heroic reality, which can be neither belittled by being seen at close quarters nor magnified by monumentalization. In his articles he has time and again depicted these manifestations of a new heroic humanity in a movingly simple and accurate way. And a great deal in *Henri IV* reveals this new spirit, which no longer has anything in common with Hugo's stylization and Heinrich Mann's old dilemma.

But *Henri IV* in this respect, too, is a transitional product. Conceived originally under the influence of Hugo, with a monumentalized hero as the eternal champion of an ideal, it won through in many directions to a concrete and straightforward richness of life. However, the framework of the original conception stood in the way of a really concrete portrayal of this richness of life in its simplicity and humanity. And one can say with as much justice of Mann's dilemma of belittling and magnifying insight what was said before of Alfred Döblin's dilemma of fairy tale and report: it is not an invention of aesthetics, but proceeds from life itself into aesthetics.

Nevertheless, it proceeded from a phase which life itself—and with it Heinrich Mann—has already left behind. Heinrich Mann's present artistic struggle is with the legacy of a past which he has overcome both politically and humanly. The substance of the struggle is to find a fully appropriate form for his new sense of life. If we call *Henri IV* a transitional product, this does not lower its literary significance, on the contrary, only emphasizes it. It is a product of the transition of the best section of the German intelligentsia, and the German people, to the decisive struggle against Hitler's barbarism and to the revival of revolutionary democracy in Germany.

2. *Popular Character and the True Spirit of History.*

We can see the transitional character of the historical novel of anti-Fascist humanism at its clearest if we examine the artistic methods and means by which the role of the people in history is presented. All these writers portray the destinies of nations. What distinguishes them from the preceding period of the bourgeois historical novel is the fact that they have broken with the tendencies which make history private, which turns it into an exotic, colourful panorama based upon some eccentric case of psychology. The stories at the centre of these novels are deeply connected from the very beginning with the fortunes of the people, socially and humanly. Thus as far as content is concerned they take an important step in the direction of the classical historical novel.

But artistically there is as yet no decisive break with the forms and methods of portrayal of the modern historical novel. As regards composition, structure, action, particularly where the relation of the main hero and his adventures to the broad sphere of popular life is concerned, the classical inheritance remains as yet untouched. For the new humanism the classics of the historical novel are almost as much the forgotten figures of literary history as they were for the writers of the previous period; they can be safely ignored.

But what appears to be a formal-aesthetic or, if one likes, literary-historical matter in fact goes far beyond aesthetics or literary history. Heinrich Mann, Feuchtwanger, Bruno Frank do indeed portray the fortunes of the people, but not from the standpoint of the people. The classics of the historical novel were politically and socially far more conservative than Heinrich Mann or Feuchtwanger—think of Sir Walter Scott. There was no question of any such passionate involvement with the revolutionary transformation of society in their case, nor could there be. But in their experience of history, in their concrete and living regard for history, Scott and the other classics of the historical novel are much nearer to the real life of the people than even the greatest democratic writers of today. History for Scott means in a very primary and direct way: the fortunes of the people. His first concern is the life of the people in a given historical period; only then does he embody a popular destiny in an historical figure and show how such events are connected with the problems of the present. The process is an organic one. He writes *from* the people, not *for* the people; he writes from their experiences, from their soul.

The anti-Fascist humanists are much more strongly and passionately drawn to the people than most of the classics. This very passion is a sign that the best section of the democratic intelligentsia, under the influence of the terrible and magnificent events of the last years, is resolved to break down its previous isolation from popular life. This resolve, which has already been realized in political-publicist writing, is an enormously significant step forward. The modern historical novel constitutes a high artistic expression of this resolve. However, where it is a question of changing every principle of composition so that the voice of popular life should be heard for itself and not just the writer's attitude to popular life, such a resolve can only be realized gradually and unevenly, only after searching questions have been asked in the domains of history, ideology and art. The writers of today do write for the people and about popular events, but the people themselves play only a secondary role in their novels. They provide a counter for the artistic demonstration of humanist ideals, though these ideals are certainly closely connected with the important problems of popular life. Seen artistically, then, the people provide simply a stage for the principal action, which takes place on a different plane, not directly connected with popular life.

Thus, insofar as its action takes place largely in the upper spheres of society, the historical novel of the new humanism follows on from the later bourgeois historical novel. We have already shown that this resemblance conceals a very deep difference, indeed contrast, as far as social content, psychology, etc., are concerned. But the conception of "above" and "below" in society easily gives rise to misunderstanding, and the conception of popular character in connection with the presentation of history from "below" can very easily be vulgarized, so that a brief clarification of these concepts is necessary here.

First of all, let us once again stress what will certainly not be new to the reader of this work: by presentation from "below" we on no account mean the exclusion of the historical protagonist, that is, an historical novel which portrays only the oppressed sections of society. An historical novel of this kind is *also* possible; it was realized, for instance, in the works of Erckmann-Chatrian. But we hope that our arguments have left no doubt that it can in no way provide a model for the historical novel. On the contrary, this type of historical novel brings out the problematic sides of modern literary development in a new but no less pronounced form. The overwhelming majority of Scott's, Pushkin's and Tolstoy's heroes come from the upper sections of society, and yet the life and destiny of the whole people are reflected in the events of their lives.

Thus one must define these antitheses a little more clearly, both as they relate to the historical novel and to the novel in general. What is the aim of the historical novel? First, it is to portray the kind of individual destiny that can *directly* and at the same time typically express the problems of an epoch. The modern novel in its shift to the world "above" has portrayed destinies which are socially eccentric. Eccentric because the upper sections of society have ceased to be the leaders of progress for the entire nation. The only proper way of expressing this eccentricity is to indicate its social basis, to show that it is the social position of the characters which distances them from the everyday life of the people. They must appear eccentric from a social standpoint. For as the characteristic of a particular stratum of society this eccentricity is *also* typical. But the decisive thing is the social and psychological content of the particular personal destiny; that is, is this destiny inwardly connected with the great, typical questions of popular life or not?

The lack of such a connection can just as easily be the case in novels which seem to deal directly with popular life, which aim to portray life from "below". To quote one typical example: Franz Biberkopf in Döblin's *Berlin Alexanderplatz*. Biberkopf is a worker; his *milieu* is presented externally with the utmost exactitude. But when Döblin has wrenched him out of working-class life, turned him into a ponce and criminal and then, after taking him through various adventures, endowed him at the end with a mystical belief in fate—what, in terms of psychology, has all this to do with the German working-class of the post-war period or with the German people as a whole during this period? Obviously, very little. This does not mean that Döblin's individual case is not possible, nor that it could not be repeated in just this *milieu*. But it is not a question of the psychological truth of an individual case or the sociographic and descriptive authenticity of *milieu*. It is the content of the story that matters. And in Döblin this content is eccentric as far as the German people are concerned. As eccentric as the personal destinies portrayed by Joyce or Musil with whom Döblin's book inwardly belongs. By placing his action in a Berlin working-class environment Döblin, far from removing this eccentricity, only increases it.

In contrast to this, take Pushkin's Tatiana in *Eugene Onegin*, or, to cite a contemporary German example, Thomas Mann's *Buddenbrooks*. From a social angle both works take place "above". Nevertheless, Belinsky was quite right in calling Pushkin's novel-in-verse an "encyclopedia" of Russian life, and the story of Tatiana is precisely an example of an important, general destiny in which the most important problems of Russian popular life during a period of transition appear concentrated. It is no longer possible for Thomas Mann to have Pushkin's direct and broad universality. Nevertheless, the fate of his Lübeck patrician family is only outwardly, from a formal artistic point of view, that of a self-contained and isolated family. The most important spiritual and moral problems of Germany's transition to modern, developed capitalism are given major typical expression here. And this transition is a turning-point for the German people as a whole.

Thus, if we reproach the modern novel for not portraying history from "below", it should be clear what we are getting at. Yet the rejection of historically and socially eccentric fates is only the first step towards clarifying the problem. A subject which is socially and psychologically typical can also be unsuitable for an epic work. And this brings us to the central artistic question of the contemporary historical novel; for there is little tendency today to portray the openly eccentric. Why are the minor aristocrats in Scott or Tolstoy popular figures, why is the fate of the people reflected in their experience? The reason is simple. Both Scott and Tolstoy created characters in whom personal and social-historical fates closely conjoin. Moreover, certain important and general aspects of popular experience are expressed *directly* in the personal lives of these characters. The genuinely historical spirit of Scott or Tolstoy appears precisely here. Through personal experience these characters come into contact with all the great problems of the age; become organically linked with and inevitably moulded by them; yet lose neither their personality, nor the immediacy of their experience. With Andrei Bolkonsky, Nikola and Petya Rostov, etc., in *War and Peace*, the influence of each particular war is felt directly in their private lives, both in the outward transformation of life and in the inner change of social-moral behaviour.

This indirect contact between individual lives and historical events is the most decisive thing of all. For the people experience history directly. History is their own upsurge and decline, the chain of their joys and sorrows. If the historical novelist can succeed in creating characters and destinies in which the important social-human contents, problems, movements, etc., of an epoch appear directly, then he can present history "from below", from the standpoint of popular life. And the function of the historical figures in the classics is this: when problems and movements such as these have been rendered concrete for us so that we may experience them directly, the historical figure steps in to raise them on to a higher level of historical typicality by concentrating and generalizing them. In this way one is not imprisoned in the simple immediacy of popular life, in the simple spontaneity of popular movements, the typical example of which are the novels of Erckmann-Chatrian. For this reason, as we have already shown, the historical figures of the classics are only minor figures but indispensable to the total historical picture.

From the standpoint of popular character then there are two possible dangers for the historical novel. The first we have already treated at length, namely the lack of organic connection between personal fates and the historical problems of popular life, the essential social-historical contents of the period in question. Thus the personal fates may come to life humanly and psychologically and may be socially typical in a certain sense, but they remain nevertheless private destinies, and the function of history becomes merely that of a background, a decorative stage.

The historical novel of anti-Fascist humanism courts the opposite danger. The important writers here approach their theme from a high level of abstraction to begin with. Their historical protagonists embody emotionally and intellectually the great humanist ideas and ideals for which they themselves are fighting. As a result the immediacy of historical experience disappears or at least runs this risk. For the importance of the important characters of history lies in their ability to generalize, raise to a high intellectual level problems which in life itself are scattered and appear in purely individual forms and purely private fates.

We emphasize once more: this is an important positive feature in the historical novel of anti-Fascist humanism, a step towards eliminating that lack of connection between past and present from which the historical novel of the previous period suffered even in the work of its most outstanding representatives. But the restored connection is nevertheless too *direct*, too *intellectual*, too *general*.

We have already mentioned the danger of intellectual generalization (struggle between reason and unreason as the content of history) and shown how it weakens specific, concrete historical character. Now we must point to another closely related danger: namely the elevation of immediate historical experience into too intellectual a form. That is, the path from immediate historical experience to its generalization and summing-up is too short and therefore abstract. It is so short and abstract because the whole process takes place *within one person*, namely the historical protagonist himself, the champion of the humanist ideals. Two things follow from this. On the one hand, the immediate experience cannot be shared in the same kind of breadth and many-sidedness by characters who do not have this generalizing function. On the other, the single path leading from experience to generalization, i.e., within the soul of a single person, is necessarily too narrow, straight and simple. Compare it with what happens in the classical historical novel. Here, very divergent paths leading from the experiences of characters very different humanly and socially are drawn together by another character, namely the historical protagonist, who in the classics is always a minor figure. In addition, the generalization of one's own experience is necessarily a process of abstraction, whereas the "answer" which the protagonist of the classical historical novel gives to the "questions" of those immediately experiencing history is not at all an answer in a logical sense and does not need to be directly linked with their experiences. It is sufficient if his summing-up answers their question in an inwardly historical sense. This gives the writer greater freedom of movement; it extends the range, richness and complexity of life which he can portray.

Let us take Tolstoy's *War and Peace* once more. When the French army invades Russia the various characters react to the event in the most varied ways, but in every case they react directly and personally, so that the war's transformation of their lives is expressed in their transformed feelings and experiences. None of these characters, neither Andrei Bolkonsky nor any of the Rostovs, nor Denisov, etc., is obliged compositionally to generalize his experiences any more than his given state of feeling demands. Even in such conversations as between Bolkonsky and Bezukhov on the eve of the battle of Borodino, Bolkonsky's theoretical remarks are no more than generalizations of his subjective feelings. They are intended as a dash of colour to the total canvas, not to carry the meaning of the whole.

When, however, in Heinrich Mann the young King of Navarre learns that his mother has been poisoned by Catherine de Medici, he, as the leader of the Huguenots, must react immediately; he has to confront the cunning queen in the guise of a diplomatic enemy. His emotional and intellectual reactions form the central axis of the novel. Its entire development passes through his soul. Whatever else is simply illustrative. The central figure is thus overloaded—he is expected to make an adequate historical response at every stage of the story. And this means that the already short and narrow path from experience to generalization is further artificially curtailed. In important situations where this curtailment does not occur, where the central figure remains for some length of time on the level of immediate experience, he inevitably falls in stature. His central position compels the reader to expect from him something significant, some kind of lead in every situation and to see his immediate and purely personal experiences solely as a vehicle of the historically general, not as an end in themselves. Tolstoy, too, concentrates the experiences of the Russian people at war in the figure of Kutuzov. This old man no longer has any personal desires or experiences, nevertheless he is never as abstract as Heinrich Mann's *Henri IV* often is, despite Mann's outstanding powers of portrayal. The explanation is simple: Kutuzov is a minor figure, the experience of the people has been lived in the experience of the most varied characters, the artistic generalization thus has an extremely broad basis to it and a representative figure whose position in the novel and whose psychological make-up are particularly suited to this summing-up function. The people "below" thus experience history directly, either as participants or victims. "Above" both groups become blurred and abstract, lose contact with life and sometimes even leave the domain of the historical. Thus, the fact that Kutuzov is a minor figure creates the basis for his profound and authentic role, artistically and historically, of mediator between "below" and "above", between the immediacy of reaction to events and the highest possible consciousness in these particular circumstances.

The manner of portraying history which we have criticized here is connected with the outlook of a period which has been overcome only in a political-social sense. Popular destiny is not yet felt as the really concrete destiny of the people, but as abstract historical destiny, in which the people play a more or less accidental role. And this accidentality is often increased in the very attempt of these writers to close the gap between themselves and the people. They are ardently and passionately involved in the present fate of the German people. Yet the specific, historical destinies they portray in the past often have no individual complexion or independent significance. For the past is used simply as illustrative *material for the problems of the present.* Nevertheless despite the unevenness and contradictoriness of this development, it is plainly leading beyond this estrangement from the people.

Let us look at Lion Feuchtwanger's development from this point of view. His first historical novels (*Jew Süss* and *The Ugly Duchess*) essentially conform to his stated theory of the historical novel. In both, history is no more than a decorative costume for specifically modern psychological problems. The fate of the Tyrol in the struggles for power between the Luxemburgs, Habsburgs and Wittelsbachs has very little to do with the individual love tragedy of Margarete Maultasch. The tragedy of the gifted, but ugly woman, which consitutes the human interest of this novel—for there is very little in the actual political power intrigues that could interest the present-day reader from a historical-human angle—is woven into the plot of political intrigue with great skill, but humanly has hardly anything to do with it. It is a similar case with *Jew Süss*. The main theme here is also a specifically modern psychological conflict, a clash of outlooks. Feuchtwanger himself says of his subject: "For years now I have wanted to show a man's path from doing to not-doing, from action to contemplation, from a European to an Indian outlook. There was an obvious example of this development in our own times: Walther Rathenau. I attempted it: I failed. I transferred the subject two centuries back and attempted to portray the path of the Jew Süss Oppenheimer: I came nearer my goal."

Feuchtwanger's mistake is very instructive. He says that his failure with Rathenau and success with the Württemburg Jew proves the suitability of historical themes for the embodiment of abstract-intellectual collisions. We think that it was neither the proximity nor the unfavourableness of contemporary material which caused Feuchtwanger's failure with the Rathenau theme, but the fact that his collision has little to do with the inner tragedy of Rathenau. Thus the familiar personality of the latter and the well-known circumstances of his life strongly and successfully resisted the writer's attempted "introjection". Rathenau's Jewishness certainly plays an important part in his tragedy and there is some kind of split between activity and contemplation. But Rathenau's real tragedy is the tragedy of the liberal bourgeoisie of Germany. Because of the discreditable political and cultural position of the economically dominant bourgeoisie under the Wilhelmine régime the liberals proved incapable of changing over to a democratic-republican policy even when the Hohenzollerns had fallen and German social democracy had placed state power into their hands. The doing not-doing theme could only form an episodic abstraction from this vast subject; it certainly could not master it.

Feuchtwanger realizes his aim in *Jew Süss*, because he is able to do what he likes with this remote historical figure. However, as far as the story as a whole is concerned he is not successful, nor could he be. His aim was to take the Jew Süss from action to inaction. Action meant the fearful exploitation of Württemburg with the help of a minor branch of the dynasty which had come to power. Now when the turning-point occurs and Feuchtwanger's hero takes the "Indian path", everything which has preceded it is made to appear a chain of aberrations, incidental and episodic. This, however, produces a grotesque and distorted perspective in which the fate of a whole country and of millions of people appears as an irrelevant stage background to the spiritual conversion of a Jewish usurer. An aureole of Cabbalist mysticism presides over the end of the story when Süss undergoes his martyr's death. Such is the conclusion to a development in which we have watched the ceaseless suffering and downtreading of a people—if only in the background.

Thus the personal destiny portrayed here is as eccentric to the historical events as in Flaubert, for example. Yet Feuchtwanger is passionately concerned with historical and human concreteness; he chooses a type for whom the problem of action and inaction is a real one, arising from the actual conditions of his life, namely those of a Jewish financier and usurer of the seventeenth century scarcely out of the ghetto. The direct juxtaposition of extortionate money manipulations and religious mysticism corresponds to social and historical truth. Considered in himself, the hero is both psychologically and historically true to life. Feuchtwanger departs from inner historical truth and hence artistic truth in two ways. First, in the disproportion between the action itself and the twist he gives to it. A writer who deals with history cannot chop and change with his material as he likes. Events and destinies have their natural, objective weight, their natural, objective proportion. If a writer succeeds in producing a story which correctly reproduces these relationships and proportions, then human and artistic truth will emerge alongside the historical. If, on the other hand, his story distorts these proportions, then it will distort the artistic picture as well. Thus it offends if the suffering of an entire people during a decade should appear as a "pretext" for the spiritual conversion of a none-too-important individual.

The other way in which Feuchtwanger offends against proportion and artistic truth is by surrounding his hero's conversion with an "eternal", "timeless" halo as if it has resolved some universal human destiny. The conversion of a seventeenth century Jew to the mysticism of the Cabbala is socially and psychologically understandable and portrayed by Feuchtwanger with sensitive psychological insight. But the underlying philosophy—the abandonment of fickle, practical Europe for the contemplative heights of the orient, where the deceptive illusions of action and history dissolve into nothingness—is but a voice of a past period in literature. It was Schopenhauer who discovered for Germany that Indian philosophy was the appropriate antidote to Hegel's "superficial" view of human progress. And since then this theory has been re-echoed in every possible variation in the philosophy and literature of the German intelligentsia and the intelligentsia of other countries.

If the literary representatives of decadence do not see that their flight from history already has its ideology, this is entirely understandable. They wish (consciously) to have no part in history's reactionary, capitalist development, while they fear to take part in its revolutionary overthrow. In the case of a progressive writer and fighter of Feuchtwanger's rank this position stands in harmful contradiction to his work. For a decadent, who was only interested in décor and psychology, everything preceding the conversion in *Jew Süss* would indeed be no more than a pretext for the latter. Such a writer would have presented all this in decorative abbreviation, unlike Feuchtwanger, who aims at a genuine realism. The structure could thus have been more unified—but Feuchtwanger's importance lies in the fact that the "pretext", the fate of the people of Württemburg, grips him deeply as a writer and a man. He portrays it in vigorous, realistic colours, but precisely by so doing reveals the eccentricity of his final statement. Feuchtwanger is too honest a humanist and too realistic a writer to be able to master this theme adequately.

Hence the step which Feuchtwanger takes in his Josephus Flavius novels is a vitally necessary one. We have already pointed out that the general theme of these novels, the antithesis between nationalism and internationalism, really grows out of the historical material itself. For this reason alone the proportions here between Feuchtwanger's general-humanist ideas and the historical events and figures he portrays are quite different and much more correct. The big collision is no longer transferred *into* past history, it is developed *out* of it. This is an extremely big step forward towards a real historical novel; at the same time it considerably sharpens the contradiction between Feuchtwanger's own stated theory of the historical novel and his practice as a writer.

What is of decisive importance for us in this connection is the portrayal of popular destinies. In this respect not only is *The Jewish War* an enormous step forward in comparison with Feuchtwanger's early novels, but the same is true for *The Sons* in comparison with *The Jewish War*. The first portrays the actual dramatic tragedy of the Jewish people, the destruction of Jerusalem, the smashing of the Jewish state. But this violent drama of an entire people takes place almost entirely "above": what is most important and most plastically brought out is not the popular destiny itself, but the reflections of important personalities on this destiny. The people themselves here are only the object, in the fullest sense of the word, of what is happening "above", the object of the subtle dialectics with which their destiny is pondered from the most varied points of view.

This conception of popular life comes out most clearly in the fact that Feuchtwanger, who portrays various types of Jewish, Greek and Roman intellectual with a fine sense of intellectual and personal differentiation, sees in the radical champions of Jewish national resistance a mere horde of wild fanatics blindly tearing one another to pieces. As a result of this attitude the image of the heroic resistance of the Jewish people becomes intellectually chaotic and merely decorative in presentation. The fighting people have no clearcut, changing social-political physiognomy which we can understand: subtle intrigues "above" and chaotically wild outbreaks "below" succeed one another without any clear and concrete connection between them.

This weakness of Feuchtwanger's historical picture is linked with survivals of liberal ideology. Feuchtwanger has too great an admiration for *Realpolitik*, for subtle diplomatic intrigue and shrewd compromise. In *Jew Süss* Rabbi Jonathan Eybeschütz says: "It is easy to be a martyr; it is much more difficult to appear in a shady light for the sake of the idea." And similar ideas crop up time and again in the Josephus Flavius novels, even in the second part. Such theories and attitudes are closely connected, as we have seen, with the isolated position of progressive intellectuals in the great class struggles of late capitalism, a position which the best intellectuals, among them Feuchtwanger himself, are overcoming from day to day with the help of the practical example of the popular front.

But ideological survivals have a long after-effect. One consequence here is a gross over-rating of the individual decisions of individual persons. This gives rise on the one hand to an exaggeration of individual responsibility, sometimes bordering on mysticism, and on the other to a psychological justification of liberal compromise. Both tendencies are rooted in the fact that the isolated intellectual, if he is honest, cannot get beyond a self-confessed relativism; to absolutize his individual standpoint would appear to him narrow-minded.

Josephus Flavius's rival, Justus of Tiberias, expresses this standpoint in the second novel with great psychological truth and honesty: "If a truth is to last, it must be mixed with lies. Pure absolute truth is unbearable, nobody possesses it, it is not even worth striving for, it is inhuman, it is not worth knowing. But each person has his own truth and knows very well what his truth is ... and if he strays from this truth by one iota, then he feels it and knows that he has committed a sin." Justus of Tiberias always criticizes Josephus Flavius with the greatest severity. What he criticizes, however, is the fact that the latter's policy of "shrewd compromise" has never led to any conscious and responsible form of ethics, that Josephus has fluctuated between a spontaneity, which made him join the extreme wing in the Jewish uprising, and egoistic compromise.

This antithesis includes Josephus's own work. In the second volume we see his book which treats the Jewish uprising as a purely ideological-national question of the opposition between Rome and Judea, between Jupiter and Jahve. Justus, on the other hand, writes a book which is full of "ciphers" and "statistics".

In this question we see a not unimportant change and development in the author himself. The second volume was already written before Hitler's seizure of power, but the manuscript was destroyed by the Fascists, and Feuchtwanger had to write the book afresh. The material, according to his account, broadened considerably and he felt the need to write a third Josephus novel, which so far has not appeared. It is extremely interesting and of the highest importance for the further development of the anti-Fascist historical novel that this breadth was very much due to the greater space which Feuchtwanger allocated to descriptions of the people, their economic position and the ideological problems which sprang from it.

This change is stated in the novel itself clearly and programmatically in the form of a discussion on Josephus Flavius's book about the Jewish war, the general spirit of which tallies very much with Feuchtwanger's own conception in the first volume. In one such discussion at the house of the Roman senator Marullus, John of Gischala, a former leader of the extreme plebeian wing of the Jewish uprising and now this senator's slave, tells the famous writer some home truths about his book: " 'When the war began I knew its causes no better than you (Josephus, G.L.), perhaps I didn't want to know them any better ... It wasn't a question then ... of Jahve and Jupiter: it was a questiion of the price of oil, wine, corn and figs. If your temple aristocracy,' he said turning to Josephus with a friendly counsel, 'had not imposed such shocking taxes on our meagre products and if your government in Rome,' he said turning to Marullus with the same friendly and informative air, 'hadn't inflicted such duties and tariffs on us, then Jahve and Jupiter would have got along together perfectly well ... Let me, a simple farmer, tell you: your book may be a work of art, but after reading it one is not a bit the wiser about the whys and wherefores of the war. Unfortunately, you have left out the most important thing.' "

The great importance of these discussions for the re-orientation of Feuchtwanger's writing is shown in the final part of the second volume which deals with the differences which emerge among the Jewish people after the defeat of the national uprising and where, in connection with this, the beginnings of Christianity are portrayed. There is no doubt that Feuchtwanger here, in connecting "above" and "below", in relating the problems of popular life to the ideological movements of the age, gains enormously in concreteness over the first volume.

But precisely because this development is so very clear, one needs to determine the limits of its present stage. The attentive reader of John of Gischala's remarks will have already noticed that while Feuchtwanger is seeking here the real economic and social causes of the Jewish war, he does so in still too simplified, too abstract, too direct, too "economist" a fashion. It is not possible even in an historical work, let alone an artistic portrayal, to connect taxes and duties *directly* with the complicated ideological problems of an epoch, one cannot so reduce the content of a national war of liberation. The historian has to examine concretely the varied and differing effects of the economic situation of the classes, he has to disclose the most varied, complex and very indirect connections in order to really explain the ideological problems of a past epoch.

The historical novelist must go another way. He can only disclose these connections if he is able to see in economic problems the concrete problems of existence of concrete men. When Marx says that the economic categories are "forms of existence, determinants of existence", he is not only defining the material character of economic categories philosophically; he is also providing a key to the literary portrayal of economic determination. That is, the economic categories must not be seen fetishistically as abstractions—as in the vulgar economics of the bourgeoisie or in Menshevism and vulgar sociology —but as immediate forms of existence of human life, forms in which the metabolism of every individual person with nature and society takes place.

And to observe this concretely, as a writer, one does not need to be a Marxist. Defoe or Fielding, Scott or Cooper, Balzac or Tolstoy in most cases grasped this living side of economy correctly and deeply. And this portrayal of the basis of life could produce extraordinarily accurate and profound pictures of society, even when the writers concerned drew economic conclusions which were entirely false. This falseness remained as it were (in the case of Balzac or Tolstoy) the private falseness of the writer, a false commentary upon a picture of life in which the real interaction between the economic and spiritual-moral life of men has been correctly portrayed and corresponds with objective truth.

But for this the writer must have deep ties with popular life in its most varied ramifications, with the real life of all classes in society. And should the correct observations then give birth to false theories artistic truth is not likely to be endangered. The reverse position, is well-nigh impossible: that is, to penetrate to the concrete problems of popular life from the standpoint of abstract, though correct, economic truths.

And this at present is still Feuchtwanger's position. What is wrong with it primarily is not the rightness or wrongness of his individual views, but his method of approaching the facts themselves. At present he sees economic categories as fetishized abstract concepts and not as concrete forms of life, not as the concrete foundations of life of real people. As a result he is faced with two kinds of difficulty.

In the first place, it is impossible, as we have shown, to portray the concrete events in the life of a popular character on the basis of such abstract categories. Feuchtwanger at present shows the economic determination of life less in a portrayal of actual life than in reflections *upon* this life. And this again transfers us to "above". The decisive factor is once again the views and ideas of the characters "above" on the social-historical trends in popular life. What happens "below" is important not for itself, it appears not as the real driving force of the action, but as the content of the reflections constituting the life of the upper stratum of intellectuals.

In the second place, these fetishized abstract categories necessarily have a fatalistic character, and a writer like Feuchtwanger, who feels and experiences life keenly in all its ramifications, cannot possibly be content with such fatalism. For if the economic categories are grasped in their living concreteness, they will appear in the case of each individual person in accordance with his individual economic position, education, traditions, etc. And economic necessity will assert itself in the form of a law which, amidst the tangle of individual accidents, will emerge as the ultimately dominant, triumphant tendency of development. If economic necessity is portrayed in this way, there is not longer anything fatalistic about it. (Think of Balzac's portrayal of the relation between capitalism and land divisions in *The Peasants*.) But if economic categories are grasped abstractly, they are inevitably related rigidly and abstractly to the problems of life, and can only assert themselves fatalistically. Thus the writer must either depict or deny this fatalism; if he does the latter, he must also deny the economic determination of life. Or he may set a mechanical limit to this fatalism. This has been Feuchtwanger's path up to now. In his recent novels he acknowledges the necessity of economic categories, of figures and statistics, but only for a certain sector of human life. And to this he opposes an equally autonomous sector of life—the inner, moral life. The dualism in the determination of human life which marks Feuchtwanger's present crisis is expressed clearly in a hymn of Josephus Flavius in *The Sons*:

> So our destiny forms us
> The world of dates and figures around us . . .
> But the world of dates and figures
> Has its limits too
> Above it is
> Something inscrutable, supreme Reason,
> And its name is : Jahve.

Finally, this dualism inevitably involves the modernization of history. For this can only be avoided if the thoughts, feelings, attitudes and experiences of the characters in an historical novel are developed organically, in all their concrete complexity, from the concrete conditions of life in a given age. Here any approximation of the characters' psychology to our own age will be confined to the demands of "necessary anachronism". If however, the basis of life is abstractly conceived, then it is solely by means of psychology that the characters can be brought to life and this necessarily involves modernization. For what will be missing is the controlling function of concrete facts of existence which alone can tell the writer the kind of feelings and thoughts that are possible for a character belonging to a certain period. To which must be added that abstract economic categories are very apt to blur the specific differences between the representatives of the "same" class in different periods. If a writer starts from conditions of life, then he will make an enormous difference between a merchant of the thirteenth and a merchant of the seventeenth century. (In Scott these differences are very finely emphasized.) If, however, capital, for example, is not a form of life, but an abstract concept, then the psychology of the Roman capitalist or financier will inevitably be much more like that of the present-day stock exchange king than is in fact the case.

We see that all these problematic sides of the new historical novel are connected with the nature of the change which the anti-Fascist writers have undergone: they have become revolutionary democrats but this has not fully penetrated their art. What remains of their liberal and intellectual alienation from the concrete problems of popular life has not yet been fully overcome. And with this is linked the weakness in the basic conception of these novels. The old, classical historical novel was historical because it provided a *concrete prehistory of the present*. It portrayed the evolution of the people through the crises of the past up to the present. The historical novel of the present-day humanists is also closely related to the present, and in this respect has already overcome the period of bourgeois decadence, is indeed sharply opposed to it. But it has not yet produced a concrete prehistory of the present, merely the historical reflections of present-day problems in history, an *abstract* prehistory of *problems* preoccupying the present. Hence the accidental character of the subject-matter which has still to be overcome; hence the starting-out from idea, reflection or problem rather than from actual life. Therefore modernization or abstract generality so often replaces the historical; therefore the concrete role of popular destiny in these novels is still weak in comparison with the reflected form in which it appears in the minds of those "above"—the principal characters in these novels. In short the people are still only object, not acting subject, not the protagonist. This is shown perhaps at its crudest in Gustav Regler's portrayal of the German peasant revolts in his book *Saat* (Seed)

(Regler later became a renegade). The German peasantry appears all the time; nevertheless, the relations are inverted. The central characters are Fritz Johst, organizer and leader of the revolt, and his closer associates. As propagandists and leaders they come into contact with the peasants. In the course of this contact all the sufferings of peasant life are revealed, but they are always seen as the *object* of revolutionary propaganda, as *problems* of revolutionary tactics.

Propaganda and tactics do not spring from the life of the oppressed and exploited peasantry; we see no conflicting tendencies in this respect; nor are the propaganda and tactics accepted because they give the clearest and most energetic expression to peasant life. On the contrary, they are introduced *into* this life, tested against it, so that everything in it provides either a positive or negative example, simply illustrates the correctness or shortcomings, etc., of the propaganda and tactics. As a result the picture of peasant life in the sixteenth century is extraordinarily constricted, indeed quite distorted: everything is related to this central revolutionary theme, there are no by-currents or complications, no one stands aside, etc.

In novels where there has been a conscious attempt to multiply the connections between the central theme and the problems of popular life, these features may emerge even more sharply. In his interesting novel *Cervantes* Bruno Frank puts the popular character of his hero in the forefront—intellectually. Cervantes' artistic depth as opposed to the playful facility of Lope de Vega and other contemporaries is one of the most important motifs in his novel. And the main theme, too, the very effective contrast—which, unfortunately, is never translated into human action—between the radiant, humane and popular figure of Cervantes and the dark, counter-revolutionary figure of Philip II, serves to underline the popular qualities of the author of *Don Quixote*.

But how are these popular ties portrayed? What do we see of the Spanish people? What do we see of Cervantes' relations with the people? A few passing love affairs and friendships. The rest is presented in an abbreviated chronicle or essay form. No more than would be required in an essay on Cervantes' popular qualities. Not a single event in popular life really comes alive for us. Nor do we ever see how such an event might affect Cervantes as a living person.

Let us take one example. The tired and despondent Cervantes has been persuaded by his parents to marry an aristocratic girl of semi-peasant stock. His life with her is very unhappy, he becomes terribly bored and goes off frequently to the tavern to while away his time with the peasants. Slowly he overcomes their mistrust, and they tell him of their life and lot. This is narrated as follows: "They spoke

as always of their transactions, with long pauses in between. Of the
bad market, how in the towns they were paid only four maravedis
for a hen's egg, so that only half a maravedi was left over for them.
No, nothing was left over for them! Not even the last drop of the
river of gold pouring over Spain came near them. Nobody gave a
thought to them, they were ridiculed and despised. Once it had been
different, in their grandfathers' times. Then the peasant had been free,
he had chosen his own mayor, the land had belonged to him and he
had had his rights. Today three quarters of Mancha belonged to two
fine dukes who lived near the king. Their officials and tax collectors
squeezed the peasantry. Whoever still had a title to a piece of land
suffered from taxes, interest payments and payments in kind.
Cervantes listened to all this. They talked to him as to one of their
own. He looked at their chiselled brows and thought that a truly
noble aristocrat, a prince of a free and undissembling spirit, could
have made of these the most splendid people in the world."

And that is all. The weakness of this passage, its purely essay-like
character does not result from any lack of literary ability on the part
of its author. Where Frank, in accordance with his plan, brings
Cervantes into human relations with other characters, he shows considerable plastic powers. His abstract treatment of this side of Cervantes' personality is intended; it is not a failure of literary ability.
But the fact that this can be his intention, that he can be satisfied
with merely intimating the most important part of Cervantes' literary
and human personality in an abstract, essay-like form shows that
Bruno Frank, too, is still at a transitional stage of development with
regard to real popular character. He too starts not from the trends
of popular life in order then to portray the writer as their highest
embodiment but *vice versa* from Cervantes' personality, using the
people merely as an abstract means of illustration, as a stage background.

As a result of such a conception the problems of popular life take
on an abstract sociological, merely descriptive, lifeless and falsely
objective character. And this appears at its crudest when the subject
is a revolutionary movement. The isolated leaders are portrayed in the
customary literary manner while the popular movement appears as a
homogeneously chaotic mass impelled by some mystical natural force.

This kind of portrayal of mass movements begins with naturalism.
In Zola the old, Balzac-Stendhal legacy still conflicts with the new
sociologism. In *Germinal* the struggle of the two tendencies is still
clearly visible; in *Le Débâcle* the new principle has already
triumphed. And the development of the later period strengthened
these tendencies, giving them further support in a host of scientific
and pseudo-scientific theories (mass psychology, etc.).

Mass movements thus assume a fetishist mystical character. The masses do not consist any longer of real, living people with living aspirations; mass action is no longer the continuation, the intensified expression of popular life hitherto, but something autonomous, a historical symbol. We have already pointed to the weakness in Feuchtwanger's portrayal of the national uprising of the Jews. There are traces of the same weakness even in Heinrich Mann's *Henri IV*, where he portrays the night of St. Bartholomew. The events of St. Bartholomew's night which he portrays relate directly to his hero and his surroundings, and they are conveyed with great poetic power. Yet all of it takes place "above", at court. The people of Paris, misled by the demagogy of the Guises, appear as some kind of uniform mystical wild beast. If one looks at the corresponding scenes in Prosper Mérimée one sees how very differently the older writer translates these movements into human actions and human destinies. And even Mérimée, as we have seen, is by no means on the same level in this respect as the classical historical novelists. His description of St. Bartholomew's night nowhere reaches the level of, say, Manzoni in his portrayal of the hunger rising in Milan or of Scott in his portrayal of the Edinburgh rising (*Heart of Midlothian*).

The modern writers simply create symbolist *tableaux*. Their novels are conceived as biographies of individual great men; the events are grouped accordingly round the psychological development of these individuals so that when the people actually appear—that is, not simply as the object of the hero's reflections—this chaotic-mystical character becomes inevitable. And as long as the spirit of democracy and popular feeling is not sufficiently strong for writers to treat popular revolts as necessary continuations and intensifications of normal popular life, as long as they are unable to embody these intensifications in human stories, this kind of fetishistic symbolism remains unavoidable.

What must be stressed in this respect is the falsely objective, to a certain extent sociographic manner of describing popular life to which important writers fall victim. The individual representatives of the oppressed and exploited, appear as exemplars of a sociographically fixed species rather than as independent figures; their outer and inner lives seem to be deduced from general sociological principles: i.e., how would such an exemplar think, feel, etc., in such circumstances? But in a genuine prehistory of a popular movement it is the complex, contradictory and very individual way in which the oppressed *really* think about their situation which is important. To portray the revolutionary awakening of buried popular energies with artistic and historical truth, this must first of all be shown.

The real historical greatness of a subject depends upon the inner greatness of the popular movement it portrays. This inner greatness lay at the centre of the classical historical novel. The classical novelists were able to convey a very genuine and unpretentious greatness very simply, very economically. If this centre is lacking the writer will inevitably resort to those questionable substitutes which we have discussed in connection with Flaubert and Conrad Ferdinand Meyer.

For example, the portrayal of the brutal and cruel features of past ages. Unfortunately, very few writers today have entirely freed themselves from the false tendencies of the late bourgeois novel. They only too often revel in descriptions of cruel executions and torture, etc., not realizing that the reader will very soon become accustomed to these brutalities—especially in an historical novel—and regard them only too soon as a necessary peculiarity of the age in question, so that they lose all effect, even that of propaganda against the inhumanity of earlier forms of class rule. The strength of the old historical novelists lay in the fact that they gave central place to the *human* collisions which resulted from the inhumanity of the old class tyrannies. In this way it was often not necessary to show the cruelty of the law in action, so soon did its inhumanity move the reader to sympathy for its victim. We mention only the story of Effie Deans in Scott's *Heart of Midlothian*. Of course the older writers depicted executions, etc., too, but they did so very sparingly and always emphasized the human premises and consequences rather than the brutal-descriptive character of the executions—that is, of the execution *qua* execution. The fact that such tendencies as atrocity and even exoticism have still not been overcome gives a precise artistic indication of the present position of the contemporary historical novel in its process of conquering the harmful legacy of late capitalist ideological development.

3. The Biographical Form and its "Problematic"

The important modern historical novels show a clear tendency towards *biography*. The direct link between the two in many cases is most probably the contemporary fashion of historical-biographical *belles lettres*. But in the really important cases this is barely more than a formal link. The popularity of the biographical form in the present-day historical novel is due rather to the fact that its most important exponents wish to confront the present with great model figures of humanist ideals as examples, as resuscitated forerunners of the great struggles of today.

And given the conception, which we have analysed, of the relations between historical protagonists and the people, it is inevitable that biography should appear as the specific form of the modern historical novel. If the great figure of the past is really the sole embodier of the great historical idea, if the historical novel is interested in the prehistory of the ideas which are being fought out today, then writers may understandably see the real historical genesis of these ideas and therewith of present-day problems in the development of the historical personalities who have championed and embodied these ideas in the past. Some overhasty and over-"sensitive" critics have a habit of creating a new aesthetic as soon as any new kind of writing appears. Thus any new manifestation of literature is immediately and uncritically raised into a criterion which is binding on literature in general. We have experienced this repeatedly from naturalism to expressionism, and now we fortunately possess a whole museum of such abortive aesthetic criteria. Yet the facts show that as a rule the few works which have survived the literary fashions of our time have done so *in spite of* such criteria. This should counsel caution and a look at mankind's artistic experiences during the past few thousand years. And there is every reason for such caution in regard to the present fashion of biography. The task of aesthetics and criticism in the case of a widespread practice like the use of the biographical form in the historical novel should simply be that of an impartial examination of the possibilities and limits of the form. Any artistic canonization of present-day practice is of no use either to theory or practice. If we derive the aesthetic criteria of a particular trend simply from the works belonging to this trend, then they have ceased to be criteria. And an aesthetic which is afraid to approach the question of criteria, of the rightness of a particular trend or genre, has abdicated from aesthetics.

Let us therefore look at literary practice rather more broadly and examine how the great writers of the past went about the problem of biography, how far they used a biographic method or presentation in their art. Goethe's practice is perhaps the most instructive here. In particular, because Goethe portrayed certain problems of his own life both as straight biography and as material for his novels. *Dichtung und Wahrheit (Poetry and Truth)* contains the material of both *Werthers Leiden (Sorrows of Werther)* and *Wilhelm Meisters Lehrjahre (Wilhelm Meister's Apprenticeship)*. Now if one follows through these works from their inception, one sees that they verge away from the biographical. Since we now have the first version of

Wilhelm Meister, we can see exactly how much more autobiographical it is than the final version.

The reasons for this trend away from the biographical are easy to see. The most conscious and planned life is full of accidents which cannot be portrayed. Certain features occur in a way that cannot be sensuously embodied. To give them the same significance as in reality, one would have to invent a whole new set of circumstances. The external appearance of dramatic collisions does not always correspond with their inner significance; sometimes collisions of slight significance in themselves lead to tragic consequences, sometimes the tragedy which would be the only adequate expression of a collision does not take place in life at all, the collision is blunted and leads to consequences which are only biographically, theoretically or creatively important, but not to a viable drama. The people, with whom the evolving hero of an autobiography has to do, come and go by chance, the outward history of the relations of the people to one another never corresponds really to their inner, dramatic or epic, significance. For this reason Hegel said with full justice of the epic constructed round biography: "In biography the individual admittedly remains one and the same, but the events in which he is involved can happen quite independently and retain the subject only as their quite external and accidental point of connection."

If one compares *Werther* with the Lotte Buff episode in the autobiography, one can see clearly what Goethe has added in the novel, where as a writer he has left the autobiographical behind. In *Werther* he has introduced the social element into the conflict and lifted the love collision onto a tragic plane. In a word, everything which gives *Werther* its lightning effect and eternal freshness is biographically untrue. No biographical account of the Lotte Buff episode could have remotely attained to the poetic greatness of *Werther*; for the elements of this poetry lay in Goethe's experience of this episode, but not in the episode itself as it actually occurred. But even then these were only elements and germs in Goethe's experience. It still required an enormous amount of poetic *invention*, the supplementing, extending and deepening work of generalization, before the story and the characters of *Werther* could take shape in the form we know them today.

This is the universal position of great writers in regard to reality in general and hence to the reality of their own lives, to their own biography. Since reality as a whole is always richer and more varied than even the richest work of art, no detail, episode, etc., however exactly copied, however biographically authentic, however factual, can possibly compete with reality. If one wishes to re-create the richness of reality, the whole context of life must be refashioned, one's composition must take on an entirely new structure. If biographically authentic details, episodes, etc., can be used here, just as they are, then this will be a particularly fortunate accident. Although even in these cases they cannot be left quite as they are, for their environment, what came before and after them, will have been decisively altered, and these alterations will transform the artistic quality of the biographical episode.

These are well-known facts, observable in the practice of the most important writers. However, they provide only the general premises of the problem which specially interests us here: namely the question of whether and in what way a biographical portrayal of *great men* in history is possible. Goethe portrays many things in *Wilhelm Meister* which he recounts autobiographically later on in *Dichtung und Wahrheit*. He makes of Wilhelm Meister a representative of those tendencies in life which were decisive for his youth and for his development to manhood, a representative of those trends among the best section of bourgeois youth at the turn of the eighteenth century which led to a new flowering of humanism. As such a figure Wilhelm Meister bears many personal traits of Goethe himself and his development contains innumerable episodes from the life of his creator. But apart from those basic alterations, the nature of which we have just analysed in the case of *Werther*, Goethe undertakes one further correction of his hero's character: he deprives him of Goethean *genius*. Gottfried Keller does the same in his even more pronouncedly autobiographical novel *Der Grüne Heinrich* (*Green Henry*). Why? Because both great narrative artists—Goethe and Keller—clearly saw that a biographical portrayal of genius, a biographical account of the development of a man of genius and his accomplishments, conflicts with the means of expression peculiar to epic art.

One would have to portray the growth of the genius *genetically*, that is, by presenting, recounting, describing, etc., facts and episodes from his life, and this always involves some kind of "short circuit", as we shall soon show in detail. For the circumstances of life in which a quality of genius manifests itself, in which genius is kindled, and in which the achievements of genius make their first appearance (from a biographical-psychological standpoint) in fact do no more than provide a particular occasion against which such qualities or achievements may be revealed. And the connection between occasion and achievement cannot do other than appear accidental even in the best portrayal; the objective character of the accidental connection will not be dispelled by literary creation. The better the writer's work, that is, the more truthfully he portrays the particular occasion on the basis of scrupulously checked and selected material from the given life, the more noticeable and striking will its occasional and objectively accidental character appear.

If we deny the practicability of portraying genius by the bio-graphical-psychological, genetic method we are certainly not denying that genius can be genetically explained, nor do we wish to surround genius with a mystery of inexplicability. On the contrary. We are denying that this kind of portrayal is possible because we know how very much the man of genius is bound up with the entire economic-social, political and cultural life of his time, with the struggle of the great movements, the class struggles, the development of the material and cultural heritage of his time, etc., and that he proves his genius by the originality with which he extends, concentrates and generalizes these most important tendencies in the life of an epoch.

But it is precisely this connection which cannot be made immedi-ately evident in the biographical facts and episodes with which the artistic biographer or autobiographer has to work as a creator of character. These connections can only be brought to light on the basis of a broad, deep and very generalized analysis of an epoch. Not only must they be investigated by scientific means, it is only by scientific means that they can be adequately presented. If one looks at Goethe's Dichtung und Wahrheit in the light of these connections, then one realizes that every time Goethe wishes to clarify some synthesis between himself and the big movements of his time during certain stages of his development he forsook the means of narrative. In every such case Goethe uses scientific, historical means of the highest intellectual and artistic kind.

This scientific approach, as a method, needs to be quite specially underlined in our own day. For it has become increasingly the fashion to look down upon the scientific method with a kind of snobbish relativism, while sanctioning acknowledged scientific achievements by knighting them with the title of "art". Naturally the important works of historical science have often used artistic means, too. And this does not mean simply good and expressive prose, it means subtle description, plastic representation, forceful irony, satire, etc. None of this will undermine the basic character of scientific method, which is to disclose connections in accordance with the objective laws governing them. The destinies of individual persons, experienced as individual destinies, cannot provide a means for clarifying objective connections and laws. To create a really good historical portrait of an important figure one needs to show his personal singularity, his intellectual physiognomy, the singularity of his method, the objective significance of this method in the context of the most important movements which lead from past to future, at whose crossroads he stands and to whose development he has contributed in an original way—all of which must be shown in a very generalized and, because generalized, scientifically concrete, form using the correct scientific means.

This will produce a very high level of writing, but it will not be art. One of the comical aspects of our time is that the only praise one can find for works like Hegel's *Phenomenology of the Spirit* and Marx's *Eighteenth Brumaire* is to place them in the same category as Arthur Schnitzler or James Joyce. This is not only more-than-questionable praise for scientific achievements—it is also a sign of the diminishing understanding for the real principles of art.

We shall take a characteristic example to illustrate the tasks facing a scientific biography of a man of genius. One of the most important turning-points in the history of knowledge was Marx's description of the sole commodity which the wage labourer could sell as "labour power" instead of "labour". For any real biographer of Marx a central task would be to uncover the path which led to this brilliant insight which revolutionized economics. He would have to show how far pre-Marxist economics had got in this question, what contradictions it had become entangled in as a result of the unclearness of the category "labour" and the social reasons for these limitations. At the same time he would have to show against biographical material from Marx's life and career how this problem developed until it reached its conscious and clear formulation, how long Marx still used the old concept "labour" during his youth not only in word, but also in meaning, where he begins to attribute a new, enriched and precise meaning to the old term until the path is completely laid bare. However, even given that one knew the precise moment at which Marx reached this formulation, the representation of this moment could be of no more than episodic importance. For the discovery itself was a necessity of the class struggle between proletariat and bourgeoisie, a struggle which required the disclosure of the true character of capitalist economy—and which thereby paved the way for an adequate understanding of all forms of economy. From the standpoint of this objective necessity it is a matter of pure accident whether Marx came to his formulation in a conversation with Engels, on his own walking up and down his study or elsewhere.

Every biography of an important person will contain an abundance of such problems. And the biographical *belles lettres* of today, instead of showing the large social connections and their reflection in science and art, revel in pseudo-artistic, psychologically "deepened" portrayals of individual "occasions". Against this we must stress with all vigour the necessity of presenting the large objective connections. We must say there is no path which leads from Schiller's rotten apples to *Wallenstein* or from Balzac's black coffee, bust of

Napoleon, monk's garb and walking-stick to the *Comédie Humaine*, etc.

But even the "deepest" psychological analyses of the various loves and friendships of great men do not really help us to understand their works any better. On the contrary, as far as really important human relations are concerned, these are much better explained by the large objective connections than by mere biographical psychology. The friendship of Marx and Engels was forged by the objective necessities of the revolutionary working-class movement. It was the complete devotion of both to the emancipation of the proletariat, their genius in founding and extending revolutionary theory, in leading the revolutionary working-class movement, which gave their friendship that human depth and inseparable unity which so moves us. The more intimately we know these objective connections and their material content, the more deeply can we comprehend the human character of the friendship between Marx and Engels. For only by understanding these connections can we really understand the personal part which each played in their common life's work and the so happily complementary character of their collaboration. The personal facts of their lives which have been transmitted to us provide an enormously important supplement to these connections. But it would be an illusion to think that one could start from these individual facts of life and produce an immediate picture of the large connections.

We repeat: the facts of a great man's life tell us at best the particular occasion on which something great was achieved, but they never give us the real context, the real chain of causation as a result of which this great accomplishment played its part in history. One could object to this that the historical novelist, too, can portray no more than the particular occasion against which his heroes perform their deeds. But this objection overlooks the difference in the relation of chance to necessity in the two cases. It is a characteristic of human life that the occasions which produce the most important feelings, experiences or deeds are accidental. If, however, the real character of the given literary figure is properly revealed in his deed, then although the occasion of the deed remains accidental it occupies precisely the position which would be required of it in reality. For it is part of life that necessity asserts itself through accidents of this kind.

Yet the true writer will keep the right proportions even in this case. That is, before introducing the occasion he will clarify the social forces encompassing his characters as a whole and at the same time indicate the psychological qualities of the particular character in question. The connection between the two will then be translated by the occasion into the deed. Thus the occasion will occupy a position in the given context of life appropriate to its corresponding position in objective reality; at the same time necessity, as is natural in literature, will make its appearance more clearly and deliberately than normally happens in life.

It is different with an historical achievement, the nature of which is to take mankind a step forward in a certain field. This is what gives every great historical achievement an objective and necessary character. Its essential quality is the fact that it accords with objective reality more richly and profoundly than previous such steps forward. Its significance therefore lies in this objective content and, as we have shown, can only be understood if the objective connections surrounding it are disclosed. Faced with these connections the immediate occasion loses all value. Whether we are acquainted with it or not has no effect, either in a positive or negative way, upon our knowledge of the real connection. Whereas with actions in the normal course of life it is quite indispensable to know the occasion in its right combination of chance and necessity in order to understand the deed.

Here we see the principal reason why the achievements of the great men of history *as achievements*, as works, lie beyond the reach of literature. Goethe once said of the poet's task:

> "Und wenn der Mensch in seiner Qual verstummt,
> Gab mir ein Gott zu sagen, wie ich leide."
> (And when man in his agony is dumb,
> God gave me a voice to say how I suffer.)

Naturally, it is not just a question of suffering if we are to define the mission of poetry. Nevertheless, Goethe describes its main task rightly—a task which only it can fulfil: it imparts to all manifestations of life a more distinct, more articulated, more understandable and essentially truer voice, closer to the essence of life, than these manifestations possess in life itself. It is precisely for this reason that the great achievement or work lies beyond the reach of literature. The writer cannot clarify it any further. He can show how it is connected with life and the effect it has on life, but he cannot portray the work itself. An important literary task might be to show how people at the time of the Church persecutions went bravely to the scaffold, bravely endured the tortures of the Inquisition for the truth of the newly arisen sciences, for the truth of the legitimacy of the godless universe; it would also be an important literary task to show the human, intellectual and moral foundations of such behaviour, and in such a portrayal the world-historical significance of the scientific achievements of Copernicus, Kepler and Galileo would shine forth in a hitherto undreamt-of light. But even the greatest writer (and most learned in science) could add nothing to Galileo's law of falling bodies. He could only insert it into his work.

For this reason the great writers of the past, who knew the possibilities and limits of literature, always portrayed the achievements of great individuals *by their effects*. In the same way all great epic writers of the past always portrayed beauty by its effects—from Homer's Helen of Troy to Tolstoy's Anna Karenina—and never by direct description. Goethe once said of the conquest of Troy that it was unportrayable, "as a moment of fulfilment in a great destiny" it was "neither epic nor tragic, and in a true epic treatment" could "only be seen in the distance either from in front or behind". The achievements of great historical individuals also have this character of fulfilment.

It is a modern prejudice to suppose that the historical authenticity of a fact will guarantee its poetical effectiveness. This prejudice is strengthened when it is a case of the utterances and facts in the lives of men who are justly loved and revered by the masses. It is quite understandable that the liberated mass of workers in the Soviet Union should wish for lively, comprehensible and moving accounts of the lives of their loved and revered leaders Marx and Engels, Lenin and Stalin. These wishes can and must be satisfied. They can only be satisfied, however, by *scientific* biographies on a high literary level, intellectually thorough and at the same time popular. For it is only in the large objective connections, scientifically presented, that the features for which these men are loved and revered will emerge humanly as well. No assemblage of authentic documents can possibly satisfy these wishes, just wishes, of the masses.

If a writer, for instance, were to portray Marx, what would be the result? Marx would walk diagonally up and down his room, as we know from Lafargue's reminiscences, he would smoke cigars, his desk would be littered with books and manuscripts (see again Lafargue, Liebknecht, etc.); this would all be historically true, but would it bring us any nearer to Marx's great personality? Despite the authenticity of all the individual features this study could be that of any mediocre scholar or bad politician. Admittedly the writer would let Marx *speak* as well. And again we should get an authentic text— quotations, say, from the letters to Kugelmann. The ideas pronounced would, of course, be true, significant and important, but their origin in the given conversation, their character as intellectual manifestations of Marx's life could *not* appear convincing. In their original context they are both more powerful in themselves as well as more humanly immediate than they could possibly be in any such literary adaptation.

Now let us take a contrary example. Lenin's *State and Revolution* includes a large number of quotations from Marx, but obviously there is nothing remotely "literary" in the modern sense about Lenin's straightforward manner of presentation. Nevertheless, the reader of this magnificent work gets a powerful impression of the political and intellectual personality of Marx. Why? Because Lenin sums up the major viewpoints of the European revolutions of the nineteenth century in a theoretically brilliant, lucidly outlined and popular way and this enables us to cast a glance, as it were, into the intellectual workshop of the founder of scientific socialism. We see how the great revolutionary events fructify his thinking on the central questions of revolution, how his bold and always correct generalizations bring to light the still hidden tendencies of historical development, how his insight into reality races prophetically ahead of historical development. Such presentations, but only such, bring out the human significance of Marx's personality which is not to be separated from his greatness as a thinker and politician. It is undoubtedly a major scientific and literary task to write biographies of the great leaders of the proletarian struggle of emancipation which really correspond to these demands, just demands, of the masses. But they can never be replaced by biographical *belles lettres*, by the insertion of authentic biographical facts into novels. Franz Mehring's biography of Marx contains many ideological errors and limitations. Nevertheless, it allows one to get to know Marx's human personality much more clearly and adequately than any belletrist treatment would.

Let us illustrate this by a further example which we quoted in the first section of this study—the fine passage from Lenin's *Will the Bolsheviks Retain State Power?* The example of the effect of a worker's remarks as to the better bread following the July rising of 1917 is not only a very convincing argument in Lenin's chain of thought, it also throws an unusually brilliant light into the workshop of his mind, bringing the leader of the Great October very near to us in a human and personal way. We suddenly see by this example how sensitively Lenin observed the apparently most insignificant facts in the lives of the working people and with what lightning speed and accuracy he drew far-reaching, generalizing conclusions from these experiences. But let us not forget that the powerful effect of this passage is due to the fact that Lenin had built it into the scientifically unbreakable chain of his argument. True, the passage would be just as correct and profound without the remarks preceding and following it, but it could not have this surprising, stirring and truly human impact.

This episode in Lenin has a very rounded effect. But were a writer tempted to reproduce it in a belletrist manner what would we have?

A description of the room, an atmosphere of work; the table would be laid, the wife would bring in the bread, the man make his remarks about its good quality in connection with the July rising—and then "suddenly", like a pistol shot, Lenin's profound and correct reflections would follow. What in the context of the original pamphlet was humanly moving and intellectually inspiring would now have become a banal piece of montage. Can the genius, then, the great man of history, be portrayed artistically at all?[1] To this question we gave a clear and positive answer in the first two chapters of this work. We showed that the "world-historical individual" has his organic place in the novel as a minor figure and in tragedy as the chief figure. Our present arguments as to the impossibility of epic-biographic portrayal do not contradict this, but indeed confirm it from a different, negative angle. For why was this portrayal possible in the classics of the historical novel and historical drama? The reason was that they portrayed the great men upon the basis of their concrete historical mission, upon the basis of the totality of the objective social-historical determinants. The writers of the classical period, as a result of their broad and deep social experiences, saw the task of the great man in history clearly (however wrong they may have been at times in their theoretical pronouncements on this problem). From these experiences the classics of historical drama portrayed great, crisis-filled collisions of human history, and the "world-historical individual" appeared in their works as a great figure because in his own person he sensuously embodied the colliding social forces. From these experiences the classic of the historical novel portrayed a broad and rich picture of popular life and presented the "world-historical individual" as the supreme concentration and em-

---

[1] Note (written in 1953). To-day someone will perhaps take issue with the preceding remarks by pointing to Thomas Mann's portrayal of Adrian Leverkühn in his Faustus novel. I should be the last to question Mann's unique achievement ; his characterization, both individual and typical, of a distinguished musician from the standpoint of his artistic career. (Cf. my studies on Thomas Mann). One must never forget, however, that Leverkühn was portrayed from the standpoint of his (typical) 'problematic'; not as a genius, but as a miscarried great talent. Thus the unsurpassably portrayed genesis of this 'problematic' has inwardly nothing to do with the question we have been dealing with here, the biographically depicted genesis of genius. To which must be added in passing that Thomas Mann's biographical method turns out on closer examination to be hardly biographical at all. The genetic connections between the life and work of Adrian Leverkühn proceed only in the very rarest borderline cases from particular occasions in his life ; in the main, the genesis of the stages of development, the works and crises of the central figure is Mann's broad and deeply grasped presentation of the social life from which—objectively historically—work, crisis etc. grow. The double time-sequence of the novel also serves to illuminate these connections : Zeitblom's reflections while writing Leverkühn's biography throw a genuine historical light on the real historical genesis from the standpoint of the consequences.

bodiment of the important tendencies of an important transition in popular life. The determination and genesis of the "world-historical individual" arises in the classics of the historical novel upon the basis of the unfolding and broadening of these tendencies. We experience in these novels the objective path of social-historical development which at a certain point causes Kutuzov or Pugachov, Cromwell or Mary Stuart to become those centres of force in which the social forces of a crisis are united. (And it should be noted that a "world-historical individual" by no means needs to be a genius).

Only in this way can the new, the qualitatively special that the "world-historical individual" represents be given expression. We experience in the most varied forms the movement of popular forces in a certain direction, we experience their inability to grasp adequately the content of this direction, their weakness in fulfilling the deeds required to transform this direction into a reality. When then the "world-historical individual" appears and—in accordance with the concrete historical circumstances and his own personal conditioning—finds an answer to this question and translates it into action, then and only then does the genesis of what is historically new become evident for us and so, simultaneously, does the role of the important man within this development.

In this kind of portrayal the occasion which gives expression in words and deeds to what is new receives a position which corresponds to its real character. Its accidentality is not eliminated. But the accidentality of the occasion here is no more than the irreducible accidentality of any individual event in human life: this individual event, however, exists in organic-historical connection with that infinite chain of individual events which in themselves are similarly accidental and in and through whose totality historical necessity always asserts itself. The necessity itself is produced by the complex inner social-historical unity of the popular movements over and above the immediate and psychological connections. The individual occasions which serve to portray the different stages at which historical necessity reveals itself need not be directly linked with one another. It is only necessary that the action, in its complex and intricate paths, should make the inner dialectics of this development clear to us.

It is easy to see what ideological inhibitions work against this kind of portrayal in modern writers. The development of capitalism inevitably alienates writers from popular life, they find it more and more difficult to see into the inner active forces of capitalist society, and as a result the same tendency comes to dominate their outlook as dominates the general philosophic development of the imperialist epoch. This tendency may be briefly stated: of all the factors which determine the complex context of life only the immediate causal connection between two related spatial-temporal phenomena is recognized.

Should there be dissatisfaction with the cognitive value of this conception it does not in general lead on to any deeper philosophical enquiry, to the discovery of the real and more complex connections where even causality, though more deeply conceived, appears as only one important category among many others. It leads rather to a doubting of the immediate causal connection itself (Machism) and, as a direct consequence of this, to a more or less mystical conception of the totality of society and of its total development. The literary greatness of the classics of the historical novel, who philosophically often stood at a relatively unadvanced level, lay in the fact that they were sufficiently intimate and well-experienced with popular life to be able to portray the real connections in life itself which went beyond immediate causality. In contrast to this the alienation which modern writers feel from popular life leads them to over-rate immediate causation, which they generally and inevitably see in terms of biographical-psychological causation, and so to acquire their preference for biographical form.

With the classics and their conception the historical figures practically never *develop before our eyes*. The genesis and development of the "world-historical individual" take place *among the people*. The great figures appear, as Balzac showed in the case of Scott, only at such points where the objective necessity of the popular movements imperatively requires their appearance. And then they appear as complete characters, as concentrations, as supreme forms of expression of this development. They are great because they possess this concentrating power, because they are able to answer the problems most deeply affecting the life of the people at this moment. Like the Homeric heroes physically, they are intellectually taller than the people by a head. But their historical greatness lies in the fact that they are taller *only* by a head and that they give the socially-historically possible and necessary concrete answer to the concrete questions of the people. In many cases this greatness is at the same time their limitation. If Vich Ian Vohr or Rob Roy, as well as being intellectually superior to the clan members, did not share with them a common attitude to life and hence certain common limitations, they could not be the leaders they are. Similarly, Cromwell or Burley in Scott are linked not only with the revolutionary tendencies of the Puritans, but also with their limitations. The same is true for Pugachov and the rebellious peasants in Pushkin and for Kutuzov and the patriotic spirit of the Russian army fighting Napoleon in Tolstoy.

It is this objective social context, portrayed in breadth and depth, which makes it possible for the characters to appear before us already complete, yet without producing any impression of lifelessness. Their inner vivacity and development is but an unfolding of the qualities which make them into the representatives they are of the popular movements in question. Their proof or failure in the given historic mission is thus essentially more a development than a genesis in the psychological-biographical sense. In most of the classical historical novels the prehistory of the important figures occurs before the action of the novel itself and is not recounted at all; we simply learn from a few scattered indications what is necessary for our understanding of the nature of their personal relations with the other characters. Where the personal prehistory is given at all, it is told only after we have long become familiar with the character concerned. And then our acquaintance with his past takes on a quite specific character: that of a special story inserted into the main narrative revealing to us the development of an important character with whom we are already familiar. This retrospective account is another of the artistic means used to put the accidental nature of any experience occasioning a deed or event into its rightful place.

May we again take an example from life. Say we have carefully followed the part played in Lenin's career by his fight against the Narodniks; we know precisely the enormous significance for the Bolshevik party of his two-front struggle against the Narodniks and Struvism; we then learn that after the execution of Lenin's dearly loved brother for his part in a plot against the Tsar Lenin immediately realizes the incorrectness of his brother's path, that it cannot lead to the liberation of the Russian people. Now let us reverse the picture. The Ulyanov family, Lenin's admiration for his elder brother, the news of the imprisonment and the execution—and then the theoretical reflections condemning the Narodniks. We do not deny that there is significant material here for a historical, literary portrayal of the great crisis of transition undergone by the Russian working people during the decline of the Narodniks. But if one were to use this material really effectively, one would have to rob the story's hero of Lenin's genius and make of him a still significant, but only typical, representative of this transitional period.

The portrayal of "world-historical individuals" from the standpoint of their success or failure in their historic mission frees them of all the trivial and anecdotic characteristics of biographical portrayal without making them forfeit any of their human aliveness. For, as we have seen, they have become "world-historical individuals" because the deepest personal core of their being, their most passionate personal aspirations are bound up in the closest possible way with the historical task they have had to fulfil, because their most personal passions tend towards precisely this goal. Thus his success or failure tells us in a concentrated manner all we want and need to know about such a personality. And a good writer who treats history not in the abstract, but as the complex destiny of the people, will be able to portray this central task so that it allows very different, very complex personal features in such a character to gain expression. But, as we have already argued from Otto Ludwig's apt pronouncement on Scott—only the humanly and historically *significant* features of his personality. He must not be placed on a pedestal in order to appear as a great figure, for the events themselves will raise him in imposing upon him their task: he appears only in situations which are significant, and hence only needs to unfold his personal qualities freely in order to appear significant.

This anti-biographical method at the same time provides an artistic answer to the question of why it was such a figure—why Cromwell or Burley, why Kutuzov or Pugachov—who took on this leading role. There is an irreducible element of chance involved. In a letter Engels examines the dialectic of necessity and accident which arises in this respect, the ultimate triumph of economic necessity in history: "This is where the so-called great men come in for treatment. That such and such a man and precisely that man arises at that particular time in that given country is of course pure accident. But cut him out and there will be a demand for a substitute, and this substitute will be found, good or bad, but in the long run he will be found. That Napoleon, just that particular Corsican, should have been the military dictator whom the French Republic, exhausted by its own war, had rendered necessary, was an accident; but that, if a Napoleon had been lacking, another would have filled his place, is proved by the fact that the man has always been found as soon as he became necessary: Caesar, Augustus, Cromwell, etc." In his further remarks Engels uses Marx himself and the rise of historical materialism to illustrate this relationship.

Belletrist biography, the biographical form of the historical novel sets itself—whether it likes it or not—the insoluble task of reducing this irreducible element of chance. It is the personality of the man portrayed which is to be the guide to his special calling, his biography will provide the inner, psychological proof of this calling. As a result the character is inevitably exaggerated, made to stand on tiptoe, his historical calling unduly emphasized while the real objective causes and factors of the historical mission are inevitably omitted.

A scientific treatment of history and also a scientific biography of important men assumes the *fact* that this element of chance has already established itself in life. The task of such writing is no longer to "deduce" this fact in some way or another, but simply to explain it by its presuppositions and consequences, and to show the necessity of development expressed in it. For this reason the objective achievement of the given figure must be at the centre of a scientific biography. The theoretical significance and historical position of the achievement has to be *scientifically* demonstrated, and only in this way can the personality of the "world-historical individual" also be drawn humanly and brought personally close to the reader.

The classical historical novel also starts from the fact that in crises of popular life in past ages certain important figures have played a leading role—whether this was a profitable or harmful one. And the actual portrayal answers *artistically* why it should have been just this particular individual at this particular time who secured the leading role: he is capable of giving answers to the diverse problems of popular life, while both his shining qualities as well as his human limits and limitations are woven out of the same material as the popular movement itself. Chance is preserved here and there is no attempt to reduce it. The novel simply reflects, profoundly and authentically, how necessity and chance interlock in historical life. Thus chance is reduced here only in the sense in which history itself reduces it. It is reduced by our being shown in human terms how the concrete historical forces of a particular period have become concentrated in the life of this particular individual.

It would be both wrong and unjust to suggest that the important writers of our day do not see the connection between popular movements and historical figures. Heinrich Mann indeed states this connection very correctly in his novel: " 'In short', said Agrippa d'Aubigné while they rode amongst the troop, 'you are no more, Prince, than what the people have made of you. And that's the reason why you can stand higher than they: a creation is sometimes higher than its artist. But woe betide if you become a tyrant!' " But unfortunately this correct insight gets no further than an insight even with Heinrich Mann and has no decisive influence upon the action and composition of his novel. Of all present-day writers he is the most deeply aware of this connection and of the need to portray it. Thus he gives Henri IV the national characteristics of the French people and portrays them in a most captivating way. In all the scenes where his hero comes into contact with the people his popular character comes across simply and convincingly. Yet these parts of the novel are the briefest; they contain the least action and are in the nature of reports. This of course is the right of every epic writer. No real narrative would be possible without such summaries of none-too important events and stretches of time. But the characteristic and decisive thing here is what receives detailed narrative treatment and what a brief report. In Heinrich Mann the role of the hero's relation to the people too often falls under the heading of report and even where it is really narrated remains largely episodic. Let us take an example from Henri's early youth. Heinrich Mann sums up briefly: "He slept with his people in the hay if necessary, neither undressed nor washed more often than they, stank and cursed as they did." This is then followed by a full portrayal of his relations with Condé and Coligny, although Mann knows quite well that it is Henri's new relation to the people which is at the basis of his differences with the admiral. We can see here how the biographical conception of the novel becomes an artistic obstacle to any real expression of the hero's popular characteristics. For the people, their joys and sorrows, their own spontaneous and conscious endeavours cannot be portrayed except through direct contact with the person of Henri IV. Thus very little can be shown of the popular movements which tend in his direction, which raise him to the heights he attains or which guarantee his ultimate victory in dangerous situations. Too little to explain his victory in terms of the lives of the French people. The biographical-psychological portrait of the hero, however fine in itself, provides too narrow and frail a basis on which to demonstrate this convincingly.

The position is similar with regard to Feuchtwanger's Josephus Flavius novels. In Josephus's conversations, particularly with Justus of Tiberia, one frequently finds shrewd and correct reflections on the relation between hero and people. However, when Josephus entering revolutionary Jerusalem in a spirit of compromise instead throws in his lot with the leaders of the extreme nationalist wing, Feuchtwanger has set himself a task which the biographical method cannot convincingly solve without defaming the person of Josephus. For let us imagine a classical portrayal of this episode. Through the lives of a number of individuals portrayed in the round we should be given a broad picture of the Jewish people with their different parties and trends. We should be humanly and politically enthralled by their determined national resistance, and Josephus's transformation would be made fully intelligible, personally and politically, by his interaction with this dynamic popular movement. But Feuchtwanger, as we have seen, portrays popular life in a very abstract and general way. When Josephus arrives in Jerusalem it is only his contacts with the conservative temple aristocracy which can be shown to us in concrete human terms. As a result his defection from them smacks unpleasantly of the behaviour of a disappointed climber. And we find similar features in other crises of his life.

Those who defend the present biographical form of the historical novel will perhaps contend that it is only details such as these that have been transmitted to us about the lives of these characters and that we know too little about popular figures to be able to portray them as living characters. But the objection is invalid. If we know nothing about the popular life of a period, then we may say of it what Sainte-Beuve said of Flaubert's *Salammbô*—that it cannot be made to live for us artistically. But the great task of the historical novel is to *invent* popular figures to represent the people and their predominant trends.

It is natural that bourgeois historiography in general as a discipline of the ruling classes, should have consciously neglected, omitted or even slanderously distorted these factors of popular life. Here is where the historical novel, as a powerful artistic weapon in defence of human progress, has a major task to perform, to restore these real driving forces of human history as they were in reality, to recall them to life on behalf of the present. The historical novel of the anti-Fascist humanists sets itself the same task in intention. And it defends the principles of human progress against the slanders and distortions of imperialism as well as the attempts at total annihilation on the part of Fascism.

But at the present the task is conceived too abstractly. Given the conditions in which they live, it is natural for the leading intellectuals of the imperialist period to believe that the real bearers of humanist ideals are the isolated intelligentsia who take a stand against society. But however natural and socially explicable this belief, it is nevertheless burdened with liberal traditions of alienation from the people and its attendant distortions. The major charge undergone in recent years by the writers we are studying has taken them a long way from these traditions—Heinrich Mann most of all. In the intellectual problems posed in their historical novels this change is very clearly visible—again most clearly of all in Heinrich Mann. But the biographical method takes them back to the old conception of progress and humanism and prevents the full and adequate expression of their new revolutionary-democratic outlook.

The attitude behind the biographical form is one which views human progress exclusively or predominantly in ideal terms and sees its bearers as the more or less isolated great men of history. This raises the insoluble problem of how to connect in a direct way a detailed presentation of a character's private life with a convincing portrayal of the genesis of great, indeed "timelessly" magnified, ideas. Since these are important writers with whom we are dealing no detailed analysis is required to show that the personal life very often receives authentic and subtle portrayal. In this respect both Bruno Frank's *Cervantes* and Lion Feuchtwanger's novels attain to a not inconsiderable degree of human truth and psychological depth.

Here once again we must stress the quite special significance of

Heinrich Mann. Henri IV much more than the characters of Mann's contemporaries is a concrete person, the son of his country and his age. He is also, as we have been shown, much more closely involved with the popular life of his time. As a result of this more pronounced and more vital popular element Heinrich Mann produces a wonderfully fine figure: Henri IV is full of personal charm, honesty, courage, intelligence, cunning; he is able to talk to every person in his own language; shows a broad vision, theoretically and politically, human tolerance and a strong will in carrying out his great designs. And the way the light-minded and easy-going youth is educated by the hard facts of life into this representative of the best and most popular traits of the French people is full of true poetic beauty. Heinrich Mann, moreover, is able to portray this development with all the psychological complexity of real life; it follows no didactic and pedantic straight line. Its way is intricate, full of doubt, despair and error. All this constitutes a peak of achievement in contemporary literature. And what must be specially emphasized is that Heinrich Mann has succeeded here in creating a really *positive* and vital figure who concentrates the best human qualities of those fighters who for centuries have struggled to extend human culture in the teeth of reaction and who today are defending this culture against Fascist barbarism.

But Heinrich Mann's novel is not simply an enchanting portrait. It sets itself the task of presenting a great historic turning-point in the history of the French people. This turning-point is embodied in Henri IV's conversion to Catholicism and the period of religious tolerance which succeeded the generations of civil war between Huguenots and Catholics and to which France owed its great resurgence right up to the age of Louis XIV. This turning-point is expressed much more weakly in Heinrich Mann than the personality of Henri IV himself. What is new and significant about Henri IV historically is that he ceases to be the mere leader of a party, i.e., the Huguenots, and with the help not only of the Huguenots but also of the other progressive elements in the country is able to consolidate national unity by means of religious tolerance. This great turning-point, however, is all too brief in Mann's portrayal. Because of the whole conception of the novel it is presented merely in a biographical-psychological manner—in the form of the hero's lonely reflections.

Admittedly it is biographically prepared. After the poisoning of his mother Henri meets Coligny in secret. The admiral says of Paris: "... 'They hate us because they hate religion.' And perhaps because you have plundered them too often, added Henri to himself, recalling the wretched inn ... 'It should never have been allowed to come to this,' he said, 'we are all Frenchmen.' Coligny answered: 'But some have earned themselves heaven and others damnation. That must remain fixed—as truly as the Queen, your mother, lived and died in this belief.' The son of Queen Jeanne bowed his forehead. There was no reply once his mother's great companion-in-arms had brought her into the field. Both of them, the old man and the dead woman, stood together against him, they were contemporaries and shared the same unshakeable firmness in their opinions."

The deep difference between Henri and Coligny comes out very strongly here, especially as in the previous inn scene Heinrich Mann has given Henri a living picture of the Parisians' hatred. But here again this opposition escapes into the realm of lonely reflection and remains a dumb mental accompaniment to Henri's subsequent experiences at court which are recounted very extensively and vividly. And even after his flight from court, when he engages in open struggle, his opposition remains the lonely reflections of an isolated genius who—by a miracle of history—becomes the leader of his people. "He was to be leader of the Protestants: now another has taken his place, his cousin Condé, who was there before. He is zealous and rash, does not see beyond the war of the parties. You are putting your trust in a simpleton, good people of religion! He still lives in the times of the admiral. Does not realize that to divide up the kingdom for the sake of religion is tantamount to tearing it apart for one's own advantage like a will-o-the-wisp."

The times of Admiral Coligny are past: this is the great historical truth which Heinrich Mann has set himself to portray. For it is only against this change of the times that the thoughts of Henri IV can become more than the ponderings of a lonely eccentric, can assert themselves triumphantly in the civil wars and act as a guide to the history of France during a major period of resurgence. The secret of his victory then, as with every important historical figure, is his ability to understand the pressures of popular life in favour of some historic change, to give consciousness to these pressures and translate them into deeds.

In Heinrich Mann, however, this change remains a biographical fact in the life of Henri IV. For this reason his victory appears much less convincing than his psychological development and education. We think it unnecessary to repeat at length the reason for this weakness, namely that the biographical-psychological path to Henri's understanding is much too narrow a one. It is the understanding of a lonely great man, and however deep and correct, Henri IV cannot overcome all resistance in his own and the enemy's camp simply by understanding. This cannot appear convincing.

The victory of Henri IV's ideas could only appear convincing if we knew something about the varied trends in French popular life through the lives of individual characters travelling with greater or less consciousness, greater or less determination in the same direction; and if we experienced Henri IV as the leader of these trends. That is, if the difference between Coligny's period and Henri de Navarre's could be made clear to us in artistic terms as the difference between two phases in national life. This does not and cannot happen given the biographical form, despite Mann's fine psychological analysis of the spontaneous differences of temperament between Henri and his mother, between Henri and the Admiral.

Nevertheless this tendency of French development is visible even in its reflection among the ruling circles. However, certain abstract-humanist prejudices hinder Mann from seeing it. He does not see that the introduction of religious tolerance by Henri IV is only a step along the path to the then progressive establishment of absolute monarchy in France, that Henri's conquest of Coligny's period was a stage in the struggle between absolute monarchy and feudalism. This struggle in France proceeds in a very complicated, very uneven manner. It is certain that Catherine de Medici encountered similar problems and made similar endeavours, that she objectively was in some respects a forerunner of Henri IV and his endeavours. We are thinking of the period in which, with the help of the great bourgeois Chancellor L'Hospital, she used the Huguenots to break up the predominance of the Guises; in which supported by L'Hospital and the party of "politicians", she endeavoured to exploit the balance between the religious parties in order to strengthen French absolutism. The historical causes which led to the collapse of these plans lie beyond our scope. What is important for us is the fact that the party of "politicians" and the figure of L'Hospital are completely absent in Heinrich Mann. That they should not receive a place in the *biography of the hero* is proper. But it is precisely this which reveals the historical weakness of the biographical form of the novel. Henri's psychological development has to do service for what was an important objective tendency of the time and the real precondition of his ultimate victory. (Obviously, we should expect an historical novel dealing with this period to have less to say about L'Hospital and his friends than about the real popular movements which to their activities gave political expression.)

Another consequence of this narrowing and abstract-making conception is that the so very contradictory and significant figure of Catherine de Medici does not receive her historical due in Heinrich Mann. She is made into a kind of stylized phantastic witch, an embodiment of the evil principle. Here Heinrich Mann's Enlightenment traditions create an obstacle to a really artistic grasp of historical reality. At the same time all this is cause and effect of the biographical form of the historical novel. The form itself is born out of these abstract tendencies, which it then reinforces by simplifying human character. Characters lose their individual concrete and complex dialectics; they become planets revolving round the sun of the biography's hero.

We have stressed the weak sides of this important work because they reflect not so much Heinrich Mann's individual failure, as the limits which the biographical method imposes upon even so outstanding a writer as him; particularly as he has now reached a point in his development where his extraordinary gifts of characterization are emerging in full maturity and strength. We may generalize this weakness of the biographical form of the novel by saying that the personal, the purely psychological and biographical acquire a disproportionate breadth, a false preponderance. As a result the great driving forces of history are neglected. They are presented in all too summary a fashion and relate only biographically to the person at the centre. And because of this false distribution of weights what should be the real centre of these novels—the given historical transformation—cannot make itself felt sufficiently strongly.

But this false proportion affects the psychological portrayal too. Here too it is less important features and episodes which gain predominance. And even in a work like Henri IV which on the whole is narrated in a masterly fashion there remains a certain element of the merely circumstantial. This is to be observed in all novels of a biographical kind. They abound in embellishments, with the effect that the big crises and turning-points, even in the hero's own life, are given too brief, too summary a treatment.

The important writers of today take exception—and rightly so—to an excess of the psychological. They try to translate the psychological development of their heroes into living action. This is a very healthy and progressive tendency. But again the biographical form with its inevitable constriction of action checks the unfolding of this tendency. For, as we have shown in the case of Heinrich Mann, the most important changes in the hero's life take the form of lonely rumination, of lonely discussion with himself. Hence the result of this justified dislike for the psychologism of declining bourgeois literature is a false curtailing of the big moments of crisis.

This failure at precisely the points where writers are trying to portray the most important historical changes in the lives of their heroes is no individual literary weakness and also no accident, but the necessary consequence of the biographical form in the historical novel, or rather of those ideological tendencies which still mislead writers into using this form.

4. The Historical Novel of Romain Rolland.

We have so far confined ourselves—with deliberate onesidedness—to the German form of the historical novel. This was necessary because it commands the fate of the historical novel today. But it is by no means the sole important trend in the historical novel of our times. We have had occasion earlier to mention the novels of Anatole France and in particular his outstanding, truly historical portrayal embodied in the figure of Abbé Jerome Coignard. The path which was begun here immediately before the imperialist World War is significantly continued in the fine historical novel of the great humanist, Romain Rolland, *Colas Breugnon*.

By juxtaposing these two works we are not suggesting that Romain Rolland was "influenced" by Anatole France in any narrow philological sense. On the contrary, we think that if such an "influence" was present at all, it was quite minimal and had no bearing on the inception of Rolland's novel. That the two works belong together from the standpoint of the theory and history of the historical novel, that Romain Rolland in a certain sense continues along the same path as Anatole France is due to deeper, objective, social-historical causes.

Both the merits and limitations of these two extremely interesting novels—the limitations we shall examine later on—are linked with the special conditions surrounding the struggle for humanism and popular roots in the literature of pre-war imperialist France. The chain of revolutions which preceded the founding of the Third Republic had raised the political consciousness of writers, even of those who had for long been consciously "apolitical", to a level which could not be matched by German development even in its most outstanding and most politically concerned writers. Naturally, the general effects of imperialist economy were the same. All the problems of literary form which arose from the unpropitious nature of capitalist society and which the epoch of imperialism reproduced in a heightened form and at a higher level apply equally to France. Since we have dealt with these problems at length, we need not return to them here. In the previous chapter we established that certain reactionary features belonging to both imperialism proper and its preparatory stage were particularly apparent in French literature. Among these—and very important for our problem—was the transformation of revolutionary democracy into a cowardly and compromising liberalism which coquetted with every kind of reactionary ideology.

Primarily, however, we are concerned with certain specific features of French development which have had positive consequences for literature. We shall mention briefly only those which are specially connected with our problem. Foremost, the fact that the great tradition of the bourgeois-democratic revolution is much more alive and more immediately felt in France. Such glorifications of the Revolution as Victor Hugo's novel *1793* or Romain Rolland's drama of the Revolution would not only have been impossible for writers in Germany of the same period, but would have had nothing like the same effect upon readers. One has only to think of the history writing of Social Democracy in imperialist Germany (Blos, Cunow, Conradi, etc.), which set its entire "Marxism" into motion in order to make the revolutionary aspects of this period appear "immature" and "obsolete" in the eyes of the present.

With all Jaurès's ideological weaknesses one cannot for a moment compare his historical conception with conceptions such as these. The few Germans, such as Franz Mehring, who thought differently about the French Revolution, were isolated exceptions, whereas in France a relatively broad section of French scholars (e.g., Aulard and his school) endeavoured to explore the true history of the French Revolution, even in its plebeian-revolutionary aspects.

The important progressive writers of France feel the bourgeois-democratic revolution to be part of a still living, still potent heritage. And the continued life of this heritage simultaneously throws a bridge to the ideology which prepared the Revolution: to the Enlightenment and, beyond that, to the progressive, revolutionary, popular intellectual currents of the Renaissance. Again, this ideology is not only understood, but felt.

This sense of heritage also enables the materialist traditions in French literature—the zestful epicureanism of the spirited men of the sixteenth to eighteenth centuries—to live on, while among the German intelligentsia Feuerbach more or less ceases to exert an influence, the philosophical materialism of Marx and Engels remains unknown and uncomprehended (except in the form of crude vulgarization) and the only materialism which lives at all in the consciousness of the intellectuals is the barren schematism of a Büchner or a Moleschott. In France the spirited tradition of epicureanism is never entirely broken. This continuance of the heritage of Rabelais and Diderot, of Montaigne and Voltaire, does not of course demand a consistent philosophic materialism on the part of writers in our time. In literature it is not the philosophic consistency which matters, so much as whether the spirit of Enlightenment epicureanism has fruitfully affected the portrayal of characters and the world they inhabit.

We have already mentioned the immortal figure of Jérome Coignard. The principal character in Romain Rolland's historical novel, the artist craftsman Colas Breugnon, receives his best spiritual and human values from this common source. In both cases there is a cheerful, detached and harmonious respect for reality, an intellectual, spiritual and artistic self-enriching through a naïve and matter-of-course, yet cunning and self-preserving, abandonment to its inexhaustible richness. Colas Breugnon expresses this attitude to life very well indeed when he speaks of his relationship to art and nature: "As to art I have many times unravelled its secret: for I am an old fox, I know all the tricks, and I laugh into my beard when I discover they are stale. But as to life, I have often come off the worse. It outdoes our cunning, and its inventions are far superior to our own."

Naturally, this living-on of an old tradition always means that is being fashioned afresh; and in keeping with the general trends of the imperialist period this refashioning is often mixed with reactionary tendencies. Thus the spontaneous, but not consistent, materialism frequently becomes a nature mystique which is not always free of reactionary elements.

One can best observe this complex blend of progressiveness, attempts to transcend the limits of bourgeois democracy and reactionary criticism of the great revolutionary traditions, in the widespread influence exercised upon the French intelligentsia by the ideas of syndicalism—particularly as formulated by Sorel. It is easy to discover and criticize the reactionary tendencies in Sorel. But one has to see the reason for this influence. In the case of the most important writers of the age it starts from their dissatisfaction, as democrats, with the events and results of the bourgeois-democratic revolution. They feel the insoluble contradictions of bourgeois democracy very keenly and see only one way out of them—the myth of syndicalism. The occasional references to syndicalist ideology in *Jean Christophe* undoubtedly have their source here. And once again it is not primarily a question of the influence of syndicalist theories upon literature, but of the necessary intellectual reflection of France's social position. This is shown by Anatole France's conception of the Revolution in *Les Dieux ont Soif*, which we have already briefly mentioned, where the criticism of bourgeois society has no syndicalist foundations.

There is an essential unity underlying these contradictory standpoints which comes out particularly strongly in political life. Take the attitude of the best section of the French intelligentsia to the Third Republic. During the "normal", peaceful course of events the predominant mood is one of disillusion and ironical criticism of the shortcomings and limitations of bourgeois democracy. The best of this criticism expresses disillusion with the results of the bourgeois revolution and dissatisfaction with capitalist society in its most advanced and democratic form. But in general it can very easily give the impression of indifference towards democracy and towards the Republic as a form of state. However, recent French history shows that whenever reaction mounts a conspiracy or attack and creates a situation of crisis in the Republic the best section of the intelligentsia, the most talented and farsighted writers leave their "splendid isolation" and come actively to the rescue of democracy. This was the case with France and Zola and many others at the time of the Dreyfus campaign; and again with the best spirits of France when Fascist aggression threatened.

And this political emergence of the best writers is linked with the movement of the working masses. It is as typical of Wilhelmine Germany that Heinrich Mann's political radicalism should have isolated him among broad sections of the intelligentsia as it is of French development that Zola and France, Barbusse and Romain Rolland should have increased their authority and popularity after and as a result of their vigorous entry into politics. Of course, we must not forget the violent attacks made upon them by countless and not unimportant reactionary writers, the almost pogrom-like hue and cry against Zola, etc. But precisely these passionate struggles around the social content of literature distinguishes Wilhelmine Germany sharply from French democracy. Heinrich Mann has often stressed this difference in his publicist and critical essays and found the reason for the superiority of French literature in this connection with public life.

This vigorous involvement of French literature in the important struggles of the day prevented the historical novel from gaining the leading role which it acquired in post-World-War Germany. For Romain Rolland the historical novel is even more of an episode in his career than it was for Anatole France. History certainly plays a decisive part in his work—particularly the summits of humanist endeavour and the great Revolution. But the first he treats in a series of interesting and penetrating monographs of an essay-like nature, and the second in an ambitious cycle of historical dramas. In neither case is the choice of literary form accidental.

Romain Rolland's essay has firm scientific foundations and his choice of this form shows how emphatically he rejects the vogue of historical belles lettres. He knows from his own rich artistic experience that to reveal the personal and human greatness, the individual human tragedy of a Michelangelo, Beethoven or Tolstoy, one must first analyse their time and their works with patience, thoroughness and objectivity.

His dramatic treatment of revolutionary subjects is equally deliberate. Anatole France was interested in bringing out the social dialectics of the realized bourgeois Revolution, the inevitable disappointment with its limitations. This was not Rolland's concern although of course political and social questions are central to these dramas. Rather he wished to portray the huge explosion of the tragically interlocking passions released by the Revolution. Romain Rolland's attitude to the period of the French Revolution is somewhat similar, given the difference in historical situation and personality, to Stendhal's attitude to the Renaissance. Romain Rolland, too, sees the revolutionary period as a tragic school in which passions run their full course. He says himself of his attitude as a dramatist to this period of history: "For me it is a reservoir of passions and natural forces ... I make no attempt at likeness; for they are eternal ... The artistic power of the drama of history resides less in what it was then in what is always is. The tornado of '1793' is still circling around the world."

The historical novel *Colas Breugnon* is born of quite a different spirit. In Romain Rolland's own words it is a kind of interlude between his large epic and dramatic cycles, a secondary line, an episode in his total production. But this placing of its origin and position in the writer's life-work should not depreciate its artistic significance. It should simply confirm afresh the social-historical role of the historical novel within French humanism today.

It is an interlude, cheerful and life-affirming, even though its story is full of sad, indeed tragic events—like that of Anatole France's *Rôtisserie de la Reine Pédauque*. This tension and the triumph of life that springs from it is the decisive thing: here the old life-affirming, epicurean materialism, the great tradition of the French humanists breaks through. The historical theme is not accidental because, with the action taking place in the time of the Regency under the young Louis XIII, it expresses the continuity of this attitude to life among the French people.

Indeed Romain Rolland intends much more than an uninterrupted historical development. The outlook of this great humanist, his belief in the eternity of human feelings and passions goes beyond mere continuity. "Bonhomme vit encore" he writes as the motto to this novel, and in the preface where he gives his reasons for publishing the work unchanged (it had been completed just before the imperialist World War) he says that the grandsons of Colas Breugnon, the heroes and victims of the bloody epic of the World War, had proved to the world just how right this motto was.

Colas Breugnon, then, is conceived by his author not only as a son of his time, a time long past, but also as an eternal type. And—which is decisive—a type representative of French popular life. With

Anatole France the epicurean wisdom and blithe affirmation of life "despite everything" was the intellectual property of a declassed intellectual of the eighteenth century. Romain Rolland's outlook has deeper roots in the people. To be sure Colas Breugnon, the artist craftsman also feeds his spirit and outlook on literature, but his wisdom is essentially more native, more directly drawn from life, from popular life.

Here resides the imperishable beauty of this work, which makes of it a unique product in our time. Romain Rolland nowhere idealizes his hero. In fact he deliberately sets a whole series of negative features in the foreground: a tendency to loaf, a certain laxness and negligence about life, etc. Colas Breugnon is anything but an "ideal hero" modelled on perfection; his faults and merits correspond in no way to those images which, at different times and on different sides have been used to glorify the French people.

But if Romain Rolland refuses to throw a false gloss over the French people in keeping with these traditions, he is even more strongly opposed to those modern literary trends which seek to provide a natural picture of the people by stressing human brutality; even though they would make "circumstances" responsible for this. Romain Rolland's portrait of a popular hero is throughout blunt and robust. But inseparable from these qualities, which have more to them than their form suggests, is the hero's human genuineness, subtlety and tenderness in his relations to people, his simple and shrewd decisiveness which in moments of real trial and danger soars into true heroism, heroic steadfastness. Certain scenes are hardly to be equalled in any other writer of the present: the hero's encounter and farewell with the sweetheart of his youth, from whom we learn the humorous and moving story of their love; his farewell to his efficient, prosaic wife with whom he has lived all his life in humorous discord. One has to go back to Gottfried Keller's scenes of popular life to find the equal of this popular humanism.

This is enough to show the unique position of Romain Rolland's historical novel in the literature of our time. His manner of presentation is if anything a polar opposite to that of the German anti-Fascist humanists. What is missing in their novels, and constitutes their chief weakness, even in so important a work as Heinrich Mann's Henri IV, is concrete popular life in its native, human fullness; and it is precisely this which distinguishes Colas Breugnon. This contrast deserves to be particularly emphasized today when, with the gathering of all democratic forces against Fascism, the question of popular roots is even more actual than it was when Colas Breugnon was written.

Naturally, this is not the only way in which Romain Rolland

proves his enormous superiority over his German anti-Fascist com-
rades-in-arms. The contrast also comes out in the attitude expressed in
these two types of historical novel to the political and social struggles
of the age portrayed and, thereby, to the class struggles of the present.
In the following remarks we shall discuss the reasons for the over-
directness of this attitude in the historical novel of the German anti-
Fascists and its disadvantages for a truthful presentation of the past.
The historical novel of the German anti-Fascist writers gives us the
poetry of the struggle for humanism and culture, against reaction
and barbarism; but as yet this poetry is still abstract, not fed by real
popular forces.

It is quite different in Romain Rolland. We have already stressed
the lofty and vital poetry of popular life in his novel. This, however,
rests on a conscious *aloofness* from the political struggles of the time
portrayed, an aloofness which has been raised into a philosophy. Not
that Colas Breugnon and his author do not take sides in these
struggles. But the position they do take is one of blunt plebeian
mistrust, repudiating *both* contending parties of the age, the
Catholics as well as the Protestants. Romain Rolland has his hero
say: "One party is worth as much as the other; the better one is not
even worth the rope with which it ought to be hanged. What do we
care whether this or that good-for-nothing plays his knavish tricks
at court?" And even more clearly at another point: "God protect
us from our protectors! We are quite capable of protecting ourselves.
Poor sheep! If it was only a question of defending ourselves against
the wolf, we'd soon know what to do. But who will protect us against
the shepherd?" Romain Rolland not only has his hero state this
view repeatedly, but shows by striking examples during the course of
the story how right the plebeians of the time were to mistrust
both sides in this way and how they attempted to translate their mistrust into deeds, now slyly, now boldly.

Romain Rolland also shows great artistic wisdom in choosing this
particular period in which to portray this plebeian mistrust for all
that happens "above". The great period of the Huguenot struggles
is past. The time of the last decisive battles between absolute
monarchy and the party divisions produced by feudalism, the age
of the Fronde, the struggles in the Cévennes, lies far ahead. The
parties exist, but their clashes take the form of court intrigues "above"
and pillaging "below", whether the people concerned are friends or
enemies. The intelligent plebeian Colas Breugnon judges these
struggles of his time on the whole correctly; especially if one adds
that he expresses a warm admiration for Henri IV, regarding him as
"his man".

But I think one would not be doing justice to Romain Rolland's artistic intentions if one simply accepted this justification of Colas Breugnon's standpoint and left it at that. For it is only a temporary justification, valid for a certain phase. We repeat: Romain Rolland shows great artistic wisdom in having chosen an historical theme in which all his hero's arguments, thoughts and actions appear to be confirmed by the reality of the time. But the author wanted to say something else here, something broader and deeper; he certainly did not wish to restrict his conclusions to the concrete stretch of time covering his hero's activity.

Let us recall his remarks on de Coster's novel, quoted in the previous chapter. He praises it both for its opposition to Rome and for its refusal to support Geneva in the Netherlands independence struggle. Now if we compare this attitude with what he says about the contemporaneity of the Colas Breugnon type in his preface to the novel, we see that Romain Rolland wanted to do more with his hero's indifference to the contending parties "above" in the time of Louis XIII than lovingly portray an historically understandable sentiment. He also wanted to hold up for posterity an ideal figure who should typify a correct plebeian standpoint.

Shortly after the completion of this novel the imperialist World War broke out. Everyone will remember vividly and gratefully the manly, brave and self-sacrificing stand taken by Romain Rolland against the universal slaughter. But Romain Rolland knows today, after the experiences of the last, eventful decade, which he has lived through with all the awareness of a great writer and thinker, that his slogan "Au dessus de la mêlée" only incompletely expressed his fighting spirit and opened the way to a great deal of misunderstanding and indeed distortion of his intentions.

Romain Rolland's temporary abstract pacifism was never inwardly related to the pacifism of those who called themselves his disciples and followers. Colas Breugnon indeed shows the fundamentally different social and ideological sources of his specific, personal position. And this plebeian quality which stems from a deep and genuine spontaneous popular sense distinguishes his position sharply from those which seem to use a similar language.

One has only to place Stefan Zweig's Erasmus next to Colas Breugnon to see this contrast clearly. There we have an over-refined, anxious and nervous shrinking back from any decision, a cautious balancing between "on the one hand" and "on the other", the conceited intellectual's attempt to transcend intellectual contradictions and social antagonisms. Here, on the other hand, is a powerful plebeian repudiation of the repulsive courtiers and adventurers who suck the people's blood, a rejection of both contending parties who are cleverly outwitted and whenever possible and necessary fought with cudgel and sword. There a refined and subtle product of the decadent liberalism of a once revolutionary bourgeois intellectual stratum. Here a native plebeian rebelliousness which has not yet ripened into the conscious activity of democratic revolution. Artistic pallor and fragility in the case of Zweig, blossoming richness of colour in the case of Rolland reflect this contrast clearly and adequately.

Colas Breugnon and the entire corresponding phase of its author's development have nothing to do with the latter's so-called followers. The book reflects those peasant-plebeian moods which we have already seen objectified in a number of important instances in certain parts of Tolstoy's War and Peace, in de Coster's Ulenspiegel.

But the similarity is only a general one of social trends. Romain Rolland has not de Coster's blind, spontaneous hatred which leads him to naturalism. His attitude to the parties "above" is more an intellectually superior contempt than a pathetic hatred. Colas Breugnon, despite his plebeian status, is nearer intellectually and humanly to Jérome Coignard than to the modern Eulenspiegel. He is a popular hero and yet rooted intellectually and humanly in the native soil of the new humanism. This combination spares Rolland's manner of presentation the naturalist excesses of carnal lust and cruelty that we find in the important Belgian author. But the delight which Colas Breugnon takes in woman, wine and good food shines forth everywhere in the gentle pastel colours of a translucently humane, deeply cultivated and yet somewhat crafty epicureanism. Colas Breugnon is a more earthy character than his eighteenth century brother because of this happy transposition into plebeian spheres, where the basic humanist outlook is not only preserved, but strengthened.

These two works reflect the best that has been produced in France by the humanist protest against the capitalist present. But they also reflect the social and historical limits of this protest. In both cases the epicurean wisdom and detachment reflect a refusal, veiled in irony and humour, to enter into or alter the hostility and meanness of social reality. And this refusal is clearly expressed artistically in the fact that the whole context of historical reality, if it appears at all, does so in much vaguer outlines than the humanist principal figure himself; in the fact that such works, however vividly drawn many of the minor characters, however powerfully executed many of the individual scenes, are in their totality *portraits* rather than world pictures.

Romain Rolland underlines this portrait character still more by his first person narrative. He is not so much drawing a picture of the times as mirroring them through the life and experiences of Colas Breugnon. But this induces a certain immobility and staticness in the work despite its very varied and interesting happenings. Development in this novel is only apparently a progression in time and events. Its inner essence is more a revelation. We see the portrait of Colas Breugnon growing feature by feature, as the author wields the brush of life in his experienced hand. When the picture is finished, the novel finishes too. However, we feel that nothing really new has happened. We simply see the portrait more clearly and comprehendingly now than at the beginning. But the model is no different. Colas Breugnon undergoes no development. And it is not the kind of no development which we have observed in the case of "world-historical individuals" who appear as minor figures. The revelation of their human qualities provides an answer to the social-historical questions which have arisen in the course of the novel and thus constitutes a factor in the objective dynamic of the given historical theme. Colas Breugnon's lack of development is much more literal. For all human and historical problems are concentrated within his character and psychology. Question and answer alike are contained within the compass of his life. Hence a geat deal happens in the novel, but only to show from as many angles as possible an identical attitude to life. In this sense the novel has no action. Whatever happens externally is intended neither to take men a further stage along their paths, nor to disclose some universal crisis, but simply to explain a *human attitude*.

Romain Rolland is a writer who has assimilated and learned from the best and noblest traditions of classic art. Nevertheless the unpropitiousness of the times has driven him far from the classical traditions of the historical novel. His outstanding humanity and artistry are revealed in the inner perfection which he has given to his novel despite the unfavourable circumstances of the age. But this perfection has been achieved at the expense—a conscious expense—of a comprehensive historical world picture. By failing to portray the interaction of all classes in society, Rolland is unable to reveal to us those unknown human strengths in people which flower forth historically.

From a purely artistic point of view this renunciation cannot be sufficiently admired. And similarly the choice of period: after the author's brief indications the reader is not that sorry at all to have Colas Breugnon's portrait rather than a picture of the period. But measured against the historical pictures produced by the classics of the historical novel and the picture of society in *Jean Christophe*, there is a certain resignation and artistic self-limitation in this wisdom of choice.

This purely artistic concern comes out in the language, too. Romain Rolland depicts Colas Breugnon through the latter's own words, which give to his portrait a very directly authentic ring. This delicately achieved renewal of the old language constantly and vividly emphasizes the hero's native plebeian character. Yet it is un-avoidable that the present-day reader should feel a slight, often barely perceptible, touch of artificiality, of studied artistry in this langu-age. And the two consequences of the first person narrative—both this tie to the old language and the quality of static portraiture which we have mentioned—underline the all-too-artistic and experi-mental character of this fine novel. It is one of the many tragic manifestations of our time that such a lofty portrayal of the old, native plebeian life should not be possible without these undertones of arti-ficiality.

5. Prospects of Development for the New Humanism in the Historical Novel.

We see that all problems of form and content alike in the historical novel of our day centre upon questions of heritage. All aesthetic problems and valuations in this sphere are determined by the struggle to liquidate the political, ideological and artistic heritage of the period of declining capitalism, by the struggle to renew and fruitfully extend the traditions of the great progressive periods of mankind, the spirit of revolutionary democracy, the artistic grandeur and popular strength of the classical historical novel.

This statement of the problem—both here and, we hope, in our previous analyses—will suffice to show how more than purely artistic these questions are. Artistic form, as the concentrated and heightened reflection of the important features of objective reality, both regula-tive and individual, can never be treated purely as such, in isolation. Precisely the development of the historical novel shows most clearly how what appear to be purely formal, compositional problems—e.g., whether the great figures of history should be principal heroes or minor figures—so obviously conceal ideological and political problems of the highest importance. Indeed, the whole question of whether the historical novel is a genre in its own right, with its own artistic laws or whether it obeys essentially the same laws as the novel in general can only be solved on the basis of a general approach to the decisive ideological and political problems.

We have seen that the answer to all these questions depends upon the writer's attitude to *popular life*. The resumption of the traditions of the classical historical novel is not an aesthetic question in a narrow, professional sense. It does not matter whether Sir Walter Scott or Manzoni was aesthetically superior to, say, Heinrich Mann, or at least this is not the main point. What is important is that Scott and Manzoni, Pushkin and Tolstoy, were able to grasp and portray popular life in a more profound, authentic, human and concretely historical fashion than even the most outstanding writers of our day; that the classical form of the historical novel was a form in which authors could express their feelings adequately; and that the classical manner of story and composition was specially designed to bring out the essentials, the richness and variety of popular life as the basis for changes in history. Whereas in the historical novel even of important writers of the present we are confronted every moment with a conflict between the ideological content, the human attitude that is intended and the literary means that are used.

If then, to judge the outstanding works of contemporary writers, we take our aesthetic measure from a study and analysis of the classics of the historical novel and the laws of epic and drama in general, we are justified in two respects. First of all, the fact that a given literary trend arises as a result of social and economic necessity and the class struggles of its time is still no gauge for aesthetic judgment. To be sure, reactionary-relativist historicism and equally relativist vulgar sociology preach the contrary. Since Ranke all mechanistic vulgarizers say that each product of historical development is "equally near to God" or, in vulgar sociological phraseology, a "class equivalent". This sounds—according to how one likes it—either extraordinarily "deep" in the sense of a mystically irrational conception of history or extraordinarily "scientific" in the sense of a vulgar-bourgeois, liberal-Menshevik theory of progress.

But both conceptions sever the real connection between art and reality. Art appears simultaneously as a fatalistic and purely subjective mode of expression of an individual. Thus it is not a reflection of objective reality. Yet the criteria of a genuine aesthetic derive precisely from this basic characteristic of art. Because the historical novel reflects and portrays the development of historical reality the measure for its content and form is to be found in this reality itself. But what is this reality? It is the uneven and crisis-filled development of popular life. Writers like Flaubert and Conrad Ferdinand Meyer create a "new" form of the historical novel for profound and necessary reasons: the development of society produces an ideological decline in their class, they are no longer in a position to see the real problems of popular life in their extended richness, their picture of history is socially and historically impoverished, inadequate, accordingly they fashion it into a "new" form. However, it is the duty of Marxist aesthetics not only to *explain* this impoverishment and inadequacy in a social-genetic way, but also to *measure* them aesthetically against the highest demands of the artistic reflection of historical reality and to find them lacking.

Criticism must be allowed the right to judge and condemn the artistic products of entire periods, while acknowledging their social-historical necessity—indeed, the whole aesthetic judgment rests upon this acknowledgment. But this proclamation of the right of criticism by no means disposes of the problem of the historical novel in our day. For we have repeatedly established the deep ideological *contrast* which separates the literary activity of the important representatives of the historical novel in our own time from that of bourgeois decadence. Thus the problem of assessing the present historical novel is a much more complex one. Our classical yardstick is by no means as opposed and alien to the latter as it is to the products of the beginning decline of bourgeois literature and especially to those of fully-fledged decadence. There are also deep and important similarities between the classical period of the historical novel and the historical novel of our time. Both aim at presenting the movement of popular life in history, in its objective reality and simultaneously in its living relation to the present. This living political and ideological relation to the present is a further important element of outlook which inwardly connects the present-day writing of our humanists with the classical period.

But the unevenness of historical development makes this relation an extremely complicated one. This applies to both important questions, both to the question of popular roots and to that of the connection with the present. It is interesting and characteristic that in a political and ideological respect the views of many humanists of the present are much more radical than those of the classics. One need only think of the contrast between the moderate Tory, Sir Walter Scott, and the revolutionary democrat, Heinrich Mann. But the unevenness of development comes out in the fact that Scott was much more livingly bound up with, much more intimate with, the life of the people than the outstanding writer of the imperialist period, who has had to struggle both against the isolation from popular life imposed upon the writer by the social division of labour of advanced capitalism and the growth of an ever more reactionary liberal ideology under imperialism.

This link with popular life was still a natural, socially given state of affairs for the writers of the classical period of the historical novel. In the period in which they lived the forces of the social division of labour had only just begun to exert a decisive influence upon literature and art in the direction of the writer's isolation from popular life. In many reactionary Romantics of the time this influence is already clearly tangible; however it does not become the dominant basis of literature as a whole until much later.

The humanists of our time start in their writing from a *protest against the dehumanizing influences of capitalism.* An extremely important part is played in this protest by the writer's tragic estrangement from popular life, his isolation, his complete dependence upon himself. However, it is also part of the situation that this protest can advance only gradually, unevenly and contradictorily from *abstractness* to *concreteness.* And this is not only because generally one's links and familiarity with popular life can only be made concrete in a gradual, step-by-step way, but partly because of the inner dialectic of the writer's struggle against the socially isolated position of literature under imperialism.

This dialectic determines the slowness and unevenness of the way in which the writer settles his accounts with the liberal ideology of imperialism. The genuine writers of this period begin with an ardent wish to conquer the isolation of literature and the aestheticism, the artistic self-satisfaction and self-sufficiency which flow from it; and in their desire to make literature an effective force in the society of their time—which they take as given—they naturally look round for allies. The result has been that they have clung passionately to any social current or human manifestation which seemed to offer the slightest hope of being moved to protest against the inhumanity of the social present.

Thus the reawakening of the revolutionary-democratic spirit in German literature has been extremely difficult. The most varied obstacles have been placed in the path of its development by liberal compromise on the one hand and abstract negation of a bohemian-anarchist kind on the other. Hence if, in analysing the development of the most important anti-Fascist writers, we come across all manner of attempts to ally themselves with currents of this kind—because of insufficient critical judgment or even uncritical over-estimation—we must understand this as part of the general line of development of Germany (and in many respects, though not so markedly, of the rest of Western Europe). The fall of the Hohenzollern régime and the Weimar Republic was able to produce a certain advance in this respect, but no radical change. This took place only with the victory of Fascist barbarism in Germany itself and the experiences and victories of the popular front in France and Spain.

It would be a mistake, however, to see nothing but weaknesses in the earlier literature which everywhere reveals traces of this slow emergence of the revolutionary-democratic spirit. It is not possible here to analyse German literature of the pre-Fascist period in all its detail, particularly since its essential achievements lie outside the scope of this study. But in order to illustrate this general position of protesting humanist literature let us quote one example: that of Thomas Mann. In his youthful work this great writer makes a harsh and deep self-criticism by contrasting the world of the isolated writer with that of the sound, straightforward citizen. Now it would be quite superficial and erroneous to see this as something negative. Thomas Mann discloses deep contradictions in bourgeois life, in its lack of culture, with a dialectic of extreme subtlety and complexity, and there is no doubt that he combats the dominant human type produced by German capitalism. But the more deeply he sees into the problems of isolated literature, the more firmly he repudiates the writer's withdrawal into an "ivory tower" and abstract negation of the present as a whole, the more he is compelled to look round everywhere in reality for positive (at least, relatively) human types. His honesty as a writer also comes out in the fact that while he may present a type positively in one context he will criticize him ironically in another, and in this way add strong reservations to his affirmation; thus his writing never sinks into apologia or glorification of the present.

In all this one has to recognize a double tendency. On the one hand Thomas Mann, like every important writer, endeavours to portray an all-round and comprehensive picture of the society of his time. The universality of this picture depends upon the variety of the characters and whether, even when they are felt to be bearers of hostile principles, they are portrayed as living, many-sided human beings and not as poster-like caricatures. In this respect both Thomas Mann as well as a few of his important contemporaries went far beyond the horizon set by the prejudices of the liberal bourgeoisie. On the other hand, the manner in which these types are humanly and artistically understood reflects the slow and contradictory form in which this separation from the bourgeois-reactionary prejudices of the Wilhelmine period takes place. We stress once again: it is not the fact that hostile types are humanly portrayed that points to this slow and hesitant overcoming of prejudices, but the uncritical attitude to these types in their social and human totality, the failure to recognize their social and human limits. It will suffice if we mention here Thomas Mann's presentation of Frederick the Great's Prussia and its traditions in the First World War.

But we find similar forms of conception and portrayal—admittedly, of a less pronounced kind—even in the earlier period of Heinrich Mann with regard to representatives of the liberal bourgeoisie; and in Arnold Zweig with regard to decent, venerable types of the German military. This sort of artistic conception of reality naturally has its political and ideological roots. Here again a few examples will suffice; it suffices if one mentions the false estimate of Bismarck or

Nietzsche. These cases show how certain prejudices of the past period or, at least, their survivals are still alive today.

This slow and contradictory process of overcoming liberal ideology and its estrangement from the people is reflected, too, in the historical novels of the anti-Fascist humanists.

We showed earlier how one of the most important weaknesses of these novels was their portrayal of the problems of popular life from "above"; the people themselves played a part only when they came into direct contact with whatever was going on "above". This gives us a clear picture of the liberal-bourgeois traditions still to be overcome. Thus the return to the traditions of the classical type of historical novel is not primarily an aesthetic-artistic question. It is a consequence rather of the decisive and complete victory of the spirit of revolutionary democracy, of the concrete and close involvement of the important humanists with the destiny of the people. (Our earlier analyses have, we hope, shown the reader sufficiently clearly that the new plebeian tradition in the Latin countries, whose phases are marked by the names of Erckmann-Chatrian, de Coster and Romain Rolland, suffer from a lack of historical concreteness in quite the contrary way. Thus the ideological-artistic problem of reawakening the spirit of the classical historical novel holds good for this tradition, too and is likewise connected with the political and social concretization of revolutionary democracy; except that the literary conclusions to be drawn in this case are of a different, often quite contrary, character.)

The question of the relation of past to present is very closely connected with this problem. Again we must stress sharply the contrast between the present-day historical novel and its immediate predecessors. The historical novel of the humanists of our day is closely linked with the great and urgent problems of the present. It is on the way to portraying the *prehistory of the present*—very much in contrast, say, to Flaubert's type of historical novel. Its topicality— in a large historical sense—is one of the great advances achieved by the anti-Fascist humanists; it marks the beginning of a *change* in the history of the historical novel.

Yet only the *beginning* of a change. For the change itself leads back to the traditions of the classical historical novel. The difference which still exists between the two today has been stressed by us at different points. To recapitulate briefly: the humanist historical novel of today gives only an *abstract prehistory of ideas* and not the concrete prehistory of the destiny of the people themselves, which is what the historical novel in its classical period portrayed.

As a result of this general and conceptual rather than concrete and historical relationship between past and present the distortion of historical figures or movements is at times inevitable; there is thus a falling-away from that superb faithfulness to historical reality which was the strength of the classical historical novel. But beyond that, this all-too-conceptual and therefore all-too-direct relationship with the present has an abstracting effect upon the totality of the world represented. If the historical novel is the concrete prehistory of the present, as it was with the classics, then artistically the popular destiny represented in it should be an end-in-itself. The living relationship to the present should be expressed by the movement of history itself. The relationship is then objective in an artistic sense; it never breaks the limits set by the human-historical frame of the world represented. (That this depends also upon a "necessary anachronism" we have already fully explained.) The direct and conceptual relationship with the present which prevails today reveals an immanent tendency to turn the past into a *parable of the present*, to wrest directly from history a "fabula docet", and this conflicts with the real historical concreteness of the content and the real (not formal) self-containment of the form.

It may sound paradoxical, but is nevertheless true that this direct relationship with the present has an abstracting and hence weakening effect upon the very problems of the present placed in the foreground. This can be seen most clearly of all in Feuchtwanger's novel *The False Nero*. No other artistic work of our time burns with such hatred of Fascism. The satirical pathos of this hatred takes Feuchtwanger a great step forward along the revolutionary-democratic path. But this is not the only merit of the work. Feuchtwanger portrays popular movements here much more concretely than in his Josephus Flavius novels, more so even than in the second part of the cycle. True, these popular movements are also seen and presented from the standpoint of the wirepullers in the background and the leaders in the foreground, yet they have gained a much higher degree of concreteness and differentiation than in his earlier works. Nevertheless, despite its greater liveliness and concreteness this interesting work is but an extensive parable: we see how a pathetic buffoon, incited by the intrigues of big capitalists, assumes the leadership of a popular movement, exercises dictatorial power for a long time and then collapses once the people have come to their senses. No other satire written against Hitler and his gentlemanly and mob accomplices has such deadly accuracy. It is so sharp and convincing, its meaning so immediately clear that *The False Nero* deserves an important place in the anti-Fascist struggle.

But what is missing in this interesting and powerful work? We believe—a sufficiently deep and concrete relationship with the present. It expresses only the immediate emotions aroused by Fascism. For the real and deeper question which stirs all true democrats is this: how could these bands of murderers come to rule in a country like Germany? How was it that thousands and thousands of convinced people could fight fanatically on behalf of these mercenary, murderous hirelings of capitalism? What Feuchtwanger's satirical novel does not do is to unravel the mystery of this mass movement, the mystery of this German disgrace. It simply accepts as a fact that the people may become temporary victims of the crudest demagogy.

But how this crude demagogy was able to exert such an influence upon millions of people is not even asked, let alone answered. And this question is not an academic historical one, but a practical issue of the highest order: the question of the concrete perspective of the collapse of the Fascist rule of murder. This is indeed shown by Feuchtwanger's novel itself. By not portraying the concrete, social-historical origins of the rule of his false Nero, he is not in a position to portray its concrete, social-historical collapse. A "miracle" occurs: a satirical song travels from mouth to mouth, unmasking the inner hollowness of the usurper and his band, the people come to their senses and the barbaric dictatorship collapses. This perspective of the future no longer expresses the feelings of the progressive anti-Fascist fighters, but— very much contrary to Feuchtwanger's intention—the feelings of those who see in Fascism not so much a concrete political-social movement of the imperialist age as a "social illness", a kind of "mass lunacy" and who hence passively wait for the people to "recover", to "come to their senses"—in a word, for the automatic collapse of the Hitler régime, for a miracle.

We see that there is no substitute for a concrete relationship to the present or, what comes to the same thing, a concrete familiarity with popular life. This is true, however high the intellectual level or brilliant the artistic expression of an abstract relationship to the present. This problem must be emphasized again and again because the way in which it is solved determines the artistic fate of the historical novel in every period. The transformation of the historical novel into an independent genre which plays a considerable part in Feuchtwanger's work—particularly in his theoretical pronouncements—is still a symptom today of the weakness of these relationships. The cause of this weakness is quite different today from when the decline of bourgeois realism began, but the result in both cases is the same: modernization and abstractness in the portrayal of historical characters.

This can be confirmed by positive examples. In the first place, we see that given a deeper and more complex, less direct, abstract and allegorical relationship to at least certain aspects of popular life in the present, a writer may produce more significant and convincing historical portrayals. It is interesting, and characteristic of the new position of the historical novel, that this should come out most clearly in its *positive* characters. The sheer fact that positive characters can be created at all is extraordinarily important. Since Balzac's Michel Chrestien and Stendhal's Palla Ferrante the modern bourgeois novel has been unable to create a positive character who takes an active part in public life. But even Balzac and Stendhal, as clear-sighted and consistent realists, were forced to make their democratic and popular heroes episodic figures.

The anti-Fascist popular front and the spirit of revolutionary democracy which it has revived have once again made it possible to embody a people's yearning for liberation in positive characters. This is the extraordinary historical, political as well as artistic significance of figures like Heinrich Mann's Henri IV. These positive portrayals are politically deepened polemics against the mendacious demogogic leader-cult of the Fascists; and the breadth and accuracy of their polemical impact depends upon their artistic stature. These characters must visibly embody the deep longing of the broadest popular masses for a solution to the most terrible crisis ever experienced by the German people during the course of their long and arduous history. The less direct the portrayal, the deeper are its roots in these popular sentiments. In this way it brings to light and gives voice to the most varied and obscure popular strivings; in this way it not only expresses what today may be seen upon the surface of life and is consciously known, but can delve into the real origins both of the oppression and degeneration and of the path to liberation. It creates *models* which *accelerate* the consciousness and resoluteness of the longing for liberation.

Bruno Frank's Cervantes constitutes a serious coming-to-terms with the divorce of German writing from popular life. Hitherto this kind of self-criticism in literature had been predominantly elegiac and satirical (at its profoundest and most moving in Thomas Mann's *Tonio Kröger*); here a positive example is portrayed. Frank succeeds at many points in portraying the human side of a great writer who was primarily a fighter and for whom literature—literature at its highest cultural and artistic level—was an organic, all-crowning part, yet only a part, of his social activity; and by so doing Frank shows a way out of this estrangement not only for writers, but also for the masses who had been painfully deprived of such a literature and such writers, even if for them this has been an unconscious deprivation and they only now realize what they have been missing.

This connection between political-polemical effectiveness and artistic quality is still more striking in Heinrich Mann's Henri IV. Here for the first time after a long period we have before us a figure who is at once popular and significant, wise and resolute, sly yet brave and undaunted. And Heinrich Mann, as we have seen, stresses the fact that Henri IV has drawn his strength and adroitness from his links with popular life, that he has become the leader of the people because of his sensitivity to the real desires of the popular masses and his ability to fulfil them courageously and wisely. The artistic subtlety of this portrayal strikes the Hitler cult far more mortal a blow than the majority of direct attacks. For Mann discloses the connection between people and leader; he answers in an indirect polemic the question which concerns the masses: what is the social content, the human essence of leadership? If one compares Mann's indirect polemic with his direct satire on Hitler in the figure of the Duke de Guise, one sees how much more politically effective is the superior artistic portrayal.

These remarks must not of course be misinterpreted: we are not depreciating negative and satirical portrayals of the enemy. We are simply criticizing the limitations of a too direct, unhistorical approach to these questions. Precisely the lessons of classical literature show how highly artistic, historical and inclusive of all important determinants such portrayals can be. And the positive portrayals, particularly of Heinrich Mann, are so significant because they go a long way towards overcoming a direct, abstract and therefore unhistorical, merely allegorical relationship with the present.

But there is still a long way to go. As we have seen, Bruno Frank and even Heinrich Mann have produced portraits rather than real pictures of the times. The popular character of their heroes, in human terms, in terms of the individual person portrayed, is true and genuine. Yet the real basis, the real interaction with popular forces is not portrayed. Hence the organic link with popular life is lacking, both politically and polemically; there is lacking the concrete interconnection between the concrete popular movement and the hero who leads it. Only when the emergence of the positive, popular hero is shown artistically from a social-historical and not merely individual-biographical standpoint can the full political effect occur: that is, the literary unmasking of the pseudo-hero of Fascism.

This step has already been taken in life, and the literary achievement of a Heinrich Mann is the fact that he has seen this step in German life correctly and embodied it in art. Further advance along this path will again depend solely upon this growing involvement with popular life.

In this way life corrects and guides the work of true writers. And the recognition of this brings us to our second example from contemporary writing of a positive relationship with the present. In the previous chapter we showed how when Maupassant and Jacobsen took their subjects from the present many of their prejudices, which assumed a rigid and abstract form in their "autonomous" historical novels, were corrected by the immediate experiences of life; how a "triumph of realism" occurred in their best novels on the present. One can often observe a similar "triumph of realism" in Feuchtwanger. One can criticize in many ways the conception of Fascism both in *Erfolg (Success)* and in *Die Geschwister Oppenheim (The Oppenheims)*. And it would be interesting to show how these false conceptions of Fascism have been enlarged and vulgarized in his historical novels. But this is not so important for us as the fact that Feuchtwanger has created really living and really popular characters in these novels, who express plastically and convincingly all that is best in the popular forces rebelling against Fascist barbarism. Characters such as Johanna Krain in *Erfolg* or the young grammar school boy Bernard Oppenheim are nowhere to be found in Feuchtwanger's historical novels. In these characters especially, but also in many other of his contemporary novels, Feuchtwanger's outstanding talents emerge unobscured by false theories and contemporary prejudices. He is converted to the historical novel because its self-contained material seems to promise lighter artistic labour and easier success. It seems to us that this "lightness", this insufficient resistance of the historical material to false constructions is one of the sources of the shortcomings of these novels, whereas the contradictory hardness of the living life of the present wrests from the writer his highest artistic talents.

This connection is not an accidental one. If we look at German literature in the imperialist period as a whole, then we have to admit that the historical novel—despite the luminous figure of Henri IV—cannot compare with the monumental portrayals of the present, with Thomas Mann's *Buddenbrooks*, Heinrich Mann's cycle on Wilhelmine Germany, etc. And the same is true for post-war literature. Thomas Mann's *Magic Mountain*, Arnold Zweig's World War cycle, Feuchtwanger's anti-Fascist novels are artistic peaks with which only *Henri IV*, in the field of the historical novel, can compare.

This literary-historical and aesthetic phenomenon tells us something important about the social mission of literature. On what does the significance of these novels rest? On the fact that their authors have tried to show artistically the concrete *historical genesis* of their time. It is this which is so far lacking in the historical novel of German anti-Fascism and in this that its central weakness lies. The great task facing anti-Fascist humanism is to reveal those social-historical and human-moral forces whose interplay made possible the 1933 catastrophe in Germany. For only a real understanding of these forces in all their complexity and intricacy can show their present disposition and the paths which they can take towards the revolutionary overthrow of Fascism. The ever stronger spirit of revolutionary democracy among the best representatives of the literary popular front against Fascism must take this direction ever more insistently if it is to overcome those ideological and literary traditions of liberalism still alive in the imperialist period today.

The historical novel of the anti-Fascist humanists risks taking the path of least resistance. It enables writers to avoid the question of the historical genesis of the present by resorting to the path of abstraction, the abstract prehistory of problems. To point out this danger, to criticize ideologically and artistically the weaknesses which follow from it, is not to repudiate the historical novel and its great artistic, cultural and political importance for the present. Quite the contrary. Once writers as writers—that is, in terms of the portrayal of characters and destinies—learn to see this concrete, historical genesis of the present in the spirit of revolutionary democracy, the real perspective is opened for the development of the historical novel in the narrower sense. If we have confronted the historical novel of our time with some of the most outstanding works of our time dealing with the present, then it has been chiefly in order to stress how much more *historical* they are compared with the historical novels. Only the consciousness of this historical spirit and its artistic application will conquer the past, in the true sense of the word, on behalf of anti-Fascist humanism.

Here is not the place to subject the above-mentioned contemporary novels to a detailed criticism. These too are products of their time, and though they arose in struggle against imperialism, against the decline of realism in the imperialist period, they could not possibly remain untouched by the weaknesses and limitations of this decline. But whatever criticism is possible and necessary here, it is striking how many of the most important of these works approach the classical type of social novel much more closely than the historical novels of anti-Fascism their corresponding classical type. Our previous arguments have shown why this had to be: the cause was not a purely aesthetic one; it was simply that these works looked at the present much more historically. They did so because of the breadth and wealth of their author's experiences. And this stronger historical spirit became the basis of their greatness.

This historical spirit is the great new principle which Balzac learnt from Walter Scott and passed on to all the really great representatives of the modern social novel. When realism declines this spirit becomes abstract and evaporates, and the problems of the present, its people and its destinies, are conceived metaphysically. The modern social novel is as much a child of the classical historical novel as the latter is of the great social novels of the eighteenth century. The decisive question of the development of the historical novel in our day is how to restore this connection in keeping with our age.

This restoration necessarily leads artistically to a renaissance of the classical type of historical novel. But it will not and cannot be a purely aesthetic renaissance. The classical type of historical novel can only be aesthetically renewed if writers concretely face the question: how was the Hitler régime in Germany possible? Then an historical novel may be achieved which will be fully realized artistically.

The perspective for the development of the historical novel depends then on the resumption of classical traditions, on a fruitful assimilation of the classical inheritance. We have repeatedly shown that this is not an aesthetic question; it does not mean a formal imitation of the manner of Scott, Manzoni, Pushkin or Tolstoy. And since the prospects for the development of the historical novel tie up so closely with the problem of our approach to the classical heritage, we must stress energetically the two closely connected aspects of this heritage: one, its popular, democratic and for this reason truly and concretely historical spirit; secondly, its high artistic concreteness of form. But popular character, democratic spirit and concrete historicism have a *radically different content* in our time. And, moreover, not only in the Soviet Union where the radically different content follows necessarily from victorious Socialism, but also for the fighting democratic humanists in the capitalist West.

The classical historical novel portrayed the contradictions of human progress, and with the means of history defended progress against the ideological attacks of reaction; in this struggle it depicted the necessary destruction of the old, primitive democracy and the great heroic crises of human history. But its historical perspective could only be that of the *necessary decline of the heroic period*, the necessary march of development into *capitalist prose*. The classical historical novel portrays the *sunset* of the heroic-revolutionary development of bourgeois democracy.

Today's historical novel has arisen and is developing amid the *dawn* of a *new* democracy. This applies not only to the Soviet Union where the tempestuous development and vigorous construction of Socialism have produced the highest form of democracy in human history, Socialist democracy. The struggle of the revolutionary democracy of the popular front, too, is not simply a defence of the existing achievements of democratic development against the attacks of Fascist or near-Fascist reaction. While it is this, it also goes beyond these limits in its defence of democracy; it must give revolutionary democracy new, higher, more advanced, more general, more democratic and more social contents. The revolution unfolding before us in

Spain shows this new development at its clearest. It shows that a democracy of a new type is about to be born.

The struggle for this new democracy, which throughout the world is evoking an enthusiastic revival and development of the traditions of revolutionary democracy, everywhere awakens unsuspected and extraordinary heroism in the people. We are in the midst of a heroic period, whose heroism moreover does not rest on historically necessary illusions, as was the case with the Puritans in the English and the Jacobins in the French Revolution, but upon a real knowledge of the needs of the working people and the direction in which society is developing. This heroism does not rest on illusions because its historical conditions are not so constituted that a period of prosaic disenchantment must follow upon its victory. The heroism of the Puritans in England and of the Jacobins in France—much against the will of the revolutionary fighters—helped the prose of capitalist exploitation to victory. The heroism of the fighters of the popular front, however, is a struggle for the true interests of the whole working people, for the creation of material and cultural conditions of life which can guarantee their human growth in every respect.

This perspective, that the heroism of the struggle does not have to be an episode—however historically necessary, yet still an episode—in the triumphal march of capitalist prose, also changes our attitude to the past. If a writer of today, enriched by the experiences of the heroic struggles of the people against imperialist exploitation and oppression throughout the world, depicts the historical forerunners of these struggles, he can do this in a quite different, much truer and deeper historical spirit than Scott or Balzac. For them the heroic periods of mankind could only appear as episodes and interludes, albeit historically justified and historically necessary.

This new perspective which has opened up as a result of the events of recent years not only makes possible a deepened conception of the past, but simultaneously broadens the field of portrayal in our concrete prehistory. Let us refer to just one example. Up to now oriental subjects have necessarily been of an exotic and eccentric character in bourgeois literature. The importation of Indian or Chinese philosophy into the declining ideology of the bourgeoisie could only increase this exoticism. Now, however, when we are contemporaries of the heroic liberation struggles of the Chinese, Indian, etc., people, all these developments flow concretely into the common historical stream of the liberation of mankind and are therefore portrayable in literature. And in the light of this common direction the past of these peoples is illuminated in a new way or at least can be so illuminated through the work of their important writers.

The rule of prose set in after the heroic period because objectively the only result of the people's colossal heroic efforts was the replacement of one form of exploitation by another. From an objective social standpoint the victory of capitalism over feudalism is of course a great historical advance. And the great representatives of the classical historical novel always acknowledged this progressiveness in their work. But precisely because they were great writers, and felt really deeply with the people in their misfortunes, it was impossible for them to be unconditional admirers of capitalist progress. Together with the economic progress they always portrayed the fearful sacrifices which it cost the people.

With this realization of the contradictory character of progress the representatives of the classical historical novel do not glorify the past uncritically. But nevertheless their works do clearly mourn the passing of many moments in the past: in the first place the fruitlessness of the heroic upsurge of past popular movements of liberation; secondly the many primitive democratic institutions, and the human qualities associated with them, which the march of progress has pitilessly destroyed. In really important writers, writers with a really live historical sense, this mourning is very divided and contradictory, dialectical. Humanly, aesthetically and ethically repelled by victorious capitalist prose, they not only feel its necessity, but also, despite all the horrors associated with it, that it marks a step forward in the development of mankind.

This dividedness disappears for the writer of today. His perspective of the future rests neither upon illusions, nor upon a disenchanted awakening from them. It shows not a degradation of heroic and human manifestations of life from the standpoint of a victorious future but on the contrary, the broadening, deepening and raising to a higher level of all the valuable qualities of man which have emerged during his previous development.

It suffices to point to one example in order to show clearly this difference of perspective, which is a difference of development in historical reality. In the first chapter of this work we quoted Maxim Gorky's fine analysis of Cooper's novels. This analysis shows the divided attitude of the classics of the historical novel clearly. They have to affirm the downfall of the humanly noble Indian, the straightforwardly decent, straightforwardly heroic "leather stocking", treating it as a necessary step of progress, and yet cannot help seeing and depicting the human inferiority of the victors. This is the necessary fate of every primitive culture with which capitalism comes into contact.

Now Fadeev, in his new cycle of novels, has raised an enormous problem with a similar theme, although—in those parts of his work so far published—not solved it: namely the fate of the surviving tribe of the Udehe, living still in a state almost of primitive communism, as it comes into contact with the proletarian revolution. Obviously this contact must vigorously transform both the customs and the economic life of the tribe; but it is also obvious that this transformation must take a completely opposite direction from the one which Cooper depicts as movingly tragic.

The revolutionary liberation of the people from the yoke of capitalism produces a heroic upsurge among the masses in exceptionally broad numbers and in a very profound manner. But—and this is the important thing—this upsurge is not an episode to be followed by a fresh suppression of popular energies. On the contrary, it clears away all obstacles which hinder the unfolding of human energies in the popular masses; it creates institutions which help to accelerate and deepen, economically and culturally, this unfolding of the people's energies. This perspective of the real and permanent liberation of the people alters the perspective which historical novels have of the future; it gives quite a different emotional accent to their illumination of the past from that which we find, and inevitably find, in the classical historical novel; it is able to discover entirely new tendencies and features in the past, of which the classical historical novel was not and could not be aware. *In this respect* the new historical novel, born of the popular and democratic spirit of our time, will indeed *contrast* with the classical historical novel.

From what has been said up to now it is clear that this new perspective exists not only for the writers of the Soviet Union, but also for the humanists of the anti-Fascist popular front; although, of course, these tendencies are inevitably more distinct and developed, both objectively and subjectively, in the Soviet Union. But the struggle for a democracy of a new type, the realization that the problems of this democracy are connected with the economic and cultural liberation of the exploited—something we have seen especially vividly in the writings of Heinrich Mann—show that this perspective is also a reality for the fighters of the popular front. Thus, it can also become a reality for their literature.

If these tendencies are to be realized, deep-going changes will have to take place in a formal-artistic respect as well, both in the novel in general and therewith in the historical novel, too. Very generally this tendency may be described as a *tendency towards epic.* This tendency is plainly perceptible in some of the best products of the most recent period. Think of some of the familiar features of Heinrich Mann's *Henri Quatre.*

This tendency is born of a deep historical necessity. It expresses artistically the same historical phenomenon which led us to contrast the new, emerging historical novel with the classical historical novel.

But it must not be overlooked that this is *only* a tendency. Only in fully developed socialism can the cessation of the antagonistic character of contradiction, with its consequences for the whole of human activity, become a determining principle of the structure and movement of social life. As long as there exists a capitalist economy the antagonism of contradictions must prevail. Admittedly, the concrete and actual prospect of liberation does produce a different subjective attitude to the contradictory course of history though of course without being able to change its real character. Thus in such changes of style it can only be a question of tendency.

We are still far from being able to look on capitalist prose as a period we have fully done with, as one which really does belong simply to the past. The fact that a central task of the internal policy of the Soviet Union is the conquest of capitalist survivals in economy and ideology shows that even in socialist reality capitalist prose is still a factor to be reckoned with, although it has suffered defeat and is condemned to ultimate extinction.

What Marx said of legal institutions applies in wide measure to literary forms. They cannot stand higher than the society which brought them forth. Indeed, since they deal with the deepest human laws, problems and contradictions of an epoch they *should* not stand higher—in the sense, say, of anticipating coming perspectives of development by romantic-Utopian projections of the future into the present. For the tendencies leading to the future are in fact more firmly and definitely contained in what really is than in the most beautiful Utopian dreams or projections.

Naturally, this reservation applies still more to the anti-Fascist literature of the West. For there the capitalist system rules in its most repulsive, barbaric, inhuman form. The popular front today can at best only gather together all forces of democracy to resist Fascism, as in Spain. But the victory, the liberation of the people from the Fascist yoke, the new social order of democracy, not to speak of the abolition of exploitation, is today at best an object of struggle, in most cases a real, but nevertheless future, perspective. That a literature of the kind we have seen in the anti-Fascist historical novel could arise in capitalist countries under these social and political conditions is a very important sign of the times—of the maturing revolutionary situation and the enormous international significance of the victorious construction of Socialism in the Soviet Union. But our recognition of this new situation should nevertheless not mislead us into twisting perspectives and tendencies intellectually into present-day realities.

For this reason the contrast between the historical novel today and the classical type is only a very relative one. We had to stress the tendency for this contrast so as to avoid the misunderstanding that we intended a formal revival, an artistic imitation of the classical historical novel. That is impossible. The difference in historical perspectives causes a difference in principles of composition and characterization as well. The more these perspectives and tendencies are transformed into reality, the more therefore the novel develops generally in the direction of epic, the greater will this contrast be. But it would be idle to worry one's head today over how radical a contrast this will be.

The more so, since the principal front of struggle in the artistic sphere, too, is the conquest of harmful legacies. We have shown that in many respects the tendencies present in the new historical novel contrast with those marking the decline of bourgeois realism. So far, however, these tendencies have nowhere been fully realized. The liquidation of harmful legacies is still far from complete. And we have seen how much the problems of the historical novel of our day, both ideological and artistic, depend upon a radical settling-of-accounts with these legacies. At the same time we must stress particularly strongly that any Utopian anticipation of the future, any transformation of the future into a supposed reality can very easily cause a slipping-back into the style of the period of decline by blunting the antagonistic contradictions which operate in reality.

In this struggle the study of the classical historical novel will play an outstanding part. Not only because we possess in it a literary standard of a very high level for our portrayal of the real tendencies in popular life, hence a measure for the popular character of the historical novel, but also because the classical historical novel, as a result of this popular character, realized the *general laws of large epic* in a model form, whereas the novel of the period of decline, severed from life, largely destroyed these general laws of narrative art—from composition and characterization down to choice of language. The perspective of the novel's return to true epic greatness, to an epic-like character must reawaken these general laws of great narrative art, recall them to consciousness, translate them again into practice, if they are not to disintegrate into a self-contradictory "problematic". This "problematic" we can observe in the very highest achievement of the modern historical novel, Heinrich Mann's *Henri IV*, where the grand, epic character of the positive hero, the monumentality of the narrative style conflicts strangely and unresolvably with the necessary, unavoidable and irremovable pettiness of the biographical manner of presentation.

And in a quite different, but—in a large historical sense—similar way, we were able to discern in Romain Rolland's *Colas Breugnon* a contradictory combination of this artistic strength, which points to the future, and a specific "problematic" of the present.

This historical novel of our time, therefore, must above all negate, radically and sharply, its immediate predecessor and eradicate the latter's traditions from its own work. The necessary approximation to the classical type of historical novel which occurs in this connection will, as our remarks have shown, by no means take the form of a simple renaissance, a simple affirmation of these classical traditions, but, if one will allow me this phrase from Hegel's terminology, a renewal in the form of a negation of a negation.

Index

Works are included under their respective authors. Page numbers in *italics* indicate detailed discussion.